Rethinking Meter

Rethinking Meter

A New Approach to the Verse Line

Alan Holder

Lewisburg
Bucknell University Press
London: Associated University Presses

Associated University Presses
440 Forsgate Drive
Cranbury, NJ 08512

Associated University Presses
25 Sicilian Avenue
London WC1A 2QH, England

Associated University Presses
P.O. Box 338, Port Credit
Mississauga, Ontario
Canada L5G 4L8

The paper used in this publication meets the requirements
of the American National Standard for Permanence of Paper
for Printed Library Materials Z39.48-1984.

Library of Congress Cataloging-in-Publication Data

Holder, Alan, 1932–
    Rethinking meter : a new approach to the verse line / Alan Holder.
      p.   cm.
    Includes bibliographical references and index.
    ISBN 0-8387-5292-6 (alk. paper)
    1. English language—Versification.   2. English poetry—History
and criticism—Theory, etc. I. Title.
PE1505.H58   1995
821.009—dc20   94-49336
                                   CIP

For Barbara
who has helped me scan my life anew

"English prosody has tended to be a subject for cranks."
—John Hollander

"who can avoid mania writing on this subject?"
—Roy Fuller

"in an age in which the critic must gain note through ingenuity in interpretation or rigor in exotic science, it must be admitted that prosodic criticism is but a hand-maiden."
—Alan T. Gaylord

"Again and again I must repeat, that the composition of verse is infinitely more of an art than men are prepared to believe, and absolute success in it depends upon numberless minutiae."
—William Wordsworth

Contents

Preface

COMMENTARY on the nature and function of sound patterns in English and American poetry has, for the most part, long operated within the boundaries of a "foot"-based concept of meter. That concept and its applications constitute the core of prosodic criticism. The present study, as it engages such criticism, may often appear to exhibit a spirit of slash-and-burn. I can only defend my approach by saying that traditional prosodic theory and practice, while in need of supplementation, are first in need of a severe clearing out.

My frequently antagonistic treatment of the works of various prosodists locates me, willy-nilly, within a countertradition, a history of deep unease with foot-based metrical analysis. (In expressing my views, though, I do not necessarily march in step with all my fellow grumblers). The countertradition has obviously not prevailed, and seemingly timeless precepts about feet and substitutions and tension and counterpoint continue to be promulgated or assumed in poetry textbooks and in much critical practice. The traditional concept of meter is, for many, one that is carved in concrete; nothing will make them question it. But I hope to show readers with open minds that it is a notion scratched in quicksand, that it must be seriously modified, de-centered, and supplemented if we are to arrive at an accurate and fruitful (not merely wistful) way of analyzing the contours of verse movement, the structurings of its flow, and the effects of those structurings. It is toward realizing such a project, at least partly, that this book is directed. I will suggest procedures that are applicable to all verse, and thereby hope to accomplish a portion of what Eniko Bollobas describes as "an immense task, the ultimate one, perhaps for any prosodist," namely, constructing "A prosodic theory which is not based on the opposition of free and strict, of non-metrical and metrical, but holds equally for all degrees of tightness. . . ."[1]

Acknowledgments

In writing this study I received aid or encouragement in one form or another from the following: Robert Morgan, M. L. Rosenthal, Diane Wood Middlebrook, Steven Gould Axelrod, and T. V. F. Brogan. My naming them here, in gratitude, does not necessarily imply that they agree in whole or in part with my views.

I wish to thank the Research Foundation of the City University of New York for the award of two summer research grants.

I am grateful to the following friends for having been in my life: Richard Abrams, Fred Bornhauser, Arthur Goldberger, David Hoddeson, Stanley Moses, Charles Persky, Jim Weaver, Jim Williams, and the late John Potter.

Portions of Chapters I and II appeared in "Mired in Meter," in the Spring 1990 issue of *The CEA Critic.* A slightly different version of Chapter IV appeared as "The Haunting of Free Verse: Towards a Method of Metrical Ghostbusting" in the Summer 1991 issue of *The Southern Review.*

Quotations from George Wright's *Shakespeare's Metrical Art,* copyright 1988 The Regents of the University of California, are being used with the permission of The Regents of the University of California and the University of California Press.

"Acquainted with the Night" is reprinted from *The Poetry of Robert Frost,* edited by Edward Connery Lathem. Copyright © 1956 by Robert Frost. Copyright 1928 ©, 1969 by Henry Holt and Company Inc. Reprinted by permission of Henry Holt and Company, Inc. Jonathan Cape is the British publisher.

"Ariel" is reprinted from *Ariel* by Sylvia Plath. Copyright © 1965 by Ted Hughes. Copyright Renewed. Reprinted by permission of HarperCollins Publishers, Inc., and Faber and Faber Limited.

Introduction

OVER twenty-five years ago, in the course of his spirited effort to move prosodic commentary beyond the dark and muddy ground that has been its characteristic turf, John Nist made the following observation:

> The discipline of English metrics has suffered for centuries because it has been forced to tell lies to every schoolboy who has ever filled up a bluebook with exercises in its scansional systems. And those lies, with all the deadening grace of metronomic boredom, have alienated the classroom student from his early rhythmical interests and have turned his teacher into a deaf mathematician who can clip, inlay, and fit (with the cement of certainty) the brightest language moments of musical genius into the muffling white-washed rigidity of a tomb.[1]

As we move through the 1990s, we might well look back to an era where schoolboys still did scansion as both distant and charming; even Nist might wish to recover it. (Still more distant and charming is the time when, in response to Robert Bridges's account of Milton's versification, "public protests appeared in the newspapers, one of which actually advertised 'prosody' on its street posters as an item of considerable interest."[2]) For in the years since Nist delivered his polemic, scansional exercises have disappeared from the curricula of many schoolpersons, at least in this country, even at the college level.

What may have happened is that teachers no longer believe in their students' willingness or ability to engage poetry in the painstaking way that scansion requires. Or perhaps, in the course of a century that has seen an explosion of free verse, those teachers have implicitly come to regard the concept of meter as something less than urgent. Perhaps, too, they have simply lost interest in the subject of prosody. While there is (and has been) a good deal of critical activity in the field, it is largely confined to specialized journals; prosody, when compared to other areas of literary criticism, occupies something of a backwater. Prosodists themselves have acknowledged the relative obscurity of their discipline and sometimes see it as a just fate. One might almost say that there has been a tradition of apology and self-denigration among prosodists, reinforcing the aspersions cast by others.[3] In poetry reviewing and criticism, one finds an occasional reference to prosodic matters, but this often amounts to little more than flashing a kind of membership card in The Metrics Club, an assurance in passing that the commentator can scan a line with the best of them, and knows all about amphibrachs and ionics. Such a gesture is often anomalous, since the commentator is likely to be dealing with free verse, resorting to inappropriate terms for want of better ones. Some might find an additional anomaly in such scanning, arguing that many poets today write from an ignorance of or indifference to traditional prosody.[4]

That alleged ignorance or indifference created something of a flurry in the 1980s, resulting in what has purported to be a countermovement. Advocates of a "New Formalism" emerged, denigrating much that had been written under the banner of "free verse," while championing and/or producing poetry in traditional modes. But the New Formalism and the response to it have as yet done little to move prosody from its marginal position in the field of criticism, and have certainly not advanced metrical theory and its applications a single inch. For one thing, to the extent that the New Formalism has become a live issue, it seems to partake more of the political than the aesthetic.[5] For another, the New Formalists have proceeded by simply swallowing whole old notions of meter.

Witness the case of Timothy Steele. Although his *Missing Measures: Modern Poetry and the Revolt Against Meter* (1990) never actually uses the term "New Formalism," the hardcover jacket copy characterizes the book as providing that "vital movement with a brilliant critical statement." Meter, Steele claims, "is of no less value today to poets and readers than it ever was."[6] But while he mounts a substantial attack on the theoretical underpinnings of free verse, he eschews any reexamination of the concept of meter, claiming that "Its basic statutes are few and clear" (283); he thereby ignores a whole history of confusion and controversy that has attended the exposition of those "statutes." For him, meter simply is a great good: " . . . I believe that our ability to organize thought and speech into measure is one of the most precious endowments of the human race."[24] Unsupported as it stands in Steele's book, this statement is pure piety, and on a grandiose order to boot. Apart from the failure to demonstrate meter's virtues in an allegedly crucial critical text, works exemplifying the New Formalism are, judging by the two principal anthologies the movement has produced, more focused on the use of rhyme and stanzaic modes than on the employment of meter per se.[7]

But while the concept of meter has failed to experience a meaningful or triumphant resurrection under the aegis of the New Formalism, while it has languished in the classroom, and while it has been marginalized to a great extent by the widespread use of free verse, that concept is in an important way still with us, enjoying at the very least a kind of persistent half-life. It occupies an a priori status in any number of recent works of prosodic criticism (though it may sometimes seem to undergo some refurbishing there). Perhaps more notable, it is as enshrined as ever in many of the texts used in our colleges to introduce students to verse. There it functions as a given, one that is often skirted in actual teaching, but a given nevertheless, its avoidance cause for pedagogical guilt.

This positioning of meter in the academy makes for a curious cleavage in the culture of poetry, at least here in America. Over the last three decades or so, the care and feeding of many of our poets has in effect been taken over by colleges and universities. The emergence of poet-teachers is an increasingly familiar phenomenon, as is the proliferation of creative writing courses or programs in which most of them are employed. Not noted nearly as often as these developments, perhaps because it has been simply taken for granted, is the fact that the care and feeding of poetry itself has become a function of our institutions of higher learning. It seems safe to say that, on any given day in these United States, the number of people reading poems is made up largely of college students who have been assigned such reading (with a majority of them having received their assignments in introduction-to-literature courses). The sheltering of many poets as well as verse itself under the same roofs may seem to have given the culture of American poetry an unprecedented coherence (some might say an undesirable narrowness), but it has also made for a large anomaly. Whatever buddings of a "New Formalism" may be taking place, ours is an era in which free verse remains the dominant mode, and in which the academy is home for many poets writing in that mode. At the same time, most of the texts and manuals through which poetry is presented to the students of the academy not only take the concept of meter as central to prosody, but, in a complementary maneuver, tend to see free verse as intrinsically hampered, a kind of poor relation to traditional or metrical verse.

We need, both in the academy and outside it, neither to espouse the concept of meter unquestioningly nor to sidestep it guiltily, but to confront and demythologize it. This will help eliminate the cleavage I have noted,[8] and remove free verse from under the cloud where, for many, it is still situated. Most importantly, it will aid us in arriving at a more accurate sense than we now have of the sonic contours of the poetic canon in English, of "metrical" works as well as nonmetrical works. Muted though they may be in much current verse, poetry's sonic dimensions are or should be regarded as essential, and a good many readers outside college, including poets and critics, are carrying around notions of those dimensions acquired from a misguided prosodic pedagogy. So while, in this era of free verse and scansion-free classrooms, the dead hand of the past, in the form of the concept of meter, may be resting relatively lightly on the transmission of the poetic canon, it has been and still is enough of a presence to be attended to. If we disestablish the standard notion of meter not only in our texts but in the general literary consciousness, it will enable us to develop an approach to the sound qualities of the whole canon of our poetry that is closer to our experience of individual poems than traditional prosody has been able to get. The concept of meter stands between us and our reading of poetry, displacing or devaluing our perceptions with its precepts. Prosody has been fettered in "feet" long enough.

In the first two chapters I will discuss the orthodox concept of meter and its principal corollaries, challenging their usefulness in reading particular texts. In chapter 3 I will demonstrate the tenacity of orthodox metrical thought by a consideration of some recent prosodic writings, including writings that may *appear* to be making important concessions to the sort of critique I advance or that seem themselves to be effecting breakaways from conventional formulations. In the fourth chapter, I will show how the concept of meter has pervaded even the analysis of supposedly free verse. Chapter 5 will consider some basic issues that arise in attempting to characterize how a poem moves, and will lay the groundwork for a prosodic approach that will not only modify the concept of meter but will shrink the role that meter plays in our consideration of poetry. Chapter 6 will trace a kind of minority prosodic tradition, that of "phrasalism," which extends to the present and lies behind my proposed revision of prosodic theory. That chapter will furnish my own approach to meter and will provide some readings both of metrical and free verse in a phrasalist manner. The final chapter will consider the difficult matter of intonation and offer a preliminary sketch of how that element of speech might be incorporated into our prosody.

Rethinking Meter

1

In the Muddled Kingdom of Meter

PERUSING the critical literature of prosody is useful for defining the issues regarding poetry's sound patterns, but the sad fact is that the bulk of that literature is wrong-headed or irrelevant, forever warming up dubious pieties.[1] It appears to be a law of metrical studies that once a notion is advanced, it persists, as stubbornly as Richard Nixon, in never going completely away. Paradoxically, metrists are also capable of a kind of amnesia—or is it only ignorance?—with respect to those who have gone before them. This is attested to by T. V. F. Brogan, who has the distinction, at once heroic and unenviable, of having read more of the critical literature of prosody than probably anyone else, living or dead, and who has gifted us with an indispensable annotated bibliography of the subject, *English Versification, 1570–1980: A Reference Guide with a Global Appendix*. Brogan notes that the "virtual explosion" of interest in prosody in the two decades prior to the appearance of his book had been accompanied "by a very palpable ignorance of the historical tradition and resources."[2]

Such ignorance of the past, or at least indifference to it, is not a recent phenomenon. For example, some years ago Karl Shapiro pointed out that Sidney Lanier, advocating a time-based prosody that presumes a very close tie between the sound relations of verse and those of music, did not give proper credit to his "true ancestor," Joshua Steele, author of *Prosodia Rationalis* (1779), who advanced just such an approach.[3] Ignorance of the work of others may extend to that of contemporaries: In 1985, Donald Wesling, referring to the period of 1855 to 1910, spoke of "prosody *then as now* being remarkable for the lack of logical contact between discussants" (my italics).[4]

But there is more plaguing the field of prosody than not knowing or adequately acknowledging the work that has already been done, for in fact much of that work might well be consigned to oblivion. Brogan, who above all others should know, has said that "versification" (his term for prosody), is "a field which in historical terms has been (it is not too extreme to say) a great mass of ignorance, confusion, superficial thinking, category mistakes, argument by spurious analogy, persuasive definitions [sic!], and gross abuses of both concepts and terms." The field "has been prey to more eccentricity and confusion, more nonthink and doubletalk, than probably any other discipline in the realm of letters" (pp. xii, xix). Perhaps Brogan should have added to this sorry catalog the use of tautology and a weakness for high-flown, rhapsodic abstractions.

At any rate, this is hardly the first time such a note as Brogan's has been sounded. He records in his bibliography the statement made several decades ago by René Wellek and Austin Warren: "the very foundations and main criteria of metrics are still uncertain; and there is an astonishing amount of loose thinking and confused or shifting terminology even in standard treatises" (p. 48).[5] Brogan also lists a book on Robert Bridges put out in 1914 that characterized "the whole of English versification [as] one long gross 'mistake'" (p. 289). T. S. Omond, who might well be thought of as the Brogan of his time (the early years of this century), cited, in his survey of English metrists, a work published in 1774 that denounced "the errors of 'all who have written on English prosody, and their utter inability to form any system for analysing English verse.'"[6] Omond, extending his survey to American metrists, apparently noted, and Brogan might have noted, Edgar Allan Poe's contention in "The Rationale of Verse" (1848) that "There is, perhaps, no topic in polite literature which has been more pertinaciously discussed [than "verse," in the sense of "rhythm, rhyme, metre, and versification"], and there is certainly not one about which so much inaccuracy, confusion, misconception, misrepresentation, mystification, and downright ignorance on all sides, can be fairly said to exist."[7] Much evidence is available to support such gloomy denunciations of prosody, which come from within the field itself; unfortunately, the denouncers can become part of the problem. This is certainly the case with Poe, as I shall show later.

It seems reasonable to conclude, though Brogan himself does not make the point, that the sorts of faults he and others before him point to are largely located in treatments of meter, for that is the subject that has gotten the lion's share of writings on prosody. The section devoted to meter in Brogan's bibliography proves to be by far the longest. Apart from this quantitative testimony to the way the concept of meter has monopolized the writings of prosodists, we repeatedly come upon explicit affirmations of meter's centrality, affirmations that go back for centuries. O. B. Hardi-

son has spoken of an *ars metrica* tradition in Latin prosody that
was standardized by the fourth century, and that made "the use of
meter the fundamental characteristic of poetry."[8] The entry on
poetry in the ninth edition of the *Encyclopedia Britannica* (published in the late nineteenth century) cites Hegel's claim in his
Aesthetics that "metre is the first and only condition absolutely
demanded by poetry, yea even more necessary than a figurative
picturesque diction."[9] Seymour Chatman says that "the difference
between prose and verse must be accounted for, and meter is obviously central to that distinction."[10] In the original edition of his
widely praised *Poetic Meter and Poetic Form,* Paul Fussell claimed
that "Attempts to 'escape' from meter are . . . almost equivalent
to attempts to escape from poetry."[11] Even when, in the revised
version of the book, he included a chapter on free verse, he retained this statement, though he modified it to read "Attempts to
'escape' from meter—or at least some kind of governing rhythm—
are . . . almost equivalent to attempts to escape from poetry."[12]
For J. V. Cunningham, "the repetitive perception that this line is
metrical or that it is not, that it exemplifies the rules or that it does
not, is the metrical experience. It is the ground bass of all poetry"
(cited in Brogan, 148). The so-called generative metrists (who will
be discussed in a later chapter) certainly appear to be in agreement
with Cunningham, having made the definition and testing of the
metricality of lines the core of their enterprise. Brogan himself
observes that "Meter is so much the principal component of verse-
structure that the part and the whole are routinely conflated and
the terms for their study commonly interchanged" (p. 141).

The prominence accorded to meter in the critical literature of
prosody is reflected in such texts as are employed to introduce
college students to poetry. Meter is certainly featured in what is
perhaps the most influential such textbook of our century, *Understanding Poetry* by Cleanth Brooks and Robert Penn Warren, originally published in 1938 and put through several editions. (I shall
be referring in this chapter and others to the third edition unless
otherwise indicated). The treatment of prosody by Brooks and
Warren may be taken as typical of the sorts of things students are
likely to encounter in comparable books or in the poetry sections
of introduction-to-literature texts. Meter, which is used at least
once in the book as synonymous with "rhythm," is placed in a
context of remarks on the inescapable and honorific place of
rhythm as it operates in the scheme of things: "the seasons . . .
day and night . . . the solar system."[13] There is the notion that the
use of meter sets up a pattern that we unconsciously expect will

continue, and that there are departures or variations from this pattern, some of which can be "deeply expressive (pp. 125, 128; more on these matters later). There is the advancing of the "foot" as the metrical unit, and the scanning or diagramming of lines of verse in terms of feet, together with the contention that one kind of foot may be "substituted" for another. There is a disclaimer to the effect that the sort of "rudimentary system" of scansion employed in the book cannot do justice to the subtleties of "rhythm and texture in language when it is well used," together with the insistence that the system will nevertheless help us (p. 146). There is, in fact, a domination of the pages on prosody by the application of that system of scansion.

Other features of *Understanding Poetry* that reappear in subsequent texts (though they may undergo some revision there) include the notion that there is a "positive tension" between "a principle of metrical regularity which conditions our reading toward a fixed recurrence of stress and tends to level out divergencies from the norm," and "a principle of dramatic and rhetorical emphasis which demands stresses that sometimes coincide with those of the metrical pattern and sometimes diverge from them" (p. 137). (Other writers put the matter more concisely, saying that the desirable tension arises between metrical regularity and the divergences from it.) The concept of tension is standard and crucial in what may be called traditional prosodic theory, and will be addressed more fully in the next chapter.

Typical of prosodists who assume meter to be the central component of a poem's sonic dimensions (such prosodists constitute an overwhelming majority), Brooks and Warren manage to see it as functioning in two ways that seem diametrically opposed, or, better, that combine antithetical effects. (This may be seen as the notion of tension writ large.) The presence of meter is said by them to establish "a pervasive impression of unity" and an "authority" that assures us that the poem, in spite of its frequent defiance of common sense, "will ultimately make sense." At the same time, the variations from the meter enable the poet to impart a "dramatic significance" to his work, by which Brooks and Warren appear to mean that the movement of the lines "seems indivisible from the movement of the thought and feeling . . . " (pp. 125–26). Achieving unity and authority on the one hand, registering the shifting contours of mental and emotional processes on the other—this impressive synthesis is effected by the meter operating in combination with the variations from it. Such a synthesis is truly alluring, the core of what might be called the Mystique of Meter, taking a number of shapes in the critical literature. Thus, meter is said to bring together unity and variety, repetition and change, form and freedom, artifice and reality, control and expressiveness, regulation and arousal, the conventional and the experiential (these pairings have even been extended to include death and birth).[14] The notion of some such synthesis may be traced back at least as far as the eighteenth century, but for modern criticism probably has its genesis in Coleridge. Its different formulations typically appear in the context of general celebrations of verse, celebrations suggesting a single dominant sonic-aesthetic effect emerging from that genre, at least from its metrical subset, whereby any individual poem is dissolved and ascends to the heady stratosphere of Poetry. Apart from the doubtfulness of allowing such homogenization and evaporation, it should be observed that when operating at the humble level of individual poems, many prosodists put the concept of meter to work in very questionable ways, as I hope to demonstrate.

While allowing for rhetorical overkill in the remarks of John Nist that I quoted at the start of my introduction, one can only applaud his attributing a stultifying certainty and rigidity to traditional metrics and their pedagogic perpetuation. Not only do the usual presentations of meter in our textbooks (including Brooks and Warren) purvey notions that need to be questioned, they manage to impart to those notions an air of the timeless and absolute by ignoring or just barely acknowledging the problems and controversies that have beset the discussion of English metrics for a long time. To put the matter as simply as possible, we might note Seymour Chatman's observation that "1. Metrists do not agree upon the number of syllables in a given word or line; 2. Metrists do not agree upon whether a given syllable is prominent or not; 3. Metrists do not agree upon how the syllables are grouped."[15] But the disagreements and difficulties go well beyond these elementary and elemental considerations. Among the matters that have been debated are the following (here readers should brace themselves for a plethora of questions):

Is the foot, the unit that the concept of meter is based on, a truly operative entity in our poetry, or is it an arbitrary imposition on the English verse line, wistfully appropriated from Classical prosody?

What is a foot anyway? Is it strictly spatial, a grouping of syllables (usually two or three in number) exhibiting a particular arrangement of stressed and unstressed components, with these corresponding to other such groupings in a line of verse? Of is it a unit of time, equal in duration to its fellow feet in the line, with the corollary that lines of equal numbers of like feet are of equal duration, that is, are *isochronous*?

More fundamentally, should the differences between syllables, on which meter is based, be thought of as a matter of stress (if so, how many degrees of stress should we see operating?) or of duration (quantity)? Or is it a matter of pitch? Or is it some combination of these?

Assuming the meaningfulness of the terms, is English verse basically iambic, or trochaic? Does our poetry contain genuine spondaic, or pyrrhic feet? Should the recognition of a metrical pattern, that is, the dominance of a particular kind of foot, affect one's reading of a given line, whereby there is a "promoting" or "demoting" of certain syllables, or should that reading proceed without such deliberate alterations? Is meter a kind of purified version of a sound pattern intrinsic to English at large (in terms of placement of stresses or timing) or is it something that goes counter to the language, serving automatically to "foreground" verse?

What is the function of meter? Does it serve to excite us, producing a kind of hyperattentiveness, or does it work to lull or hypnotize us? Is it meter's principal job to set up a recurring pattern that pleases an intrinsic human appetite for repetition, or is it designed to create such a pattern simply in order to deviate from it in an expressive manner? Or, since having things both ways is a favorite sport of metrists, should meter be seen as doing both?

Are the effects of meter, whatever they maybe, inseparable from the sense of the words in which the metrical pattern is operating, or does the meter have a force of its own, and are there such things as representative meters, meters that fit certain themes or that tend to elicit or are appropriate to particular emotional ranges?[16]

One final question: In the light of all these unresolved (if not always acknowledged) issues that arise with the conventional application of meter to verse, can one really put one's faith in "the recognition of the few homely and sound, traditional and objective, principles of prosody," embodied in the concept of meter and its corollaries, a recognition apparently advocated by Brooks and Warren (p. 570)?

The point of asking this last question is not primarily to indicate that a particular, if highly influential, textbook is being simplistic (and some might argue that students beginning their study of poetry are best not deluged with the controversies of prosody). Rather, posing that question points up the dubious advocacy or employment of the concept of meter in sophisticated or scholarly contexts. For we should take note of two things. First, the statement about "the few homely and sound, traditional and objective principles of prosody," was borrowed by Brooks and Warren from a landmark essay by W. K. Wimsatt and Monroe Beardsley, published in 1959 in one of the central journals of academic literary studies, *PMLA*. Second, the principles referred to have commanded the assent of many prosodists, past and present, including that of Timothy Steele, who, as already noted, has said of meter that "Its basic statutes are few and clear . . . ."[17] A detailed look at the concept of meter might well begin with the Wimsatt and Beardsley essay.[18]

The piece in question, "The Concept of Meter: An Exercise in Abstraction," is ostensibly intent on upholding traditional meter against two competing systems, one the musical or temporal approach, and the other a linguistic approach. But it is really intent on fending off the latter, and it is this aspect of the essay I wish to focus on. Structural linguistics, more particularly *An Outline of English Structure* (1951) by George L. Trager and Henry Lee Smith, Jr., had contended that English is characterized by, among other things, four discrete levels of stress. The traditional concept of meter, at least in its pure form, recognizes only two sorts of syllables, stressed and unstressed. Wimsatt and Beardsley, in a determined rearguard action, attempt to undermine the linguists, first by outdoing them, saying that there may not be merely four degrees of stress in English, but five or eight—"How can one be sure?"—and then by circumventing them, saying that what counts as far as meter is concerned is *relative* stress. "What one can nearly always be sure of is that a given syllable in a sequence is more or less stressed than the preceding or the following. . . . How *much* more is always irrelevant" (p. 593; italics in original). In short, by looking on stress as a relative matter, the two-stress system of traditional meter is saved.

But we immediately run into a difficulty that Wimsatt and Beardsley appear not to detect. If a given syllable in English always receives a greater or lesser stress than that adjacent to it, we lose the spondee, which consists of two stressed syllables. Wimsatt and Beardsley, in fact, like some other prosodists, explicitly chuck that hapless foot overboard. But the greater-or-lesser-stress principle should also mean the dissolution of the anapest, consisting of two unstressed syllables followed by a stressed syllable, for the simple reason that one of the first two syllables would have to be regarded as stressed in relation to the other. (A similar process would apply to the dactyl, made up of a stressed syllable and two unstressed syllables.) The anapest is certainly not a foot Wimsatt and Beardsley are ready to get rid of; indeed, they invoke it when scanning Blake's

Ah, Sunflower, weary of time

as "unmistakably an anapestic line." They say that while the "flow-" of "flower" is a "strong" syllable, "'sun' is even stronger . . . a fact which is crucial" (p. 593). This of course preserves a distinction between the two syllables, relegating "flow-" to the domain of the unstressed, which ostensibly makes it available as the first component of the "anapestic" foot, "flŏw ĕr wéa." But regard that foot. Are we seriously to read "flow" and "er" as equally unstressed? In fact, apart from the matter of ordinary pronunciation, we *can't*, if we go by Wimsatt and Beardsley's own contention that two successive syllables in English do not possess the same degree of stress. The two critics have taken care of "flow-" on its left flank, but not on its right, and we are left with a disappearing anapest, both theoretically and in fact.

Putting aside the ontological status of the anapest (and the last thing in the world I wish to do, as will soon be made evident, is to defend the legitimacy or continued use of any sort of foot), consider the adverb in Wimsatt and Beardsley's contention that Blake's line is "unmistakably . . . anapestic." Consider next their contention that Shelley's "Hail to thee, blithe spirit!" has "an unquestionably iambic movement following the very strong first syllable . . . " (p. 593). Consider, finally, their characterization of Marvell's line from "The Garden," "To a green thought in a green shade." Having dismissed the notion of the spondee, they say "whatever we do with the two pairs of weak syllables [to a, in a], it remains absolutely certain that 'thought' is stronger than 'green,' and that 'shade' is stronger than 'green.'" They thus presumably salvage a pair of iambs from an otherwise troublesome line (594–95). "Unmistakably anapestic," "unquestionably iambic," "absolutely certain"—Wimsatt and Beardsley seem to take the rhetoric of unqualified assertion as a substitute for persuasive demonstration. It is my contention that not only are their scansions open to question, but that in the cases of both Blake and Shelley those footbound readings are manifestly at variance with a commonsense, expressive processing of the lines, and that in the case of Marvell their reading ignores the thematic importance of "green," as well as the more general consideration that the repeating of a term other than, say, an article or preposition, tends to give the term importance. In confronting their scansions, we have arrived at the heart of the morass that is meter country. (While touring it I am going to use as a guide the assumption that, with respect to proso-dists, by their scansions shall ye know them.)[19]

Let us look more closely at the Wimsatt-Beardsley reading of Blake's line as "unmistakably anapestic," which would be tanta-mount to the following scansion:

$$\overset{\text{x}}{\text{Ah}} \ \overset{\text{/}}{\text{Sun}} \mid \overset{\text{x}}{\text{flow}} \ \overset{\text{x}}{\text{er}} \ \overset{\text{/}}{\text{wea}} \mid \overset{\text{x}}{\text{ry}} \ \overset{\text{x}}{\text{of}} \ \overset{\text{/}}{\text{time}}$$

First, we have the suppression, or "demotion" (the technical term), of a syllable—"Ah"—which for most of us would seem to call for stress out of expressive considerations; I have treated it as unstressed in keeping with Wimsatt and Beardsley's virtual banish-ment of the spondee. (They say, unhelpfully, that "Ah Sun-" can be taken as "iamb, trochee, or spondee (if there is such a thing) . . . " (593).) Then we have the demotion of another sylla-ble—"flow"—which would ordinarily be stressed, at least second-arily, if we go by the word's lexical (according-to-the-dictionary) pronunciation. Consider the resulting two "anapestic" feet:

$$\overset{\text{x}}{\text{flow}} \ \overset{\text{x}}{\text{er,}} \ \overset{\text{/}}{\text{wea}} \mid \overset{\text{x}}{\text{ry}} \ \overset{\text{x}}{\text{of}} \ \overset{\text{/}}{\text{time}}$$

In the first case, the foot ends with a fragment of a word, and, by putting itself forth as a unit, has the effect of ignoring the strongly marked caesura within it. In the second case, the foot begins with a fragment of a word. Apart from Wimsatt and Beardsley requiring us to supress the sort of stressing we would ordinarily do in the initial portion of the line ($\overset{\text{/}}{\text{Ah,}} \ \overset{\text{/}}{\text{Sun}} \ \overset{\text{/}}{\text{flow}} \ \overset{\text{x}}{\text{er}}$), there is a question to be asked, however naive some might find it: What do the two units into which the last six syllables allegedly fall have to do with the experience of reading the line, an experience that surely incorpo-rates, without our even having to think about it, a regard for word boundaries and syntactical groupings?

In the case of the Shelley citation ("unquestionably iambic") the presumable Wimsatt-Beardsley scansion is as follows:

$$\overset{\text{/}}{\text{Hail}} \mid \overset{\text{x}}{\text{to}} \ \overset{\text{/}}{\text{thee}} \mid \overset{\text{x}}{\text{blithe}} \ \overset{\text{/}}{\text{spi}} \mid \overset{\text{x}}{\text{rit}}$$

The first thing to note is how the important term "blithe" is de-moted. But the supression of normal stressing aside, we find our-selves looking at what one might call a hemi-foot both at the beginning and ending of the line, the first consisting of a stressed syllable (Wimsatt and Beardsley concede it this status), the other of an unstressed syllable, "rit." In other words, two of the line's six syllables, the first and last, are both outside the allegedly iambic pattern. In such an array, what meaning does the notion of the foot as the constitutive "unit" of the line have, for that is what it is supposed to be? (I should note that, in a solo reading of the line, Wimsatt so marks the word "spirit" that it *might* be taken as a monosyllable.[20] This would then assimilate "spirit" into a "foot" pronounced "blithe spírt," and remove one of my objections to what I have taken to be the Wimsatt-Beardsley reading of the line. But then, of course, I would continue to object to the demotion of "blithe" and take exception to the violation of the line's terminal word.)

Whether in terms of foot divisions or stress assignments or line characterizations, the Wimsatt-Beardsley readings can be taken as all too typical of the history of scansion, insofar as it has employed the concept of meter, or more precisely, the concept of the "foot" (for the overwhelming majority of prosodists the two concepts are inseparable). I offer a list of samples, selected more or less at random:

> For at e | ventide, lis | tening earn | estly
>> (George Saintsbury, applying
>> the "foot system" to a
>> line of Tennyson)[21]

> I do not set my life | at a pín's |ʌ fée
>> (Egerton Smith, a "timer" (explained
>> below), marking a line from *Hamlet,*
>> in which his notation appears to
>> indicate a pause just before "fee")[22]

> Weep nó | more, wóe | ful Shép | herds, weép | no móre
>> (John Crowe Ransom's marking of a
>> line from Milton's *Lycidas*)[23]

> Rocks, Caves, Lakes, Fens, Bogs, Dens and shades of death
>> (Henry Lee Smith, Jr. scans this line
>> from *Paradise Lost* as "iambic meter
>> . . . perfectly maintained")[24]

> Seen, and unknowne; heard, but without attention
>> (John Thompson says of this line
>> from Sidney that "two of its feet
>> depart from the metrical

pattern. . . . Word for word,
however, it does fit the
metrical pattern, even the exact
iambic pattern")[25]

Speech af | ter long | si | lence; it | is right
    (Harvey Gross's scansion of a line
    from Yeats)[26]

If he | risk to | be wound | ed by | my tongue
    (Gross's scansion of a line from
    Ransom)[27]; it seems only fitting
    that Ransom should have done
    unto him the sort of thing he does
    unto Milton)

                4   3   2   1
When to the ses | sions of | sweet si | lent thought
                    4   3   2   1
I summon up remem | brance of | things past
    (Wimsatt's reading of lines from
    Shakespeare, where the numerals
    1–4 represent degrees of stress in
    descending order, thus giving us two
    iambic feet in each of the portions of
    the lines marked by the numbers[28];
    this reading is assented to by
    Thomas Cable)[29]

Yet utter the word Democratic, the word En-Masse.
    (Annie Finch describes this line from
    Whitman as "almost perfectly
    dactylic, with an initial
    hypermetrical syllable. . . .")[30]

While there might well be differences in rendering from reader
to reader, no enunciation of these lines that honored the usual
stress patterns of the words as well as their sense and their syntactic groupings would be accurately mapped by even a single one of
the above formulations. Devoid of this accuracy, how meaningful,
how useful are the scansions? (Assemblages not nearly as hokey
as these were rightly labeled by Nist as "little coffins of unreality."[31]
They are the result of a kind of prosodic foot fetishism, a will so
determined to behold particular "units" making for an overall design within a verse line that the most factitious sorts of packets
are shamelessly marked off and "exhibited" to us.
    I am certainly not the first to question the usefulness of scansion

by feet, as will be made evident in the next chapter.[32] But such questioning has not triumphed in the field of prosody, *pace* Donald Wesling, who, in his historical study of English and American poetry, says: "Curiously the foot hypothesis is dethroned at the same time it is given its most detailed defense in the theorists between Patmore and Saintsbury."[33] Wesling's statement assigns too much weight to the practices of some poets in the period 1855–1910, the time span that he is focusing on when he makes the statement.

Prosodists *after* Saintsbury have continued to think like him, as my earlier listing of scansions would indicate. In fact, there is no doubt that the concept of meter as it has operated over many years and up to the very present has had at its heart that small but imperious entity, that Napoleon of notions, the foot.

Here is George Saintsbury proclaiming its centrality:

> the clear universal principles which govern the province of English versification . . . are the foot, the line, and the stanza or paragraph, but, above all, the foot, the ground at once of stability and motion, the secret and *idea* of English prosody, the be-all, if not the end-all, of English verse (italics in original).[34]

He also says that "The birth, progress, and perfecting of the foot under the guidance of equivalent substitution [the convention whereby one foot may be substituted for another in a given line] . . . this is 'the mystery of this wonderful history,' the open secret of English prosodic life."[35]

Saintsbury embraces the "be-all" of the foot without any clear conception of the nature of its elements, as has been recognized; he appears not even to desire such a conception. Such is the effect of his telling us early in the course of his monumental work, *A History of English Prosody: From the Twelfth Century to the Present Day*, that he will make only minimal reference to the problem of "the particular agency which constitutes that difference of the value of syllables out of which rhythm and metre are made."[36] Composed of syllables of different character, the foot has a worth simply known to Saintsbury, though its measure has not been taken.

Saintsbury rejects (in a characteristically fuzzy way) the temporalist approach to meter, that is, the notion that lines of a poem written in a given meter take approximately the same time to say, or to put it a little differently, the assumption that the feet of the line are equal in duration, or to put it still differently, that the time elapsing between stressed syllables is roughly equal, or isochronous, whatever the number of intervening unstressed syllables may be.[37] Given Saintsbury's dismissal of the timer approach, we must ask why he should have characterized Edgar Allan Poe as "an instinctively and generally right . . . essayist on points of prosodic doctrine," though he does qualify that approval by saying that Poe was "in detail, hasty, ill-informed, and crude. . . ."[38] For Poe was a timer, pure if not simple, conceiving of syllables in terms of their length, and taking, as so many timers do, music as his model. Referring to what he regarded as an erroneous scansion of a line in Horace, he said it violated "the inviolable principle of all music, *time*" (Poe's italics).[39] He said, too, that in attempts to relieve verse of "monotone," "men soon came to see that there was no absolute necessity for adhering to the precise number of syllables [in a foot], provided the time required for the whole foot was preserved inviolate" (p. 43). The time values of individual syllables in a line were to be kept under tight rein: "every long syllable must of its own accord occupy in its utterance, or must be *made* to occupy, precisely the time demanded for two short ones" (p. 35; Poe's italics.) To keep his timer approach afloat, Poe had to resort, among other things, to the notion of some short syllables being only one-sixth the length of a long syllable. But no matter how much he fiddled with syllable length, Poe never for a moment abandoned the idea of the foot, and perhaps this was enough to keep him in Saintsbury's good graces.

The concept of the foot, in fact, constitutes a crucial overlap between the stresser and timer approaches. Egerton Smith's book, *The Principles of English Metre* (1923), is described by Brogan as "The most authoritative statement of the Temporal theory of metrics . . . " (p. 206). But while differing so sharply from Saintsbury, Smith is as staunch an advocate of the foot. He says that "ordinarily the system of grouping [of feet] shows itself unmistakably, and the intention of the poet discloses itself to the reader's perception or even forces itself on his attention."[40]

To some more recent metrists, temperamentally the opposite of Saintsbury in being intent on specifying everything, and conceiving of themselves as radically revising traditional prosody, the foot remains a given. Henry Lee Smith, Jr., writing a piece called "Toward Redefining English Prosody," continues to employ the foot, though he casts aside not only the spondee, à la Wimsatt and Beardsley, but also the dactyl and anapest. (The tossing away of this last must have set the corpse of Saintsbury spinning; for him, the anapest was not only among the "commonest English feet,"[41] but, when employed continuously, "perhaps the chief enlivening and inspiriting force in English poetry. . . .")[42] Smith, introducing a monograph by Edmund L. Epstein and Terence Hawkes, describes them as developing "a theory of English prosody differing markedly from the traditional statements. . . ."[43] Do *they* reject the foot? Not at all. Taking into account not only stress, but also the linguistic considerations of pitch and juncture (the latter refers to the various boundaries that may exist between syllables), they exponentially multiply the various kinds of feet, and seem disappointed that they have not come up with more. They state, without irony, that there are "*only 6192 possibilities of iambic units*" in English, and "*only 2376 possibilities of trochaic units*" (pp. 21, 30; underlining in original). Only! While they are certainly right in their desire to bring our attention to the presence of pitch and juncture, is their obsessive exhaustiveness an improvement on traditional scansion?

Readers may judge for themselves by looking at how Epstein and Hawkes deal with one of Ariel's songs in *The Tempest*. Here is the song:

> Full fathom five thy father lies,
> Of his bones are coral made;
> Those are pearls that were his eyes:
> Nothing of him that doth fade
> But doth suffer a sea change
> Into something rich and strange.
> Sea nymphs hourly ring his knell:
>   Ding-dong.
>
> Hark now I hear them,—Ding-dong, bell.

If we approach the lines through traditional prosody and read them as trochaic, Epstein and Hawkes argue, we come up with, out of thirty-three possible feet, fifteen "impurities," that is, feet that are either monosyllabic or spondees—an "unbearably ragged" result. But if read as iambic, the lines can be shown to have (though only through a procedure that an unfriendly observer might call the Higher Finagling) merely three impurities, and reveal themselves as—iambic. Carrying their analysis further, but now drawing on their huge collection of feet, they discover that the poem is in iambic tetrameter (pp. 44–47).

It seems to have escaped Epstein and Hawkes that they have labored only to bring forth a tautology, and that traditional scansion, with its smaller collection of feet and its own tautological mind-set (I shall take note of this later) would have been perfectly capable of yielding their final result. Readers may decide at their leisure how well the iambic tetrameter grid (x / | x / | x / | x /) fits Ariel's song. Let them, for example, contemplate the fact that only two of the song's lines display the eight syllables the grid would appear to call for. But what I chiefly wish to point out is that, under the aegis of Epstein and Hawkes, an originally troublesome piece of verse—troublesome only to foot fetishists—has been safely embalmed under a standard label. After all this, is it any surprise that these alleged revisionists should say that in general "Saintsbury's ear and modern descriptive linguistics complement each other . . . "? (p. 30) Epstein and Hawkes have turned out to be metrical good old boys.

Working the side of the street opposite that of Epstein and Hawkes, with their veritable warehouse of feet, is Sheridan Baker, who carries the willed simplifications of Wimsatt and Beardsley to their ultimate expression. (It should also be noted that Baker, unlike Epstein and Hawkes, is a timer.) Baker declares "We need feet . . . and we need to remember the predominance of the iambus. . . . Fancier systems of scansion tend to destroy the conception of meter with which the poet began . . . thinking . . . simply of *ti-dum, ti-dum, ti-dum*. . . ." That Baker really means this is indicated by his approach to a verse line that is problematical for metrists who measure by feet: "It is not impossible that [Shakespeare] first thought 'Let ME not TO the MArriage OF true MINDS,' and discovered afterwards that his five stresses would migrate to where they belonged in the language. . . ."[44] *Where they belonged*—that is the question. One has to doubt the usefulness of a reading of the line that begins where Baker's does, with an array of uniform feet, and doubt even more such a reading of another line from Shakespeare's Sonnet 116—"Or bend with the remover to remove." *Ti-dum, ti-dum, ti-dum* is a hard notion to swallow.[45]

The sort of simplification represented by Baker may be an overreaction to the multiple considerations and relatively elaborate notation brought to the study of sound in poetry by linguists (including Epstein and Hawkes, who, ironically, as has just been indicated, have strong affinities with traditional metrics). Showing himself a member of the school of Baker (and Wimsatt and Beardsley) is John Frederick Nims, who declares that "No good English poet has ever devised a rhythmical system using more than the two intensities (accented and unaccented)." Presenting a line as it might be marked by a linguist to indicate both degrees of stress

and pitch change, he says that "a system that turns a simple line
of Yeats into

$$\overset{2}{\underset{\wedge}{\text{Speech}}} + \text{after} + \text{long silence; it} + \text{is} + \text{right} \dots$$

is more complex than we need. Readers do not listen that way;
poets do not write that way."[46]

But that readers do not listen and that most good poets (one
hopes) have not written the ways *traditional* scansion would have
us believe is precisely the point I have been trying to make. One
need not enjoy perusing lines bristling with a linguist's notations
in order to consider the possibility that such notations have much
more to tell us about verse movement than does the foot system,
the heart of traditional scansion.[47] Of course, if such notations are
put at the service of that scansion, we get the mind-boggling figures
of an Epstein and Hawkes.

2

A Further Look at The Foot: Prosody's Persistent Problematic

HOW or when did commentary on poetry written in English come to be mired in the mind-set of regarding the verse line as made up of feet? We might begin by taking note of a crucial observation made by Derek Attridge; should it receive proper attention it might well begin to undermine the domination the foot has enjoyed over the minds of too many prosodists for too many years. Attridge points out that in the sixteenth century, for want of a more appropriate, native frame of reference,

> the terms of classical prosody [specifically, 'the iambic'] became lodged among the commonplaces of English metrical analysis. . . . [But] the main tradition in prosodic theory until the end of the eighteenth century was based on syllables and accents rather than feet, and only with the new interest in Greece and Rome in the nineteenth century did foot-scansion come into its own as a mode of analysis. . . .

Subjecting meter to this historical contextualization is important in order that "its sheer familiarity does not confer on it any unwarranted authority."[1]

Attridge's statement about the nineteenth century giving prominence to foot-scansion strips from the foot the aura of timelessness and inevitability it is endowed with (if sometimes only implicitly) by many modern treatments of prosody. (Paul Fussell's *Poetic Meter and Poetic Form* is a notable exception, with its chapter on "The Historical Dimension.") For example, while Karl Shapiro and Robert Beum recognize objections to the foot, they attempt to sweep them aside by saying:

> It would be foolish . . . to disregard in a modernist or intuitionist frenzy the whole business of the foot and its attendant implications. If any point in prosody matters does *not* require debate, it is that English

35

poets were early made and long kept acutely conscious of the classical tradition.[2]

I am frenzied enough to continue to question "the whole business of the foot," and to say that while English poets (and prosodists) certainly did know of the classical tradition, that does not mean that they adopted it mindlessly and monolithically.[3] Attridge, in fact, advocates our not "allowing ourselves to be awed by [the foot's] classical pedigree."[4] Looking closely, as I now propose to do, at that classical pedigree and then at its purported transfer to English in the Elizabethan period can only confirm Attridge's less-than-reverent stance.[5] (Attridge himself has given us the definitive study of attempts to imitate classical, that is, quantitative meters in English, one of the works I shall draw on in the remarks that now follow.)

The Greek term from which "prosody" comes originally referred to the accentuation of syllables as determined by musical pitch, but the word gradually expanded to mean "the facts concerning the 'quantities' of syllables, i.e., the time taken to pronounce them."[6] But ancient grammarians had two ways of regarding syllables in terms of quantity. The first divided them into short and long, the second "found a whole scale of durational values." (This is somewhat analogous to the current situation, in which some prosodists wish to recognize only two degrees of stress while others prefer three and still others four.) The two classifications could not be and were not resolved.[7] Latin prosody worked with the simpler scheme, that of long and short syllables, which were grouped in various predetermined combinations within a verse line, with the units of combination constituting feet.

But in the would-be assimilation of Greek prosody by Latin prosody, even the apparently simple procedure of employing just two kinds of syllables produced oddities. For one thing, a reversal of terminology eventually took place. Donatus, a fourth-century writer, attributed "arsis" and "thesis" to every foot. In Greek prosody, the first term, which meant "lifting up," and the second, which meant "setting down," refer

to the upbeat and downbeat of a melodic line and are related by etymology to the uplifting and placement of the feet during a dance. The Romans, however, came to equate arsis and thesis with "raising" and "lowering" of the voice. . . . Since the "lifting up" of the voice is a way of "marking time" and thus of defining a rhythmic interval, arsis (rather than thesis) is associated with ictus [this last term may be equated with "metrical beat"].[8]

Moreover, in Latin prosody, according to the rules of versification, but for reasons not clear, "consonants at the beginning of a syllable play no part in determining its quantity, while consonants at the end are of crucial importance;" even with this distinction, "a long vowel or diphthong followed by two or more consonants . . . is no longer than a long vowel or diphthong alone."[9] In short, the notions of long and short are divorced from physical actuality. This is not the last oddity in classical prosody. In some meters, certain feet, though mathematically correct, cannot, by tradition, be used as substitutes; "in other metres, substitutions of certain feet, though mathematically faulty, are allowed." Moreover, "Many verse forms seem organized not according to feet but according to larger groupings of feet: dipodies and cola."[10]

There are gaps or anomalies, then, both in the transition from Greek to Latin prosody, and within Latin prosody itself. Attridge, in *Well-Weighed Syllables,* notes that "quantitative Latin verse was the result of an attempt to impose upon one language a metrical system natural to another, and very different, language, Greek . . ." (17) So while the Romans "devoted their theoretical attention" to quantitative meters, "it nevertheless seems possible that, as far as rhythmic organization of sound is concerned, they actually responded to the stress patterns when reading and listening to verse" (p. 18). But this is not the end of the matter. "The rules of Latin verse prevent the complete coincidence of accent and ictus [the metrical beat, enunciated or *imagined*] in the great majority of lines . . ." (p. 14). Attridge further says, *nota bene,* that the idea of judging the quantity of a syllable by what one actually heard in pronouncing its vowel "would have made the whole art of Latin prosody impossible" (p. 72).

This observation, along with the other materials I have been citing, indicates that to survey our classical prosodic legacy is to view as dubious an inheritance as one can find in literary history. We begin with a prosody, the Greek, that slides from an interest in a musically defined component of language—pitch—to a codification of another, more strictly linguistic component—quantity—possibly without noticing that it has done so. Latin prosody then attempts to force this codification on itself, while asking for more trouble by setting up a conception both of quantity and of stress patterns at variance with normal pronunciation of words. What concerns us is that to a large extent (*but certainly not entirely*—a qualification I shall pursue shortly) English prosody then links up with Latin prosody as Latin prosody had linked up with the Greek, taking over the notion of foot-based meter, and carrying into our language a way of thinking of the verse line that would prove to be at variance with the actual nature of its constituents.

The point at which English prosody took the concept of meter to its bosom, or more precisely, the point at which it *allegedly* established the foot-based iambic pentameter line at the center of poetic practice, is, if we go along with John Thompson's acclaimed study, *The Founding of English Metre,* the late sixteenth century. George Gascoigne's treatise, "Certayne Notes of Instruction" (1575) is Thompson's prime exhibit as he attempts to show "how and why" the iambic line achieved "a vigorous and triumphant realization."[11] He claims that Gascoigne doesn't say

> there *should* be alternate weak and strong stresses in a pentameter line . . . he says there *are* alternate weak and strong stresses in a line, whether the speech fits or not. It was a profound change, even if it was largely only the conscious recognition of a principle that sometimes operated in verse whether the poets liked it or not (pp. 69–70; italics in original).

Thompson further says of Gascoigne that "The iambic foot is the only one that counts for him" (p. 73).

That there was some attempt to incorporate classical prosody into English poetry is undeniable; it should probably be seen as part of the effort at the time to establish the worth of English literature. But I have several problems with Thompson's widely accepted assertions about the triumph of meter, or at least of the foot-based iambic pentameter line. For one thing, just what was the source of the power of this principle that "sometimes" imposed itself on poets allegedly powerless to withstand it? Judging from what he says, I gather Thompson would argue that it was the nature of the English language itself: "The iambic metrical pattern has dominated English verse because it provides the best symbolic model of our language" (p. 12). But if so, why did the principle not *always* impose itself? Elsewhere in his book, Thompson appears to forget his qualification and suggest that it did; he asserts that "In one sense Gascoigne's 'Certayne Notes' contained nothing new at all. He only described what *everyone* was doing or trying to do. It was all implicit in the use of iambic metres from the beginning" (p. 75; my italics). Thompson has effected a double shift here, from saying that the weak-strong metrical pattern *sometimes* operated to saying it *always* did (more or less), and from saying the pattern imposed itself to saying the poets were imposing it or trying to.

But apart from this slipperiness, the chief problem I see in

Thompson's book is his focus, in treating Gascoigne, on the imperiousness of meter:

> The metrical pattern is absolute and admits of no variation whatsoever. . . . The most important point in the ["Certayne Notes"] essay is [this]: When the language and the metrical pattern come together in the line of verse, it is the metrical pattern that rules. If language and metrical pattern do not coincide exactly, the metrical pattern takes precedence . . ." (p. 73).

In reading this we need to ask: whatever happened to Gascoigne's concern with maintaining ordinary stressing, which Thompson himself cites? Gascoigne wrote: " . . . in your verses remember to place every worde in his natural *Emphasis* or sound, that is to say in such wise . . . as it is commonly pronounced or used" (quoted in Thompson, p. 71). Gascoigne goes on about this for several sentences, indicating its importance to him. Thompson has chosen to see as the most notable principle emerging from Gascoigne the notion that meter tyrannizes the line, so to speak, admitting of no exceptions. In doing so, he does not give enough weight to Gascoigne's concern that ordinary pronunciation not be violated. Where Gascoigne would appear to be intent on avoiding a clash of meter and normative pronunciation, Thompson posits such clashes and declares meter the undisputed winner.[12]

Moreover, it appears that Thompson is, like it or not, giving his assent to sonically defective poetry, poetry that mechanically thumps out an endless series of iambs on the theory that meter *must* be preserved. To the extent that the iambic line triumphed in Thompson's sense, flexible and engaging verse movement suffered, a Pyrrhic victory if ever there was one. George T. Wright (himself a traditional prosodist, and one whose work I shall engage in later chapters) has observed that " . . . Gascoigne and poets of his generation wrote a verse that sounded essentially the same in every line. . . ."[13]

Thomas Cable has suggested that "there are two quite different modes of the English iambic pentameter, one based on an alternating pattern, the other based on the foot."[14] He so names Gascoigne in this view of the matter as to undermine the claim Thompson puts forth for that poet-metrist's founding role in the establishment of foot-based meter. Cable contends that "the meter of Chaucer and . . . Gascoigne (based on alternating stress and syllabism) is significantly different from the English iambic pentameter from Sidney to Yeats (based on the foot and syllabism)."[15]

But Cable's overall mind-set is much closer to Thompson's than not, and there are other grounds for believing that a tyrannical, meter-imposed regularity did not necessarily have as wide or as lasting a victory as Thompson would suggest, with his talk of the "founding" of English meter as an assemblage of five iambic feet, a formulation that implies the laying down of a permanent bedrock. We might do well to remember O. B. Hardison's observation that "Much English sixteenth-century verse is [like medieval English verse] more irregular than one would expect if it had been written according to the formulas of accentual foot meter."[16]

Actual poetic practice aside, the notion that meter was to be lord of the line was not an uncontested one in the period in question. Hardison informs us that "Testimony on the priority of syntactic rhythms to meter in verse is given by sixteenth-century grammarians who observe that only schoolchildren read poems in a way that gives precedence to meter. Experienced readers emphasize meaning . . ." (p. 4). He quotes in particular one John Brinsley who said: "in all Poetry, for the pronuntiation, it is to be uttered as prose; observing distinctions and the nature of the matter; not to be tuned foolishly or childishly after the manner of scanning a Verse, as the use of some is" (p. 100). If we give weight to this, it can be said that Thompson is taking the view that English poetry was "founded" on a basis uncomfortably akin to schoolboy scansions.

Resistance to scanning by feet in the Elizabethan period can be found not only in the materials cited by Hardison, but in George Puttenham's *The Art of English Poesie,* which Brogan has called "the most extensive and important English treatise on verse-making" (p. 269). It was published in 1589, only fourteen years after the appearance of the document allegedly crucial to meter's "founding," Gascoigne's "Certayne Notes. . . ." Puttenham describes Greek verse as having meters composed of feet, but says "Meeter and measure . . . with us [consist of] the number of sillables, which are comprehended in every verse, not regarding his feete. . . ."[17] After playing with the possibility of incorporating classical feet into English, where the role of quantity would be taken by ictus or stress, he ends up saying "in very truth I thinke [my remarks] but vaine & superstitious observations nothing at all furthering the pleasant melody of our English meeter . . . and rather wish the continuance of our old maner of Poesie, scanning our verse by [count of] sillables rather than by feet. . . ."[18]

Puttenham's position is not unique, according to Hardison, who says that "English Renaissance critics regularly refer to English verse as though it is syllabic . . ." (p. 13). Even George Wright, who speaks of "the alternating accent that seems to us so palpable a feature of iambic pentameter practice and that poets and readers had obviously aimed at and responded to from Surrey on," notes that "For Elizabethan readers . . . iambic pentameter was perceived essentially as a line whose pattern was entirely defined when you stated that it had ten syllables."[19] We can conclude, then, that even if a strict foot-based prosody in English, modeled on Latin poetics, can be found operating as far back as Gascoigne (and again I would point out that Thompson's version of Gascoigne does not give us the whole story of that poet's concerns), the embrace of such a prosody was not universal in the Elizabethan era. Nor was it universal in ensuing periods right up till our own time. There has been not only avoidance of it but conscious resistance to it, beginning with Puttenham. So we can say that while too much has been made of the pedigree of "classical" prosody, centered on the foot, not enough has been made of the pedigree of the opposing camp. Questioning of the foot has not necessarily been, as Shapiro and Beum would have it, a frenzied "modernist" stance.

It was certainly present in the eighteenth century. Edward Bysshe's *The Art of English Poetry,* originally published in 1702, brought out in many more editions, and characterized by Brogan as "very likely the most influential prosodic handbook ever written" (p. 242), presented as its opening statement the following: "The structure of our Verse . . . consists in a certain Number of Syllables, not in Feet compos'd of long and short Syllables . . ." (quoted in Brogan, p. 243). Much later, coming after the nineteenth-century rise of scansion by feet that Attridge refers to, but before Saintsbury's work, which can be thought of as the apotheosis of foot-enamored metrics, we have two great scholars, W. W. Skeat and Otto Jespersen, declaring war on the foot.[20] The latter spoke of it as a "paper idea," and noted that the use of it sometimes joined

syllables which are not to be heard together . . . and whose relation to one another is therefore of no consequence, while the syllables that have to be weighted against one another are by the same means separated as if they did not concern one another. Could anything be more absurd?[21]

Writing two years after Jespersen, in 1902, the experimental phonetician E. W. Scripture treated the poetic line as a continuous sound stream rather than as an assemblage of individual "feet."[22]

About three decades later, inspired by Scripture, and using electronic equipment, Wilbur Schramm measured the acoustic properties of lines of verse. In the spirit of Jespersen, he concluded, according to Seymour Chatman, that

> in many respects the traditional foot was not a real phonetic entity. The foot was not set apart by sense, nor by pauses, nor by the psychological grouping effect nor by equal time spans. Neither did it 'express the rhythm of the line'. . . .[23]

The Russian Formalists, whose work has made itself felt in English poetics, chiefly through the writings of Roman Jakobson, questioned the applicability of the foot to Russian verse, thinking of the line as the basic unit of verse rhythm. George R. Stewart, even as he retained references to "feet," told us that the terms "iambic" and "trochaic" had been "so variously used and misused" that he was going to do his best to avoid them,[24] and in his scansions he did just that. A friend of the foot of Stewart's sort might prove as deadly as any enemy (and if we combine his rejections with Saintsbury's dismissals of spondees and dactyls, we have to wonder what is left for foot-metrists to work with—anapests and choriambs?) The same could be said of Seymour Chatman, who, while aware of the views of Jakobson, Scripture, and Schramm, is not willing to relinquish the foot, but concedes that it is "a pure metrical convention with no relation to English or to the sense of the poem."[25]

James G. Southworth defines the "native tradition" as

> rhythmical rather than . . . metrical. . . . With Surrey the tradition is altered, but not basically changed. Although contemporary writers [i.e., of the Elizabethan era] begin to use classical terms and to speak of feet, poets continue to write in units longer than the foot.[26]

Southworth cites the work of Catherine Ing, whose study of Elizabethan lyrics has been highly praised by Brogan. Ing contends that in order for us to enjoy such poems as "Slow, Slow, Fresh Fount," "it is essential to allow whole phrases to remain undivided by any attempt at ordering into simple repeating 'feet,' and to read the phrases with sufficient care to make their rhythm perceptible."[27] She does not use feet in any of her scansions. In 1970, Charles L. Stevenson, noting that T. S. Omond had remarked that the foot was borrowed "without enquiry into the actualities of English speech-sounds"[28] and acknowledging George R. Stewart as a forerunner, proposed an approach to English verse that would do away with the foot altogether. He made as important an observation as any to be found in prosodic criticism:

> Our poets have led, rather than followed our prosodists. And their thoughts, like their intentions, are best judged from their work itself. If the concept of a foot poorly illuminates their work, that is a reason for suspecting that they did not think in terms of it.[29]

(Perhaps he should have added that while poets may have *thought* in terms of it, they did not necessarily let it operate as their master.)

Much of the work in so-called generative metrics, which focuses on defining metricality and testing lines for its presence or degree, dispenses with the notion of the foot.[30] Another approach, in a study that can lay claim to being the leading treatment of prosody in recent years, Derek Attridge's widely-informed and strenuous *The Rhythms of English Poetry* (1982), conducts its scansions without invoking feet. Attridge quite properly refers to feet as "ghostly divisions." (Without his saying so, or necessarily agreeing that it is the case, this nicely turns the tables on those who regard free verse as "haunted" by meter, a matter I shall consider in a later chapter—for such prosodists, meter per se is hardly ghostly.) Attridge further says that classical scansion "tends to conceive of metre as a visual and spatial phenomenon rather than a dynamic one; it is satisfied if it can find five feet in a line by its analytical procedures, even if these do not coincide with the five recurring beats perceived by the reader."[31] I would add that it is questionable, as with Shakespeare's line, "Or bend with the remover to remove," whether the reader always does perceive five beats, let alone perceive them where the metrist may place them. (Attridge's own approach to scansion will be discussed in the next chapter).

Given the long and substantial pedigree of attempts to avoid or eliminate scansion by feet,[32] given the persistent gaps between the conventional precepts and the reader's perceptions, why has the concept of the foot endured? What accounts for its perverse vigor, and its finding new territory to encroach upon in the domain of free verse? Why haven't all modern prosodists (and poets, in their criticism) heeded John Nist's' declaration that "the classical foot is a dead metrical concept. It is time to bury it"?[33] Why have we continued to encounter metrists who feel free to inform us that Blake's chimney sweeper cries out his calling—"'weep! 'weep! 'weep! 'weep!"—in two iambs,[34] and that one of Prufrock's outbursts could be scanned as

It is | im pos | si ble | to say | just what | I mean! ?[35]

Why did John Berryman think he was telling us something useful in scanning a line from *The Pisan Cantos,* "So old Elkin had only one glory," as having "a spondee-two dactyls-and trochee?"[36] What does it add up to for a free verse poem to have, according to Paul Ramsey, one line that consists of "iamb amphibrach," another of "pyrrhic spondee," yet another of "dactyl dactyl?"[37] (As Eliot once pointed out, "Any line can be divided into feet and accents"[38]; but where does that leave us?)[39] Why does Miller Williams say "the nature of the foot at the end of a line is as relevant to nonpatterned poetry as it is to what we call formal poetry . . .?"[40] Wherever do these shadowy limbs spring from?

It is a passion for abstract pattern that seems to inform the continued use of the foot, the core entity of conventional prosody. The explicit registration of that passion can be traced to the late nineteenth century,[41] the very period designated by Attridge as having given us a preoccupation with foot-based scansion. Wimsatt and Beardsley's landmark essay, "The Concept of Meter: An Exercise in Abstraction," echoes Victorian prosodists, and is reechoed in much critical literature appearing after it. John Thompson says that metrical pattern "does for language what the forms of any art do for their materials. It abstracts certain elements from the experience of the senses and forms them into patterns."[42] Harvey Gross, who talks of Wimsatt and Beardsley's "brilliant deductions," states that "Meter, the specialized form of rhythm, is an abstraction from a realm of linguistic possibilities; consequently no mere linguistic 'facts' (given us by phoneticians or oscillographic analysis) can explain what is intimately a part of symbolic process."[43] I might note here that this contempt for the mere linguistic facts has been the curse of prosody from the Greeks onward; it is a most dubious instance of mind over matter.

On the other hand, a concern for facts provides no automatic immunity against the appeal of abstraction. Marina Tarlinskaja, an amasser par excellence of facts about stress patterns, notes that in studies of metrical theory "meter is rightfully considered . . . as a sequence abstracted from the sequence of stresses in concrete lines. . . ."[44] Moreover, it should be acknowledged that a passion for abstraction can survive even when the foot has been left behind, as it is by most generative metrists. Donald C. Freeman contends in an article published in 1972 that "Research here characterized as generative metrics has argued that the best kinds of generalizations can be captured about metrical form when meter is conceived of as an abstract pattern." His own proposed solutions to the problem of Emily Dickinson's metrics "argue for a far more abstract concept [more abstract than generative metrics?] of deep metrical form. . . ."[45]

We reach perhaps the apogee of allegiance to abstraction in an essay by Thomas Cable, who, while calling Wimsatt and Beardsley's essay "brilliantly written," dismisses their dismissal of a reading of Donne that would keep one of his lines perfectly regular, at least at an abstract level. Hoisting them with their own petard, Cable says "The metrists who argue most convincingly for meter as an 'exercise in abstraction' fail to abstract far enough, basing their reading upon the syntactic pattern. . . ."[46] Elsewhere he says that "The process of stepping back and abstracting is of course central to metrics."[47] Cable is so enamored of abstraction (on the level of duration as well as stress) that he argues, with a modicum of self-deprecation, for observing a pause before reading the first line of a particular poem in order to make up for a deficient foot at the start of that line and to achieve a "conceptually more satisfying" reading than would otherwise be the case.[48]

The continuing allegiance of metrists to the foot might proceed from something a little different from a fascination with abstraction. To think of a poem in terms of regular patterns of iambs, trochees, etc., is simply to piece out the idea that a poem is governed by, or at the very least contains, a *system*, and one of elegant simplicity; the foot is its constituent element, its atom so to speak. (Brooks and Warren define meter as "the systematization of rhythm. . . .")[49] The presence of such a system serves as a heady source of pleasure, implying the "unity" of a given poem, and providing the comfort of something that can be invoked automatically as a framework for analyzing the sounds of that poem.

The accentual-syllabic, foot-based prosody I have been discussing is referred to as "a received paradigm" by Donald Wesling, who goes on to say of it: "the tendency of the whole reigning-paradigm enterprise is to forget that feet are theoretical entities, so that feet are somehow found, reified, and believed in—and once exceptions and anomalies are reduced, prosody's work is done."[50] It would be hard to find a more admirable and concise formulation of the matter. But, even while issuing strong qualifications, Wesling is willing to grant the paradigm far more acceptance than I do. Such a gesture may well derive from his *own* attraction to the idea of a system, which he extends to specimens of verse that would seem blatantly resistant to the accentual-syllabic paradigm. He says:

In Hopkins, the number of verbal systems . . . is extremely in excess of the systems in the Tennysonian norm. . . . [i]n Whitman, by con-

trast, the system of parallelism of syntax is basic, and infinitely changeable; this is clearly systematic enough for the creation of strong
poetry. . . .[51]

The contrast Wesling is drawing between Hopkins and Whitman is
not put as clearly as it might have been, but the celebration of
"system" is clear enough.

The satisfaction in having a system is sometimes explicitly recognized by prosodists. Harvey Gross, for example, has said that
"Meter, with its flow of syllables, stresses, and feet, may set up a
self-referring system, a *Gestalt,* to which our sensibilities respond
as if to actual feelings" (italics in original).[52] The setting up of
meter has been seen by Frederick Turner and Ernest Pöppel as an
example of the system-seeking inherent to the human mind: "The
human nervous system has a strong drive to construct affirmative,
plausible, coherent . . . models of the world, in which all events
are explained by and take their place in a system. . . ."[53] Free
verse, on the other hand, is the absence of system. Brad Leithauser
claims that what has not emerged from the un-iambic verse innova-
tions of the nineteenth century "is an ongoing, evolving prosodic
system that might compete in vigor and adaptability with the iambic line. To most contemporary poets, anyway, the only genuine
competitor is a nonsystem—that of free verse. . . ."[54] What Leithauser thinks of free verse, of nonsystem, is indicated by his ag-
gressive advocacy of the New Formalism. (I shall take up the
hostility to free verse in Chapter 4.)

A variation on the notion of system is the notion of verse "laws."
Thus, Saintsbury declares that "The most important law of English
prosody is that which permits . . . the substitution of equivalent
feet."[55] Dennis Taylor tells us that "Understanding metrical law is
important because metrical law enables us to read poetry as the
poet intended it. . . ."[56] But shortly after this axiomatic declaration, Taylor makes the following observation:

> Our standard English rhythm, with its complicated heritage in 'French
> and Anglo-Saxon principles . . . with music, religious and secular, and
> Latin for intermediaries' . . . has remained a rich and puzzling phe-
> nomenon (p. 8).

Moreover, Taylor goes on to note that metrical theory has been
"peculiarly dependent on analogies and world views" (p. 9), and
talks of the distinctive ways in which metrical laws have been
defined in different periods: "as classical law, as mechanical law,
as musical law, as organic law, as dialectical law, as statistical law,

as structural law, as generative law" (p. 9). This list of laws would appear to comprise an array of superannuated items, not an enduring entity among them. Taylor himself, for example, says that "the classical law, muddled in itself and applied to English verse, was hardly a law at all" (p. 11). What has happened to his original claim that a knowledge of the metrical law guides us in the reading of a line "as the poet intended it?" Taylor's historicism, which gives us, as Wallace Stevens might say, "the squirming facts," is plainly at war with "the squamous mind," which shows forth in Taylor's appeal to the abstract frame, the law.

In a self-sustaining circular process, the assumption of a system or law in a poem prepares the way for having that system or law displayed in terms of the reified, prefabricated units known as feet. For remember that scansion in conventional prosody is not as innocent an activity as merely marking stressed and unstressed syllables, letting them fall as they may. This may be how scansion *begins,* but behind such marking is the intention, the *will,* to find groupings of syllables that match each other and that conform to one or more of the kit of feet the traditional prosodist keeps always at his elbow. Under its entry for "scansion," the *Princeton Encyclopedia of Poetry and Poetics* speaks of the reader

> first mark[ing] stressed and unstressed syllables, not according to any pre-conceived pattern, but according to the degree of sense emphasis transmitted by the syllables. . . . After ascertaining whether the lines are generally in ascending or descending rhythm . . . the reader next marks the feet. . . .[57]

Following upon such "ascertaining," this marking is virtually tautological; the metrist "finds" what he was looking for. The *Encyclopedia* entry thus fails to detect that it has brought into the procedure the element of the preconceived that it originally attempted to banish.

The determination to "discover" a foot-defined system in a poem, and *to ensure that the system does not topple through the appearance of seeming irregularities,* accounts for a good deal of the time the traditional prosodist puts in on the job (though I should add that the same passion for system may be attributed to the foot-eschewing generative metrist). If the line has to be broken up into peculiar pieces, if ordinary pronunciation has to be deformed, so be it, say the system-mongers.[58] The devices for keeping the system up include not only matters already spoken of or illustrated— grotesque groupings of syllables, the squelching of a stressed syllable, the upgrading of an unstressed one, the allowance of monosyllabic feet—but also the following: a proliferation of categories or terminology (if a name for something can be invented, that apparently constitutes its assimilation into the system), the invention of the concept of "headless lines" (lines missing their first syllables), the scanning of a line starting at its end, and the borrowing of a syllable from a line that has too many syllables to piece out an adjoining line that has too few. Reading a poem becomes an exercise in system maintenance. Whether one is a "stresser"—a prosodist who conceives of the line as composed of stressed and unstressed syllables set in recurring sequence—or a "timer"—one who conceives of a line as grouping syllables, defined as short or long, in units of uniform duration—the poem is treated, in effect, as a mechanism for grinding out clonelike lines, in the sense of their having the same number of a particular kind of foot, or of some permissible "substitutions" for that kind.

From this point of view, there is little reason for preferring stressers over timers or vice versa; in fact, scratching a stresser may reveal a closet, if unwitting, timer. After all, what does it mean for a foot of three syllables to be the "equivalent" of a foot of two syllables, unless one is thinking implicitly of duration?[59] The poem is supposed to display a system, and both the stresser and the timer, the traditional prosodist and, in his own way, the generative metrist, by a series of nips and tucks, nudges and fudge factors, will make sure that it does. (After seeing this happen repeatedly, it is a relief to come across Robert Bridges' statement that "A consistent prosody is . . . so insignificant a part in what makes good English poetry, that I find that I do not myself care very much whether some good poetry be consistent in its versification or not. . . .")[60]

What has characterized conventional prosody's love affair with the idea of system is the equivalent of the development Harold Rosenberg once attributed to art criticism: "Instead of deriving principles from what it sees, it teaches the eye to 'see' principles."[61] We might say that instead of deriving principles from what the mouth articulates or the ear hears, conventional prosody teaches us to articulate and/or "hear" principles.

The notion of working with a system can lend an aura of the scientific to the prosodist's procedures, at least in his or her mind. Marina Tarlinskaja tells us that:

Metrics is, in general, one branch of philology where the application of precise methods is particularly rewarding and appropriate. This is because the basis of verse structure is the principle of rhythmic repetition: so many lines to the stanza, so many feet, or syllables, or stresses to a line, and so on. . . . The application of precise methods is also rewarding in the sense that analysis "according to the ear" is often subjective and imprecise. . . . the metrist, in comparing 18th and 19th century verse, will choose several features which may be inventoried so as to calculate the precise difference between the metrically strict 18th century verse and the more irregular, slacker 19th century verse. Then the subjective evaluations "slacker," "less regular" and "stricter," "more regular" receive an objective scientific foundation.[62]

Given the impressionistic readings of poetry's sound patterns that are all too common, one can understand Tarlinskaja's attraction to the "objective" and "scientific." But the alternative to impressionism need not be Tarlinskaja's arid, statistical "stress profiles," which assume a foot-based prosody, and which survey whole bodies of poetry while having nothing to say about the texture of a particular set of lines. Detecting and formulating the sound patterns of poetry should be regarded not as a science but as an art, exercised upon individual specimens, yet an art that is finally more scientific than Tarlinskaja's approach, in the sense of rooting itself in the sound patterns that actually emerge from the articulation of a poem, and not in traditional prosody's a priori groupings of syllables into feet.

Apart from the hunger for system, and the desire to set prosody on a scientific basis, what has kept the foot alive for many persons is its connection to a kind of sonic Platonism. In this conception there always exist, in effect, two lines for each line of verse. One is the line per se, the line as it sounds when read in accordance with normative pronunciation. The other is an Ideal Line, hovering above the first one, and consisting, for any given meter, of the prescribed number of perfect feet, each syllable and stress in place. The physical ear receives the first of these lines, the "mind's ear" the second.[63] The first line corresponds to the irregularity of the actual, the second is a kind of Platonic form. (This Platonism can be found among both stressers and timers; for timers, what is heard by the mind's ear is not an ideal pattern of stressed and unstressed syllables, but one of feet of equal duration.) Speaking of a metrical "type," Joseph B. Mayor says "It is Plato's one in the many, the permanent in the changeable, the persistent background in the mind of the poet and the reader."[64] John Crowe Ransom tell us " . . . I find myself construing the meter as a characteristic Platonic form or idea, whose seat is in the Platonic Heaven. . . ."[65] Sheridan Baker (he of *ti-dum, ti-dum, ti-dum*) suspects, unsurprisingly, that the iambus had existed "as a kind of Platonic *ta-dah, ta-dah, ta-dah* in [Shakespeare's] head, long before Shakespeare moved his pencil. . . ."[66] Elias K. Schwartz, like Baker a timer, contends that "The relation between the spoken words of the poem and the meter is analogous to those between Plato's Ideas and their concrete images."[67] Attridge has identified the most important "emblematic function" of rhythm in the history of verse as "the Neoplatonic notion that language which obeys the rules of a strict metre represents an ideal reality governed by order and harmony."[68] It seems fair to say that most of the devotees of meter-as-ideal-form define it in terms of feet moving in flawless procession, and further, that to such devotees the unheard melodies generated by this movement are sweeter than the heard melodies of the actual sounds of the lines. Not for them, apparently, an acceptance of both "heavenly labials" and "earthly gutturals" of the poem as sounded (the terms have been borrowed from Wallace Stevens); they have their ear on mind-perceived feet supposedly floating above the spoken lines.[69]

What this entire strain of criticism comes down to is making a sharp distinction between the Platonic (unspoken but heard, universal, pure) and the performative (spoken, individual, imperfect). Even when the former is not evoked, its silent influence can be seen in the denigration of the latter. Harvey Gross for example, speaks of "the old performative fallacy. The meter remains what it has always been, revealed by the traditional method of scanning the stressed and unstressed syllables."[70] The attraction to dogma implicitly accompanying this sort of judgment emerges when Gross, sounding like a prosodic inquisitor, says "There is considerable evidence that Hopkins gave assent to the performative heresy." (Hopkins' sin was to say "above all remember what applies to all my verse, that it is, as living art should be, made for performance and that its performance is not reading with the eye. . . .")[71] Wellek and Warren caution us to

> distinguish between performance and pattern of sound. The reading aloud of a literary work of art is a performance . . . which adds something individual and personal and . . . may distort or even entirely ignore the pattern. Hence a real science of rhythmics and metrics cannot be based only on the study of individual recitals.[72]

So, in pursuit of that will-o'-the-wisp, a science of metrics, we are to beware giving too much weight to what happens when we actually read a poem. Wellek and Warren go on to defend the usefulness of traditional scansion even after acknowledging its insufficiency, doing so on the grounds that "It concentrates frankly on metrical patterns and ignores the minutiae and personal idiosyncrasies of the performer. . . ."[73] C. S. Lewis distinguishes between meter, "an imaginary archetype or paradigm," and performance, the latter being delivered either by "Minstrels" (who bring out the meter but not the rhythm or tempo that "the words would have in ordinary speech") or "Actors" whose recitation recognizes rhythm or tempo but fails to recognize the meter at all.[74] In this view, sounding the poem appears doomed to distorting it. Taking a tack that is not so much, like Lewis's, contemptuous of performance as it is grudging, Wimsatt and Beardsley concede that

> There is, of course, a sense in which the reading of the poem is primary: this is what the poem is *for*. But there is another and equally important sense in which the poem is not to be identified with any particular performance of it, or any set of such performances. . . . A performance is an event, but the poem itself, if there *is* any poem, must be some kind of enduring object.[75]

Even Seymour Chatman, who has said that it seems to him "dangerous to consider metrics abstractly—that is, dissociated from what a poem sounds like when it is read aloud,"[76] and whose *A Theory of Meter* features performances of Shakespeare's Sonnet 18 by several individuals, appears intent on keeping actual vocalizations of verse in a subordinate place. Invoking Roman Jakobson, who in turn had invoked the passage from Wimsatt and Beardsley just cited, Chatman refers to a "common denominator" emerging from the various renderings of a poem, which is "part of the poem itself, the 'enduring object' in contradistinction to the many performances of it, which are merely 'events.'"[77] This is ungrateful to the specific readings that have produced the abstract matrix, the poem's meter. They are being accorded an ontological status inferior to that of their progeny; it is plainly a case of the original Many being made to defer to the succeeding One. Chatman admits that "scansions can only derive from recitations—whether actually vocalized or 'silent,' that is, the scanner cannot but proceed by actually reading the words. . . ."[78] Yet Chatman still seems to give meter privileged status.

From the important pulpit of the *Princeton Encyclopedia of Poetry and Poetics*, James Craig La Drière goes so far as to say that "The datum of a prosodic analysis is ideally an oral performance (actual or conceived) rather than a written text," but immediately proceeds to qualify this by claiming that "every performance is governed by norms supplied by a text, and performance itself is to be judged by its conformance to the textual norm."[79] There seems no question here as to what has priority.

Happily, we can find prosodists who are not contemptuous or grudging of performance, or quick to qualify any concession they make as they contemplate the matter of a poem's overt articulation. John Nist, as might be expected, has listed as one of the "lies" of traditional prosody the notion "That a line of English poetry is an 'ideal' metrical form that transcends its local limitations in a kind of platonic world separated . . . from the vocalizing organs of its performer. . . ."[80] Alan T. Gaylord, not nearly as disposed as Nist to challenge orthodoxy, has nevertheless said, to his credit, that "in order to accomplish a significant increase in what I might call 'total' prosodic criticism, an important change must take place: 'performance' must be more eagerly anticipated and put closer to the center of the critical enterprise."[81] Roger Fowler, in effect, challenges La Drière's text-dominated perspective when he offers the refreshing notion that the performance of a poem

> is not to be viewed as an implementation of the written record . . . but an independent realization; because the written record is not the poem, but is itself only an implementation of it. The distinction is not between the poem on paper and the reading of it but between the poem (an abstraction) and two ways of realizing it.[82]

Fowler has brought to bear on the poem the linguist's characteristic concern with spoken language, a much-needed corrective when we regard the humble status assigned the articulated poem by too many metrists. Another linguist, David Abercrombie, has said that "we are all, when it comes to language, performers."[83] As students of poetry, we would do well to keep this in mind; whether before us on the page, or in our minds, or in our mouths, the words of the poem cannot escape being performed. Even silent reading apparently brings into play the vocalizing muscles.[84]

I would argue, moreover, that in performing the poem, what we say is what we get, and *all* that we get. A syllable that is stressed is heard as stressed; it is not heard simultaneously as stressed and unstressed. A corresponding statement can, of course, be made for an unstressed syllable. What the Platonists would have us believe is the very opposite, that while we articulate in mono, so to speak, we hear in stereo, registering both the sounds we are making and the silent contours of a sequence of perfect feet. To continue invoking the other artistic medium so many prosodists are fond of calling on, would the Platonists claim that a jazz soloist taking liberties with a given tune hears the notes he is producing as those of a duet generating two intersecting but not identical melodies? Isn't articulating a line of poetry while attending both to its sounds and its meaning about all any of us can do? There are those who would pity this position as the expression of a disadvantaged sensibility,[85] looking down as they do from a paradoxical paradise where the "pure iamb or foot exists in silence . . . invisible, unspeakable. . . . A music of the spheres."[86] So be it. Readers must judge for themselves what it is they are *experiencing* as they read a poem silently or aloud, as opposed to any ex post facto celebrations of celestial music made up of pure feet. A prosodic monism, as opposed to the Platonists' dualism, seems to me the only sane approach to poetry.[87]

Not all believers in the foot are Platonists, that is, people who claim to register two lines of poetry occurring simultaneously for every line on the page or in the mouth. Here, as a matter of fact, we see a clean break in the ranks of those assembled under the banner of the foot. Where the Platonists view meter operating as a species of ongoing aural superscript, a separate ideal entity, the non-Platonists conceive of it more prosaically, exerting its presence not as a pure form floating above the line, but as a dynamic force operating within it. For them, there is only one line in question at any given moment, but that line is to be read with a consciousness of the poem's alleged metrical design. Wimsatt and Beardsley, for example, see observance of the meter as a necessary if not sufficient condition for a correct reading of a poem.[88] G. S. Fraser (for whom, writing in 1970, Saintsbury's *A History of English Prosody* is still "the greatest work in English on the subject") finds that "A knowledge of metric can stop us from reading a line of verse aloud wrongly.[89] Samuel Levin contends that "in a sensitive reading of a poem the stresses and intonations will be modified as they are submitted to the demands that the meter makes. . . ."[90] Karl Shapiro and Robert Beum, attending to the question of how to read a poem properly, wish performance to be checked by a consciousness of the metrical pattern, which has somehow already been "discovered." (How, one wonders, if not by performing the poem?) The oral delivery of the poem is to proceed as "a compromise between a 'natural' reading . . . and a metrical reading."[91] Wimsatt, writing without Beardsley, would appear to share this position when he claims that the meter of a poem "exerts a certain kind of coercion. . . . A quiet 'promotion' of certain weaker syllables . . . and a partial 'suppression' (or demotion) of certain stronger ones would appear to take place in much of our reading.[92] In statements such as these, the performative and the metrical do not, as they do with the Platonists, occupy segragated domains; rather, they come together. The apartheid of the Platonists is replaced by a kind of benevolent despotism.

The second arrangement seems to me as wrongheaded as the first. It would appear to make for enormously strained, self-monitored renderings, putting the reader in the position of continuously attempting to keep one ear on the meter, lest he or she betray it. (Given what they require, it is no wonder Shapiro and Beum find that "few people manage to deliver verse with maximum effectiveness."[93] Both the Platonist and non-Platonist positions share a distrust of or dissatisfaction with the spoken language delivered with normative pronunciation. The non-Platonist shows as well a distrust of the poet's ability to create a steady pattern of stressed and unstressed syllables, *if that is the desired goal,* by a selection of words standing on their own usual pronunciation, rather than requiring a fussy interventionism, whereby the accented is sometimes patted down and the unaccented sometimes pulled up. As we shall soon see there is a timer equivalent of this meddling. Neither stressers nor timers, neither Platonists nor non-Platonists, offer us much to choose between when it comes to the question of a poem's performance.

As a matter of fact, in addition to their mutual embrace of meter, these last two schools sometimes come together in an essential way, and this converging is made even more interesting by also serving as the occasional meeting point of the first two schools. This fairly busy intersection goes under the name of "tension," or "counterpoint." (The latter is an example of prosody's long-time and mainly harmful habit of regarding poetry in terms of music.)[94] Either word is capable of a good deal of semantic slippage as we move from one metrist to another, both doing their bit to contribute to the Tower of Babel effect one sometimes gets in the critical literature. But as a rule, both terms are used to refer to the interplay of two systems or schemes assumed to be simultaneously at work in any given line of verse. Calling them "the metrical system . . . and the suprasegmental system of English (with its stresses, intonations, and junctures, however they are analyzed)," Seymour Chatman and Samuel R. Levin have attempted to summarize the various names by which the two elements are designated: "meter vs. performance, (traditional) meter vs. 'rhythm . . .' meter vs. its actualization, abstract frame vs. actual instance, schema . . . vs. particular. . . ."[95] However conceived, the presence of tension between the two elements is always regarded as a good thing. (Richard Cureton has remarked that "Formal tension is . . . one of the central features of aesthetic form.")[96]

For the stressers, the tension is between, on the one hand, the theoretical placement of stressed and unstressed syllables, arranged in feet, and, on the other, the actual locations where stress does and does not occur, when the verse line is spoken in a normative or "prose" manner. For the timers, the interplay is between the theoretical isochrony of the feet as well as the lines, and the actual durations of these units when the poem is uttered.[97] Platonists, who may be either stressers or timers, clearly pave the way for tension or counterpoint by assuming the presence of an ideal line for every actual line; the two are regarded as pulling against each other. Non-Platonists, who tend to be stressers, are not in nearly as strong a position as the Platonists for positing interplay, for they think in terms of only one line, whereas "counterpoint," in its strict, musical sense (and would it had never been allowed to stray from that sense), involves the simultaneous presence of two independent series of notes. "Tension," too, would seem to require two separate elements acting at the same time.

But far be it from the non-Platonists to forego the pleasures of tension or counterpoint, even at the cost of some theoretical muddiness, wherein they exhibit the penchant of prosodists for having things both ways. Thus, we find John Thompson telling us that Donne gave up neither the effect of his phrases nor the metrical pattern: "his phrases demand the living voice, and at the same time the line can be reconciled to the metrical pattern, not in speech, it is true, but in that counterpoint of speech and metrical pattern which today we usually recognize and value."[98]

But what does "reconciliation" through counterpoint mean? And what does that counterpoint sound like if it is not realized in speech? In fact where, in what medium, does that counterpoint exist? Similar questions can be raised about Seymour Chatman's envisaging "a tension between *two* systems: the abstract metrical pattern, as historical product of the English verse tradition, and the ordinary stress-pitch-juncture system of spoken English, determined as it is by requirements of meaning and emphasis."[99] As Chatman goes on, he says "What I have called 'metrical tension' can conveniently be described as 'promotions' or 'suppressions' of the stress levels of normal nonverse speech under the pressures of the abstract metrical pattern."[100] *But this is no longer tension; it is the resolution of tension, in the form of a kind of compromise* between metrical set and prose speech, the sort of thing advocated by Shapiro and Beum, as well as Wimsatt. As Chatman himself says elsewhere, in reading a poem "a choice must be made. The voice has no mechanism for 'hovering,' at least if it is to remain an English voice speaking English."[101] With the choice made, any original tension dissolves.[102]

To be evenhanded, I should point out that the sort of theoretical inconsistencies or fuzziness I am pointing to in Thompson and Chatman are not confined to non-Platonists. Elias K. Schwartz, a Platonist and timer, says that once the meter of a poem is established, it strongly affects the poem's performance, "So that, though the duration of syllables and feet will vary, a proper reading will tend to *adjust* these variations with periods of silence . . . so as to make the actual line more closely approach the ideal equivalence of the meter" (italics in original). This is the timer equivalent of Chatman's promotions and suppressions. After thus forsaking a pure Platonism by having the meter, in effect, descend into the line through the line's being read, Schwartz goes on to attempt a recovery of that Platonism by saying that the rhythm of the poem

involves what has been called "double audition." The listener is simultaneously aware of the actual sound of the poem and of its ideal norm (its meter), which is "heard" by the mind's ear. It follows that, if the listener is aware of both the actual and the ideal, he is also aware of discrepancies between them and feels these discrepancies . . . as more or less significant.[103]

In their reply to Schwartz, Wimsatt and Beardsley properly note that the "double audition" of which he speaks corresponds to the "tensional patterns" in their essay "The Concept of Meter: An Exercise in Abstraction," to which Schwartz was responding.[104] What I am adding here is that Schwartz has already foregone doubleness when he speaks of "adjustments," which presumably make for a kind of rapprochement between the ideal line and the usual durations of its syllables. His talk of "double audition" is an attempt to take back what he has just given up. Thus we see that tension or counterpoint or their equivalent can evaporate from the Platonist position as much as from the non-Platonist one, though its disappearance may go undetected or be qualified.

The Platonists, moreover, need to worry about another flaw in their theory. To the extent that they talk about tension (or counterpoint) they embrace it. But if a metrical pattern gives us the equivalent of a Platonic form, why should the poet ever deviate from this perfection? Why should he or she introduce tension? The non-Platonists, when they are not making a case for the expressive value of tension, argue glibly, from their mundane position, that unity needs to be leavened with variety (it would be interesting to be told at what point, in any given case, unity becomes monotonous). But why should Platonists countenance straying from the realm of Ideal Form? As far back as 1902, Mark Liddell, a declared enemy of foot-prosody, pinpointed the curious nature of such approval, though he did not designate the position he was questioning as "Platonist," and in fact his queries could be directed, though to lesser effect, against the non-Platonists as well. Citing the example of Shakespeare, he asked:

> is it not a strange state of affairs that the aesthetically imperfect should produce greater pleasure than the aesthetically perfect? And is it not stranger that the poetry whose verse most consistently and violently deviates from our assumed aesthetic form should be the best poetry which our language affords? . . . There must be something wrong with an aesthetic system whose norms exist only to be violated.[105]

The inconsistencies and gaps I have been pointing to in both the Platonist and non-Platonist conceptions of tension seem to me of considerable interest in themselves, and of some importance with respect to the invidious distinction that has often been made between metrical poetry and free verse. Because, if there is a central argument put forward by advocates of meter for the inferiority, or at least limitation, of free verse, it consists of saying that by relinquishing the structure or norm of a metrical set, and the attendant departures from that set, free verse has lost the crucial element of tension, or counterpoint, with its alleged effects of pleasurable surprise and expressiveness.[106] What I have been trying to argue is that to the extent that they allow the alleged meter to impinge on the performance of the poem, to enter the lines, so to speak, rather than simply hover above them, Platonists and non-Platonists, stressers and timers alike, are in danger of giving up, without recognizing that they are doing so, their beloved tension, or counterpoint, insofar as either requires, in one way or another, the *simultaneous presence of two different lines.*[107]

But even if counterpoint dissolves, there remains a means whereby metrists *appear* able to hang on to the abstractions of metrical patterns and at the same time engage the waywardness of the verse line as it sounds in performance, in short, a means for them to retain a particular form of "tension." This consists of say-

ing that meter sets up an "expectation," which the line either ful-
fills, thereby creating the effect of satisfaction, or fails to fulfill,
thereby generating tension (with its accompanying effects of variety and/or expressiveness).[108] Such an approach has the advantage
of not positing an a priori Platonic form continually unfolding
above the actual line; rather, it has us focus on the line itself. The
element of expectation is created through a reading of the poem,
which will supposedly detect a meter whose pattern is broken
from time to time, with such breakage designated as "syncopation"
rather than "counterpoint" if one wants a musical term. Dispensing
with the superscript line allegedly heard by the mind's ear, the
expectation approach is altogether superior to the notion of counterpoint. But it too has problems, as well as limitations.

The concept of expectation-based tension is grounded on a faith
that reading a given poem will clearly reveal a metrical pattern, as
exemplified by Egerton Smith's declaration that "ordinarily the
system of grouping [of feet] shows itself unmistakably, and the
intention of the poet discloses itself to the reader's perception,
or even forces itself on his attention."[109] The meter shows itself
promptly, or at least it is supposed to. Chatman has spoken of "the
traditional idea that the 'real' meter should be indicated as soon as
possible to guarantee the reader's early recognition of the metrical
'norm.'"[110] But one wonders what sort of pattern and, thereby,
expectation is created by the following opening lines:

> When to the sessions of sweet silent thought
> >   (Shakespeare, Sonnet 30)

> Let me not to the marriage of true minds
> >   (Shakespeare, Sonnet 116)

> 'Tis the year's midnight, and it is the day's
> >   (Donne, "A Nocturnal upon S.
> >   Lucy's Day, Being the Shortest
> >   Day")

> Of man's first disobedience and the fruit
> >   (Milton, *Paradise Lost*)

> Earth has not anything to show more fair
> >   (Wordsworth, "Composed upon
> >   Westminster Bridge, 3 Sept. 1802")

> Back out of all this now too much for us
> >   (Robert Frost, "Directive")

If the poet, in any of these cases, was intent on establishing a metrical pattern as early as possible, he has to be judged incompetent.

But perhaps it will be argued that this sampling of first lines is not fair, that if we read through enough of the succeeding lines of each poem, the metrical pattern will quickly become clear, and therefore the notion that meter sets up an expectation that the poet will either satisfy or not is a viable one. Roger Fowler doubts even this position, but apparently still believes that the notion of expectation holds.

> It is sometimes claimed that poets make the openings of poems dense with 'regular' lines to fix metrical set early. The truth of this claim is doubtful, and in fact it does not matter where the design-fixing lines are sited: understanding is a tentative and cumulative process, and a second reading refines one's perception of the first.[111]

To answer this, I will cite not individual lines of the kind just given, but the entire verse category to which all but one of them belong, that of iambic pentameter, the most prominent division of poetry in English. *Its* most prominent subdivision is blank verse.

T. V. F. Brogan evinces a curious determination to question the eminence of blank verse, saying that it is

> in fact no staple meter at all but rather a limited transitional form in the history of English metric: it appears for only [sic] 300 years (say, 1557 to 1855), 100 of which are a virtual interruption, and then largely falls into desuetude in the present century, having no recent example of a great English poet to be its impelling force. . . .[112]

Brogan's effort to shrink the space blank verse occupies in the usual conception of the history of poetry in English may derive from an unconscious recognition on his part that such verse presents a serious challenge to the concept of meter. For in spite of his awareness of the questionable practices and assertions that permeate the writings of prosodists, Brogan, in my reading of him, is essentially a conservative, taking the validity of the notion of meter for granted.[113] Be that as it may, his attempt to minimize blank verse in the scheme of things appears to represent the view of a minority of one. Saintsbury, who, whatever his theoretical limitations, had read through enormous amounts of poetry, declared that blank verse in English "has . . . grown to be one of the greatest metres in the world's prosodic history."[114] Otto Jespersen, while taking in more than blank verse, made a comparable statement, declaring that iambic pentameter "may without any exaggeration be termed the most important metre of all in the literatures of the North-European world."[115] Paul F. Baum, in 1923, said that 'Perhaps three-fourths of the greatest English poetry is in the unrimed 5-stress line called blank verse."[116] John Thompson, writing in the *Princeton Encyclopedia of Poetry and Poetics,* declares blank verse to be "the distinctive poetic form of our language. . . ."[117] Qualitative judgments aside, Paul Fussell, in the early 1970s, estimated that "about three-quarters of English poetry is written in blank verse."[118] The explosion of free verse has undoubtedly diminished this figure, but the reduced percentage must still be formidable. Blank verse and other forms of iambic pentameter include much of Chaucer, Shakespeare, Milton, Dryden, Pope, and Wordsworth, and almost all the sonnets in our language. Any theory of "metrical" poetry in English that cannot account for or that misrepresents iambic pentameter cannot be taken seriously, no matter how well it might do for, say, poems written in rhymed tetrameter quatrains. It would be like a theory of planetary motion that covered the paths of Mercury, Venus, and Earth, but not the grander orbits of Saturn, Neptune, and Uranus.

How does the notion of tension, in the form of disruption of expectation, fare when applied to iambic pentameter? The reading of such verse would presumably lead us to look for the following metrical pattern to operate as the norm: x / | x / | x / | x / | x / |. But consider Dennis Taylor's citations of a number of late nineteenth-century prosodists:

> Symonds said of the iambic pentameter: "so various is its structure that it is by no means easy to define the minimum of metrical form below which a Blank Verse ceases to be a recognisable line." Masson noted that English blank verse admits trochees, spondees, pyrrhics, and trisyllabic feet "in almost any place in the line" . . . "the number of accents, unless in a peculiar sense of accent, not realized in actual pronunciation, is also variable. . . ." Stevenson exclaimed: "in declaiming a so-called iambic verse, it may so happen that we never utter one iambic foot." Bridges concluded that in Milton's *Paradise Lost* "there is no one place in the verse where an accent is indispensable."[119]

Now consider the estimates and statistics a number of twentieth-century prosodists have come up with, independently of each other (statistics are good for *some* things). Ian Robinson has said that "Ordinarily Chaucer's lone line has five feet and they are most frequently iambs, though the line with five iambs is perhaps not even in a majority."[120] R. M. Alden found it safe to state that "in

English five-stress iambic verse, read with only the ordinary ety-
mological and rhetorical accents, twenty-five per cent of the verses
lack the full five stresses characteristic of the type."[121] A considerably higher figure can be found for Milton. Roger Fowler notes
that judging by Robert Bridges' criteria in his study of Milton's
prosody, "about 60 per cent of the lines in Book I of P[aradise]
L[ost] have less than five ictuses."[122] Sampling the works of Shakespeare, Milton, Thomson, Cowper, Wordsworth, Tennyson, Brow-
ning, Arnold, Robinson, and Frost, John D. Allen found that "all
ten of the poets used more irregular than standard blank verse
lines. . . ."[123] Marina Tarlinskaja, perhaps the most encyclopedic
of metrists who employ statistics, claims that in the lines of Shakespeare (his nondramatic verse), Jonson, Dryden, Pope (Pope!), and
Arnold, we get variations from the iambic pentameter norm anywhere between 27% and 39% of the time.[124] Assuming that our own
impressions had not already conveyed it, statistics like these
should make us realize that iambic pentameter is awash in variations, or "deviation[s]," in Tarlinskaja's terms.[125]

With a verse medium possessing so many deviations or variations, the sophisticated reader's expectations, as John Hollander
says, "are going to get more flexible the more of a total stock of
iambic pentameter lines he has experienced."[126] To put the matter
more strongly, the experienced reader of such lines will have
learned to carry a decidedly qualified "expectation" of regularity,
or, even better, will have learned to expect irregularity.[127] Raymond
Southall said of A. K. Foxwell's work on Wyatt that she

> failed to appreciate . . . that the more numerous the departures from
> the strict iambic pentameter line become, the less schematic the verse
> becomes until, suffering death by a thousand qualifications, observa-
> tion of the rule or norm becomes merely fortuitous.[128]

With the sort of slack found in the actual practice of iambic pentameter, the vaunted element of tension, dependent on the presence of a strongly maintained norm, will be decidedly less
operative than many traditional prododists would have us believe.[129] Touters of tension had better look to more than iambic
pentameter for their occasions. They should not be including it in
the category of "metrical" poetry, insofar as they use that category
as a stick with which to beat free verse for its absence of tension.
Their weapon is a good deal smaller than they seem to have
thought.[130]

What else can we say about the large number of variations in iambic pentameter? If variation, in metrical poetry in general, is used primarily as a good in itself, a relief from the monotony of regularity, the percentages of deviating lines, as calculated by Tarlinskaja, would seem to constitute overkill. On the other hand, the primary function of variation is often thought to be that of expressiveness. Coleridge asserted that "'variation . . . is not introduced wantonly, or for the mere ends of convenience, but in correspondence with some transition in the nature of the imagery or passion.'"[131] Paul Fussell, who traces the idea of expressive variation back to eighteenth-century prosodists, has claimed that in poetry of the "most sophisticated metrical kind. . . . the poet establishes regularity only to depart from it expressively," and that "it is to locate and interpret and finally to value these variations . . . that we scan at all."[132] John Hollander has called the notion "that poets seem to adopt strict forms and meters *in order that* they may proceed to violate [them] slightly" a "critical commonplace" (italics in original).[133] It seems fair to say that the doctrine of expressive or significant variation is a crucial component of the conventional theory of meter. But one must wonder how many of the numerous variations in iambic pentameter could be assigned a specific expressive or functional role. It is good to keep in view D. W. Harding's skeptical position on the whole matter of expressive variation: "To say that metrical variations, through the mere fact of being variations, are always producing slight—but unspecifiable—expressive effects is one of those completely untestable and unprofitable assertions that leaves us where we were."[134]

The questionable habit of looking for foot-based expressive variations in a mode, iambic pentameter, that is permeated with deviant feet to begin with, is carried a step further in David Dooley's remarks on some lines by Dana Gioia, lines that may be said to flirt with blank verse. Here is the passage in question:

> But no, it never lasts. The alluring voice
> cracks reaching for a high note that would join
> two passages; the fingers stumble on a piece
> of brilliant bridgework. Bows scrape.
> The second part falls half a step behind.
> And the sunlight fades. The distant hills
> become drearily familiar. Other voices,
> the usual ones, start up behind us.

Dooley, who himself characterizes these lines as having only one "complete end-stopped phrase of regular iambic pentameter," the fifth line, says that "the reversed fourth foot of the [second] line ('note that,') creates additional emphasis on the phrase 'high note,' [a] fine imitative effect."[135] It would be hard to find a better example of dubious hunting for significant variations and of the sort of reading I have been questioning in much of this chapter.

First, we might observe how Dooley's foot-approach violates, in a way typical of such scansion, the phrase structure of the second line—after all, "note" is more tightly connected with the preceding word, "high," than with the following "that." Next, in a passage of such admitted irregularity, in a *line* of such irregularity—it contains at most two "iambs," namely "a high" and "would join"—we might well ask why we should be expected to concern ourselves with or even register "a reversed fourth foot."[136] Finally, we might ask how that foot has a kind of *backwash* effect on the phrase "high note," the very phrase that Dooley's foot-approach dismembered to begin with. (This is yet another instance of a meter-minded prosodist wishing to have things both ways, in this case a foot and the phrase it violates). But the principal thing to be observed here is that Dooley, who is writing in a periodical issue partly given over to celebrating the New Formalism, might well argue that his sort of reading has been encouraged by conventional prosody, the prosody that in my view has been guilty of foot fetishism and indiscriminate variation-fondling. The New Formalism appears not to examine the Old Formalism with a critical eye, but simply to regurgitate it.[137]

Rejecting the notion of the foot, questioning the reverence accorded to a poem's allegedly governing metrical system, pooh-poohing Platonic dualism, contesting the applicability of "counterpoint" to verse, contending that the role of "tension" has been much exaggerated and allowed to operate as a kind of Berlin Wall between metrical poetry and free verse, and challenging the promiscuous assignment of significance to metrical "variations," what can I offer to replace the traditional concept of meter and its corollaries? Before formulating my own approach to line-movement in poetry, I should like, in the next chapter, to demonstrate the continuing, the stubborn hold of the concept of meter in recent criticism, and, in the chapter after that, to document the spread of the concept, during the course of this century, into the unlikely quarters of free verse.

3

Recent Prosodic Commentary:
Old Wine in New Bottles

MY quarrel with traditional prosodic thought has focused largely on its addiction to the foot as the key building block of verse; by and large, the commentators I have been questioning employ feet in their scansions, and much that is dubious follows from that. But as I have suggested, the true villain is what probably helped produce the foot approach to English verse in the first place, and what has contributed to keeping it alive, the hunger for a "system" that can be seen as governing a poem's sounds. Such a system, as I have said, helps guarantee a poem's "unity" and provides a ready-made scheme for analyzing the poem's rhythmic patterns. Unfortunately, even when traditional prosody is modified or extended, even when the foot is questioned or cast aside as a dysfunctional entity, even when meter is allegedly positioned on a physiological foundation other than the traditional one of the heartbeat, this hunger for a system can persist and do serious damage to the description of a poem's sonic features. It can also operate so as to continue to make free verse appear intrinsically inferior to metrical verse. The traditional prosodic mind-set has managed to cast its spell over a number of notable studies of the last ten or twelve years, even when they give promise of breaking new ground or of leaving some old assumption behind.

It is particularly disheartening to find that this applies to Derek Attridge's *The Rhythms of English Poetry* (1982), for Attridge has at once an impressive command of and detachment from the critical literature of prosody, and works very hard to come up with foot-free descriptions of the English verse line. But even as he makes a thoughtful case against the foot and the notion of "counterpoint" that frequently attends it, he regresses to a central assumption of traditional metrics: the line is to be conceived of as enacting an approach to "a marked regularity and at times depart[ing] from it, constantly arousing and thwarting rhythmic expectations . . . . Tension arises out of the twin tendencies of language, towards variety and towards regularity."[1] With this we are back in Brooks and Warren country, back to the assumption of a system. Specifically, that system is invoked in the reference to "a marked regularity" in the lines of a poem. If there is any doubt about this, consider the passage late in his book where Attridge makes a case for the "surrender of the liberty . . . fundamental to ordinary speech" that he sees as being effected by metrical verse. He describes the poet as "putting his words into the hands of a pre-existing metrical scheme, an external organising force from which no syllable can escape . . . ." The satisfaction, the reverence, with which Attridge contemplates this totalitarian "scheme" is indicated when he says it incorporates "the voice of divine order . . . " (p. 314).

Attridge replaces the usual division of a line into stressed and unstressed syllables with the categories of beats and off-beats, designated as B and o, respectively. This is essentially a terminological shift, accompanied by a typographical one—Attridge places his notations of beats and offbeats below the line as opposed to the above-line placement of markings in traditional prosody. As is the case with foot prosodists, he then comes up with a series of gimmicks designed to guarantee that the assumed metrical scheme of a poem will show itself, persist, and, if necessary, absorb any would-be errant syllable or other potentially subversive element in the verse line. These devices include the "deviation" rules for converting an unstressed syllable to a beat (this "promotion" is designated as B), and for regarding a syllable that would ordinarily receive a beat as realizing an offbeat (this "demotion" is designated as ȯ). In addition, taking his cue from the timers, who think in terms of musical analogues, Attridge comes up with the notions of an "unrealised beat"—[B]—and an "optional unrealised beat"—([B]). *These two shadowy entities do not correspond to any existing syllables in the poem.* They are used, rather, as padding in the description of the line's configuration. Unrealized themselves, they wonderfully enable the alleged meter to show forth.

Here is an example of the unrealized beat in action; the lines are from "The Ancient Mariner":

   And I had done a hellish thing
    B B   B   B
   And it would work 'em woe:
    B   B   B [B]

> For all averred, I had killed the bird
> B   B   B   B
> That made the breeze to blow.
>   B   B   B   [B] (p. 91)

The presumed advantage of such scansion is that it allows Attridge to describe Coleridge's lines as four-beat verse; it tidies things up. If this sort of thing satisfies Attridge's taste for regularity, all well and good—it is relatively harmless, leaving the line intact. But it seems to me a waste of analytic energy—and there is more of that to come.

Elaborating on his system, Attridge uses the notion of an implied offbeat—ô—which others might simply (and more legitimately) designate as a pause. He confuses matters by saying that implied offbeats are usually "used in the literary tradition to create a minor disruption in the rhythm" (p. 173), and yet his invention of the concept seems designed to present a schematic view of the line that *regularizes* its rhythm. Just how self-confirming Attridge's approach is can be shown by his assertion that "two [stressed syllables] can induce varying kinds of phonetic material between them to act as an offbeat—not only one or two unstressed syllables, but also a stressed syllable, or nothing at all" (p. 174). This magical bringing forth of an offbeat serves to keep intact the *system* that Attridge is so intent on preserving: the principle of alternation in the poetic line between the unstressed syllables and those that are stressed, or in his terms, between the offbeats and the beats.

A couple of examples of his scansions will illustrate his approach and, I hope, confirm my characterization of it. This is his rendering of a line from Milton's *Comus*:

> Antiquity from   the old   schools of Greece
> o B o B̄   ŏ B ó B o   B   (p. 179)

Here the ŏ represents a "double offbeat," that is, two successive unstressed syllables. The last syllable of "Antiquity" has been promoted and the successive stressed syllables of "old schools" have produced from the intervening nothing an implied offbeat. Attridge does something similar with lines from Marvell's "The Garden":

> −s−s +s   +s −s−s +s   +s
> To   a green   thought in   a green   shade
> ŏ   B ó B   ŏ   B ó B   (p. 183)

(Here the -s and +s represent, respectively, unstressed and stressed syllables as these emerge from a reading of the line. In Attridge's prosodic world these actualities, while recognized, are subordinated to the abstract system of offbeats and beats.) What Attridge's scansion has given us, however qualified, is a repeating *visual* (o B) configuration—thus have the lines been tamed into a scheme.

Attridge's readings are in keeping with his decidedly traditional notion of what scansion is all about—exhibiting a line's embodiment of a pervading pattern. Scansion "shows which metrical rules are employed at particular points to realise beats and offbeats. It therefore directly reflects the way in which *the line is perceived as rhythmically regular,* indicating the degree and exact nature of metrical deviation at every stage" (p. 361; my italics). Acknowledging deviation, he nevertheless assumes a controlling pattern operating in a given succession of lines, and repeatedly manages to find what he assumes to be there, the point of scansion apparently being to show what devices the line uses to regularize itself.

Attridge's essential traditionalism is further exemplified in his discussion of the "affective functions" of rhythm, by which he appears to mean the way the movements of verse lines embody particular mental states. These are distinct from rhythm's "iconic functions," which have to do with the way verse movement imitates properties of the external world. Affective functions are plainly closer to Attridge's heart, and, according to him, are much more the property of metrical verse than of free verse:

> Traditional metrical forms occupy a special place in this area of rhythmic function: though nonmetrical verse has all the potential for iconic effects that metrical verse has—perhaps even more, since it can range more freely in its search for imitative devices—and can embody a variety of affective speech rhythms, it is the approximation to *regular* rhythms, and the consequent play of arousal and satisfaction, which engages the deepest sources of affective behaviour: those neural and muscular periodicities that generate all mental and physical activity (pp. 299–300; italics in original).

His treatment of nonmetrical verse is accorded all of seven pages, approximately, in a volume close to four hundred pages in length. His book should have been entitled *The Regular Rhythms of English Poetry,* though even this would have been problematical, since, as I have indicated, Attridge is capable of *imposing* regularity.

Attridge has, in passing, appropriated something as deep as the "neural" in his endorsement of the allegedly superior virtues of traditional verse. A much more elaborate invoking of that realm is at work in a remarkable essay (briefly cited in Chapter 2), "The Neural Lyre: Poetic Meter, The Brain and Time," written by Frederick Turner and Ernst Pöppel. Awarded the Levinson Prize— normally reserved for verse—as the best work to appear in *Poetry* magazine in 1983, it is a piece that can only gladden the hearts of Attridge and the traditional prosodists, to whom, in my view, he is so closely related. Turner and Pöppel draw a sharp, intensely invidious distinction between metrical verse and free verse, to the detriment of the latter. Metrical verse is characterized as universal, archaic, and magical. Turner and Pöppel find a marvelous congruence between such poetry and the human nervous system, because of the latter's "strong drive to construct . . . predictively powerful models of the world, in which all events are explained by and take their place in a system . . . governed by as few principles or axioms as possible."[2] (Notice, in this passage, the echoes of Wimsatt and Beardsley's "few . . . principles of prosody.") Encountering the system of a metrical poem, the brain receives a pleasurable confirmation of its own profound proclivity; this, at least, is my understanding of a rather hazy formulation by Turner and Pöppel, which speaks of the brain's self-rewarding mechanism being "stimulated" by encountering hypothetical techniques, the criteria for which are satisfied by meter (p. 284). Put somewhat differently, metered poetry does for the brain "much of the work that the brain must usually do for itself" (p. 303). But if the brain continually craves and creates the systematic, it also has an "habituative need for controlled novelty," and this last is supplied by the variations from the norm in metrical verse (p. 303). So the brain wants things both ways and meter is there to supply it. For all their invoking of some current theories of mental processes, and their fashionable references to left-brain and right-brain functions, Turner and Pöppel have come up with long familiar notions of the virtues of meter. Their attack on free verse will be given in the next chapter. What needs addressing now is their argument for the neural naturalness of the metrical verse line.

That argument is based on their contention that for the human auditory system, the fundamental "parcel of experience" is about three seconds long. What this means is that "A listener will absorb about three seconds of heard speech without pause or reflection, then stop listening briefly in order to integrate and make sense of what he has heard." This three seconds worth of auditory information constitutes a kind of "pulse," which is sent on to "the higher processing centers" of the brain. "The three-second period, roughly speaking, is the length of the human present moment" (pp. 296–97). Turner and Pöppel set forth these contentions after stating that samples of metrical poetry drawn from a variety of languages (including English) show a predominance of lines that take somewhere between 2.5 and 3.5 seconds to articulate. What we have, then, is a norm operating in metered verse—a norm Turner and Pöppel refer to as "The three-second LINE" (p. 291)— possessed of the same duration as that of the alleged fundamental parcel of experience. In other words, built into metrical poetry is a durational feature that makes of each line just the sort of temporal unit that our neural system treats as the basic entity of incoming information. Thus we get a wonderful fit between meter's sound bites, so to speak, and our sensory-mental processes. The temporal approach to meter, the conception of meter as involving a system, and the linking of meter to human physiology each reach an apotheosis here.

If Turner and Pöppel are right about the auditory unit recognized by our neural system being congruent with the duration of the metrical verse line, they seem to have come up with a truly impressive finding, rooting meter in the biological given of the human brain. I am not competent to judge the validity of their statements about the size of the fundamental "parcel of experience," but using their own presentation of evidence, I think I can say that in their discussion of poetry they have indulged as much in dubious argumentation as have earlier attempts to display the pervasive operation of a system in verse.

If we look at the tables presented by Turner and Pöppel as listing the time measurements they have made of the duration of lines in various languages, we find, among other things, that the Chinese four-syllable line requires 2.20 seconds for its articulation, while the iambic trimeter line in Greek requires 4.40 seconds. The absolute difference between these figures, 2.20 seconds, is of course not much, but the relative difference is very great—one hundred percent. The Greek line, according to the figures, takes twice as long to articulate as the Chinese line, yet Turner and Pöppel go on to subsume these differences under the heading of "the three-second LINE."

To speak more generally, consider that the lower range of the overwhelming majority of lines examined by the two men is 2.5 seconds and the upper range is 3.5 seconds. This means that the relative difference between two lines falling within these limits might be as much as forty percent. And since Turner and Pöppel seem to be talking of averages, could we not conceivably find two such lines within a given passage, perhaps two consecutive lines, with their "average" amounting to 3 seconds? Wherever such deviations of individual lines may be located relative to each other, they are apparently assimilable by the three-second packaging process. But then, wouldn't Turner and Pöppel have to admit that a great deal of the free verse they abhor is also assimilable? If, in treating metrical lines, they can flatten out what appear to be significant disparities for the sake of coming up with an auditory "constant" that will match a neural constant, why couldn't many free verse lines be candidates for a similar process of accommodation? Moreover, the absence of feet in free verse appears to pose no difficulty, for the essential thing about metrical verse for Turner and Pöppel is that each line be three seconds long—more or less.

The Turner-Pöppel thesis is the ultimate timer approach to poetry. For all its venturesomeness, and the impressive energy the two men bring to its exposition, it is too strained to be persuasive, too much the product of a will to find a master key to prosody in a neurally-grounded three-second unit. What is likelier to prevail is the stresser branch of traditional prosody, though one hopes it will do so only in modified form, along lines to be suggested later in the book.

The continuing appeal of the stresser school is exemplified at length in the study by Susanne Woods, *Natural Emphasis: English Versification from Chaucer to Dryden* (1984). Bearing the impressive imprimatur of the Huntington Library, Woods's book is learned and thoughtful, and displays a certain amount of desirable flexibility. But her study keeps us stuck in the swamp of traditional scansion, even as she makes some concession to the linguistic facts of pronunciation as those have been formulated by Trager and Smith. Where Wimsatt and Beardsley took a hard line, arguing that traditional scansion need not give way at all to accommodate the linguists' findings, Woods adopts the Trager-Smith system of four degrees of stress, but cozily assimilates that system into readings that serve only to perpetuate doing metrical business as usual. She explicitly accepts the concept of the foot and proceeds accordingly, contributing her own dubious readings of individual lines to the long list of such readings we can lay at the feet (the pun is irresistible) of the traditional metrists who preceded her. The sonnets of Shakespeare, already abused by prosodists, suffer additional scansional indignity at the hands of Woods.

For example, Woods gives us the following scheme for the first line of Sonnet 30 (the numbers below the line designate the four levels of stress used by Trager and Smith, with "1" representing the strongest level):

$$\overset{/}{\underset{2}{\text{When}}} \overset{x}{\underset{3}{\text{to}}} \mid \overset{x}{\underset{4}{\text{the}}} \overset{/}{\underset{1}{\text{ses}}} \mid \overset{x}{\underset{4}{\text{sions}}} \overset{/}{\underset{3}{\text{of}}} \mid \overset{x}{\underset{2}{\text{sweet}}} \overset{/}{\underset{1}{\text{si}}} \mid \overset{x}{\underset{4}{\text{lent}}} \overset{/}{\underset{1}{\text{thought}}} \mid {}^3$$

The use of the Trager-Smith numbers makes some concession to the way this line would be read by any sensible reader, but Woods' commitment to the foot, combined with her rejection of the spondee and, apparently, the pyrrhus as legitimate sound entities in English, not only causes her to promote "of" (should that syllable really get more stress than "-sions" or "–lent"?) but, more importantly, to demote "sweet." Is there any justification at all for the latter procedure, except that the "display" of a line's feet must prevail over all other considerations?

Two other questionable examples of her foot-based scansions read as follows:

$$\overset{x}{\underset{4}{\text{With}}} \overset{/}{\underset{3}{\text{how}}} \overset{x}{\underset{2}{\text{sad}}} \overset{/}{\underset{1}{\text{steps,}}} \overset{x}{\underset{3}{\text{o}}} \overset{/}{\underset{1}{\text{Moone,}}} \overset{x}{\underset{3}{\text{thou}}} \overset{/}{\underset{1}{\text{climbst}}} \overset{x}{\underset{4}{\text{the}}} \overset{/}{\underset{1}{\text{skies}}}$$

She claims this line of Sidney to be "consistent[ly] iambic" (p. 167), but "shows" this only by subjecting the key word "sad" to the same sort of demotion suffered by "sweet" in Shakespeare's Sonnet 30. The subordination of "o" is also questionable.

Here is another example:

$$\overset{x}{\underset{1}{\text{I}}} \overset{/}{\underset{4}{\text{meant}}} \overset{x}{\text{the}} \overset{/}{\underset{3}{\text{day-starre}}} \overset{x}{\underset{2}{\text{should}}} \overset{/}{\underset{1}{\text{not}}} \overset{x}{\text{brighter}} \overset{/}{\text{rise}}$$
$$\text{(p. 228)}$$

This line is from Ben Jonson, whom Wood has presented as advocating that "Meters and rhythms should derive from and convey natural speech . . . " (p. 215). Here, she abuses the Trager-Smith notation, which is meant to reflect actual speech, by demoting the important word "starre" to a status below that of the adjacent "should," presumably to exhibit an iambic foot in the third position of the line. Is this what she thinks "natural speech" (or Gascoigne's "Natural Emphasis") would generate?

If Woods's method of scansion is all too familiar, so, too, are her treatments of deviations from the supposed metrical norm of a poem. For example, taking the line from Jonson's elegy for his son

BEN. JONSON his best piece of *poetrie*

she gives us three possible readings. The first two, holding exactly or nearly to a straight iambic reading, are decidedly forced. The third comes closest to a reasonable rendering, but is not without its dubieties:

BEN. JÓNSON his bést piece of *póetrié*

Regarding this last, which slights "piece" and elevates "rie," Woods says that it involves a "Jonsonian kind of mimetic rhythm, with the wrench toward the unmetrical mirroring the speaker's sorrow and painful recognition" (p. 224). What is troublesome about this is that it makes its really peculiar reading of "piece of poetrie" Jonson's responsibility, and it assumes that the alleged wrenching is set in a context of regular verse, when, in fact, Jonson's poem exhibits metrical "irregularities" throughout, starting with the first line's "of my right hand" (would Woods scan this "of my | right hand" ?)

The notion of "mimetic rhythm" that she cites in connection with Jonson is a central conception of her book. The problem with its application is the same as that with the application of "expressive variation," the notion that it partly overlaps. Both presume a greater degree of regularity in "metrical verse" than in fact often obtains, and both then proceed to locate in departures from that alleged regularity considerable effects; the results are not persuasive. In one notable instance, buried in a footnote, Woods combines the notion of representative meter with mimetic rhythm (established through variations), finding in Wyatt's "My galley charged with forgetfulness" an "underlying ocean rhythm (strongly iambic)," along with "effectively variant movements" that "imitate the speaker's unsettled situation . . . " (p. 100). An unfortunate image of Wyatt's speaker suffering seasickness comes to mind here, at least for this reader.[4]

To her credit, Woods is occasionally able to depart from traditional foot-based prosody, and to find that with Wyatt and Donne we need to think in terms of "phrasal" rhythms or movements. While she seems tempted to approach Chaucer this way as well, she rejects such a procedure as "impressionistic"—this from a dealer in "oceanic rhythm" (pp. 41, 44, 76). But interestingly, she identifies phrasal rhythms with the movements of prose:

> prose rhythms are tied to phrase rather than line, and while phrasal rhythms are an unquestionable feature of all verse rhythm, they more usually work in conjunction with and in part at the direction of the emphasis suggested by the metrical model . . . (p. 254).

So even as she seems capable on occasion of casting off the fetters of feet, she ultimately keeps meter as king of Parnassus, virtually synonymous with "poetry" for the great bulk of the English verse canon. The truth of the matter, as I shall attempt to argue later in the book, is that the phrasal considerations Woods admits into her prosodic deliberations only in a very limited or highly qualified way should be embraced wholeheartedly, as offering us an escape from the forced or arid readings that we are continually subjected to by traditional prosody. To put it a little differently, we must look not for arbitrary groupings of syllables but for semantically linked groupings of words as they operate in our articulation of a poem; such will save us from the morass of meter. Anticipating the approach that will be formulated in later chapters, I will say now that where feet were, let the phrases of our spoken language be, with true natural emphasis in the pronunciation of individual words prevailing.

By and large, the prosodic school of "generative metrics" allows words their natural emphasis, and, at least in one version, does away with the notion of the foot. So far, so good. Where does that school stand in relation to traditional prosody's hunger for a poem-controlling system? In answering that I shall eventually draw on another recent work of prosody. But the beginnings of an answer can be supplied by taking time out for a fairly extensive, if incomplete, overview of generative metrics.

Gilbert Youmans notes that literary scholars have had some trouble with generative metrics because of, in part, a misunderstanding of the term "generative." Even writers who should know better, he says, misuse the word, and by way of example, he quotes the author of a text on syntax as claiming that "Another way of saying that the grammar's rules produce sentences . . . is to say that the grammar *generates* them . . . ."[5] But it seems to me that the writer's use of the term here is in keeping with the understanding many of us have of "generative," or transformational, grammar, which Brogan has characterized as the model for generative metrics.[6] According to that grammar, the encoding of certain "deep" rules in our brains enables us to generate or create an endless number of legitimate sentences. Be that as it may, Youmans attempts to correct the alleged misuse of "generative" by observing that

"generate" is a formal term drawn from mathematics and set theory. Sets may be defined in one of two ways: by listing their members or by giving explicit conditions for membership. Definitions of the latter

sort are GENERATIVE . . . . the set of permissible iambic pentameter
lines in English is astronomically large . . . . Such a set, too, must be
defined generatively.[7]

Youmans's invoking of mathematics is significant, in that the formulations of generative metrists not infrequently assume a mathemati-
cal appearance, giving such formulations an impressive aura of the
precise and the arcane. For example, in "Chaucer and the Study
of Prosody," by Morris Halle and Samuel J. Keyser, we get the
following formulation of the *"Branching rule"*:

$V \rightarrow \#$ $P_1 P_2 P_3$ . . . . P_n $\#$ (s(s)) where V = verse, P = position,
s = syllable.[8]

While the term "generative metrics" is to be credited to Joseph
C. Beaver, the urtext of this particular prosodic school was the
Halle-Keyser essay just cited, which appeared in 1966.[9] Halle and
Keyser take the position that "principles, first adhered to by Chaucer, have provided the system of prosody for a major portion of
English poets" (p. 215). They also claim that traditional prosodists
"have tried to shore up the theory [of iambic pentameter] by giving
a list of allowable deviations" (p. 191). The two authors are troubled
by this because the theory "fails to provide any explanation for
the fact that only certain deviations are tolerated and not others"
(p. 190). Wimsatt and Beardsley's "Concept of Meter" is cited as
an example of this omission. Traditional theory, even when modified, say Halle and Keyser, "fails to capture the features that [per-
missible] deviations have in common" (p. 214). To *capture*—that
is the essential impulse of generative metrics, to arrive at a set of
rules that will bring under a single tent virtually all the lines of
such poetry as is considered, on an intuitive basis, "metrical."
There will then be no need to talk of arbitrary deviations, for they
will be covered by the rules.[10] That is, they will have been assimilated by a system. So generative metrics can be seen as carrying
the system-building tendency of traditional prosody to a maximum
degree of comprehensiveness.

Of course there may still remain *some* recalcitrant lines; separating these from the metrical lines and consigning them to a kind of
prosodic Siberia appears to be the primary function of Halle and
Keyser's system in the first place (p. 191). Also, *within* the domain
of metricality, there will be lines that differ in some way from the
model of the iambic pentameter line, which is conceived of as
consisting of ten "positions," designated as weak or strong, and

possessed of as many as four "stress maxima." (A stress maximum was defined originally by Halle and Keyser as a syllable that bears relatively greater stress than the syllables on either side of it in the same verse; this definition was later somewhat modified). Lacking the full complement of stress maxima confers on a line the quality of metrical "complexity." In general, the greater the deviation of the line from the model, the greater the complexity.

Halle and Keyser's approach is troublesome on several counts. For one thing, have they really provided an *explanation* of the deviations to be found in iambic pentameter, or only established a common denominator among them? These are not the same thing. It can be said, for example, that all the planets, while differing in their distance from the sun and in the speed of their motions, move in elliptical orbits, but to state this is not to explain why they do so.[11] Also, although Halle and Keyser are to be commended for dispensing with the notion of the foot,[12] their treatment of a particular passage from Chaucer does not inspire confidence in the usefulness of their characterization of iambic pentameter. Under the heading of "CHAUCER'S ART POETICAL," they examine a group of lines from "Complaint of Venus." They talk of Chaucer's "use of stressed variants for purposes of variety and interest" (this is an echo of the standard argument that *metrical* variations are there at least in part for variety's sake), and they comment accurately enough on Chaucer's use of syntactic mirroring, saying that this is reflected in his phonetic devices as well (p. 216). But none of these points requires invoking Halle and Keyser's conception of the *line* as a matter of positions and stress maxima.

Moreover, Halle and Keyser say they do not want the distinction between more complex and less complex lines to be confused with the distinction between irregular and regular lines, but as far as I can see this is a distinction-between-distinctions without a difference. In addition, their notion of metrical "complexity" appears to exhibit a curious inconsequence. Is a metrically complex line a good thing? A bad thing? What is its significance? How does it function in its context? Halle and Keyser are silent on these matters. This is part of a larger silence. Generative metrics has been accused of letting its preoccupation with establishing the conditions for metricality displace the question of how that metricality functions. Harvey Gross observes, for example, that "nothing in [the generative metrists'] approach has been able to demonstrate that the metricality or nonmetricality of a line of verse has much to do with either its aesthetic effect or its aesthetic value."[13] Charles O. Hartman rightly contends that Halle and Keyser's system "prevents them from explaining, or even considering, how a poem *uses* its meter."[14] Donald C. Freeman, who could himself be considered a generative metrist, properly inquires "What are we to ask beyond metricality? What does such a theory allow us to say about metrical style? What are appropriate criteria for the description of metrical styles?"[15]

Generative metrics has more than one branch. The second is the creation of Karl Magnuson and Frank G. Ryder. Interested readers can get a sense of the Magnuson-Ryder school by consulting Brogan; I do not wish to comment on it here, being content to rest with Brogan's statement that "It is fair to say that so far their approach has been considered unfruitful by most metrists."[16] The third branch is the work of Paul Kiparsky, who criticised Halle and Keyser for, among other things, not taking into account the question of the degrees of stress that syllables might exhibit (this is a notion found, as indicated earlier, in structuralist linguistics). Kiparsky's theory, first advanced in 1975, appeared two years later in a substantially revised version, which replaces the number designations of stress by a tree notation of the kind used in transformational grammar to depict sentence structure.[17] But whatever the form Kiparsky's work has taken, it shares with the Halle-Keyser approach a preoccupation with distinguishing metrical lines from nonmetrical lines and an interest in defining degrees of metrical "complexity." Moreover, his revised theory includes a return to the notion of the foot, which Halle and Keyser had rejected. In this later version, then, generative metrics has, from my point of view, lost the one thing that recommended it, the eschewing of the foot.

The recent work about prosody I now wish to examine is contained in a volume of essays by divers hands, presided over by Gilbert Youmans and Paul Kiparsky. While they themselves are both generative metrists, that is not true of all the contributors to *Phonetics and Phonology, Volume 1: Rhythm and Meter* (1989). For example, the book contains a piece by Derek Attridge, who has pointed to the limits of the generative approach, as well as essays by others who write outside that approach. But the majority of the contributors work within it, and/or are identified with linguistics, which, more than traditional literary criticism, has been the source of generative metrics. Whatever the critical allegiances involved, and whether or not claims to breaking new ground are put forth, if only implicitly, the book as a whole appears to me to have the effect of perpetuating the assumptions of the traditional prosodic mind-set that I have been questioning.

Marina Tarlinskaja is characterized by Youmans as one who is "critical of generative metrics" but who, at the same time, "has agreed . . . that she, too, is a generative metrist" in the sense that "her work is intended to establish explicit conditions for membership in the set of permissible verse lines rather than merely to list such lines."[18] Her allegiance to one strain of *traditional* prosody shows when she tells us that the reading of a given verse is subjected to the demands of the metrical pattern, that "it is only at the earliest stages of the canon formation that the meter passively follows the language givens."[19] Regarding a line from *As You Like It*— "He said mine eyes were black and my hair black"—she says she would "assign a strong stress to both *hair* and [the terminal] *black*, the first for semantic, the second for metrical reasons."[20] It seems to me that this is the only reading that makes sense, but one would like to know why semantic considerations are displaced by metrical ones in the case of the second "black," particularly since even a casual perusal of the play will show that Shakespeare does not commit himself to invariably stressing the last syllable of each line.

Writing in a vein similar to that of Tarlinskaja, Edward R. Weismiller, another contributor to the volume, whose main point seems to be that "triple rhythms [for example, anapests] from one side of our poetic heritage . . . invaded the . . . duple rhythms we learned . . . from Romance syllabic verse," states that "TO SOME DEGREE, we shape linguistic material to meter in order to maintain meter."[21] Here, however qualified, is the predilection for system-maintenance I spoke of earlier.

Elizabeth Closs Traugott combines the generative metrist's style of notation with the traditionalist's concern for showing how the presence of an alleged meter can contribute "to a critical interpretation of a poem . . ."[22]; she is listed, appropriately enough, as a member of Stanford's Departments of Linguistics and English. Her chapter in *Rhythm and Meter* focuses on Auden's "Streams." Like a good generative metrist, she strenuously goes about discovering a rule that would apply to virtually all the lines of the poem—more precisely, in this case, to all the beginnings of the lines. Like the traditionalist, she discovers that one line, the twelfth, which constitutes a decided exception to the rule, stands out in terms of its matter as well: it marks the beginning of what Traugott calls the "narrative" section of the poem (pp. 294, 295). Here I would say that the generative engine has labored mightily to produce a small result.

Traugott finds that a variation in another line, an extra stress, may be mimetic of the meaning of a phrase in that line ("jumps helter-skelter"); this strikes me as valid. Yet another line with an extra stress supposedly emphasizes the "ironic modality" introduced therein; this strikes me as forced. But I do not so much wish to make judgments of Traugott's readings of variations in individual lines as to point out that while her essay has the virtue of trying to illuminate the nature and function of a *particular* poem's sound structure (the most useful thing prosodic studies can do) it finally comes up with something all too close to a favorite *generalization* of traditional prosody, though given a special twist here. Traugott finds that the *theme* of "Streams," as opposed to the aesthetic *effect* so often attributed to metrical poetry as a whole, is "unity in diversity, freedom within boundaries" (p. 296). But that effect *is* eventually invoked by Traugott. According to her, we have in "Streams" a metric (a combination of pentameter and tetrameter, iambic and anapestic), obeying constraints, "but giving the appearance of a far freer metrical form" (p. 303); this pattern meshes nicely with the poem's matter. Apart from the question of the accuracy of Traugott's statement of the theme, she is, in effect, resorting here to the traditionalist's great fallback category for defining the effect of the employment of meter: unity in variety, form *and* freedom. To put the matter somewhat differently, it is as if Traugott's essay itself had succumbed to the principle embodied in the waters of the poem, which "transfer[. . .] the loam from Huppim/ to Muppim and back," mocking human efforts to set up distinct domains. For even while she is interested in characterizing the individual contours of Auden's poem, they tend, in her handling of them, to dissolve and to join the vast body of metrical poetry, as conceived of by traditional prosody. The particular specimen has been swallowed up by the genre.

In one of his own contributions to the Kiparsky and Youmans volume, Youmans, who is intent on showing that there is no clearcut distinction between metricality and unmetricality, declares himself as taking "a Platonic stance," defining Platonism in this context as the measuring of all lines "against an abstract metrical prototype (the Platonic Form)."[23] The traditionalism shown here by this generative metrist is only too apparent. But it is on the contribution by Paul Kiparsky that I wish to concentrate.

Kiparsky does something interesting and challenging, and does it with the patience and energy that must be conceded to generative metrists. He attempts to show that there is a set of rules governing Gerard Manley Hopkins's use of "sprung rhythm," and an auxiliary set of rules governing what Kiparsky calls "semisprung rhythm," also practiced by Hopkins. In arriving at these rules, Kiparsky is able to claim that lines regarded by other students of Hopkins's verse as wayward are really law-abiding, and that his interpretation of sprung rhythm "fits rather well with Hopkins's own attempts to explain what he was trying to do."[24] Even more, Kiparsky demonstrates that Hopkins's own scansions of his lines (these appear in the manuscripts), some of which have baffled even Hopkins specialists, "are entirely consistent with the theory of sprung rhythm proposed here and that, for the most part, they are the ONLY scansions consistent with it" (p. 334). This is no small feat. After a considerable period of time, Hopkins, both as poet and explicator of his poetry, has apparently found his proper critic.

But if this is indeed the case, there is a distinct cost involved in Kiparsky's seemingly large achievement. For he does to Hopkins in general what Traugott does to a particular poem of Auden, that is to say, he assimilates the apparent idiosyncrasies of Hopkins into the poetic mainstream, in effect asking us to play down the evidence of our ears: "in spite of the novelty of its rhythmic effects, Hopkins's poetry really is based on quite traditional principles. It applies modified versions of the familiar metrical rules to the familiar English meters . . . arranged in largely familiar stanza forms such as sonnets" (325). Reading this, one can only ask why all the fuss over the years about the sound of Hopkins's verse. And why did Hopkins himself fuss?

Also, one might well be bothered by a number of Kiparsky's treatments of individual lines, even as he reproduces them with Hopkins's own diacritical notations. He observes of those notations: "Hopkins put various accents and squiggles into the text of his poems to 'mark where the reader is likely to mistake.' . . . They show [among other things] the location of the strong [stressed] position ('in doubtful cases only') . . . " (p. 332). One of Kiparsky's examples is drawn from "Spelt from Sibyl's Leaves" (the underscorings are Kiparsky's, used to indicate strong metrical positions):

Where, se̲lfwrung, se̲lfstrung, she̲athe-and she̲lterless, tho̲úghts
aga̍i̲nst thoughts i̲n groans gri̲̍nd"

Kiparsky cites Norman MacKenzie's observation that "Most readers will want a stress upon *groans*." Kiparsky, who thinks of Hopkins as incorporating both stress and quantity, informs us that

this is ruled out by the principles of sprung rhythm, as are all other more "natural" scansions. If the strong position were shifted forward from *in* to *groans,* the long syllable *thoughts* would land illegally in a disyllabic weak position. If the strong position were shifted forward from *against* to *thoughts,* the same problem would be there with *-gainst* (p. 333).

Kiparsky's observations may well be consistent with Hopkins's notations, and he may be keeping the "principles" of sprung rhythm intact, but he leaves us with what would appear to be a perversely stressed line, which certainly constitutes a real aesthetic problem. However, such is not Kiparsky's concern.

    This is again the case when he discusses another Hopkins line (from "Hurrahing in Harvest"), which reads—again with Hopkins's diacritical notations and Kiparsky's underscorings—as follows:

I wálk, I líft up, Í lift úp | heart, éyes

How does Kiparsky respond to MacKenzie's understandable observation that "*heart* seems far more deserving of stress than *I* or *up*"? He states that "any scansion other than Hopkins's own puts a stressed or long syllable into a disyllabic weak position . . . .*Whether the line is a rhythmic success is another matter,* but there is at any rate nothing arbitrary about its metrical analysis" (p. 333; my emphasis). Here, as clear as can be, is an example of the generative metrist's distinct inclination toward neutrality (is this supposed to be scientific?), a withdrawal of judgment as to the appropriateness of a line's movement, a concern instead with whether the line conforms to the rules or not. To put the matter a little differently, the generative metrist, in the name of uncovering the "deep" structural principles governing a line of verse, makes relatively little of that line's "surface" quality. As a general principle, depths may well be honored over surfaces, but as far as the sounds of verse are concerned, I would suggest that surface is genuine, depth spurious.[25]

    Readings of isolated lines aside, how much do Kiparsky's formulations make for an understanding of a given poem? Discussing Hopkins's "That Nature is A Heraclitean Fire," he says it "projects a more dynamic view of nature" than that found in "Spelt from Sibyl's Leaves," and that the poem's metrical style "contributes to the expression of this dynamism through its predominantly rising rhythm, numerous outrides, and many stressed weak positions" (p. 331; "outrides" is Hopkins's term for extra syllables within a line). One can see the relevance of "many stressed weak positions," but is "rising rhythm" intrinsically more dynamic than "falling rhythm" (the latter a term that could be applied to, say, Blake's "The Tyger," quite a dynamic poem itself)? And why do extra syllables make for dynamism? Above and beyond this, how much do Kiparsky's observations, linking, for a change, the "metrical style" of a given poem to its content, depend on his particular formulation of Hopkins's metrical rules? Is there anything he says about the style of "Heraclitean Fire"— rising rhythm, extra syllables, and extra stresses—that a traditional metrist could not say? In short, Kiparsky's rules, for all their alleged capacity to account for all the poet's lines, do not, at least in Kiparsky's hands, add anything to our ability to characterize the sound quality of a given poem in relation to its matter. (This is similar to the charge brought against Halle and Keyser earlier.)

George T. Wright's *Shakespeare's Metrical Art* (1988) is a formidable work, a learned labor of love, love of the idea of meter and of the idea of expressive variation, chiefly as these function in Shakespeare's poetry and plays. I do not think traditional prosody has anything better to offer us, but I hope (in vain I am sure) that Wright's book may prove to be a near-last hurrah for that prosody, because for all its eloquence and for all its *apparent* willingness to surrender the notion of a prosodic staple, counterpoint, his study is still committed to the sort of scansions I have been quarreling with throughout. Moreover, Wright acknowledges the "phrasal" approach to poetry as a legitimate one, but where it threatens to displace scansion by feet he rebukes it in no uncertain terms (more of this in a later chapter). Wright's book, then, is of interest here not only because it is an important representative of traditional prosody, but because of its suspiciousness of the method of analysis this book will go on to advocate.

Before investigating *Shakespeare's Metrical Art* itself, I should like to characterize Wright's mind-set by looking at another prosodic document of the 1980s, his article commenting on the poem "Shall I die? Shall I fly?," that highly dispensable lyric that has recently been claimed for the Shakespeare canon. Wright decides that, while the poem may first strike us as anapestic, it really exhibits "an English stress-equivalent of the Latin cretic measure." Moreover, "The rhythm is essentially dipodic," and "The characteristic foot of the meter is \ x / (x)," where \ represents a secondary accent, and / a primary one.[26] He scans one two-line passage as follows:

$$\overset{\textstyle \backslash\ \ \text{x}\ \ /}{\text{Wantonly}}\ |\ \overset{\textstyle \backslash\ \ \text{x}}{\text{to make}}\ \overset{\textstyle /}{\text{fly}}$$
$$\overset{\textstyle \backslash\ \ \ \text{x}\ \ /\ \ \ \text{x}}{\text{her gold tresses}}$$

He comments:

> Most readers, if left to their own devices and free from any metrical
> pressure, would be inclined to stress 'want-' more strongly than "-ly,"
> "make" more strongly than "to," and "gold" more strongly than "her."
> What the poet appears to ask is not that we suppress such inclinations
> entirely, but that we moderate them in the interests of maintaining the
> meter . . . . (p. 12)

This is a modified version of Wimsatt and Beardsley's approach—
they mark syllables as either stressed or unstressed— but a version
nevertheless. The reading of the poem must serve the meter.

Here is Wright's scansion of another line:

$$\overset{\backslash}{We} \overset{x}{sat} \overset{/}{to} \mid \overset{\backslash}{re}\overset{x}{pose} \overset{/}{us} \mid \overset{\backslash}{for} \overset{x}{our} \overset{/}{plea}\overset{x}{sure}$$

He says "Hardly any reader will claim that such a line, so scanned
and read, is one of the high metrical moments of the poem . . .
but my purpose here is only to describe the pattern, not to justify
all the lines in which it is found" (p. 12).

In these scansions Wright gives us a good deal of traditional
metrical analysis in a nutshell: a text in English is contemplated, a
classic foot base is invoked, sometimes accompanied by impressive
terminology (dipodic cretic), individual syllables are managed so
as to make the foot appear continuously. Never mind that those
syllables are denied the stress values the reader might otherwise
give them, or that a given phrase may have its integrity dissolved
by the foot divisions (in many scansions, as indicated earlier, the
words themselves are broken up by those divisions). Readers must
not be left to their own devices but must modify their performances
or conceptions of the lines *in the interests of maintaining the meter,*
conceived of in terms of the foot. For traditional prosodists there
is no question as to what shall be master in the house of poetry.

Wright's book, *Shakespeare's Metrical Art,* is considerably less
specialized than his title would indicate. He is conversant with
much of the critical literature of prosody (though there are some
important gaps in his bibliography), and he begins with a supple
disquisition on the nature of the iambic pentameter line, the form
that is at the heart of his study, and that he celebrates. He follows
this with an investigation of the pentameters of Chaucer and Wyatt,
surveys "The Sixteenth-Century Line," and examines specimens
drawn from Surrey, Gascoigne, Spenser, and Sidney, before devoting most of the rest of his book to Shakespeare, though extending

his reach to Donne and Milton in later pages. Since Wright is, as already indicated, a most substantial representative of traditional scansion, it seems to me fair and fruitful to have the assumptions and procedures of that scansion further tested through an examination of his book.[27]

He starts, as I do (see Chapter 5), by assuming that the line "is the indispensable unit of verse and the one by which we recognize its nature" (p. ix). Consistent with his treatment of "Shall I die? Shall I fly?," he divides the constituents of the line into three groups: stressed syllables, unstressed syllables, and a third group, whose range "seems stronger than unstressed but weaker than stressed (here marked as ')" (p. 3). This is a standard and reasonable variation on the scheme of traditional scansion, and one found, for example, in Brooks and Warren. Like Wimsatt and Beardsley, Wright talks of stress as a "relative" matter—this helps greatly to keep the notion of meter intact—though unlike them he incorporates, with great frequency, the spondee as well as the pyrrhic in his analyses. The particular foot so beloved of Saintsbury, the anapest, is seen by Wright as delaying its appearance in nondramatic iambic pentameter until the eighteenth century. It goes without saying that he takes the general notion of the foot for granted.

There are no surprises as Wright tells us we may not pick up a metrical pattern right away, but when we do "we can recognize it as it is realized differently in all the succeeding lines; we listen for the returning pattern" (p. ix). Once established, the pattern, at least the iambic pattern, at least in cases where there are not "many feminine endings," is inescapable: "the pattern we come to know as we keep listening to iambic meter is one that moves inexorably, through several different modes of passage, to a final confirmation of iambicity" (p. 2). Wright, in fact, like other traditionalists, begins by anticipating a pattern, and he finds what he is disposed to find. Sustained "listening" reifies the anticipated pattern—a given piece of verse most pleasingly proves, whatever its twists and turns, to be in the grip of meter. (Note the overlap between Wright and Attridge in their sense of the power of pattern to manifest itself and to coerce.)

Wright continues to echo much of traditional prosodic theory in insisting at once on the existence of a pattern and on its disruption: "though we must hear the beat insistently enough to establish it as a recurrent pattern, we must enjoy as well a repertoire of variations, of departures from the pattern" (p. 42). Traditional, too, is his characterization of the function of such "departures" or "divergences" from meter: these "give variety, interest, grace, and sometimes expressive character" to the poet's lines (p. 7). His formulation of this last is more modest and demonstrable than the view represented by Paul Fussell, who, as noted earlier, sees metrical pattern established only in order to make possible expressive variations. Fussell places the metrist in the position of having to define the "expressive" function of each variation; Wright does not.

But Wright does reveal the passion for ordering that characterizes traditional prosody. This shows up in his construction of a system that allegedly governs Wyatt's poetry. That system involves the following: no fewer than eight line-types, along with "Metrical variations" (including "some combinations that never became standard for iambic pentameter"), "Syllabic procedures: elision, synaloepha, syncope, expansion of monosyllables into disyllables, and so forth," and "Accentual conventions" (p. 33). In an application of this "system," Wright, examining the line

> And skorne the story that the knyght told,

treats "knyght" as consisting of two syllables (kny|ght)—which he says "lets it rhyme with Wyatt"—in order to make the verse scan (p. 35). Possibly sensing at least some readers' unease with this sort of thing, Wright confesses that "It takes considerable metrical sophistication to hear what is happening around a Wyatt caesura, and even someone who grasps the system may not see how individual lines are meant to be read" (p. 34). Wyatt, it seems, is finally as troublesome to Wright as he has been to many metrists. Try as Wright does to bring them to heel, Wyatt's lines refuse to fall into the predictable-pattern-cum-deviations mode that conventional metrists are comfortable with.

In spite of my obvious unhappiness with Wright's scansions of "Shall I die? shall I fly?," and with a number of the statements in *Shakespeare's Metrical Art,* his book offers dismissals of "counterpoint" that would seem to make him a man after my own ear. But when regarded carefully or placed in their settings, these seeming departures from standard prosody only confirm his traditionalism, which includes a willingness (already indicated in his treatment of "Shall I die? shall I fly?") to tamper with the stress values of a line's syllables. He says, for example:

Despite its great vogue through much of the twentieth century, the counterpoint theory is inaccurate. When metrical variations occur, we do not hear the actual line against a model line that is constantly ticking away in our heads. We hear only the actual line, and in it we hear the familiar pattern embodied in a particular passing form (pp. 187–88).

This appears, at least on first impression, to be a major concession by a traditional prosodist. Scrutinized, it shows itself as smuggling back the notion of counterpoint by allowing us to have simultaneously "the familiar pattern" (the meter) "embodied in a particular passing form" (that presumably incorporates variations). That is, to the extent that there exists a particularity and passingness in a given line, there must be a gap between that line and the presumably general and enduring "familiar pattern" allegedly still exhibiting itself. So a two-ness peeps out from beneath Wright's alleged oneness.

He also says:

we must often in practice, in performance, "tilt" [he is quoting Wimsatt here] the phrasing in the direction of the meter . . . if we fail to do so the divergence is likely to be so extreme that we hear a hodgepodge, not a counterpoint. In fact, we hear, not two lines, but one—one actual rhythmic line that *realizes* the meter in its own idiosyncratic way (p. 11; italics in original).

This last briefly formulates a sonic monism that Wright, as we shall see, fleshes out, but before investigating how he does so, I wish to emphasize that he arrives at the one-line notion by assigning, like a number of other metrists, a policing role to performance (when performance is recognized at all). One is supposed to make sure that the line does not fall victim to the temptation of following ordinary speech stresses; instead the line must get judicious jabs so as to stay within previously defined barriers, must be made to toe the mark in the process of being delivered. Performance becomes a matter of stress control, the voice being used against its own inclinations.

From within Wright's own perspective, there is an unrecognized irony here, one that extends to many prosodists (John Thompson, for example—see Chapter 5). Wright endorses the debatable notion that iambic pentameter is close to ordinary speech, a closeness he appears to regard as commendable. On the other hand, he seems anxious to protect the iambic line from encroachment by the way we do, in fact, speak. Where his true allegiance lies is indicated by what he says in closing out his pages devoted to Wyatt:

In the last analysis, the jointed line, [much used by Wyatt], brilliant as it is in the hands of a master, is inherently too subservient to the spoken phrase, too deficient in predictable musical pattern. Since the basic pattern is variable, we may not be sure what the variations vary from, so our sense of them as variations is diminished and confused (p. 37).

Also, while he notes that Gascoigne is arguing against setting up a conflict between ordinary pronunciation and metrical pattern, and while he acknowledges (in a footnote) that "most features of poetic language, however stylized and exaggerated in verse, have their source in spoken language" (p. 297), he leaves us with little doubt as to what must triumph for both Gascoigne and himself should a conflict occur between the configurations of spoken language and the metrical form. Even assuming he is right about Gascoigne, Wright emerges as more of a hard-liner; he speaks of Gascoigne's "mistaken belief that the stress of a word in a poem is predetermined by its earlier history," that is, its ordinary pronunciation (pp. 272–73).) All in all, Wright comes over as a disciple of John Thompson (whom, in fact, he cites).

In his supposedly taking issue with the counterpointers and in his advocacy of a "one-line" approach, Wright assigns, as might be anticipated, a prominence to the element of expectation, saying "Variant lines depart not from a form we hear but from a form we *expect* to hear. The distinction is crucial" (p. 11; italics in original). But in my view this is a meaningless distinction, for the alleged metrical paradigm continues to reign supreme for Wright: according to him we expect the line to conform to it, we do our best to ensure that it does, and even if we don't actually hear the paradigm as we read, we go on expecting to. I find it difficult to choose between what Wright gives us here and the counterpointers' claim that we always have the paradigm in our ears.

Whatever difficulties one might have with Wright's arguments, it must be admitted that he speaks with considerable love for his subject, bringing celebrations of meter and the variations therefrom to a kind of culmination in the critical literature. Devotees of the concept of meter could hardly ask for something more grand than this contention:

In effect, meter [in Shakespearean drama] looks at least two ways: toward the sentence, which it both reflects and rivals, and toward the larger world of character and character, whose relations it mirrors—ultimately, to that world's structure of authority and resistance, and of inner selves and outer layers of reality (other person, family, party, state, cosmos) (p. 258).

Similarly, he says "Meter stands (but not simply) for some such principle as order, truth, certainty, completeness—doom; deviation is energy, mischief, trouble—and beauty" (p. 261). Also, "iambic pentameter in the Renaissance symbolizes a cosmic order that limits human aspiration; human experience can be heard in the counter–rhythm . . . " (p. 262). But alas, one cannot keep an entire book focused on this exalted level, and in the process of descending to the plane of specific texts and landing there, in the process of working with the nuts and bolts of actual scansions, Wright, in his book as well as his article, proves guilty of what I hope the reader is coming to think of as the standard sins of traditional prosody.

To see more than I have yet shown of Wright's prosodic practice in *Shakespeare's Metrical Art*, let us consider his treatment of the opening line of Sonnet 30. Here is how he lays out the verse (where Wright does not specify stress values, or foot divisions, he is assuming the presence of iambs):

When in | disgrace with for | tune and | men's eyes

He recognizes that the line displays "three feet that appear to violate the expected iambic pattern: a trochee in the first foot, a pyrrhic in the fourth, a spondee in the last." Does this present a real problem? Not at all. He offers not one but several solutions (and they are as conventional as they can be):

> when the line is spoken or heard silently by a reader with some auditory experience of the tradition, it does not violate the pattern: enough of the line is still iambic to sustain the iambic feeling, especially when earlier lines (from the previous sonnets in the sequence) and later ones in this poem adhere more unambiguously to the iambic design, so that our experience of this line is influenced by our iambic set (p. 8).

So, first, Wright is saying that having only two of its five feet in the proper mode is enough to give the supposedly errant line that old "iambic feeling." (To interpose for a moment, if two feet is all its takes, couldn't we get such a "feeling" from almost any decasyllabic line in English, as well as a good many stretches of ten syllables drawn from prose?) Second and third, the line is seen, in effect, as caught in a kind of pincer movement, influenced both by what has come before and what comes after. Our reading of earlier sonnets, Wright says, predisposes us to hear this first line as iambic, and our reading of later, more regular lines within the sonnet produces a retroactive effect.

Wright's treatment of the line up to this point suggests that it never had a chance of breaking out of the iambic mold (his later remarks only confirm this impression, as I shall demonstrate in a moment). In assimilating the line as he does, Wright is showing himself to be a traditionalist par excellence. He is also exhibiting traditional prosody's curious anticipation of much contemporary criticism, its preoccupation with intertextuality or with the positing of overarching grids or systems, whereby the given work is denied autonomy, either being seen largely as referring to a prior work or as simply reenacting or extending an existing grid. The prior work is granted a degree of reality or force greater than that accorded to the "belated" work, and the grid assimilates everything to its own terms. In the present instance, the belated work is the seemingly errant line.

Of course, it is true that we do not read a given line in a vacuum; as Wright says, "a line of verse does not stand alone" (p. 15). We bring our experience of preceding lines or poems to it. It might also be observed that there can be a "backwash" effect in poetry, whereby something occurring later in the poem can alter our perception of what comes before. Still, one should be very slow to apply this second principle to the sounding of a line. Moreover, it is one thing to make a place for lines we have read, as well as, retroactively, for lines we will have come to read,[28] and another to grant *more* weight to either of these than to the line we are reading at a given moment. A poem, unless it is of the most mechanical sort, operates by having different lines work in different ways, not by one line or set of lines (some of them outside the poem!) recasting any given line in its own image.

Wright is not content to have "When in disgrace with fortune and men's eyes" assimilated by what has preceded it (other Shakespeare sonnets) or by what follows it (later, more "regular" lines in the poem). Focusing on the line per se, and invoking the principle that "absolute equality of syllable stress rarely occurs" (this of course is very much in the spirit of Wimsatt and Beardsley) he applies it so as to guarantee the regularizing of the line: " . . . it seems likely that in both [the fourth and fifth feet] the second syllable is somewhat more strongly stressed than the first (or is so perceived) and that what we have in the last two feet of the line are, essentially, a pyrrhic iamb and a spondaic iamb." (My impression is that these last two terms are Wright's inventions, but he appears to say others have used them; in any case we have here an instance of terminological proliferation working to assimilate troublesome lines.) Moreover, "The trochaic pattern in the opening foot is . . . a standard variation for iambic pentameter" (p. 9).

One cannot help but feel that the reader has been set up to start with in being presented with the "deviant" specimen here. The seemingly rogue line turns out to be one easily captured for the cause of iambicity through the intervention of Wright's stratagems. Every wayward foot has been brought into line, either as a species of special iamb or as a standard variation. Is Wright's approach here different in spirit from what he accuses textual editors of Chaucer of doing, that is, of having "tried to emend, elide, or syncopate [odd] lines out of existence"? (p. 26) Judging from his *own* practice, all is fair in love and prosody.

Having "demonstrated" the essential iambicity of Shakespeare's line, Wright is now free to talk about its deviant quality. What does he find to say about it?

> If the line had read, for example,

> *In deep disgrace with fortune, eyes of men

> > its straightforward meter would not have caught the uneasiness, the uncertainty, about "men's eyes" that in Shakespeare's line is conveyed not only by the phrase itself but by the more deeply inflected meter as well (p. 9).

There is surely uneasiness about those eyes—but where is the "uncertainty?" The term "in disgrace" indicates the speaker thinks he knows just where he stands. Wright appears to me to be extrapolating a non-existent uncertainty from the line in order to justify the meter, which, according to him, is at once uncertain and clearly iambic (another instance, I must say yet again, of traditional prosody's penchant for having things both ways).

In my own reading of the line, "When" could receive a stress or not; the heart of the line, in terms of stress allocation, is in fact "men's eyes." That one of these words *might* be slightly less emphasized than the other is not as urgent a consideration as that neither should be played down. The phrase "men's eyes" carries weight via its contrast with the abstraction "fortune" that precedes it. To refine on this, one might say that there is a pattern of increasing concreteness in the sequence of nouns in the line: fortune, men's, eyes. There is no reason, on semantic grounds, for the voice to slight the middle term. Moreover, "men's eyes" sets up the first of two kinds of looking that dominate the sonnet's octave: the speaker feels he is *being looked at by other men* with contempt, he *looks at other men* with envy. Both terms in "men's eyes" must be stressed. Wright is willing, at best, to concede some stress to "men's," but insists that it be kept subordinate to "eyes," because of his commitment to making the line safe for iambicity. Only then does he try to do something with its departure from straightforward meter. I have no interest in regularizing the line, but rather see it as a lopsided one, distinctly tilted to the right, favoring "men's eyes" as its semantic heart, and encouraging the allocation of stress to both terms.

If such allocation is carried out, "men's eyes" might be said to constitute a spondee, assuming one is intent on retaining the terminology of feet; Wright, as already noted, calls it a "spondaic iamb." This is his way of handling the apparently disturbing possibility of two syllables in a row showing the same degree of stress. Consider his *general* response to lines that are structured like the one in question, in the sense of having more than one set of syllables (or foot) apparently showing no stress differential in their respective components (for this is how "-tune and" as well as "men's eyes" could be regarded). In encountering such lines

we may well lose temporarily our sense of the meter. To avoid having that happen, our sense of the meter *may do whatever it can to restore itself* (p. 269; my italics).

Wright goes on to talk of this as meaning, in practice, the making of "some minimal adjustments," but by then the cat has been let out of the bag. Plainly, what one might call "The Principle of Disinterested Meddling" must be kicked into gear with certain lines, lest the meter disintegrate. Wright is clearly an example of the all-too-common practice spoken of earlier, that of making the scansion of a poem an exercise in meter maintenance.

If readers regard this as an overreaction on my part—after all, Wright speaks only of "minimal adjustments"—let us consider some more of his scansions. In one instance, which comes much before the passage just cited, a possible two-spondee situation threatens to arise (I have marked only the potentially offending feet:

Four lág | ging winters and | four wan | ton springs

Wright tells us to assign only secondary stress to each "four"; that way, of course, we are left with two harmless iambs—"Four lag" and "four wán." Wright's meter-saving device treats the important word "four" as if it were a not-so-important "for" (p. 55).

Here is another example of Wright's meter-maintenance scanning, this time directed at a less threatening line, a description of Falstaff in *Henry IV, Part I*:

> And lards the lean earth as he walks along.

The apparent trochee of the third food—"earth as"—appears to disturb Wright (who is preoccupied with trochees—he gives a whole chapter to them). His solution? Demote "earth," promote "as," so that each receives a "secondary stress." The line would then read:

> And lards the lean | earth as | he walks along.

Apparently sensing that this is a dubious procedure, Wright is not willing to say more than that this reading is "perhaps preferable" to reading the foot as a trochee (p. 199).

Apart from my regarding the line that emerges from Wright's scansion as deformed, I should like to observe two things. The foot "earth as" would appear to be, in Wright's treatment of it, what one could only call a "secondary-stress spondee." This is precisely what he does call it (though he does not mint the phrase for this particular occasion), so we have yet another instance of a term being conjured up to aid the prosodist in keeping a foot-based scansion intact. My second point is that humble words, such as "as," have a friend in Wright; no matter how minor, they are candidates for promotion whenever maintaining the meter requires such an upgrading. Witness, for example, his treatment of the lowly "it" in these lines from Donne's "The Triple Foole":

> Griefe brought to numbers cannot be so fierce,
> For, he tames it, that fetters it in verse.

Wright again invokes his "secondary-stress spondee," by his scansion if not by outright use of the term, marking the "tames it" foot with two secondary stresses. He says that what goes on in that foot "is a miniature taming: the verb, out of stress position, threatens to break the alternating pattern, but the word that follows is strong enough to retain the metrical stress" (p. 268). My response is that in some rare cases one might wish to regard the word "it," perhaps the meekest in our language, as of sufficient interest to merit a stress, and, in fact, such a stress will be assigned in my reading of a Shakespeare sonnet in a later chapter. But one would like to know what makes the "it" *here* deserving of stress, and what "tames" has done to be demoted to a secondary accent. The only rationale for this doubly dubious treatment of "tames it" appears to be preventing too severe a disruption of the alleged iambic pattern. Having muffled the effect of "tames it," Wright then reads the "foot" mimetically. In my view, this metrical circus act is all the work of Wright, not of the poem. But at least he refrains here from explicitly invoking his concocted terminology, denying himself not only "secondary stress spondee" but "trochaic iamb" as well.

Of course when he does invoke the latter term (204), it creates the impression that the iambic pattern is being maintained even as it is being clearly challenged—what is more antithetical to an iamb than a trochee? For as is true of so many other metrists, keeping the unstressed-stressed profile of that pattern chugging along is obviously of primary importance to Wright. At one point, after having given his readings of several lines, he says that his "barely suppressible instinct is to give some syllables a greater prominence than I am arguing for," but justifies his not doing so by saying that "excessive attention to the odd-syllable word will destroy the bond between the syllables in the foot and the bond between the phrases in the line. Iambic pentameter is a closely woven meter; if the strands are separated too far, the fabric will unravel" (pp. 201–2). As I hope the statistics adduced in the last chapter showed, the supposedly close weave of iambic pentameter is much more the result of prosodists trying to pull into place undeniably straying strands of the verse than it is of anything else. And while I too am all for respecting the integrity of a poem's phrases—in fact it is a respect my own approach to prosody will insist on—that integrity is often *threatened,* not sustained by, scansions yielding pride of place to foot integrity, as examples already adduced have shown. Where, for instance, is Wright's concern for phrasal integrity in his above-cited scanning of the first line of Shakespeare's Sonnet 30?

When in | disgrace with for | tune and | men's eyes

Wright's linkage of phrasal integrity to not giving "excessive attention to the odd-syllable word," that is, his linkage of such integrity to the maintenance of iambic feet through the supression of trochaic tendencies, is doubly odd. For not only does keeping phrases inviolate seem the furthest thing from his mind in many of his scansions, but he himself indicates that when phrases *are* allowed to function as wholes, foot integrity can suffer. In short, phrasal integrity and foot integrity tend to be *inimical* to each other, at least in Shakespeare's later plays, and this for Wright is one of their distinguishing and presumably valuable features. The opposition of phrase to foot and vice versa is what his embrace of counterpoint is founded on.

For, interestingly enough, after supposedly rejecting "counterpoint" in its standard sense—the alleged interplay between the stress configuration of a line when its words are normatively sounded and the stress pattern assigned to accord with the line's meter—he resurrects the term. Indeed, the freshest aspects of Wright's book are his dismissal of the usual conception of counterpoint, and his attempt to revive the notion of "interplay" (a synonym for "counterpoint" among many metrists),[29] but now with new components. However, if there is a problem with the first of these moves the second is also not without difficulty.

I have already indicated that in his original stance, apparently not recognizing what he was doing (the reader may notice this sort of statement cropping up more than once in this study), Wright cast his supposed repudiation of counterpoint in terms that actually permit its instant readmission, though it thereby gets reduced to a kind of contraband. More interesting is his *explicit* readmittance of the concept, but with a shifting of its usual elements. Unfortunately, Wright's notion of "counterpoint" or "interplay" is dogged by vagueness.

He says that by Shakespeare's time, English versification had become "an art of counterpoint, an art in which the rhythmic phrase may work either with or against the metrical current" (p. 46). He also says, early in *Shakespeare's Metrical Art*, that "The belief on which this book rests is that there are always at least two structural orders simultaneously audible in iambic pentameter—the metrical and the phrasal (actual lines and stanzas, and actual phrases and sentences)—and their varied rhythmic interplay constitutes the great beauty of the form" (p. 12). Late in the book he points to a "creative equilibrium" between "the continually recurring metrical pattern and the rhythmic phrase" (p. 281). So in its reincarnation in Wright's book, counterpoint, or interplay, is not a matter of normative stress patterns and foot-sustaining stress patterns differing from each other, which is a question of individual syllables, it is a matter of different *groupings* of syllables that may or may not be out of sync.

Allowing Wright his reformulation of counterpoint, or interplay, one might still ask, first, just what is a "rhythmic phrase"? Is it the same as the "actual phrase" he speaks of in connection with his book's fundamental belief, or is it possessed of some special characteristic?[30] Also, the "creative equilibrium" of the late passage suggests, to me anyway, a single sound stream, maintained in the face of conflicting pressures. But the early passage, the one about "two structural orders," clearly points to a pair of such streams. Where does this leave us? Moreover, what exactly is the function of the "interplay" Wright is obviously enamored of? Much of his discussion of that phenomenon simply points to passages in Shakespeare's later plays where "phrases run over the foot-margins" (p. 213) or run over line boundaries. These things undoubtedly occur, and frequently, but to what end?

Insofar as Wright offers us formulations on the function of interplay, he appears to say, in part, that where the breaking of foot boundaries by phrasal contours is concerned, we get what might be called an abstract *aesthetic* dividend, variety. But the question is, if the foot is simply overridden, where is the interplay? The phrases do what they want, the feet be damned. (Wright has a counterargument here that I will take up shortly.) To the extent that phrases subvert line structure, the verse medium links up, for Wright, with a *thematic* element, serving as the vehicle for "a distrust of sententious rhetoric, of the deceitful uses and users of language such as [the later plays from *Antony and Cleopatra* to *Cymbeline*] all touch and turn on." (p. 223). This is meaty enough. But we might well question whether fracturings of line endings by phrases inevitably signal or subvert dubious uses of language, or whether such ruptures might not also be found in passages where the language is untainted by sententiousness or the intent to deceive. What would be the point of mocking the medium in such instances? Witness, for example, lines from *Coriolanus* quoted by Wright himself to exemplify the pulling of phrases against line endings—this passage hardly seems a candidate for mockery:

> Your voices? For your voices I have fought;
> Watch'd for your voices; for your voices bear
> Of wounds two dozen odd; battles thrice six
> I have seen, and heard of; for your voices have
> Done many things, some less, some more. Your voices?
> Indeed I would be consul. (II, iii, 126–31)

Apart from the questionableness of Wright's generalization about Shakespeare's later plays, we might do well to hesitate before assigning *any* blanket thematic effect to the many line-breaking phrases of those plays. Doesn't such a generalization undesirably relieve us of the responsibility of attending to the consequences of particular line breakdowns in particular passages in particular dramas? As with any aspect of poetry, prosodic study would do well to give its primary energies to the Many instead of the One.

With respect to formal as opposed to thematic matters, the components of Shakespeare's later dramatic verse, *at least as Wright describes them,* do not strongly support the notion of interplay between phrase and line. He himself talks of "the *rift* between phrase and line" (p. 220; my italics); that appears to me another matter. Also, while he alludes in passing to the line's ability to "break up the phrase into bits and pieces of any description" (p. 220), he appears to give much greater weight to the reverse process, with autonomous phrases and frequent enjambment resulting in an enormous amount of line-bashing. The struggle between phrase and line seems too one-sided and destructive to admit of "interplay," just as is the case with the relationship of phrase and foot as Wright presents it.[31]

But Wright would certainly not concede this last point, and the nature of his contentions on the matter shows that, as with the other works being treated in this chapter, the more things seem to change the more they remain the same. He says that while Shakespeare's practice may *appear* to make the foot a diminishing presence, a dubious entity, the metrical pattern persists, though it is subtle and concealed: "The iambic body runs on, foot by foot, but its bones show less and less: its segments varied in length, its iambs varied in strength, its feet hidden in the phrase" (p. 213). In fact, according to Wright, at the heart of Shakespeare's elaborate verse design is nothing other than

> the meter, which . . . enable[s] the whole complex artifice to work so effectively. The midline-to-midline arrangement [of the phrasing] makes the metrical pattern less obtrusive, less evident, but it is still present to the ear and, in some sense, *more deeply emphatic for its being less insistent* (p. 228; my italics).

Finally, he says:

> verse speech, that contradiction in terms, can heighten the usual forcefulness of the spoken language by making its linguistic measures (phrase and sentence) struggle against the bonds of a strong meter, a meter that gives but does not let go, that reminds the characters' language of hidden responsibilities to an invisible order, and that fixes

their speech and their action in the grip of a benevolent but unforgiving time (p. 248).

Thus it turns out, that for all the refurbishing of counterpoint in Wright's pages, for all the admitted twistings and turnings of sylla-ble, phrase, or line, he still hears the metrical feet go marching on. Meter, says Wright, simply will not be denied; it is the central, crucial presence of Shakespeare's verse, asserting itself all the more by its apparent self-effacement. More than that, we are, in the last passage quoted, in close vicinity to the linkage made by Attridge between meter and divine order. What chance has some poor deviant stress or line-fractured and line-fracturing phrase got against a manifestation of the metaphysical? In my own view, Wright's insistence that we continue to register the presence of iambic feet, even as particular sonic events threaten to drown them out, is equivalent to wistfully claiming that, standing in the middle of the city's din, we hear the sound of the tree falling in the forest.

The reverence with which Wright treats the march of feet, the alleged persistence of meter, ultimately relegates the element of phrasing in Shakespeare's later dramatic poetry to secondary sta-tus, however much weight Wright claims to give that phrasing. In contrast, respect for phrasing appears to be central to the work of Richard Cureton, one of the most ambitious prosodists to have emerged in recent years (and one whose "theory of rhythm" carries that respect well beyond sonic considerations). But Cureton's the-ory, while commendable in its advocacy of the importance of phrasing, is not without its flaws. He does not always argue in a relevant manner or cleanly separate what are supposed to be independent concepts, and he bases too much of his theory on music. As a prosodist, he can be seen as caught between an alle-giance to conventional ways of thinking about poetry and an im-pulse to work out something significantly different. Reviewing his work will afford an illustration of how the traditional concept of meter (both in its stresser and timer versions) clings even to one who chafes at its limitations and distortions.

In "Traditional Scansion: Myths and Muddles," Cureton, focus-ing on five widely-used introductory poetry texts, extrapolates a number of "myths" he finds therein, having to do with meter and rhythm.[32] (We need not explore them all because they show a sig-nificant amount of overlapping.) One of these is: "*A Meter is an Expressive Rhythm.*" In discussing this myth he correctly claims that the poetry manuals create the impression that "a meter is the most important rhythm in the text." He presumably disagrees with this, but does not produce a true argument against the notion of expressive meters. Instead, he says that "*no* English poem of any merit whatsoever has ever been written in an iambic rhythm . . ." (p. 175; italics in original). He seems to mean that there is no such thing as a rhythm that is *purely* iambic. Defenders of traditional prosody could easily get around this limited argument by simply saying, as I have indicated earlier, that such a rhythm operates as an ideal presence. Cureton seems not to anticipate this response, even though later in the essay he will himself invoke an "ideal" metrical pattern, using Attridge's method of scansion (p. 191).) Another myth Cureton finds is that "*Variation is Valuable for its Own Sake*" (p. 176; italics in original). It turns out that he has no "inherent" difficulty with this, so one wonders at his use of "myth" here.[33] What *rightly* concerns him is the dubious procedures the myths endorse: assigning a particular label to the meter of a poem and hunting down the variations from the meter are each thought to constitute "a productive rhythmic analysis" (p. 176).

In his treatment of the next two "myths," namely, that "*Rhythm is Essentially Concrete*" and "*Metrical Shape Determines Rhythmic* Shape" (italics in original), Cureton appears to be pulling in two different directions at once, and, along the way, can be said to place himself in the ranks of those he is contesting. In response to the notion of the concreteness of rhythm (that is, that rhythm is actually experienced) he states that there are "aspects of rhythmic organization that are necessarily abstract" (p. 177)—this appears to be an echo of Wimsatt and Beardsley. On the other hand, in commenting on the notion of meter determining rhythm, he states that "metrical feet have no experiential reality" (p. 178), and such reality is apparently important to him. At least we can reasonably conclude it is if we look at his comments (to be given fully a little later) on the opening line of Thomas Gray's "Elegy in a Country Churchyard"—he uses the expression "We feel" three times in referring to the physical particulars of that line's words and phrases. While abstraction and concreteness could conceivably co-exist in a theory of rhythm (I myself am interested primarily in "concreteness") Cureton's "Traditional Scansion," in its attack on prevailing prosodic "myths," appears not to have integrated his attractions to each.

The chief value of that attack is its sense that metrical patterns can furnish only a "primitive representation" of a poem's rhythmic qualities, whose elucidation is dependent on our paying attention to "natural phrases . . . " (p. 180). If changes in foot configuration do coincide with changes in rhythm, this will happen "only where metrical feet happen to coincide with the natural phrasing of the syntax . . . " (p. 179). But as close as this emphasis on phrasing is to my own position (to be expounded more fully in Chapter 6), and as impatient as Cureton would appear to be with the "myths" of traditional prosody, his own theory of rhythm appears disinclined to throw away essential elements of that prosody, in both its timer and stresser manifestations. He has, for example, not been content simply to say that "Meter is a major component of prosodic form," he has also claimed that "Meter lays down a bedrock of physical pulsation that we feel on our nerves and establishes a precise measure of objective duration. . . ."[34] I shall not reply to the last part of this statement for now, but only note that I find an implicit discrepancy at the very least, between this picture of a pulsation registering on our nerves and Cureton's own statement that feet lack "experiential reality."

Cureton's continuing allegiance to meter, in spite of his showing the harmful consequences of allowing it to dominate rhythmic analysis,.can be seen both in his general conception of how such analysis should proceed and in some of his individual scansions. He advocates a "multilevel" approach, one that sees a given verse line as exhibiting simultaneously a number of configurations, arranged on a hierarchical scale.[35] In one such formulation, which he applies to the final line of Stevens' "Sunday Morning"— "Downward to darkness on extended wings"—his levels include "Metrical set," "Metrical realization" and "Cadence," all of which involve chopping up words and/or phrases. Fragmentation of phrases also occurs at the fourth level, that of "Words," and even at the fifth, that of "Rhythm Phrases" (and he characterizes these "phrases" by assigning them the names of feet); one so-called rhythm phrase he finds in the Stevens line is "on extended."[36] It is only on the sixth and seventh levels of his scheme, those involving "Tone Units" and "Larger Phrasing," that there emerges a commitment to keeping intact the true phrases of the line.[37]

In another formulation, Cureton says that to define rhythm we need "a theory of meter (regular beat alternation); a theory of grouping (the continuous hierarchical phrasing of the text into rhythmic equivalents); and a theory of prolongation (the hierarchical structuring of felt anticipation, arrival, and extension in the syntax)." Taken together these three theories involve a total of eight elements: anticipation, recurrence, regularity, salience, equivalence, direction, grouping, and hierarchy. He tells us that meter and prolongation *each* contribute to "only five" of them.[38]

I should say that five out of eight makes for a considerable contribution, keeping meter very important.

All in all, it's fair to conclude that Cureton does not wish to abandon or even question the traditional theory of meter, but simply to incorporate it among his levels.[39] Witness his handling of the final line of "Sunday Morning." He formulates its "Metrical realization" as follows:

$$\text{[Do}\acute{\text{w}}\text{n w}\breve{\text{a}}\text{rd] [t}\breve{\text{o}}\text{ d}\acute{\text{a}}\text{rk] [ne}\breve{\text{s}}\text{s o}\breve{\text{n}}\text{] [e}\breve{\text{x}}\text{ t}\acute{\text{e}}\text{nd] [e}\breve{\text{d}}\text{ w}\acute{\text{i}}\text{ngs]}$$

His comment is that "Both of the half-lines [i.e., "Downward to darkness" and "on extended wings"] begin with metrical deviations—the first with a trochaic inversion, the second with a pyrrhic substitution. This leaves the rhythm in both phrases appropriately unresolved (on this level)."[40] One must wonder why the rhythm isn't "resolved" on this level by what happens in the final two feet?[41] But to put the matter this way is to accede to the very sort of prosody I am trying to undo. The real point is that Cureton is playing the old game of looking for foot-defined variations and trying to link them to an expressive effect.

There is another old game being played in Cureton's work, one not so obvious (it may even be concealed from him), but one that can be regarded as ultimately central to his thought. He tells us that his definition of rhythm "might reduce some of the (largely unproductive) polemics that are so characteristic" of prosody, polemics that wield "unsupported platitudes." One of these is that "rhythm is based on isochrony . . . ."[42] He also speaks of "the temporalists' reduction of rhythm to durational differences . . ."[43]; he might better have said "durational similarities." While this comment on timers could be seen as allowing rhythm to *include* a temporal dimension rather than being confined to it, Cureton elsewhere seems more dismissive. He says:

Many isochronous repetitions are indeed judged to be rhythmic. . . . But it seems to be just an empirical fact that no English verse rhythms are isochronous in any objective sense; and I think that there are many instances of isochronous repetition that we would not consider rhythmic.[44]

But in the very same essay where this apparent dismissal or at least diminution of isochrony is found, there is something of a shift the next time the subject shows up. Cureton says "theories of isochronous rhythm in verse (whether right or wrong) are largely theories of meter" (p. 14). The parenthetical remark may, initially, not seem particularly significant, but "whether right or wrong" can ultimately be regarded as a modulation on Cureton's part, leading to an embrace of something that, if it is not isochrony per se, is a blood relative of it. For the essay goes on to say that his theory employs groupings that are built into hierarchies, and that

> The temporal "pressures" in such a [hierarchy] derive from the fact that the groups on each level represent informational equivalents and therefore equivalent units of structural time. For example, if a group at a higher level receives almost no lower-level articulation, physical time slows down (because fewer physical units are passing per narrative unit) . . . . On the other hand, if a group at a higher level receives a great deal of lower-level articulation, physical time speeds up . . . " (p. 15).

Some of my difficulties with this may simply be a function of the fact that Cureton is trying to put forth a complicated scheme in a very compressed way,[45] but as the matter stands, I am not sure what "informational equivalents" are, nor do I understand how such equivalents translate automatically into "equivalent units of structural time." What I do see is the notion of equivalent time units, and the positing of a speeding up or slowing down of physical time in order, presumably, to preserve those units. The need to preserve them is what exerts the "pressure." Is it wrong to smell essence of isochrony here?[46] Cureton has seemingly barred isochrony from his notion of meter while, in my view, allowing it in under the heading of "grouping." But was it ever banished from his conception of meter to begin with? Recall his saying that "Meter lays down a bedrock of physical pulsation that we feel on our nerves, and establishes a precise measure of objective duration . . . ."[47] If meter establishes a precise measure of *duration,* is this not isochrony?

The application of isochrony to metrical theory has its roots in a desire to see poetry operating in a manner akin to music. So, given Cureton's attraction to isochrony (at least as I read him), it is no surprise to find him featuring the word "rhythm," using terms like "counterpoint" and "polyphony," and having him eventually tell us that his theory of rhythm "has strong connections to music theory . . . and therefore holds exciting prospects for a deeper, interdisciplinary understanding of rhythmic processes . . . ."[48] Where Cureton eagerly anticipates an exciting interdisciplinary understanding, I can only foresee a continuing, disheartening confusion of realms. I think that over the years attempts to describe poetry in terms of music have done a disservice to the former. While the loose employment of musical terminology in the field of poetry criticism may never be eliminated (such terminology is very tempting, perhaps unavoidable), and while this in itself may prove harmless enough, what prosody needs is an investigation of the language-specific elements of the verse medium, not an indulgence of the hankering to restore the conjunction of words and music that we conjecture existed at one time.[49]

Paradoxically, Cureton, while making much of the alleged connections between poetry and a medium that is pure sound, music, wishes at the same time to take the notion of rhythm well beyond the sonic. He observes that

> prosodies that limit poetic rhythm to sound exclude from consideration some of the most critically central rhythms in our poetry—those deeper syntactic and semantic rhythms that are at the aesthetic center of the prosodic form of English texts from the King James Bible, to most blank verse, to much free verse that approaches a blank verse norm . . . .[50]

In the same spirit he says "phrasing is often independent of concrete phonological realization; it is a matter of sense groupings, syntactic phrasings that are indeed related in a hierarchical fashion—but structurally, not physically." In supposedly illustrating this with the opening line of Gray's "Elegy Written in a Country Churchyard," Cureton seems to me to swing, willy-nilly, *towards* a focus on the physical when he says "We feel the falling contours of the disyllabic words *curfew* and *parting*. We feel the lilt of the natural rhythm phrases . . . . We feel the length of the direct object *(the knell of parting day)* in relation to the subject *(The curfew)*."[51] All this feeling appears to be in response to entities that are demonstrably physical, concrete. Cureton's wishing to draw a line between such entities and what he calls the structural may be thought of as akin in spirit to that prosodic Platonism I pointed to in Chapter 2, the drawing of a distinction between the imperfect, actual sound configuration of a line and its ideal meter. So here, too, Cureton can be seen as at least partially under the thrall of an older prosodic sensibility.

From my sonic-centered point of view, Cureton has most to offer us when, insisting that we consider a verse line in terms of groupings that go well beyond the foot, he regards those groupings, however briefly, in terms of their sounds, and the relation of those sounds to sense. The way in which he does this and, hence, gets beyond the still-pervasive influence of traditional prosody that this chapter has attempted to demonstrate, will be taken up in a later chapter. But before getting to that material, I shall demonstrate how the traditional concept of meter has so dominated prosodic thought that it has been applied to an area of poetry where it had questionable business to begin with.

4

The Haunting of Free Verse

"Nobody knows much about free verse."
—Reg Saner

THE strong hold that the traditional concept of meter continues to exert on prosodists is shown not only in its cropping up in recent treatments of formal verse that give promise of going beyond received ideas, but also in some recent commentary on free verse. Such commentary simply *extends* the way in which the concept of meter has served in this century as a frame of reference for the handling of free verse, whether such poetry was being questioned or whether it was supposedly being embraced. For where it has not been resisted, free verse has characteristically been accepted or welcomed on grounds that tie it to the very poetry it was supposed to be putting behind. The present chapter will attempt to demonstrate this.

"The revolution is over. The war has been won. As Stanley Kunitz has said, 'Non-metrical verse has swept the field.'"[1] Thus begins the introduction to *Strong Measures: Contemporary American Poetry in Traditional Forms* (1986), an anthology that is an expression of the "New Formalism," the reaffirmation of the virtues of metrical poetry that emerged in the 1980s. Of course, such a concession statement in such a context is something of an anomaly. Ultimately it amounts to saying: "The king is dead; long live the dead king."

But this curious acceptance of the victory of free verse only as a prelude to celebrating the continuing production of formal verse is not an isolated phenomenon. It simply serves to point up the decided (if insufficiently recognized) peculiarity of the status that has long been assigned to free verse. Although widely regarded as the dominant mode of American poetry for, say, the last three or four decades, free verse has not only been challenged by the "New

103

Formalism" or "radical neo-classicism," but has, at least in the
critical literature, frequently been treated so as to make its hegemony appear tainted, its triumph begrudged. One gets the sense
that many prosodists have been, perhaps unconsciously, determined to make free verse wear its crown uneasily, remind this one-
time upstart of the doubts originally raised as to its legitimacy,
doubts that obviously still persist in some quarters. It is time both
to recognize and question the terms on which, after a considerable
struggle, free verse has been assimilated into the poetic canon,
namely, its having repeatedly been characterized as *haunted,* and
desirably so. The critical scenario in which this has taken place
might be entitled "The Ghostly Return of Meter."

The claims of free verse to legitimacy have been challenged at
least as far back as T S. Eliot's famous declaration that "*Vers
Libre* does not exist"; it is something that can be defined only "in
negatives," absences of pattern, rhyme, and meter.[2] Since the essay in which this remark occurs was entitled "Reflections on Vers
Libre," Eliot put himself in the curious position of having to discuss something akin to a vacuum. Looking back to this essay years
later, he made an equally famous remark: "no verse is free for the
man who wants to do a good job."[3] Not as well known as either of
these assertions is the fact that in the same year that Eliot published his "Reflections on Vers Libre," 1917, William Carlos Williams, who was eventually to define himself in general opposition
to Eliot, wrote an essay saying "'free verse' is a misnomer"; all
verse "must be governed."[4] Indeed, four years earlier, Williams
had said "I do not believe in *vers libre,* this contradiction in
terms."[5] And nineteen years later, in 1932, he would declare that
"Free verse—if it ever existed—is out."[6] Timothy Steele's *Missing
Measures: Modern Poetry and the Revolt Against Meter* (1990),
which might be taken as a manifesto of the "New Formalism"
even as it avoids referring to that movement, cites a number of
unfavorable remarks about free verse made by Williams later in
his career,[7] and quotes, with what I take to be implicit glee, a letter
of Eliot written in 1950 in which that poet professes to be "shocked
. . . that little girls in an American school were *encouraged* to
write in vers libre."[8]

In light of these disavowals and diapprovals, it is of course ironic
that both Eliot and Williams figured as eminent practitioners of
free verse, and were crucial in making so prominent a place for it
in our century. Richard Moore has said:

It is Williams more than any other poet of [his] pioneering generation
who faced up boldly, if not always rationally, to the problem of creating

a verse which neither uses nor alludes to any conventional, externally imposed metric; and it is for this reason that he, more than anyone else—and justly so—is virtually the patron saint of contemporary American poetry.[9]

But if Williams was crucial in clearing a space for free verse, there was decided resistance to its emergence. This ranged from Robert Frost's witty and much-cited contention that writing in free verse was like playing tennis with the net down (did he know of Ezra Pound's passionate, idiosyncratic tennis style?), to the gloomy parallel-mongering of an English essayist who compared the appearance of free verse after World War I (it had of course shown up earlier) to the alteration and complete collapse of Greek lyric poetry after the Peloponnesian Wars.[10] Taking a different historical tack but equally gloomy was Yvor Winters, who said "We have sunk into amateurism; and as a result we have in our time the meters of Eliot and of his imitators at the fifth remove, instead of meters comparable to those of the Elizabethans."[11]

Egerton Smith thought vers libre a relatively impoverished medium, relinquishing as it did the interplay between speech-rhythm units and verse-rhythm units he found in metrical verse. Paul Franklin Baum, writing at the same time as Smith (1932), found that very little free verse gave "a real place" to art, and that "mere prose printed as verse . . . may be called free-verse *par excellence*."[12] Even a friendly examination of Williams's verse by Frederick Morgan in 1947 contended that his choice of mode was distinctly restrictive, since "the elimination of meter entails the abandonment of metrical effects, which are far richer and more various than free-verse effects."[13] A year later, a seemingly respectful and close analysis of what the writer called (without making very clear what he meant) "Cadenced Free Verse," came to this conclusion:

> The only freedom cadenced verse obtains is a limited freedom from the tight demands of the metered line. Whether this is a desirable freedom is questionable. For meter, because of its circumscribing demands, does force precision of outline, condensation, intensity. And to the extent that it does spur the artist toward a firmness of outline, the conventionally metered line can generally be more successfully employed by the poet, especially if the poet is not possessed of superior genius.[14]

Such views are in the tradition of Coleridge's contention (in Chapter XVIII of the *Biographia Literaria*) that poetry without meter is "imperfect and defective." So, too, are the views of Graham Hough, stated in 1957. Subscribing to the notion of an interplay between an ideal metrical norm and syntactic structure in metrical verse, he saw free verse's abandonment of that norm resulting in a slightness of rhythm. That is why, he claimed, we find such diverse figures as Mallarmé, T. E. Hulme, and D. H. Lawrence saying or suggesting (Hough seems to me to be distorting Lawrence here) that metrical verse "remains the medium for the great permanent and public themes, free verse becoming the medium for the slighter and more fugitive ones."[15] Karl Shapiro and Robert Beum listed, in *A Prosody Handbook* (1965), the limitations of free verse, among them its lack of "the melodic and mnemonic qualities of rhymed verse."[16] The first version of Paul Fussell's *Poetic Meter and Poetic Form,* appearing in the same year as *A Prosody Handbook*, did not even include a chapter on free verse, saying that the poet working in that mode "has already chosen to eschew one of the most basic expressive techniques in poetry," namely, the variations from the meter found in traditional verse.[17] While we think of the "New Formalism" as a movement of the 1980s, Fussell, writing in the 1960s, celebrated something he might well have called that, and saw it replacing "the metrical radicalism of the 1920s." He cited a return "to a more or less stable sort of Yeatsian accentual-syllabism," as evidenced in "Frost, the Stevens of 'Sunday Morning' [published in 1915!], Robert Graves, Robert Lowell, Richard Wilbur, Randall Jarrell, and W. D. Snodgrass."[18]

Resistance to free verse has continued to manifest itself. Peter Viereck, in 1978, contended that "Free verse and unstrict form are stillborn: not because they are 'free' or lack a tennis net but because they lack the recurrences of living flesh."[19] One of the most substantial and rigorous prosodic studies of recent years, Derek Attridge's *The Rhythms of English Poetry* (1982), devotes only a few pages to what Attridge calls "nonmetrical verse." As noted earlier, while saying that such verse may have even more potential for iconic effects than metrical poetry, he goes on to assert that "it is the approximation to *regular* rhythms . . . which engages the deepest sources of affective behaviour . . ." (italics in original).[20]

But whatever the lingering resistance and invidious distinctions that have attended the emergence of free verse, it has established itself as the dominant mode of American poetry in the latter half of our century. In 1979 Fussell decided that he should do more than regard it as an inherently deficient medium, and he gave it a chapter in the revised version of *Poetic Meter and Poetic Form*. By this time free verse was so clearly in the ascendant, so widespread, that complaints had begun to surface to the effect that too much of it was being written; such complaints continue to the present time (actually, Eliot's "Reflections on Vers Libre" can be seen as implicitly registering such a complaint back in 1917!).

Still, this has not necessarily been a quarrel with the mode itself, as something inherently inferior to metrical verse, but with mediocre works being enacted in its name. Marvin Bell, issuing what might seem to be a counterstatement to Graham Hough's contention that metrical poetry was appropriate for the weightier themes, free verse for the lighter ones, said "The old forms seem exhausted, fit now only for finger exercises—witty, elegant, fanciful, safe, tepid." But he immediately went on to say that, "seen as a form of 'verse,' free verse might also seem exhausted, fit now only for noise—heavy-handed, casual, dull, safe, tepid."[21] A similar evenhandedness can be found in others responding to criticism of free verse. Reg Saner has said:

Like it or not, the average anything—sonnet, epic, or prose poem—is average. But has free verse promoted slovenliness? Of course it has. It is also true that meter and rhyme have frequently been mistaken for poetry itself.[22]

Without becoming glum about it, Donald Hall contends that

the bulk of poetry, at any moment, is *always* bad. The badness of current free verse—much of it—has nothing to do with the choice of prosody. . . . The same bad poets thirty years ago, mostly under different names, wrote equally bad poems in six-line stanzas of iambic pentameter rhyming ABABCC, not so much about the thoughts of a cactus or what I did on my vacation, more likely about Orpheus and Eurydice boarding a subway train.[23]

Still, less balanced, more hostile views have continued to be put forth. In 1983 Frederick Turner and Ernst Pöppel (perhaps replying in kind to William Carlos Williams's one-time charge that "the sonnet is a fascist form") claimed that "free verse . . . is nicely adapted to the needs of the bureaucratic and even the totalitarian state, because of its confinement of human concern within narrow specialized limits where it will not be politically threatening."[24] Do the authors mean free verse as opposed to the New Formalism, which has been given shelter in the less-than-politically-threatening *The New Criterion*? Turner and Pöppel's position here is so silly and extreme as to be self-destructing.

But if theirs is a political argument with free verse, it is also a pulmonary one. In the reading aloud of free verse, according to Turner and Pöppel, we find the frequent practice "of breathing at the end of the line—even when the line is highly variable in length and often broken quite without regard to syntax . . . ." This is "not only grammatically confusing but deeply unnatural: for it forces a pause where neural processing would not normally put it."[25] The argument here ignores the large number of prosodists, including myself, who would put a pause, however slight, at the end of any line of verse (see chapter 5); it also ignores the fact that there are a good many "metrical" lines whose endings break up syntactic units (as in late Shakespeare and in Milton), though the degree and frequency of such breakings are likely to be higher in free verse.

If Turner and Pöppel's opposition to free verse is a decidedly partisan one, it is no more so than that of the poetry editor of *The New Criterion*, Robert Richman. His introduction to the book he put together, *The Direction of Poetry: An Anthology of Rhymed and Metered Verse Written in the English Language Since 1975* (1988), superciliously puts down the collection, referred to earlier, that his might be said to rival, *Strong Measures: Contemporary American Poetry in Traditional Forms*. He characterizes *Strong Measures* as "a showcase for . . . hybrid verse, in which the pretense of a traditional form is used without employing any of its technical attributes."[26] Richman lets us know just how strictly traditionalist he is by citing George Saintsbury as his prosodic authority, and proceeding to say that "meter is clearly the best means for poets to come to terms with their experiences now."[27] That some of the poems Richman includes are not metrical Aryans appears to have escaped his attention. Such an outcropping of the "hybrid," even in an enclave designed to exclude it, would suggest that we are, prosodically speaking, and like it or not, in a mixed situation today.

This state of affairs is represented by Philip Dacey and David Jauss, the editors of *Strong Measures*, who, particularly when compared with Richman, appear to be the very embodiment of would-be mediation as they regard the jostling elements of contemporary poetry. They say that "both traditional and free verse can be called, with honor, 'artificial,' and neither can be fairly accused of being 'insincere,'"[28] making the further point that "the marriage of free verse rhythms and traditional structures is a common characteristic of the formal verse of our period."[29] This sort of tolerance is more attractive and more realistic than Richman's position. Despite the claim implicit in his title, *The Direction of Poetry*, it seems unlikely that the New Formalism is about to effect a leveraged buyout of contemporary American poetry; it stands, rather, as an alternative for poets to adopt on either a part-time or full-time basis. In short, we can say that we have *apparently* arrived at a point where free verse is neither seen, by most people, as necessarily, inherently inferior to metrical verse, nor as the inevitable form for a poet who wishes to establish his credentials as a contemporary artist. But now for my principal concern: just what have been the terms of the seeming acceptance of free verse by prosodists?

It is instructive to examine the treatment of free verse in that most influential of poetry textbooks, *Understanding Poetry* by Cleanth Brooks and Robert Penn Warren. (I am again using the third edition as the principal basis of my remarks.) Like so many other prosodists, they render the concept of meter a truly imposing one, as pointed out in Chapter 1. Where does that leave free verse? Brooks and Warren appear to take a relatively hospitable stance towards it, making the crucial observation (though it is faultily implemented) that "there is no knife-edge line between formal verse and free verse . . . ."[30] They also argue that "the shifting relations [in free verse] between the arbitrary verse lines to [*sic*] the lines based on sentence logic, and the relation among the units of varying weight based on sentence logic, provide a device capable of great subtlety of effect" (pp. 175, 76). Fuzzily formulated though this may be, it comes over as a decided endorsement of free verse. Still, the amount of space given by Brooks and Warren to considering free verse is dramatically smaller than that accorded poetry in meter (this disproportion has characterized a majority of subsequent texts, and is questionable even when we allow for free verse being primarily a phenomenon of the present century, and therefore, in fact, not entitled to equal billing).

Moreover, Brooks and Warren say that the most obvious distinction between free verse and prose is the former's use of lineation. I would argue, adding my voice to a fairly large chorus of poets and critics, that the employment of the line should be seen as the crucial formal element of *all* poetry (this matter will be taken up in the next chapter). But Brooks and Warren contend that lineation operates one way in free verse, another way in metrical poetry: in free verse, lineation functions largely as a visual element, whereas in formal verse it is "the heard, or felt, meter" that "defines the line" (p. 173n). Moreover, they quote and endorse (p. 176) what may be the most fateful pronouncement ever put forth on free verse, T. S. Eliot's statement, made in his "Reflections on Vers Libre," that the ghost of some simple metre should lurk behind the arras in even the 'freest' verse; to advance menacingly as we doze, and withdraw as we rouse. Or, freedom is only true freedom when it appears against the background of an artificial limitation.[31]

It seems that in order to be successful, free verse must invoke the very concept of meter it appears to be rejecting. Dutifully putting Eliot's contention to work, Brooks and Warren "scan," albeit tentatively, William Carlos Williams' "By the road to the contagious hospital," and announce that "most readers . . . would probably . . . feel trimeter as the ghost meter of the whole poem" (p. 179). Since Brooks and Warren themselves define "trimeter" as consisting of three feet (p. 562), this formulation could be seen as a bit sketchy in terms of traditional scansion, lacking the specification of the *kind* of foot involved. Whatever the case, their statement unpersuasively imposes a species of meter on the poem.

All in all, free verse emerges from *Understanding Poetry,* and from any number of texts that have come afterward, as simply lacking the weight, the creation of impressive syntheses (of unity and variety, for example) attributed to metrical poetry. It is therefore entirely appropriate that the last section of *Understanding Poetry,* "Note on Versification," should end, as noted in Chapter 1, with an extended quotation from the classic essay by W. K. Wimsatt Jr. and Monroe Beardsley, "The Concept of Meter: An Exercise in Abstraction." By citing the essay where it does, *Understanding Poetry,* in effect, gives traditional prosody the last word. For the Wimsatt and Beardsley piece not only celebrates the concept of meter, it takes note of free verse merely for the space of a sentence or two, and only to say that what such verse gains "in freedom and direct speech-feeling" it loses in the "opportunity for precise interplay."[32]

If we look at the fifth version of *Understanding Poetry,* embodied in *An Approach to Literature* (and done with John Purser), we find that there is some movement toward easing the invidious distinction between metrical verse and free verse made in the earlier edition, but in some ways not very much had changed for Brooks and Warren by 1975. Instead of invoking "trimeter" in connection with a Williams poem, they use it to characterize a passage in Pound's Canto XVII. They spend just a few sentences on a poem of E. E. Cummings in which they acknowledge that "metrical base [is] repudiated," and they close their section on free verse by saying that "relatively few people have succeeded in writing really effective free verse, and almost all of those have had a keen awareness of the nature of traditional verse.[33] Free verse here is not quite as spooked by meter as it is in the third edition of *Understanding Poetry,* but it comes close to being so.

The position of Eliot, reinforced by Brooks and Warren, that the ghost of some simple meter should be lurking in the vicinity of free verse, has been repeatedly echoed down through the years. We find, for example, this declaration by Theodore Roethke (which also manages to echo Williams): "free verse is a denial in terms. There is, invariably, the ghost of some other form, often blank verse, behind what is written . . . ."[34] That free verse has the status only of an intertextual dependent of metrical verse seems to me much less certain than that Roethke's remarks are haunted by the ghost of Eliot's pronouncement. Be that as it may, we can see the Eliot-Roethke theory cropping up again and again in the prosodic literature, in effect extending the domain of meter.

It might be recalled here that while the traditional concept of meter has been dominated by the stresser school—those who regard the poetic line as divided into a patterned and fixed count of stressed and unstressed syllables—it has for a long time had a timer branch, metrists who conceive of the line as measuring out equal-time (isochronous) units. The influence of this school, too, can be seen in treatments of free verse. Ernest Sandeen says "The free verse line . . . uses stress to mark off more or less equal segments of time."[35] Sculley Bradley has made an attempt to assimilate Whitman to the timer approach, yet another effort to tame his barbaric yawp.[36]

Donald Wesling has rightly complained that "Nearly every commentator on Whitman attempts to show how lines are covertly metrical, how they can be parceled into measures with the terminology and knife of the traditional prosody. But how much of value can such a method yield?"[37] Certainly, it is not only timers who have claimed Whitman for a conventional scheme, but stressers as well. Paul Fussell, having elected to include a chapter on free verse in his revised version of *Poetic Meter and Poetic Form,* examines Whitman's "When I heard the learn'd astronomer," finds "the shock of regular iambic pentameter" in its last line, and explicitly sees the poem as illustrating Roethke's contention that a ghost meter invariably hovers behind what is allegedly free verse. The "shocking" last line—"Looked up in perfect silence at the stars"— is regarded by Fussell as disclosing "the ghost meter which the poem has been concealing all along."[38] (I might note that the poem's third line—"When I was shown the charts and diagrams, to add, divide, and measure them"—with its eighteen syllables and, by my count, seven or eight stresses, does a supremely successful job of such concealment.)

It is especially striking to find Whitman, generally regarded as the ultimate progenitor of American free verse, being implicated by Fussell in the ghost theory. Just as Roethke was apparently influenced by Eliot's views on the matter, Fussell might have been influenced not only by Roethke, but by Karl Shapiro and Robert Beum's *A Prosody Handbook* (cited in Fussell's bibliography), which took the view that Whitman's lines have a tendency "to fall into a loose—and occasionally a very regular— iambic meter."[39] But Fussell is not content with one ghost, emanating from the English tradition, shadowing the Whitman ouevre. For in effect he offers us another, from the classical tradition, when he speaks of "Whitman's frequent presentation of an amphibrachic foot (u/u) at the ends of his long free-verse lines, where he seems at pains to remind the reader rhythmically of the sound of the classical heroic hexameter, the traditional medium of old-style 'epic'."[40] Leaving aside the matter of whether Whitman possessed enough knowledge to have intended any such "reminder," there is the question of whether he would have wanted his verse to produce metrical mimicking of classical epic in the first place. It was Whitman who, in addressing the Muse, said:

> Cross out please those immensely overpaid accounts,
> That matter of Troy and Achilles' wrath,
>   and Aeneas', Odysseus' wanderings,
> Placard "Removed" and "To let" on the rocks of
>   your snowy Parnassus . . .
>   ("Song of the Exposition")

Apart from these considerations, Fussell's singling out a particular kind of foot allegedly occurring at the ends of Whitman's lines is an example of what I have elsewhere called "the curious sport of foot-spotting,"[41] in which a given line of what appears to be a piece of free verse is scrutinized for what it might yield up in the way of feet, however diverse. An especially blatant example of this procedure can be found in Elizabeth K. Hewitt's study of Eliot's "Ash Wednesday." Hewitt claims to find in one of Eliot's lines the following "cadence feet": "a third paeon, an iamb, an amphibrach (undulating), and a final anapest."[42] (Not surprisingly, Brogan calls Hewitt's scansions "easily the most complex I have seen.")[43] Paul Ramsey has noted that "One can *describe* any discourse, with some give-and-take and room for arbitrariness by musical metrics [i.e., by an approach through isochrony] just as one can by accentual-syllabic metrics, but description is not as such a discrimination of pattern."[44] As noted earlier, Eliot himself once remarked, "Any line can be divided into feet and accents."[45] Hewitt appears to have taken him at his word. Charles O. Hartman has observed, in responding to a similar attempt to see Eliot's poetry in traditional prosodic terms, that "The concept of the foot has meaning only metrically—that is, within a numerically regular system."[46] To expand on Hartman, in metrical theory, a given foot has meaning as a standardized constituent; the line is supposedly generated by its recurring a particular number of times, with an allowance for *some* variations (or, in classical poetry, for standardized combinations of different feet). Hewitt has given us a hodgepodge of nonrecurring entities. If there is a "system" operating in Whitman or Eliot it has nothing to do with feet, whether amphibrachs or third paeons or any others. The same might be said of Ezra Pound, who has also been subjected to having his poetry regarded in terms of classical metrics.[47]

Perhaps the most explicit and sweeping endorsement of the notion that free verse should be seen not as an entity unto itself but largely in terms of antecedent modes is that put forth by G. S. Fraser. He claims that free verse

> will always be found, when it works, to be not really 'free' but to be an adaptation of one of . . . four metrical principles . . . —stress verse, stress-syllable verse, quantitative verse, pure syllabic verse.[48]

Harvey Gross's widely admired *Sound and Form in Modern Poetry* (1964) appears to take a similar position. Permeated by a commitment to traditional scansion of "syllable-stress meter," Gross's book matches the often forced readings produced by such scansion with his readings of free verse texts. (He is aware of Roethke's reprise of Eliot's remarks on the desirability of those texts being attended by ghost-meters). Isolating a single line from Pound's *Cantos*, "So old Elkin had only one glory," Gross says "The beauty of this line emerges from the interplay of quantity with a brief procession of syllable-stress anapests. We hear the meter (υυ/) . . . ."[49] What we "hear," according to Gross, must sound like this:

$$\text{So old \'El} \mid \text{kin had \'on} \mid \text{ly one gl\'or} \mid \text{ry.}$$

For no good reason, in such a reading, both "old" and "one" are downplayed, at least in terms of stress, and the final syllable—ry—is left to fend for itself.

A kind of circle is fittingly closed when Gross addresses the opening lines of Eliot's *The Dry Salvages*:

> I do not know much about gods; but I think that the river
> Is a strong brown god—sullen, untamed and intractable,
> Patient to some degree, at first recognised as a frontier;
> Useful, untrustworthy, as a conveyor of commerce:
> Then only a problem confronting the builder of bridges . . .

Gross says "the meter is anapestic pentameter with dactylic and spondaic substitutions . . . ."[50] As in his treatment of Pound, the anapest has been kidnapped from traditional scansion and pressed into very dubious service. Readers can determine at their leisure how well an anapestic pentameter grid fits Eliot's lines. But for this particular ghost story, Eliot can be said to have only himself to blame.

Eliot's conception of a kind of dogging of free verse by a ghostly meter exerts a pull even on Charles O. Hartman, one of the most important and sympathetic commentators on free verse, and a critic who has a problem with Gross' attempts to subsume Eliot's poetry under traditional categories. Hartman argues in his *Free Verse: An Essay on Prosody* (1980) that defenders of free verse were hampered by their assumption that "the most obvious way to give free verse a place beside accentual-syllabic verse was by discovering or inventing for it an equally abstract pattern."[51] In effect, Hartman suggests that rather than having free verse simply acted *upon*, by being assimilated within the mindset of traditional metrics, it *acts* so as to provide

> new insight . . . into the whole question of prosody in *any* verse. It neither aids nor distracts the reader with an abstract pattern he can transfer in detail from poem to poem and codify in a formally closed, quasi-mathematical system that bears only incidentally on the experience of poetry. Because the reader cannot pretend to account for its rhythms in abstract isolation, free verse confronts him directly with the complex relation of rhythm to meaning (p. 28; italics in original).

These trenchant observations, which I wholeheartedly endorse, might well be taken by conventional prosodists as fighting words, since they suggest the notion that even "metrical" poetry ought to be read without the application of traditional scansion. Unfortunately, Hartman appears to retreat from his stated position. For his views on metrical poetry finally appear quite traditional, operating within the parameters of Wimsatt and Beardsley's "Concept of Meter" piece, an essay characterized by him as "one of the best modern treatments of meter" (p. 14). (That essay, as I noted in Chapter 1, endorses, to use its own words, "the few homely and sound, traditional and objective principles of prosody,"[52] which it equates with the conventional notion of meter and its corollaries.)

Moreover, while Hartman displays discomfort with readings of Eliot by Harvey Gross and Sister M. Martin Barry, which attempt to herd that poet's verse "into a metrical corral" (p. 116), he himself cannot escape a metrical coerciveness in his own treatments of Eliot. Thus, he sees the lines of a passage from "The Hollow Men" as corresponding to a variety of "iambic pentameter" lines, with only a single specimen corresponding to a stretch of pure iambic pentameter. His reading here seems to me to be a forced attempt to make the short lines of "The Hollow Men" echo the longer lines of the form in question. Indeed, Hartman ends up calling "The Hollow Men" a "nonmetrical" work (p. 120). His scansions of lines from *Four Quartets* repeatedly produce what he himself characterizes, however qualifiedly, as "defective feet," or only as a "quasi-metrical" effect (pp. 124, 25.) My point is that looking at these lines through a metrical grid is misguided to begin with. It is as though even Hartman, who appears to show considerable potential for getting beyond a traditional frame of reference, has allowed Eliot's remarks about the haunting presence of meter to influence the way he scans Eliot's lines. (This is yet another example of Eliot's success in determining how critics should read his poetry.) When Hartman is able to get out from under the shadow of Eliot's monumental presence, when he confronts a poem like William Carlos Williams's "Exercise," where there can be no question of a meter operating behind the scenes, he is able to deliver an excellent prosodic analysis of a free-verse poem (pp. 93–98).

But even Williams is not immune from being subjected to a meter-bound mindset. (I have already noted this glancingly in talking of Brooks and Warren.) Witness his treatment by Paul Ramsey, who is an especially interesting prosodist to consider (and is also a poet). He appears to contain within himself a representative of those who have been all too ready to denigrate free verse, while at the same time he is willing to do sustained thinking about that mode, and is capable of responding with enthusiasm to works written in it—but not without a tendency towards allowing them to be pulled into meter's gravitational field.

Before demonstrating this, I should like to consider closely some of Ramsey's general thoughts about free verse. He cites as one of eleven possibilities for free verse that it "does not exist" (shades of Eliot) but "is really prose . . . ." Another possibility is that it "does exist, but in fragments of verse of different sorts; it is non-prose medley." He goes on to say that "prose, and . . . medley . . . are more prominent throughout the range of free verse than many of its practitioners understand or would care to admit."[53] Nothing is wrong with medley per se.

> But it is less satisfying than sustained verse with pervading unity. Fragments are not *a* poem. Rhythms are not unity. I have Aristotle and Coleridge and common sense and profound experience on my side, and the burden of proof is on the defenders of the Heap (p. 103; italics in original).

(Timothy Steele echoes this position in *Missing Measures*.)

Ramsey is impressively companioned. But unless we are willing to grant a given argument validity by association, or by mere assertion, we need to make our own judgments about his enterprise, and avoid automatically nodding to the notion and value of the "unity" that, in Ramsay (and a lot of other prosodists), is unquestioningly assigned to metrical, or accentual-syllabic, verse. That verse, he says, possesses "stresses and syllables . . . in certain statable relations to each other and to the poetic line." At the same time he makes the following crucial concessions: "Feet do not represent a linguistic or sonal group. They are a convenience for dividing up lines for counting into comprehensible units. Actual phrasing is independent of foot pattern" (p. 99). Thus, Ramsey's "comprehensible units" appear to mean countable clones. By his own formulation they stand independent of semantic meaningfulness or sonal integrity. Is not the essential justification for the foot, then, its accessibility to the simple operation of counting? And if a series of lines produces the same count, is not this the famous "unity" that a lot of free verse is supposedly lacking? Does free verse need to be put on the defensive because it cannot exhibit the alleged arithmetic regularity of metrical verse? Finally, if the foot is not a sonal unit, how can the mere accumulation of feet guarantee *a* rhythm rather than the rhythm*s* of free verse that supposedly amount to "the Heap?"

In fact, such a rhythm is not guaranteed, as we can see in Ramsey's own handling of "L'Allegro." His scansion of Milton's poem, which he offers as an example of "traditional verse," produces a reading that allows for as many as five different metrical patterns (including pure iambic and pure trochaic) in the six lines of his sample (p. 104). This makes one wonder all the more why Ramsey brings the baggage of the foot, the ghost of meter, to his examination of a nine-line passage from Williams's "The Yachts," a poem in free verse he regards as a masterpiece.[54] Not surprisingly, he comes up with a scansion in which no two consecutive lines exhibit the same pattern, and at the same time he does not relegate the poem to the dubious domain of the Heap. Williams's poem apparently falls under another possibility for free verse that Ramsey formulates, "That free verse is counterposed verse, which I define as verse in which different rhythmical patterns are played against each other to form a more complex but unified rhythm."[55] The problem is that he has not given us a litmus test by which we can distinguish counterposed verse from the Heap variety. My suspicion is that there is no such test. (Of another Williams poem, "Metric Figure," whose title might well be a joke, Ramsey says "it is not medley, but satisfyingly complete, though I cannot adequately name what makes it one in rhythm.")[56] We might do well to assume, in general, that rhythmically different lines can and do coexist *both in traditional verse and free verse* without the works falling apart, and that this is the chief significance of Ramsey's scansions, though he does not say so. (I believe some of my own scansions, to be offered later in the book, will also indicate the noninevitability of Heap.)

But the principal point to be made here has to do with what Ramsey effects in the first place, namely, conducting his examination of "The Yachts" in terms of feet, invoking iambs, trochees, anapests, and fourth paeons. Riding roughshod over the fact that the poem is printed as a series of tercets, and that a given line may contain as many as sixteen syllables, while another may contain as few as nine, he declares "The Yachts" to be a species of "blank verse,"[57] thereby moving the concept of meter to new heights of hospitality or, better, of imperialistic annexation. Here free verse is not simply haunted by metrical verse, it is possessed by it.

Numerous examples of the sort of thing Ramsey does with "The Yachts" are to be found throughout Annie Finch's *The Ghost of Meter: Culture and Prosody in American Free Verse* (1993).[58] She approaches Whitman, Dickinson, Stephen Crane, and Eliot through a "metrical code" theory, the notion that there are metrical passages in their poetry that carry particular (though not necessarily consistent) meanings in their individual canons and/or individual works. This may be seen as an adaptation of the notion of "representative" meter, the idea that a given meter is inherently suitable for a certain theme or themes—Finch calls this the "theory of propriety" (p. 3). In her view, a given meter, operating sporadically, assumes a kind of custom-made expressive significance in an individual poet or poem. Finch cites, for example, the following lines from Whitman:

> No poem proud, I chanting bring to thee, nor mastery's
> rapturous verse
> But a cluster containing night's darkness and blood-
> dripping wounds,
> And psalms of the dead.

She comments as follows:

> An embedded iambic pentameter, with a caesura after the second foot, begins the first line. This embedded pentameter performs the triple function of embodying the canonical meter, describing the confidence and strength of its own metrical tradition, and rejecting that tradition. The triple feet in the second part of the line reject the "rapturous" dactylic rhythm as well, but only to pick it up at even greater length in the second line, which evokes the vagueness, darkness and mysterious power typical in Whitman's dactylic lines. (p. 51)

This is another example of a prosodist bound and determined to find feet in what appears to be nonmetrical poetry, and, in this case, to maximize their import.[59] After the alleged "embedded iambic pentameter" in the opening of the first line, all of two "triple feet," that is, dactyls, presumably manage, at one and the same time, to establish a rapturous rhythm and to reject it. The rejected dactylic rhythm, according to Finch, is picked up in the second line—but, I am compelled to ask, where?

Finch's reading of the line must be something like the following:

$$\text{/ x | / x x | / x x | / x x|}$$
$$\text{But a cluster con taining night's darkness and}$$
$$\text{/ x x | /}$$
$$\text{blood-dripping wounds}$$

Such a reading subordinates the word "night" and the syllable drip." Focusing only on the first of these, I would argue that since darkness is a featured quality, and one "typical" of Whitman's dactylic lines according to Finch, and since it is closely attached to night, what justifies the subordination of "night"? I read the line as follows:

<pre>
 x   x / x   x / x   /   /   x   x
But a cluster   containing night's darkness and
                     /   / x   /
              blood-dripping wounds
</pre>

To speak the language of feet for the sake of the argument, I detect
<pre>
                        /   x x   /   x   x
</pre>
only two dactyls at best—"clus ter con-" and "dark ness and"—
and that is the case only if one agrees to read "But a" as a pyrrhic
foot (or possibly a trochaic one) instead of reading the line as
<pre>
                              x x /   x x   /
</pre>
opening with two anapests—"But a clus-" and "-ter con tain."
Finch's reading strikes me as another instance of the stress particulars of a given line being distorted in order to satisfy a scansion
embodying a meter-seeking mindset. If there is a rapturous dactylic
rhythm intended here, Whitman has botched the job—but he certainly has done something other than that. He uses his free verse in
the second line to dramatize the notion of a "cluster" by clustering
stresses, as follows:

<pre>
         /   /   /   /
    night's darkness and blood-dripping
</pre>

Even more questionable than Finch's imposing of meter on the
Whitman lines is her handling of the following passage from Eliot's
"The Waste Land":

> what have we given
>
> . . . .
> The awful daring of a moment's surrender
> Which an age of prudence can never retract
> By this, and this only, we have existed.

According to Finch, a dactylic rhythm has entered the poem here,
and "echoes dactylic connotations in the nineteenth-century poets
discussed earlier" (she cites specific examples from Whitman and
Stephen Crane, respectively, p. 111). Finch then goes on to say
that "Eliot's dactylic lines here tend to be much less obviously so
than those of his predecessors, particularly Whitman" (pp. 111–12).
Here I have to agree wholeheartedly with Finch, since it would
take even greater distortion than that operating in her reading of
the Whitman passage just discussed to make Eliot's lines come out
as dactylic. Eliot-the-poet can be said to have been misread here
because of the "ghost of meter" notion set loose by Eliot-the-critic.

Still, we have not yet seen how far meter-enthralled or Eliot-
influenced sensibilities are willing to go in analyzing works in free
verse. Prosodists like Fussell, Hewitt, Gross, Hartman, Ramsey,

and Finch impose feet on inappropriately chosen lines, but at least they leave those lines intact. It may have been Graham Hough who began the staking out of another position when, as noted by Donald Wesling, he said this of a passage in D. H. Lawrence's "Snake": "Alter the typography and break the line after "mused," and . . . we have two perfectly straightforward blank-verse lines."[60] Peter Viereck is doing something similar when he claims that Whitman at his strongest writes in iambic pentameter rather than free verse, "provided we can get around the way he broke up his pentameter lines."[61]

As if pursuing the Hough-Viereck line of thought, there are prosodists who have recently begun to take liberties with free-verse texts, actually rearranging the lines so as to "show" us the metrical ghost behind the arras. This approach may reflect, though not necessarily consciously, a curious feature of the contemporary culture of poetry. Even as we hear, quite rightly (as the next chapter will assert), repeated celebrations of the line as the central formal feature of all poetry, we also hear, quite rightly, repeated denunciations of the arbitrary lineation permeating much of free verse. Too many of its lines seem to have no rationale, no reason for being constituted as they are. They make us itch to rearrange them. Perhaps it is the frequent calling-forth of the impulse to redo a line that has made it thinkable for critics to act out that impulse and relineate even lines they admire.

We can see this operating in the poet-critic Jonathan Holden, who has given us a startling formulation of how prosodic devices function:

> in the hands of our greatest poets prosody is used not to capture or to measure ordinary sentiments and passions. Instead, it is used to gild them, to make them grandiose, in much the same way that the music of grand opera . . . exists in order to elevate and to inflate plots, situations, and passions which, when not too farfetched to be credible, are . . . banal. . . . Rarely is any prosody, "numerical" or "free," deployed so as to augment the particular sense of a particular poem; and this is no less true for the line in good free verse than for the line in an accentual-syllabic prosody.[62]

This remarkable passage appears to assign to prosody the sole function of a questionable, operatic heightening.

While Holden makes no invidious distinction here between metrical verse and free verse, such a distinction does soon appear, as, in effect, he displays the haunting-of-free-verse party line. For he goes on to say: "Without the author's ear for . . . older prosodies . . . verse would slip from being 'music' into mere noise: chopped up prose masquerading as poetry" (p. 3). He illustrates what he has in mind with a section of a poem by Ellen Bryan Voigt. He rearranges what are nine lines in the original into six lines. Instead of the new lineation being an improvement, the first two line-breaks are, as Holden himself says, "a bit forced. . . ." Why then has he done what he has done? To demonstrate a "secondary prosody" operating behind the original, which is "roughly speaking, that of blank verse . . ." (p. 5). The ghost of a precursor meter, compelled to "show" itself by Holden's manipulations—the critic as medium—apparently validates what is before us.

Holden's animus against free verse (which is something of a now-you-see-it-now-you-don't affair, and apparently something he is not aware of) reveals itself in his response to and application of the following statements by Robert Hillyer:

> we are metrical creatures in a metrical universe. . . . How foolish it is for defenders of free verse to maintain that . . . metrical structures are not natural. Free verse has no roots at all, and is itself an unnatural departure from the ebb and flow of all things (cited in Holden, p. 8).

This an example of a notion not infrequently found among prosodists, one that might be called "the cosmic connection," a linking of meter to the rhythms of the universe.[63] (Such a grandiose claim would appear to leave free verse without a foot to stand on.) Holden first seems to play down Hillyer's contention, though he finds "a grain of truth" in it. He then appears to use Hillyer against himself, when he cites a poem by Wendell Berry, which he says "affirms Hillyer's conception of periodic aspects of natural process . . . much more persuasively than any so-called 'numerical' prosody could, does so *because* it is in free verse" (pp. 8–9; Holden's italics). Free verse could hardly ask for a more ringing endorsement than this, but observe how, to demonstrate his point, Holden undermines it in the course of fiddling with Berry's lineation.

Here is Berry's poem as the poet has written it:

The Barn

While we unloaded the hay from the truck, building
the great somnolence of the ricked bales, the weather
kept up its movement over us, the rain dashed and drove
against the roof, and in the close heat we sweated
to the end of the load. The fresh warm sweet smell

of new timothy in it, the barn is a nut ripened
in forethought of cold. Weighted now, it turns
toward the future generously, spacious
in its intent, the fledged young of the barn swallows
fluttering on the rim of the nest, the brown bats
hanging asleep, folded, beneath the rafters.
And we rest, having done what men are best at.

Finding that scansion of the poem as it stands shows "no readily identifiable order, except that the last three lines are in tetrameter," Holden breaks the lines "at the ends of the most obvious syntactical units," and finds an initial pattern, that of "tetrameter accentuals," succeeded by "trimeter accentuals" (pp. 9–10). This result is still not satisfying. Noticing that the long *a* sound is conspicuous in the first two lines of the original ("hay," "great," "bales"), he then rearranges the passage so that this sound falls at the ends of lines. At this point he detects some other "rhymes" emerging (the qualifying quotation marks are his): heat-sweet, nest-rest-best. (Never mind that "best" does not occur at the end of a line, as do "nest" and "rest," even in Holden's reworking. Once you start to tinker with lineation to show what is "really" going on, who is to say where your forcings of sound patterns should stop?) Holden then says:

> suddenly we understand the game which Berry had been playing all along: With the poem's last two words, "best at," the "nest-rest-best" end-rhyme expectations of the trimeter syntactical prosody coincide with the "bat-at" end-rhyme expectations set up by the tetrameter syntactical units at the end of the original version. The two prosodies, which echo two different cycles—one a natural cycle, the other a human cycle—converge (pp. 10–11).

Whatever in the world is Holden talking about? What sort of "end-rhyme expectations" can we have even in the rearranged version, where there is in fact no rhyme scheme? And in the original there was not even a single true rhyme: "bats-at" is not the same as Holden's "bat-at." Moreover, he has turned the poem into an arbitrary palimpsest, where his all-trimeter version exists superimposed over the original poem, only the last three lines of which, according to him, were in tetrameter (and other readers than myself might find those tetrameters decidedly dubious). This palimpsest is then made to bear a heavy thematic weight.

In my view, we either read the poem as Berry wrote it, or we read Holden's reworkings; we do not read both, except separately.

In addition, Holden, who started off by saying that prosodic devices are strictly for heightening, has come up with, in his "two different cycles" remarks, as large a claim for the expressive or representative effects of such devices as one could imagine.

But my chief point concerns Holden's sabotagings of the free verse line in the name of celebrating it. He quotes a passage from Berry that speaks of a poem's rhythms resonating with the life rhythms of and around the poet:

> Rhyme, which is a function of rhythm, may suggest this sort of resonance; it marks the coincidences of the rhythm of the structure with the rhyme of the lines, or the coincidences of small structures with larger ones, as when the day, the month, and the year all end at the same moment (p. 11).

Holden goes on to call the free-verse line "by far the most sensitive prosodic instrument for registering and dramatizing these coincidences, because in the hands of poets of Berry's and Voigt's skill it is tied to traditional echoes which, in turn, are profoundly rooted in the cyclical aspects of natural process" (p. 11). Notice that the large claim for the free verse line is immediately made dependent upon that line's alleged grounding in metrical verse, since this is what Holden's "traditional echoes" must refer to (see his reference to "older prosodies," cited above). For the purpose of "demonstrating" that grounding, Holden has blithely rearranged the texts in question and "discovered" not only a resulting element of meter but of rhyme. Thus, "free" verse is celebrated, but only after being turned, with the best of intentions, into Silly Putty; the freedom in question is that of the prosodist to do with the poem what he will.

Or what she will. In Sandra M. Gilbert's treatment of two works by Sylvia Plath, we find another example of a prosodist feeling at liberty to re-order the original free verse text so as to exhibit its alleged metrical underpinning. Gilbert cites the final pair of stanzas from "Lady Lazarus:"

> Herr God, Herr Lucifer,
> Beware
> Beware.

> Out of the ash
> I rise with my red hair
> And I eat men like air.

Gilbert says that

> even while Plath's line breaks here transform what might otherwise
> have been fairly conventional caesuras into threatening statements
> (e.g., "Beware"—*pause*—"Beware"), the basic *beat* of her poem is for-
> tified by, even while it defies, the classical beat of iambic pentameter.
> For certainly there are whole sections of this piece that can be recast,
> not in a "sort of blank verse," but in superbly sophisticated blank
> verse, or even, as below, in highly regular heroic couplets:

> > Herr God, Herr Lucifer, beware, beware.
> > Out of the ash I rise with my red hair.
> > [italics in original]

She goes on to say:

> Behind the apparently ragged, indeed defiantly irregular lines of the
> "real" text, we sense the rhythm of a kind of ghost text, so that Plath's
> poem is at many crucial points written simultaneously in blank verse
> and in what we call "free verse."[64]

One must wonder about Gilbert's apparent assumptions (and, of
course, about the strain of prosodic thought she represents). Does
free verse characteristically *require* some shoring up by invoking
a metrical ancestor, and, in this case, does automatic honor accrue
to Plath's verse because of its alleged echoing of traditional forms?
What is the function of such echoing specific to this poem, in
particular the alleged recall of heroic couplets? What do the associations of those couplets have to do with the tone of "Lady Lazarus," its jittery compounding of self-pity and triumph? Are we
supposed to think of Alexander Pope?

Gilbert next goes to work on "Ariel," rearranging the last four
stanzas into a single stanza of four lines. Here are Plath's verses
in their original lineation:

> > And now I
> > Foam to wheat, a glitter of seas.
> > The child's cry
> >
> > Melts in the wall.
> > And I
> > Am the arrow,

> The dew that flies
> Suicidal, at one with the drive
> Into the red
>
> Eye, the cauldron of morning.

Here is Gilbert's reworking of the lines:

> And now I foam to wheat, a glitter of seas.
> The child's cry melts in the wall, and I
> Am the arrow, the dew that flies, suicidal,
> Into the red eye, the cauldron of morning.

Gilbert finds the revised version "surprisingly regular." That regularity is questionable, since the four lines vary between nine and twelve syllables and have no particular metrical pattern. Also, as Gilbert herself point out, her rearrangement has omitted the phrase "at one with the drive." But never mind:

> the very regular quatrain I have reconstructed makes perfect sense without it. Perhaps, given the prosodic norm that the poet is working against, her brilliant addition of the uncontainable phrase "at one with the drive" is a sign of *excess* . . . excess rebellion against historical conventions of lineation (p. 48; Gilbert's italics).

This astonishing passage appears to mark something genuinely new in prosodic criticism. A text is not only relineated but a section is deliberately left out, and thereby the original is seen to contain something brilliantly significant, something apparently not discernible in the complete arrangement of lines as they first stood. The critic has "discovered" a feature the poem has kept well hidden. In point of fact, there is nothing excessive about Plath's lineation within the domain of free verse, which had itself become, by the time she wrote "Ariel," another poetic convention. Moreover, Plath's lines have a good deal of their own sort of patterning. Each stanza except the last is a tercet, with marked, if irregular, expansions or contractions of line length in almost every stanza. The only element of excess and of the uncontainable that we are looking at is in the prosodist's procedures, not the poet's verse form.

Asking what the implications are of Plath's practice, Gilbert supposedly keeps the answers open, but strongly suggests their formulation through what might be called semi–rhetorical questions, the first of which should not surprise us at this point (and Gilbert's use of "merely" suggests she doesn't expect it to):

Am I merely saying that she is haunted by the iambic pentameter line in the way English itself is so haunted? And if our language is inhabited, even possessed, by such a rhythmic configuration, is that not because five iambs in a row constitute, as has often been said, a kind of linguistic bloodbeat—a point which would return us to what I've called the Romantic/modern physiological aesthetic? (pp. 49–50)

Here we find a conjoining of the haunting-of-free-verse theory and another dubious staple of prosodic criticism, one that might be called "the cardiac connection." The latter would have it that iambic meter (though there is no reason why it need be pentameter) corresponds to the systole-diastole movement of the heart and the consequent reflection in our pulse-beat. This particular "organic" approach has had to compete with the breath theory of verse, the notion that the line of a poet corresponds to the duration of his exhalation of air during utterance.

There is yet another version of the organic conception of poetry, at once very striking and very dubious, cited in the preceding chapter. It was noted there that Frederick Turner and Ernst Pöppel had propounded what is the ultimate embodiment of the timer approach to verse. According to them, there is a "universal" poetic line of approximately three seconds duration, and this span corresponds to what our neural system has determined as the length of the auditory present, the fundamental sound-bite, so to speak, of the human organism. While the breath theory has, in effect, been proposed in support of free verse, this neural theory, put forth in explicit opposition to the breath theory, accords free verse an inferior status (as does the cardiac connection, at least tacitly). Free verse, according to Turner and Pöppel, has no "physiological foundation," "forces a pause where neural processing would not normally put it," and "is likely to forego the benefits of bringing the whole brain to bear" in the reading of poetry.[65]

Turner and Pöppel, as I suggested in the preceding chapter, are obliged to allow a dubious amount of variation in individual line-lengths to make the case for the universality of the three-second line. However, what is important about the Turner-Pöppel piece for the matter at hand is its having brought out into the open, before the New Formalism was fully, explicitly upon us, what has often operated implicitly: an ongoing unease with free verse, an inclination to view that mode as an inherently inferior form, and a nostalgia for what is regarded as the indispensable component of true poetry—meter. What I have attempted to show is that even when prosodists have apparently been willing to accept or, better, celebrate free verse, they have too rarely been willing to do so on its own terms, bending their energies instead to pulling aside a putative arras so as to reveal an allegedly lurking ghost of an older form.[66]

In the unlikely event that Harold Bloom were ever to address himself to so prosaic a matter as prosody, he might well assent to the assumption of free verse being haunted, finding therein the alleged sense of *belatedness* he speaks of, the sense of a poet that he has come late in the scheme of things, after a series of masters. There is, after all, a centuries-old tradition of distinguished metrical poetry. How could the contemporary poet not fail to be aware of the weight of it, not fail to be haunted by it, not agree, in fact, to be so haunted, so as to incorporate some of its strength into his or her own work? But, I would suggest, this sense of belatedness is more the property of many prosodists than of poets themselves. Giving too much weight to that which is *prior* and too little to that which is fresh, according the old a degree of presentness that is greater than that of the new, such prosodists have obscured or distorted the contours of the free-verse texts they attempt to illuminate, through their virtual insistence that those texts are not free, but constrained by the sounds of meter they are always allegedly hearing, sounds emanating from a tradition that has itself been misunderstood. We need to examine specimens of free verse in terms of what they explicitly present, and stop insisting that they be heard only after placing them in a metrical-echo detection chamber. We need in fact to revise our notions of meter itself, as I have suggested in earlier chapters. And while we are at it, we might also let go of or at least bracket the various claims to the "organic" that have been advanced both on behalf of metrical verse and free verse.[67] Such claims for *poetry* may seem to their adherents to provide a gratifying grounding in the very scheme of things, but they do little or nothing to illuminate or distinguish among individual *poems*.

Our procedure should be, at least for a start, to take each poem as it comes, and, as Ezra Pound once advised, "LISTEN to the sound that it makes,"[68] the sound that it in particular effects. What we want is scansion without presupposition, and without the *will*, exhibited in so much prosodic criticism, towards discovering some overriding sonal pattern, some "unifying" abstract scheme. I have referred to this will earlier and to its assuming the form of a kind of sonal totalitarianism, in which the metrical poet is seen as creating "an external organising force from which no syllable can escape."[69] Instead of seeking out or positing such a force, we should think of a poem, *any* poem, in my view, as creating a series of individual entities—the lines—that may relate to each other in a variety of ways that elude prediction, setting up a dynamic array rather than an a priori magnetic field that compels everything into a particular configuration.[70]

What we are after is what Brooks, Warren, and Purser called "emergent" form in their discussion of free verse (but they rightly and hastily went on to say that "In the final sense, the form of a poem, even of the most traditional type, is always emergent. . .").[71] A poem's sound patterns are not to be accorded a life of their own but seen always in relation to the sense of the words by which they are generated. (Meter has tended to be credited with a life of its own.) The ultimate question we ask about a poem's prosody is: does it make for patterns that underscore or embody what is being said by the work as a whole or by any given part of it? But I should caution immediately that while such patterns constitute one of poetry's glories, they should not be expected of all lines; a line of a poem or a grouping of lines comes to us only as a potential for such designs. An enormous and unrealistic burden has been placed on metrical verse by the doctrine of "expressive variation," that is, the notion that the deviations from the metrical "norm" of a poem, or certainly many such deviations, convey something. In point of fact, such deviations are often not significant. The burden of proof is on those who think the opposite.

Free verse, whatever it has suffered from prosodists who resent or are uncomfortable with its freedom, has not, by its very nature, been called on to show expressive variation, at least not as a rule. Though some think this lack of such variation is a function of its inherent poverty of resources, free verse has its own way of creating significant sound patterns. Before we can do justice to that, we need to take the "free" in "free verse" at face value, to accept it as real, and, while admitting the obvious fact that a serious poet is aware of the "metrical" tradition, to hear, unconstrained by ghostly paradigms, how that poet exercises his or her freedom, using it to create ad hoc patterns. The "sound" of the poem is the sum total of the sonic dimensions of those patterns, to be discovered by painstaking tracings that do not violate the boundaries of words or phrases, and that cannot be subsumed under glib formulas (like "iambic pentameter"), formulas that confer a spurious unity and distort even the formal verse they are applied to. For if one looking at free verse were to ask "Where are the songs of meter?" I should not only reply "Aye, where are they? Free verse has its 'music' too," I should add that the "songs" of meter are not to be found in the traditional descriptions of them. This is what I have tried to indicate earlier, and I will offer my own formulations of such songs, as well as those of free verse, in later chapters.[72]

5

Preliminaries to Revision

IF the concept of meter, based on the foot, works more to obscure the sounds of verse movement than to illuminate them, what should we replace it with, or at least how should we modify it? Before attempting such a task, we need to consider some basic questions, having to do with the pronunciation of the individual words of a poem, the organization of those words into lines, and the status of pauses, if any, both at the ends of those lines and within them. These matters are both elementary and elemental, and need to be addressed if we are to arrive at a fruitful approach to prosody.

A key assumption that will be made in this study is that the words of any poem should be read in such a manner as to receive their lexical stress, or only such modification of that stress as is required by the rules of English phonology.[1] The distortion or alteration of normal stress patterns that some metrists have favored, because such is "called for" by the meter, undermines the connection of poetry to ordinary spoken language. Such a connection I regard as a given. To speak of a connection is not to claim an identity. The words of poetry, for example, are or should be spoken with greater care and at a slower pace than the words of our daily speech.

Some might argue that the notion of poetry being modeled on speech rather than music is not an absolute but is, in fact, a modern creation, a mere prejudice of the twentieth century, ranging in its expression from the calculated incorporation of colloquialisms to the conception of the poetic line as a breath unit based on the poet's speech. Roy Fuller, for example, has written about "The Fetish of Speech Rhythms in Modern Poetry" (and, not surprisingly, has given us some dubious, speech-violating scansions).[2] On the other hand, T. S. Eliot has said, "Every revolution in poetry is apt to be, and sometimes to announce itself as, a return to common speech. That is the revolution which Wordsworth announced in his

Prefaces, and he was right: but the same revolution has been carried out a century before by Oldham, Waller, Denham, and Dryden. . . ."[3]

Eliot, of course, is a modern, and Fuller might dismiss him as such on this point. Be that as it may, asserting an essential link between poetry and speech, which in Eliot's mind undoubtedly had to do with diction and phrasing, certainly implies that the pronunciation, hence stress patterns, of a poem's words should be lexical. To emphasize such grounding of poetry in ordinary speech, as opposed to the notion of the "foregrounding" allegedly effected by meter, to emphasize verse's *langue* at the expense of its *parole* if you will, is hardly to sound a new note, and it seems to me the burden of proof is on those who would simply violate lexical stress patterns.

The note of which I speak can be found in the earliest stages of prosodic criticism in English. George Puttenham contended in *The Art of English Poesie* (1589) that "there can not be in a maker [poet] a fowler fault, then to falsifie his accent to serve his cadence. . . ."[4] As indicated earlier, O. B. Hardison cites a work by an English schoolmaster, published in 1612, that tells us: "in all Poetry, for the pronuntiation, it is to be uttered as prose; observing distinctions and the nature of the matter; not to be tuned foolishly or childishly after the manner of scanning a Verse, as the use of some is."[5] Some later commentary continues to take this position. T. V. F. Brogan cites a nineteenth-century work, Gilbert Conway's *A Treatise on Versification,* as including the rule that the accent a word receives must be that of lexical stress.[6] Robert Bridges's *Milton's Prosody* asserts that "The intended rhythm in P[aradise] L[ost] is always given by the unmitigated accentuation of the words of the verse as Milton pronounced them," as opposed to the poem's abstract metrical pattern. For "accentual verse," at least, Bridges set out the rule that "THE STRESSES MUST ALL BE TRUE SPEECH-STRESSES. . . ."[7] Ezra Pound said to his fellow poets: "Naturally, your rhythmic structure should not destroy the shape of your words, or their natural sound. . . ."[8]

The kinship of verse to ordinary speech is sometimes put in more general terms. James G. Southworth quotes with approval John Speirs' contention that " . . . Chaucer's genius, like Shakespeare's, is rooted in the English language as it was spoken in his time."[9] Commenting on the treatment of Chaucer's prosody by a number of nineteenth-century scholars, he says:

> they forgot that language is a living thing and that a study of *schriftsprache* without reference to the spoken language can lead only to confu-

sion. Conservative scholars like Weymouth insisted from the outset on the spoken English of Chaucer and not on the symbols on paper.[10]

Henry Lee Smith, Jr. has reminded us that "the poet is first a speaker of his native language and the reader or hearer of his work has *internalized* the same linguistic system as the author" (italics in original).[11]

The most persuasive advocate of the position that we must give primacy to speech patterns in the sounding of verse has been D. W. Harding, in his *Words Into Rhythm*. Expanding, in effect, on Smith's observation, he says:

> In speaking and listening and reading we are not creating rhythmical patterns at our own sweet will; the basic features of the spoken language control our rhythmizing while we speak, and the rhythms we perceive as listeners or silent readers are guided, and sometimes closely controlled, by objective features of the sound sequences and by the usages of the particular language.[12]

He goes on to claim that "even the most highly organized English verse makes use of the stress patterns of ordinary speech" (p. 16). The pointing to a "linguistic system" by Smith, that is, to the organization of the language at large, together with Harding's noting of the a priori patterns of a language's sounds, indicate that the setting aside of the traditional concept of meter neither precipitates us into chaos nor sets up a naive assumption of a language that is entirely unmediated. As far as the poem's sound features are concerned, our reading *is* conditioned by something prior, but something more fundamental than any metrical scheme or contract; we bring to that reading what Harding calls the "objective features" of our language itself. He quotes Anne Ridler's observation that "the subtleties of poetic rhythm are produced by the variations of accent and speed in ordinary speech, and it is the poet's business to use these, not to violate them" (p. 94). The position I have been tracing needs to be reiterated because of the long-time hegemony of the concept of meter. That concept, as observed earlier, has led to the practice of overriding norms of pronunciation through the promotion or demotion of syllables, so as to preserve the alleged metrical pattern of a given poem.

This driving of a wedge between poetry and speech has been fueled in part by the desire of many traditional prosodists to have poetry modeled on music, the art to whose condition, Walter Pater alleged, all the other arts aspire. Just as a given piece of music has its assigned tempo and rhythm, so too the metrical poem, according to traditional prosody, has its governing, permeating stress pattern or temporal-unit design. Paul F. Baum has said "poetry . . . will always approach as close as its own conditions permit to the powers of music."[13] But such a conception seems to me wistful, an attempt to join together what history has put asunder. In "primitive" cultures and in classical antiquity, music and words may have been interwoven into a single entity, but those two components have long pulled apart, and their separation should be fully, if regretfully, acknowledged.[14] In writing his essay "The Music of Poetry," T. S. Eliot was quite right to counter the implications of his title by saying that poetry should be rooted in the speech of its era: "The music of poetry . . . must be a music latent in the common speech of its time. And that means also that it must be latent in the common speech of the poet's *place* . . . it is out of sounds that he has heard that he must make his melody and harmony."[15] While Eliot does not explicitly address the question of stress patterns of individual words, poetry's need to honor those patterns as they exist in speech, rather than alter them to match a preconceived pattern, is certainly, as I have indicated earlier, implicit in his remarks.

In a similar vein, G. S. Fraser has said "most great English poetry approximates to speech rather than to song, and . . . it is more important to relate metrical patterns in poetry to patterns of meaning—speech meaning, sentence meaning—than to purely musical patterns."[16] This is particularly significant because Fraser, for all his incorporation of the Trager-Smith system whereby the syllables of English are divided into four categories of stress, rather than the two of traditional scansion, is a conventional metrist.

Prosodists like John Thompson suggest a "compromise" between the ordinary stressing of syllables and such stressing as the alleged metrical pattern may require.[17] Thompson is a particularly significant figure, for it is he who has argued, as noted in Chapter 2, that a "founding" of English meter occurred in the sixteenth century, a founding in which he finds George Gascoigne's "Certayne Notes of Instruction . . ." playing a central role, and it is, again as noted earlier, Thompson who presents Gascoigne as *not* saying "there *should* be alternate weak and strong stresses in a pentameter line . . . he says there *are* alternate weak and strong stresses in a line, whether the speech fits or not."[18] For Gascoigne, according to Thompson, metrical pattern always takes precedence over ordinary language (p. 73). Thompson's focus on this elevation of metrical pattern over speech is curious in more ways that one.

First of all, it manages to cite a crucial statement of Gascoigne and then allocate it to secondary status. For whatever else he may hold, Gascoigne, as noted in Chapter 2, instructs the poet to "place every word in his natural *Emphasis* or sound . . . with such length or shortnesse, elevation or depression of sillables, as it is commonly pronounced or used" (italics in original; quoted by Thompson, p. 71). While it is true that Gascoigne allocates to meter the power to wrench words out of their usual stress configurations, he never, if we take him at his word, wants to see that power exercised—this is what his statement amounts to. Thus, speech as the pronunciation model for poetic language is being *advocated* by Thompson's chief exhibit, Gascoigne, in the crucial "founding" period. Thompson seems guilty of amnesia on this point, for later he speaks of Gascoigne's "two requirements, a strict metrical pattern and the observation of natural word order . . ." (p. 74). Whatever happened to "natural *Emphasis?*"

Moreover, Thompson himself argues that the iambic meter, or more generally, the rhythms of our verse, "are an imitation of speech." They represent abstracted, simplified versions of patterns that "occur naturally in the language" (p. 13). This is debatable; Harding, for one, questions it (p. 12), and he should. But putting aside the tricky question of whether the English tongue is essentially iambic, we have Thompson giving us a meter that at once realizes the latency of English speech and at the same time violates that speech. It is not Gascoigne who appears to be talking—almost literally—out of both sides of his mouth, but Thompson, who has unfortunately attempted to enlist Gascoigne in his cause. Perhaps Thompson's notion of the need to compromise between speech pattern and metrical pattern constitutes some sort of imperfect recognition of what he has been up to.

Taking a strong stand on the need for natural emphasis, Harding's *Words into Rhythm* is full of English good sense on a number of other matters (though such sense is no more assured of receiving a proper hearing than was Clarissa's advice in *The Rape of the Lock*). He puts his finger on the flawed thinking of several prosodists (Chatman, Thompson, Wimsatt, and Beardsley, *et al*), points up the centrality and function of the verse line (a matter I will address shortly), and acutely contests the dubious notions of counterpoint, isochrony, the hypnotic effect of meter, and the inevitable expressiveness of metrical variations. But the chief feature of his book, one of the most valuable works in the prosodic canon, is its insistence on honoring speech patterns, as those patterns relate to meaning: "the sense [of a poem], with the speech rhythms it dictates, must take precedence of any mechanical form of the nominal metre, and must do so decisively, without compromise" (p. 39).

In writing his book, published in 1976, Harding assumed that the realization that poetry is ordered by something other than meter had already been extended by scholars and critics to verse "which is largely metrical" (p. 18), but in my reading of the literature such a shift had not taken place to a significant degree (and still has not, though there have been some rumblings of change). The field of prosodic criticism had certainly registered and continues to register pressure from linguistics, with its interest in the spoken language; this is mostly to the good. But there has been some resistance to letting linguists into the field, and when they *have* gotten in the results have not inevitably proved salutary (witness the work of Epstein and Hawkes cited in Chapter 1). The appearance of Harding's book should have done more to bring about the sort of approach he believed was already beginning to blossom; that approach is conspicuously absent in poetry textbooks that continue to be published.[19] His lack of influence may be partly attributable to his not having sufficiently elaborated his case, but is more likely the result of the traditional concept of meter, which often encourages unnatural emphasis, being as deeply rooted as burdock.

The persistent hold of meter may be seen as operating in Harding himself as he handles individual lines. Even while insisting that speech patterns not be violated, he concedes too much, I think, to the idea that the reading of a given verse is conditioned by the verses that have preceded it, through their establishing of a "metrical set" (it is significant that T. V. F. Brogan's summary of Harding's book was able to feature the notion of metrical set).[20] What we may be witnessing in this prosodist who focuses on *rhythm* as something distinct from meter, is an attraction to what lies at the heart of *meter's* appeal, the possibility of an ongoing pattern, a uniformity, even though such uniformity runs counter to Harding's theoretical commitment to the idea of diversity: "Serious verse, even in a form as seemingly strict as the line of Dryden and Pope, is an organization of diverse rhythms, not the repetition of metrical feet" (p. 157).

Attracted to uniformity though he may be, the core of Harding's book is its insistence that we base our sounding of poetry on the stress patterns of customary spoken English, and it is this that must be the starting point for any approach desirous of escaping the tyranny of the concept of meter. If Harding's focus on such patterns is supplemented by considerations of the syntactical units of spoken English, and if we keep continuously in view his recognition that a variety of line movements may emerge in a particular poem (as opposed to the pervasive single metrical pattern that traditional prosody focuses on) we will be well on our way to a foot-free prosody that can address both traditional poetry and free verse. There are signs that such a prosody is starting to emerge, a matter that will be considered in the next chapter.

Where my first basic assumption, that the words of a poem should receive their ordinary stress, goes counter to the practice of a good many advocates of traditional scansion, my second basic assumption, in effect, declares common ground with orthodox prosodists. For implicit in and fundamental to the concept of meter is that the words of a poem need to be thought of as organized into lines. I am going to assume that the distinguishing formal feature of poetry is, from the poet's point of view, the line as the unit of production, and, from the reader's point of view, which concerns me more here, the line as the unit of consumption.

As early as 1869, we find a work on versification claiming that there are no real units in English verse except lines.[21] In our own century we have seen the Russian Formalists contend that the fundamental unit of rhythm is the line, not the foot,[22] and John Erskine argues that the line end is "the 'one fixed mark' which enables the reader to distinguish between verse and prose in audition."[23] Benjamin Hrushovski, finding that there is no absolute basis for distinguishing between poetry and prose, nevertheless says: "The differentia of poetry is the verse line; it is hard to overestimate its importance in creating the poetic rhythm and the very being of the poem."[24] Zdzislawa Kopczynska and Lucylla Pszczolowska declare that "Le vers [i.e., line] est en effet, d'un point de vue general, l'element necessaire et suffisant tout a la fois de la structure poetique."[25] In *A Prosody Handbook,* Karl Shapiro and Robert Beum point out that the line is "a nearly universal characteristic of poetry. . . . The only major exceptions to this universality are 'prose poetry' and perhaps the Hebrew poetry of Old Testament times."[26] (In fact, some recent editions of the Old Testament are using a verse format for much of the materials (see, for example, the Oxford English Bible), which still leaves "prose poetry" as a "major exception," a genre I will comment on shortly.)

The observations of prosodists about the central status of the line have been reinforced by a number of poets. We have T. S. Eliot telling us:

> After much reflection I conclude that the only absolute distinction to be drawn [between poetry and prose] is that poetry is written in verse, and prose is written in prose. . . .[27]

Charles O. Hartman declares: *"Verse is language in lines.* This distinguishes it from prose. . . . This is not a really satisfying distinction . . . but it is the only one that works absolutely."[28] The editors of "A Symposium on the Theory and Practice of the Line in Contemporary Poetry," in which the contributors were all poets, note that "questions of the rhythmic and structural basis of the line seemed fundamental to most of our contributors," and, not surprisingly, further observe that "no contributor expresses full enthusiasm for the prose poem."[29] A similar symposium, in which the participants were again all poets, and which was published in the same year as the first, 1980, produced a near unanimity of agreement as to the importance of the line.[30] Two years later, one of the contributors to this second symposium, Louis Simpson, asked if Coleridge's definition of a poem could not be applied to Flaubert's *Un Coeur Simple.* Simpson answered his own question by saying "Yes, but sentences are not lines. Verse is written in lines—this is what makes the difference."[31]

It seems fair to say that the overwhelming majority of prosodists and poets, if only implicitly, regard the use of the line as a *sine qua non* of poetry. But there are markedly dissenting opinions. Such dissent can arise from within the study of "metrical" poetry, the argument taking the form, as with George Stewart, that the use of the "verse paragraph," as it occurs in much Elizabethan drama or in Milton, "destroys the reality of the conventional line structure."[32] Similarly, Randy Weirather contends that

> A line is . . . a technological creation, whose sole reality is written. It may or may not coincide with the verse, a point of confusion that has enslaved many prosodists to the white of the page when they could have more profitably listened to declamation for their definition of the verse.[33]

As does Stewart, Weirather cites Milton, or rather G. S. Fraser on Milton; Fraser, says Weirather, claims that "some verses of Milton may be scanned equally well in different fashions," and proceeds to relineate a passage from Book IX of *Paradise Lost.*[34] (Incidentally, the relineation of Milton can be found as far back as 1765— see the instance cited by Donald Hall.)[35] One might argue against Stewart, Weirather, and Fraser by invoking the work of Ants Oras, who has observed in Milton a treatment of "terminal phonetic echoes,"[36] and a use of consonant patterns at line endings that run "counter to the traditional notion that for him the individual line was a very subordinate unit intended to be submerged in the long flow of his paragraphs."[37]

Taking a wider stance, one might contend that lineation in general is meaningful, that it is not to be trifled with by prosodists in handling either metrical or free verse, and that the continuing presence of the line in the overwhelming majority of contemporary works that put themselves forth as poetry cannot simply be waved away. On the other hand, it is precisely the nature of the line in much contemporary verse that has presented what some would regard as an Achilles heel in the argument that the line is the ineluctable component of poetry.[38] In the first of the two symposia on the line in contemporary poetry, referred to earlier, one contributor claimed that "The line as it is practiced in most contemporary poetry says no more than 'This is a poem,'"[39] and another said "A great deal of present lineation seems to me merely foolish. . . ."[40] The second symposium appears to have been provoked by Hayden Carruth's printing as prose a pair of poems by John Haines and Charles Simic, and his asking of their original form "What purpose do these lines serve, beyond making us read with unnatural emphasis and in a joggy cadence?"[41] The editors of *The Line in Postmodern Poetry* contend that "the free verse line . . . has come to signify an *authentic* self-expression, but is used everywhere, at least potentially, in *bad faith*" (italics in original).[42]

Aware of the first of the symposia I have cited, and drawing her materials from contemporary verse, Marjorie Perloff, in her essay "The Linear Fallacy," has subjected the notion of the line being the central, indispensable component of poetry to a vigorous, extended attack. But her logic is less than impeccable when she takes several lineated poems she considers weak as evidence that poetry does not require the line. Nobody would claim that lineation *guarantees* authentic poetry, only that it is a necessary if not sufficient condition for such poetry. The presence of lineation in mediocre verse does not make the use of the line dispensable, and its employment in such verse should not convict it of superfluousness through a kind of guilt by association.[43]

Perloff's argument is less dubious (though still open to challenge) where she says that "when prose foregrounds marked patterns of recurrence (whether phonic, syntactic, or verbal), calling attention to itself as language art, as in the case of Gertrude Stein or Samuel Beckett or John Ashbery's *Three Poems,* we have poetry, and often much better poetry than in the so-called free verse of a C. K. Williams or a Karen Snow."[44] Perloff is at once trying to legitimize the prose poem and, like John Hollander before her, voicing discontent with what she rightly regards as the flatness and arbitrary lineation of much contemporary poetry, though one might not necessarily agree with her examples. (Behind Perloff and Hollander and others unhappy with much of what passes for poetry today, stands the figure of Ezra Pound, with his warning—quoted by Perloff—that the poet should not "try to shirk all the difficulties of the unspeakably difficult art of good prose by chopping [one's] composition into line lengths.")[45]

But a number of things should be noted. First, one of the poets Perloff holds up as a model of good writing, George Oppen, has said that "The meaning of a poem is in the cadences and the shape of the lines. . . ." Perloff herself quotes this in an essay an Oppen that appeared in the same year (1981) as "The Linear Fallacy." In the Oppen essay she also cites that poet as saying "The line-break is just as much a part of the language as the period, comma, or parenthesis, and *it shows that there are things that can only be said as poetry*" (my italics).[46] She also quotes Oppen as saying "I . . . believe in a form in which there is a sense of the whole line, not just its ending. Then there's the sense of the relation between lines, the relation in their length . . ." (p. 120). In that same essay on Oppen, Perloff writes out one of William Carlos Williams's poems as a sentence, and says "To destroy Williams's lineation in this way is, of course, to make a travesty of his poem" (p. 123). After a similar exercise performed on an Oppen poem she says of the result "It makes no sense" (p. 124).

In yet another essay, published in 1983, two years after "The linear Fallacy," Perloff defends against Hayden Carruth's charge (made in 1950) that Williams's lines are neither "run over . . . nor are they rove over, in the Hopkinsian sense," but "hung over, like a Dali watch," and that "If this is done for typographical effect, as it sometimes appears, it is inexcusable, for it interferes with our reading." Perloff rightly calls this "A remarkable misunderstanding, implying, as it does, that typography is detachable from the poem, that lineation is just a nuisance. . . ."[47] But there is a good deal of irony in Perloff's espousal of the importance of lineation as a response to Carruth's denigration of Williams. Not only does that espousal carry her well away from the thrust of "The Linear Fallacy," there is also the fact that Carruth himself takes the line very seriously. He has said that "historically and at present the line is our basic unit of poetry . . . for my part I would not have it otherwise, and . . . ninety-five percent of the other working poets in America agree with me. . . ."[48] It is Perloff who is less than staunch in arguing the importance of lineation. It was she who wrote "The Linear Fallacy," not Carruth. Also, her defense of Williams leaves something to be desired, being inconsistent with respect to the function of lineation. Talking of Williams's "This is just to say," she asserts that "It is typography. . . that provides directions for the speaking voice. . . ."[49] I would certainly agree. But as she proceeds, intent on making a case for the "visual" aspect of Williams's poetry, her focus shifts. She speaks of how his lineation can make words stand out for the reader's *eye,* rather than serving as a guide for voicing.

She cites the following passage:

> In brilliant gas light
> I turn the kitchen spigot
> and watch the water plash
> into the clean white sink.
> On the grooved drain-board
> to one side is
> a glass filled with parsley—
> crisped green.
>   Waiting
> for the water to freshen—
> I glance at the spotless floor—
>
> .   .   .   .

She comments that "Waiting" has been "moved over toward the jagged right margin of the poem. Notice that the poem would *sound* exactly the same if 'waiting' were aligned with 'crisped' and 'for' at the left margin; the effect, in other words, is entirely visual" (p. 104; italics in original). Agreeing with the fact that the placement of "Waiting" makes it impinge on the eye, I would argue that there is also a sonic effect to that placement. The space to the left of the word delays our getting to it, so to speak, imposes a brief period of silence, so that *we* experience a kind of waiting.

To return to Perloff's attack on "The Linear Fallacy," I should like to note that the very kinds of recurrence she points to as the marks of poetry, whether they appear in verse or not, are heightened by their containment within lines. This is the result of the general intensifying of focus provided by the line format, wherein a relatively few words at a time are presented for our consideration. In encountering lines we are being given, one by one, a series of small frames. This framing increases the possibility of a given word or combination of words impinging on us more strongly than if such words were encountered among the larger units that prose sentences and paragraphs typically present to us. Put another way, a word set in the comparatively limited domain of a line has to compete less for our attention, so to speak, than the same word put in the longer flowings of prose.

Lineation, even when it does not take the radical form of giving us only one word at a time, as Williams does with "Waiting" in the poem cited above, enters into the *sonic* dimensions of a poem, whatever visual factors might be operating, if only as part of the overall effect of the intensification-by-narrow-framing that the use of verse format automatically creates. The line presents us with a relatively few words at a time to absorb, and, of course, the mere fact of lineation, claiming that we are in the presence of poetry, encourages us to take those words in by sounding them out. (Can the same be said for prose poetry?) Lineation thus works for a *slower* consumption of a given number of words than would be the case if they were set as prose. It does this because it encourages us to enunciate the text, even if only *sotto voce,* and because it creates many more breaks between groups of words than would obtain in a prose setting. Those breaks are accompanied by pauses, however slight (more on that later), and these help make for a slower pace as we put the words of the poem out through our mouths as well as take them in through our eyes.[50]

Brooks and Warren have called the line a "unit of attention,"[51] and George Quasha, in a nice variation on this, calls it an "arena of attention."[52] My point has been that it is a *small* arena, one in a series of such spaces, that this is a case of a difference in quantity making for a difference in quality, for a considerable gap between verse and prose, even prose that calls itself "prose poetry." That very term concedes a crucial distinction between such "poetry" and its verse counterpart.

This last point is driven home by Jonathan Monroe, who is certainly no enemy of prose poetry. He has put forth claims for it as large and elaborate as any devotee of that genre could wish for. But he doesn't seem to share much more with Perloff than an enthusiasm for "poetry" written in prose. As opposed to Perloff's emphasis on a formal feature, the marked patterns of recurrence she claims to find in prose that can qualify as "poetry," Monroe agrees with Tzvetan Todorov and others who have characterized the prose poem as "a genre remarkable in part for its relative paucity of formal requirements."[53] Moreover, Monroe has called such a poem

the place where [the] distinction [between "prose" and "poetry"] dog-gedly maintains itself despite itself. Whether we are speaking of the two words "prose" and "poem," or even of the collapsing of these two words into Ponge's 'proême,' the prose poem depends for its very existence not only on the continued difference of its two defining terms but even on their continued oppositional status (p. 20).

In Monroe's view the prose poem is a genre that has been practiced not simply as an alternative to verse but in conscious *antagonism* to it. He writes "the prose poem is . . . the place where the verse lyric is driven back to its own prosaic subtext, to the place where the lyrical self loses itself in the verse line's extension to the margin of the page and the disarticulated, disindividuated uniformity of the block-print of prose" (p. 27).

In fairness to Perloff it should be noted that she is arguing not so much for the prose poem, but, it would seem, for "poet's prose," a term that serves as the title of a book by Stephen Fredman, and that does not designate, say, a critical essay by T. S. Eliot or Robert Pinsky, but a supposed form of poetry. In fact, Perloff follows the distinction made by Fredman between "poet's prose" and the "prose poem," which, she states, "in its classic nineteenth-century form is, as Fredman says, 'a highly aestheticized, subjective, idio-lectal artifact, a paean to the isolated genius' "[54]

Perloff, it turns out, is championing a branch of *contemporary* "poetry," mainly American. An example of this poetry, or poet's prose, is John Ashbery's *Three Poems*. Such a work, according to Perloff, does not have Mallarmé for a forefather but Gertrude Stein for a foremother.[55] But it seems to me Perloff would be hard put to demonstrate, outside her examples from Stein, the patterns of recurrence that she appears to seize on as the essence of poetry. Ashbery himself, in his books other than *Three Poems*, has almost always used lineation, so it would appear that there is a difference for him between works written in lines and those that are not.[56]

Furthermore, from within the ranks of self-declared poets who dispense with lineation, Ron Silliman has spoken not of patterns of recurrence, but of "the new sentence" that serves as the vehicle of such poets.[57] And what characterizes the new sentence? What Silliman calls "torque," the effect created in "traditional poetry" by line-breaks, that is, by the line terminating before a unit of meaning has been completed. Such an effect is gotten by such a "new sentence" as "He lived here, under the assumptions." With such sentences, making for "polysemy/ambiguity," "poetic form has moved into the interiors of prose."[58] Apart from the question of how great a claim on our attention a series of such sentences might have, those sentences do not give us what a series of lines do, for a particular line, however severe the cutoff of a syntactic-semantic unit its line-break might effect, generally goes on to complete its thoughts, to provide us, in fact, with what Silliman might call an "old sentence." Silliman's new sentences simply hang us up. They appear to be all torque, with no semantic completions.

It should be added that line-breaks cannot only create "torque" situations, or conditions of suspended meaning that are then resolved by the line or lines that follow, they can create the impression of semantic *completion,* which in fact turns out not to be the case. The line may *appear* not to be enjambed, but as we proceed we find out that it is; the "torque" is then seen as such only in retrospect. Christopher Ricks, who has written brilliantly on Wordsworth's use of line-breaks (including the advantage he takes of the space at the end of a line), offers the following example from *The Prelude:*

> Oh! at that time,
> While on the perilous ridge I hung alone,
> With what strange utterance did the loud dry wind
> Blow through my ears! the sky seem'd not a sky
> Of earth, and with what motion mov'd the clouds!

Ricks comments as follows:

> it did not seem to be a sky at all, with this effect drawing strength from the way in which *sky* is brought to the very edge, up against that free space which is as invisible as the sky or the wind but as existent and active. And then the sense is evolved and dissolved, and Wordsworth is seen to have been about to say something both more confined and less confined than that it didn't seem to be a sky at all. . . . We cannot doubt the translatable sense: that the sky did not seem to be the sky which goes with our Earth. And yet there is . . . something audacious to the point of apparent wilfulness about such a use of *[Of]*. 'A sky of earth:' it cannot but sound as if the sky might be made of earth. . . . we are to entertain the phantasmal unimaginability of a sky of earth— to entertain it, and then with a wise relief to cleave to the other sense.[59]

In Ricks' rich reading then, we first get one sense of the line about the sky, then another, then a return to the first. The play of meaning here is partly dependent, as he points out, on the ambiguity of both "Of" and "earth," but that play is initially kicked off by Wordsworth's line-break. It is doubtful if anything but a single meaning would emerge if we were simply allowed to read "a sky of earth."

Silliman's new sentences do not produce the kind of effect Ricks points to. They do not generate a counterpoint or interplay be-

tween line unit and other assemblages of words. As Peter Townsend has said, "the verse line . . . maintain[s] a significant and
rhythmically versatile relation with at least three units of the linguistic scale: the sentence, the clause, and the group."[60] The only
unit operating in Silliman's medium is the (truncated) sentence
itself. Finally, since such sentences are set as prose and, at least
in his formulation, do not pretend to make any claims on the ear,
they do not particularly encourage us to read them differently from
the way we are likely to read other prose, silently and swiftly.

Not only, as noted above, does the quantitative difference between lines and sentences (at least "old" ones) make for a different
reading experience, but so does the increased number of distinctly
marked beginnings and endings that lineation is likely to create
within a given number of words, as compared to their setting in
prose. Karl Shapiro and Robert Beum have pointed out that "The
positions of greatest emphasis in a sentence are the end and the
beginning, in that order. These same points are emphatic in any
unit: phrase, clause, or poetic line. If a sentence, then, is broken
into lines, it obtains several additional points of emphasis."[61] Christopher Ricks observes that the verse line makes of poetry "a medium which is more totally and persistently involved in effecting
something through its recurrent sense of an ending. Poetry is involved, more than prose, in persistently stopping and starting. . . ."[62] Only in this respect might Silliman claim that his new
sentences, which are generally very short, have an effect similar
to that of verse, though he seems solely interested in pointing to
the "torque" element.

In the course of her attempt to demythologize the line, Perloff
adduces a *locus classicus,* Jonathan Culler's conversion of a news-
paper item into a "poem" through his lineation of the original account, and his accompanying commentary on the effects of that
lineation. Her response to this demonstration is to inquire, citing
John Hollander, what happens when "the look of the received free
verse poem" has become "the norm." She asks: "Does the mere
act of lineating one's phrases and sentences continue to produce
the proper *frisson* in the reader?"[63] Later, she complains that lineation is automatically taken to spell *"elevation."*[64] But lineation *per
se* should not be thought of as guaranteeing either *frissons* or elevation. It is a device that makes for a *possible* effectiveness, an interest that *may* attend on the line's having brought our attention to
focus, and that is all. Perloff and others are right to question the
dubious entities that are so often presented to us in contemporary
poetic practice. If a line appears to lack some structuring principle,

semantic, syntactic, or sonic, or fails to create some meaningful suspension, it has wasted its precious potentials. We see this only too often, and in the process, both the notion of the line and, since such lines abound in that mode, free verse, open themselves to denigration.

Stanley Plumly, whom Perloff refers to, does not help matters when he says, with apparent approval, that "the line breaks [in free verse] are more eye than ear oriented. The unit of the sentence, as in good, scannable prose, is the ear of the free verse poem."[65] Further, Plumly contends, "the intersection of the flexibility of the free verse rhythm with the strategy of storytelling has produced a kind of prose lyric: a form corrupt enough to speak flat out in sentences yet pure enough to sustain the intensity, if not the integrity, of the line . . ." (p. 27). Here is confusion confounded: a free verse that is like scannable prose, whatever that might be, with the line having no particular function. Plumly apparently is willing to accept a prosy (sentence-as-unit) poetry, finding as the one thing essential to free verse the element of "tone" (p. 23).[66] This leaves us, prosodically speaking, nowhere. But at least Plumly is assuming the desirability of intensity. Too often that quality is lacking in contemporary poetry.

The absence of intensity is far from what Denise Levertov hopes for when she says of contemporary free verse that "there is at our disposal no tool of the poetic craft more important, none that yields more subtle and precise effects, than the line-break if it is properly understood." That element registers the *"process"* of "thinking/ feeling, feeling/thinking, rather than focusing more exclusively on its *results* . . ." (italics in original). Moreover, the most "precise . . . and exciting function of the line-break . . . is its effect on the *melos* of the poem," on rhythm and pitch patterns.[67] (I might remark that with Levertov's conception of the line-break in free verse we find a curious analogy to the notion that the function of the pattern in *metrical* verse is to establish something that will be significantly broken; the free verse line for Levertov exists to be significantly enjambed.)

While I have been trying to make a case for the *virtu* of the line in general, Donald Wesling would appear to agree with Levertov in assigning particular strength to the free-verse line, or at least some specimens of it. In discussing Williams's "Asphodel, That Greeny Flower," he says:

> It seems that where the end and, less significantly, the beginning of the conventional verse lines are points of greatest interest, in free verse of

this sort each of the phrasal members of the line gains identity and weight, producing climaxes of rhythm smaller but more continuous. The difference from traditional rhythms is not one of quality but of quantity; in such cases, there are more ends, more beginnings; more scissorings of the line by grammar, more of grammar by line, more pauses—thereby, arguably, more energy.[68]

In light of such a statement it is of course ironic that, more often than not, the free-verse line rather than the line in formal verse has been the one charged with flatness.[69]

The linkage Levertov explicitly makes between the free verse line and sound effects, a linkage Wesling also makes though not necessarily in the same terms, is consistent with William Carlos Williams's remarks on his poetic practice. In an unpublished talk he said, apparently in response to a question:

> Why have I divided my lines as I have. I don't know. If I did I'd know the answer to form. I have refused to divide them according to a form I know is NOT the answer . . . Somehow or other the old line must be br[o]ken up—somehow. Pleasure, pleasure to the era [ear] is a solid guide.[70]

This passage makes for an irony similar to that referred to just above. Williams, if anybody, is the patron saint of contemporary free verse (see Bawer), so much of which has no pleasure for the ear. Moreover, it might be charged that whatever his intention, the lineation practices in a number of Williams's own poems make for fragments with no sonic charm or expressiveness.

So what truly threatens the historical centrality of the line is less the practice of "prose-poetry" or "poet's prose," or a theoretical appeal to something other than verse format as the crucial component of poetry, and more the current flood of partitionings that manage to be at once sharply enjambed and flat, generating nothing for the ear and often very little for the sense. To put it another way, many lines in contemporary verse are such as to discourage the placement of a pause at their terminations, for they seem to have little claim to constituting auditory or semantic entities. But of course, such poetry only intensifies a problem already evident with Milton (as witness my earlier citations of George Stewart and Randy Weirather), and before that with late Shakespeare.[71] The problem is simply this: should or should not the reader of poetry automatically acknowledge the fact of lineation? An ancillary question, the one of interest here, is: Should that acknowledgment take the form of invariably pausing, for however small an interval, at the end of each verse no matter how "hard" the degree of enjambment may be there (as with a line concluding with "the")? That the problem precedes the rise of free verse is pointed up by Samuel Johnson's contention, in his *Life of Milton*, that "Blank verse seems to be verse only to the eye," a remark in effect echoed by Samuel Levin, who says that "in general the line in blank verse would seem to be ill-defined for the hearer."[72] What is being asked here is whether line definition should be effected by pausing.

Early on in the history of English prosodic criticism, George Puttenham had strongly implied that every line takes a pause at its ending.[73] The explicit notion of marking a line ending by a pause can be found as far back as Sir Joshua Steele, who contended in his *Prosodia Rationalis* (1779) that there was a "stressed rest" at the beginning of a line and an unstressed rest at its end, by way of his seeing in each verse a structure like that of music, which parcels out equal units of time.[74] In our own century, Cary F. Jacob has put forth the observation that the arrangement of poetry in lines is a stage following the writing of it in "rhythmical prose" and that the line ending corresponded to a pause.[75] Egerton Smith has said that "The hearer should never be allowed to overlook . . . metrical pauses [i.e., pauses at the ends of lines]; they are always there, though at some times, in accordance with the sense, they are less distinctly marked than at others; perhaps, occasionally, even only ideal."[76] He also says "a good reader will not fail to mark the end of a line, even in verse where overflow is so abundant as in Milton's. . . ."[77] In the same spirit, Maurice Grammont has contended that "'Tout vers *sans aucune exception possible,* est suivi d'une pause plus ou moins longue.'"[78]

But these prosodists have by no means settled the matter. For to ask a question today about any kind of pause in poetry, let alone line-terminal pause, is to confront an entity of verse that is up for grabs. Brogan has remarked that, along with the matters of pitch and duration, the question of pause "has so far been either slighted or misconceived in scholarly investigations."[79] I might note that while there is an entry for "caesura" in the *Princeton Encyclopedia of Poetry and Poetics* there is none for "pause."

Harvey Gross, implicitly accepting the notion of the line as a unit, accepts also the widely practiced if not inevitable way of marking that unit. For he refers to "our usual tendency to pause slightly at the end of the line."[80] He puts this tendency to work in examining a passage from Eliot's *Burnt Norton:*

> . . . After the kingfisher's wing
> Has answered light to light, and is silent, the light is still
> At the still point of the turning world.

Gross notes that our first understanding of the terminal "still" is as an adjective modifying 'light." Once we move down to the next line, we find it can be read as an adverb.[81] I would modify what Gross seems to be saying, and observe that if we did not in fact pause at the end of the third line, the adverbial sense of "still" would dominate if not monopolize our conception of the passage. Pausing keeps the sense of "still" equally, richly poised between two possibilities of meaning. (The double effect here is related to that pointed out earlier in the citing of Christopher Ricks' treatment of Wordsworth.)

Also arguing for the importance of the end-line pause is Roger Mitchell: "The run-on line . . . is misnamed. Just as there is no syllable without stress, so there is rarely a line break without pause, however slight."[82] Mitchell goes further than this. He asks rhetorically "What other equally important reason could there be for writing poetry in lines if not to signal pause at their ends?"[83] I think this is getting cause and effect reversed. The line has its own reasons for being, or should have, as I tried to indicate earlier—the terminal pause simply honors its cut-off point.

Several commentators appear to take up positions somewhere between Randy Weirather, who is totally impatient with the notions of line-integrity and pauses in post-Anglo-Saxon poetry, and prosodists who believe in the line's centrality and, usually, as a corollary of that, in the importance of terminal pause. Samuel Levin, for example, says that even when the line *is* defined for the hearer (as opposed to what he alleges happens in iambic pentameter), it is linguistically irrelevant; also, enjambment "is not a linguistically significant phenomenon." Both are simply examples of poetic conventions. But Levin then proceeds to give back at least partly what he has apparently taken away. For he accords weight to the pause at the end of the line, and finds that enjambment creates a nontrivial effect, making for a tension between "the forward movement demanded by the syntax and the sense of completion signaled by the line-end. . . .[84] (This, incidentally, seems to me a legitimate application of the notion of tension.) Still, Levin goes so far as to say the pause "need not be expressed acoustically."[85]

Christopher Ricks plainly looks at line-ending as significant, but appears ready to have it function in an indeterminate, attenuated sort of way:

> The white space at the end of a line of poetry constitutes some kind
> of pause; but there need not be any pause of formal punctuation, and
> so there may be only equivocally a pause at all. A nontemporal pause?
> Unless the rhythm or the sense or the formal punctuation insists upon
> it, the line-ending (which cannot help conveying some sense of an end-
> ing) may not be exactly an ending. The white space may constitute an
> invisible boundary; an absence or a space which yet has significance;
> what in another context would get called a pregnant silence.[86]

Ricks' position is similar to that of Prudence Byers, who suggests
that the function of line-ending in poetry "may be more psychological than strictly phonic."[87]

I am uncomfortable with these halfway positions, which can be
placed under the heading of "mentalist," though I must say they
seem to me more justified than the mentalist claim that we "hear"
the pure meter of a line as we read it, however it might deviate.
Registering in one way or another the ending of a line is at least
in keeping with the typographic reality of the poem. But one way
or another is not enough, so while I generally hold that prescriptive
statements are best resisted in thinking about prosody, I have to
go along with Maurice Grammont and insist that a pause be registered at the end of the line and that it be actual, however slight.
Unless we are dealing with rhyme, or with poetry whose line-
endings coincide with syntactic boundaries, we are likely, without
positing a terminal pause for each verse ending, to end up in a
morass, an amorphous domain somewhere between poetry and
prose. The verse format will then amount to an empty gesture,
a claim simply to the *look* (and prestige?) of poetry, without a
commitment to meaningful frames other than the phrases and
clauses shared with prose, crucial as those are.[88]

What I am arguing for, then, is mandatory pausing at the end of
a line of verse, as a clear registration of something having been
completed. That one cannot take for granted that such pausing will
automatically occur is pointed up not only by remarks already
cited about lines of poetry not being clearly defined for the
hearer—presumably pausing would so define them—but by Prudence Byers's findings about the performances of poetry that she
studied. She claims that the acoustic features that characterized
"ordinary auditory-phrase boundaries"—such features include
pause—were not automatically generated by verse line-endings
when she had the verse read by eighteen experienced readers of
poetry. Her conclusion is that the modern poet "cannot count on
line-end to create for him a sound unit distinguishable from others
and manipulable for purposes of rhythm. Except for a few speak-

ers, and in particular circumstances, the verse line will not constitute a sound-unit at all."[89] This would suggest that insisting on the
use of the pause to mark the end of the verse line may amount to
holding one's finger in a dike that is well on its way to dissolution,
but nonetheless I think it worth insisting on.

While it may have been particularly provoked by much contemporary verse, the sense of the endangerment of line integrity has,
as suggested earlier, something of a history. John Hollander reminds us that it goes at least as far back as Dryden's belief that
blank verse, as opposed to rhymed verse, conferred too much freedom on the poet.[90] Dr. Johnson believed that every line of heroic
verse needed to be "unmingled with another," that this separation
was effected by rhyme, and that Milton's blank verse made it difficult to tell where a line began or ended.[91] Of course, Dr. Johnson
would likely not be satisfied with the use of terminal pause as a
device for making a line into an entity, as opposed to being a leaky
container, if that pause has to function as a kind of desperate seal-
ant. Nor am I so satisfied. What I am ultimately arguing for is a
poetry whose lines, through semantic and/or syntactic and/or sonic
means, generate a feeling of their individual integrity, an integrity
acknowledged, as opposed to being simply created, through terminal pauses. Of course, such pauses might also be employed from
time to time to mark lines that effect a meaningful suspension
of integrity.

By and large, lines in poetry written before the age of free verse
are likely to create a feeling of their being meaningful entities; even
in free verse many lines produce such an effect. And well they
might. For free verse has a stake in the survival of lines so felt:
To give the enjambments it so often employs some force (you can't
get much impact from transgressing a nonexistent boundary), or
to create the effect of a poetry feeling or thinking its way (as
suggested by Levertov), or to generate a rich ambiguity (as in the
example of the passage from "Burnt Norton"). Preserving the
sense of the line as a unit is also essential to the standard critical
notion of interplay between line on the one hand, and sentence,
clause or phrase, on the other. Such interplay can occur, of course,
in either formal verse or free verse. The point is, as Miller Williams
has said, "a poem doesn't work as a poem when the lines don't
work as lines" (p. 309). Pausing at the end of a line should not be
counted on to "make" the line, but should, ideally, acknowledge
that it has in some sense made itself.

In addition to end-line pausing, I am going to posit that where
the punctuation and/or sense requires it, a line be conceived of as

having interior pauses, and that these be granted as much reality in a sonic analysis as any sounded syllables. Interestingly enough, Prudence Byers's experiments with texts read aloud indicated that line-endings did not necessarily produce pauses, but punctuation, which she found to be more frequent in poetry than in prose, did.[92] Since punctuation can exist independent of line endings, we can assume that a fair amount of it, along with the attendant pauses, is line-interior.

But the notion of medial pauses being significant is not a standard one among prosodists. Randy Weirather, who has questioned the meaningfulness of the line itself in post-Anglo-Saxon poetry, takes a very dim view of internal pauses in that poetry. He links the dissolution of the Anglo-Saxon line to the replacement of the true caesura by what he regards as a promiscuous assortment of junctures within the line, a change that prosodists have failed to register: "The caesura . . . has drowned in the ambiguity of the word 'pause.' There may be several per verse, occurring practically anywhere."[93] Weirather can be seen as echoing Dr. Johnson, who spoke with some distaste of "The variety of pauses, so much boasted by the lovers of blank verse. . . ."[94] But Johnson was speaking in the name of rhyme, while Weirather's disdain for internal line pauses derives from an obvious predilection for Anglo-Saxon verse. Thus, Weirather finds by a backward look the basis for not taking medial pauses seriously: such pauses cannot begin to have the reality of the Anglo-Saxon caesura. But for other prosodists the chief justification for waving aside pauses is the commitment to the concept of meter. Meter has to do with the relative disposition of syllables; a description of that disposition is the essence of the matter, period.

This strain shows itself, for example, in T. S. Omond's response to an approach to the iambic pentameter line that saw it incorporating major and minor pauses: "To make grammatical pauses constitute rhythm is to confound elocution with structure. . . ."[95] George R. Stewart contended that the caesura results "only [!] from the physical need of drawing breath or from the desire to mark a logical division of thought. . . . Since no syllable is omitted, the caesura is really a matter of taste or judgment."[96] (While the drawing of breath might depend on the individual reader, the marking of thought divisions does not.) C. S. Lewis, while acknowledging that the pause might play an important role in creating the emotive effects of a poem, said that "It is a rhetorical and syntactical fact, not a metrical fact."[97] G. S. Fraser contends that "in the stress-syllable line the breath-pause, like punctuation generally, is essentially a device of rhetoric rather than metrics."[98] Seymour Chatman, drawing a similar distinction, says the elements of caesura and enjambment are not components of verse "in the same sense that syllable-count and ictic disposition are."[99] Harvey Gross, asking how long a pause is entailed at the caesura in a line of Eliot, dismisses the question by saying "it depends on how an individual reader performs the line. And we are back to the old performative fallacy. The meter remains what it has always been. . . ."[100]

Samuel Levin takes a middle position on the importance of the caesura as well as end-line pause. In talking of the former, he says, oddly, that it should be regarded as "the metrical progress through the line. . . ." This peculiar conception seems designed to recruit the caesura for a variant of the conventional espousal of a "tension" existing between "the abstract metrical scheme and the natural language dynamics" (much as Levin, more legitimately, recruits the *terminal* pause along with enjambment for an effect of tension involving syntax). In Levin's scheme, the caesura sets up a tension between a stoppage that would break the metrical pattern and an "impulsion" that would sustain it.[101]

Curiously enough, even while, as noted above, T. S. Omond seemed to sniff at the element of pause, he could show a good deal of respect for it, doing so as a timer. He said that when Elizabethan prosody thought in terms of quantitative measure it "sinned against the genius of English poetry" because, among other things, "It took no account of pause, no account of time underlying syllable-structure."[102] Also standing up for pause is Roger Fowler, who cannot allow Chatman's dismissal of caesura and enjambment as

"pure performance features" . . . to pass unchallenged . . . semantically and grammatically, signalled terminal junctures, both within and between lines, are an essential part of verse-structure . . . they can have a profound effect on the shape of a line and line-sequence.[103]

I welcome the support of such commentators as Fowler. But, even as I would distinguish between my own notion of an endline pause and Sir Joshua Steele's terminal "stressed rest" or Egerton Smith's "ideal" one, I would draw a distinction between my own positing of significant medial pauses in the rendering of a verse line and the isochrony-based positions taken by some other metrists. I would, for example, reject the position of Saintsbury, who, as Brogan has pointed out, ostensibly dismissed the temporalist approach even as he said he believed in "the isochronous interval," and filled whole feet by pauses.[104] More recently, David Abercrombie has spoken of "a *silent stress-pulse*" by way of bolstering his isochrony-based approach to verse.[105] Such a pulse can occupy a midline position or serve as an end-line marker. There is also the example of Thomas Cable, who follows George Stewart in distinguishing between "extra-metrical pauses" (or caesurae) and metrical pauses. The former may derive from the reader's ineptness or loss of breath (and Cable is intent on keeping anything he says free of the contamination of mere "performance"). The latter sort of pause occurs "*when a* [metrical] *position has not been filled.*"[106] Cable asserts that "Timers have generally favored pauses; stressers have had nothing to do with them [is he forgetting Saintsbury?] largely because of their faulty hearing . . . metrical pause . . . refer[s] to the abstract pattern. It is a realization of it . . ." (p. 231).[107] Cable is willing to locate a pause where the meter "requires" it though the syntax may not (pp. 235, 237); this can occur even between an adjective and its noun. Moreover, Cable hears pauses even "at the beginning of an iambic line whenever the first syllable of nonictus is missing" (p. 238). He realizes that this stance, exemplified in his citing the *first* line of a Shakespeare sonnet, subjects him to "the mischievous question" Wimsatt and Beardsley directed toward a similar-minded prosodist: "When does the pause begin?" (p. 239). But he sticks to his notion.

Derek Attridge sees silent stress, the sort of thing spoken of by Abercrombie, as part of a performance approach to verse, and, sounding a by-now familiar distinction but muting its invidiousness, he says "Pauses are an important element in the sensitive reading of a poem; unrealised beats are part of its structure."[108] Such beats, which can occur internally or at line end, constitute Attridge's addition to the prosodic lexicon, but are, as far as I can tell, indistinguishable from silent stresses.

In my own positing of interior pauses I am neither interested in setting up poetry as music nor in getting lines to generate a particular number of feet, or a uniform set of time intervals, or a fixed number of beats. Unlike my assumption of a terminal pause, which I take as *always* occurring and as marking a literary construct— the verse line—the internal pauses I am positing exist as *possibilities* within the line and are generated not because of the presence of verse but because of the presence of the English language itself. That is to say, pauses get built into poetry because they are built into our articulation of words in general. This is not a matter of individual performance, though no doubt one performance might create a particular pause where another might not. This is a matter of linguistics, and here we might turn to a number of linguists for their views of pauses in our language (*pace* Cable, who cites F. W. Bateson's attacks on linguists, and his asking "Would you let your sister marry one?").[109]

J. Milton Cowan and Bernard Bloch have stated, and this is very much to my purpose, that

> Phrasing, the grouping of sentence elements into syntactic units by pauses in the stream of speech or by other means, is acknowledged to play an important role in the grammar of spoken English and of other languages; and the conventional punctuation that we use in writing is often regarded as reflecting, at least in principle or in origin, the pauses that we make in speaking.[110]

(This is not to say that all speech pauses are occasioned by phrasal considerations, but the pause-phrase connection is a crucial one, from my point of view, as will be made evident later in the book.)

Similarly, William E. Cooper and Jeanne Paccia-Cooper observe that "Coordinate clauses, nonrestrictive relatives, and conditionals are marked by a comma in written English and are bounded by perceptible syllable lengthening and pauses in spontaneous speech."[111] They cite sources that indicate that "Clause boundaries are favored locations for breathing," and such boundaries are marked by a number of phonetic phenomena, including pausing (pp. 167–68). But clause boundaries are not the only loci for pauses: "In addition to processing major constituents—such as clauses—as units, it also appears that speakers compute representations of relatively minor phrase nodes, such as that corresponding to "old men" in the sentence "The old men and women left early" (p. 26). Syllable lengthening may be another way of marking various speech groupings. But it is of particular interest to our purposes, if one grants that the articulation of a poem is likely to be slower than a piece of ordinary speech, that "the probability of occurrence for pausing increases by a much greater amount than for segmental lengthening at increasingly slow rates of speech" (p. 188).

Cooper and Paccia-Cooper set up a "Comprehensive Algorithm," or set of procedures, for computing the relative strengths of speech boundary points, such strengths determining "the probability of occurrence of the . . . prosodic effects" they have considered, one of which, of course, is pausing (p. 182). Their algorithm is based on the "tree" model that is standard in transformational grammar, wherein the English sentence is represented by a series of schematic inverted trees, each node of which is labeled according to the sort of phrasal constituent it represents.

Several linguists, most notably Elisabeth O. Selkirk, have argued persuasively that the English sentence is better represented as a "metrical grid" than as a "tree."[112] The grid

consists of a hierarchy of metrical levels, each level in turn consisting of a sequence of positions (beats) that stand for points in (abstract) time and define the recurring periodicities of rhythm. . . . The rhythmic structure of a sentence is the alignment of its syllables with a metrical grid.[113]

What is of interest here is that not only does the grid constitute the form in which "a theory of stress patterns in language must be couched" (p. 9), but that "pausing . . . come[s] about as a result of the presence of silent positions in the metrical grid of an utterance . . " (p. 298). These silent positions are "added" to the grid under syntactically specified conditions. . . . [T]he full rhythmic structure of an utterance, its metrical grid, is constituted by the . . . silent positions of syntactic timing, as well as by the positions that represent prominence patterns. . . ." Selkirk cites J. Catford as arguing that pauses "have an integral place in an overall rhythmic structure . . . they are not merely 'performance' effects" (p. 299). So here we have, even for those metrists that are ready to dismiss "performance" effects, reason for regarding pauses as part of a line's sonic features, unless such metrists wish to contend that in reading poetry we simply leave behind this integral element of spoken English.

Selkirk presents as a working hypothesis a rule of "Silent Demibeat Addition," which indicates the degree of pausing that will occur at a given point in a sentence. A demibeat is added after every major category word, namely nouns, verbs, adjectives, and adverbs, but not after a "function word," for example, auxiliary words, personal pronouns, conjunctions, and prepositions (pp. 315–16). A demibeat would also be added after "a word that is the head of a nonadjunct constituent," that is, a word that stands on its own semantically, one that is not bound to a following word for its meaning. (For example, in "Russian is a difficult language," the word "Russian" is the "head of a nonadjunct constituent." This is not the case with that same word in the sentence "Mary finished her Russian novel.") A demibeat is also added at the end of a phrase. The fourth occasion on which a demibeat would be added would be at the end of "a daughter phrase of S," which means, in lay language, a grouping of words that results from the first breakdown of a sentence into its parts, for example, the "subject" of a sentence (p. 314). (In the sentence "Red roses make a nice gift," "Red roses" would constitute a daughter phrase of the sentence.)

That a major category word is followed by a silent demibeat, that the end of a phrase, which is often also the end of a major category word, gets an additional silent demibeat, and that a particular sort of phrase gets yet another such demibeat, provides a basis for marking off sonic entities in any sentence, including, then, the verse sentence. They are so marked by pauses. However, it is not the existence of pauses per se that is of primary interest to me, but rather that their existence marks off *groupings* of words that may well occur in the verse line.

It is such groupings or phrases, I am proposing, that contribute heavily to the sonic qualities of verse lines, and it is these groupings and their effects that should constitute much of the focus of prosodic study, insofar as such study concerns itself with the nature of a poem's line movement (or what often goes under the much-abused heading of "rhythm"). Approaching the matter this way does not call for a sharp division between the way we approach metrical poetry and the way we approach free verse. Though I have questioned David Dooley earlier in this book, regarding his foot-based scansion, I think he has made a key observation linking the two sorts of poetry. He says:

> The free verse poet, no less than the poet who writes in strict meter, is concerned with clustering and spacing of accents, regularities and irregularities of rhythm, enjambment and end-stopping, positioning of caesuras, accommodation of speech rhythms and verbal music, and incorporation of local effects into an overall flow.[114]

Of course, when we consider a "metrical" poem, we will have to take account of its theoretical paradigm as well as its pause-marked groupings, but that paradigm will, in my approach, be conceived of in a much looser way than is traditional. Such loosening will be defined in the next chapter, and will be combined with phrasal analysis of the metrical poem. Nonmetrical poetry will be examined as well. But before formulating my approach and embarking on specific readings that employ it, the next chapter will attempt to place the focus on phrases within a particular prosodic tradition.

6

Phrasalism

THE title word of this chapter is derived from "phrasalists," a term used and perhaps even coined by George T. Wright in his book *Shakespeare's Metrical Art.* This work, discussed earlier, will be returned to later at some length. For now, it suffices to point out that Wright has it in for phrasalists. Perhaps because of the focus of his book, he names such prosodists in connection with our earlier poets, though phrasalism has large implications for all our poetry. At any rate, he says that *"Phrasalists* maintain that poets from Chaucer to Shakespeare frequently wrote loose combinations of rhythmical phrases rather than metrical lines. This theory comes dangerously close to imposing an anachronistic free-verse structure on poetry of much earlier periods than our own."[1] He asks of the phrasal theory: "could it have been proposed except in an age of free verse?" (p. 301).[2]

Even if Wright were correct, and he isn't, in thinking that it took an age of free verse to regard poetry as being composed of phrases, this in itself would not necessarily mean that examining poetry of the past in terms of its phrase structures is anachronistic. (Approaching Shakespeare's plays though their chains of imagery may reflect a modern preoccupation, but does that mean the approach is wrong? Poetic practice need not be conscious of all its elements in order for those elements to exist.) As we shall shortly see, Wright himself concedes that poets write in phrases, and ostensibly honors this fact. But it is meter, traditionally conceived, that engages his primary allegiance, and he is intent on keeping phrasalism in its place, charging that it reduces the "formidable polyphonic music" of English poetry "to a meager harmony of rhythms-without-meter" (p. 12).

But to talk of "rhythms-without meter" is to set up a straw man. Of course meter has to be taken into account in the analysis of older poetry (as well as some modern verse). What I wish to advocate is an approach that will make much of phrasing while at the same time acknowledging the role of meter where appropriate, but it will not be meter as Wright conceives of it. Among other things, it will not be given the power to distort the ordinary stress patterns of our language, and it will not be the lord of the line. The crux of the matter, as I see it, is that a focus on a poem's phrases must not be *subordinated* to the matter of meter, that phrases need to be accorded real weight and regarded as functioning in ways at least as important as those credited to meter. (I should make clear that in my own references to "phrases," I am not, as opposed to Wright, prefacing them explicitly or implicitly with the term "rhythmical"—what a "rhythmical phrase" is I do not know.)

Later I shall engage Wright more fully, but for now I wish to trace what might be called the phrasalist strain in prosodic criticism. While it has certainly shown flaws and limitations, and may seem to include among its representatives one or two cranks or extremists, it has at least provided us with suggestions for making our way out of the morass of forced readings and mechanical analyses that traditional prosodic thought has brought us to. Also, it has planted the seeds for a common approach to both metrical verse and free verse. Phrasalism has grasped, however imperfectly, that we experience a line of any sort of verse in a way that registers word integrity and phrasal boundaries, rather than apprehending that line through a grid that often eliminates both.

Before sketching the phrasalist heritage and attempting to extend it, I should take some account of Donald Wesling's notable book, *The New Poetries: Poetic Form since Coleridge and Wordsworth* (1985), so as to avoid possible confusion about my use of "phrasal" or "phrasalism." Wesling, quarreling with Karl Shapiro's characterization of prosodic theory as exhibiting two "major traditions," stress prosody and temporal prosody, and a third division that combines the two, offers a scheme of his own. Here we find a categorization of prosodic theories in the years 1885–1910 under the respective headings of foot verse, syllable verse, and phrasal verse. Wesling defines the "attributes" of the last category as "optional stress; accentual; assimilating poetry toward speech; on the rise as sprung rhythm and free verse from 1855 to 1910."[3] So Wesling, at least initially, periodizes "phrasal verse." Eventually, his examples of such verse will extend beyond his original terminus, for he goes on to say that "phrasal verse . . . has made itself the major alternative way of writing [since 1910]."[4] In his own way, then, Wesling, like Wright, is linking phrasalism to free verse.

But it should be pointed out that Wesling has given the term "phrasal" a narrower application than his source for it, Josephine

Miles. She says that "Phrasal poems, and phrasal eras . . . emphasize line-by-line progression, and cumulative participial modification in description and invocation without stress on external
rhyming or grouping."[5] Notice that rather than identifying phrasal
poetry either with the 1885–1910 period that is Wesling's original
focus, or with the modern period, his later focus, Miles speaks of
"phrasal eras" and, in fact, sees "the adjectival phrasal mode" as
increasing in the period from Spenser to Thomson.[6] What I would
like to do is disengage the terms "phrasal" or "phrasalism" from
any specific period application. George Wright himself has said
"All poets compose in phrases *as well as* in lines."[7] Keeping that
elemental fact steadily in view can yield fruitful facts about the
sound patterns of poetry in all eras. It is an elemental fact because
we speak in phrases. The speech stream is not made up of a series
of individual words, each an entity unto itself, but of uneven *clusterings* of words. It is such clusterings that should be at the heart of
prosodic analysis. (Here, as in my insistence on honoring ordinary
lexical stress patterns, I am assuming that poetry is rooted in
speech—*pace* the currently fashionable preoccupation with a textuality removed from voice; see my Epilogue.)

If, as pointed out in Chapter 2, the English pedigree of traditional
accentual-syllabic scansion is shorter than many people might realize, that of phrasalism (or something like it) as an aspect of prosodic
theory appears to be a good deal longer than Wright believes. The
roots of phrasalism can be traced well back before the age of free
verse, as far back, in fact, as the late sixteenth century, the very
period alleged by John Thompson to be the one in which we find
the "founding" of English meter. O. B. Hardison, noting that the
Latin term for figures that shape syntax is *constructio,* claims that
classical and Romance-language prosody emphasized construction, and that this influenced English prosody: "Testimony on the
priority of syntactic rhythms to meter in verse is given by
sixteenth-century grammarians who observe that only schoolchildren read poems in a way that gives precedence to meter. Experienced readers emphasize meaning—in other words, their
meaning is shaped by the construction."[8] Other remarks of Hardison, made in commenting on two modern prosodists, David Crystal
and D. W. Harding, indicate that the phrasal conception of poetry
has applications extending even further back than the sixteenth
century. Hardison says that

> to argue as they do, that the important rhythms of English verse are
> not metrical but phrasal is to argue that the models provided by the

theories of construction and of syllabic prosody are at least as helpful in explaining English verse as the models provided by accentual prosody. Whatever the relevance of this position to English verse after Milton, it accords well with the shaping influence of French and Italian verse on English verse from Chaucer to Milton and also with the powerful upsurge of interest in ancient grammar and prosody at the beginning of the sixteenth century.[9]

According to Hardison, then, a very large stretch of our poetry prior to the modern period has been touched by the concept of phrasalism or something related to it. He is not the first to take this position. The nineteenth-century prosodist Edwin Guest attempted to root phrasalism in the very beginnings of English poetry. Taking Anglo-Saxon verse as his point of departure, Guest attempted to apply the "sections" or syllable groups he found there to the poetry that came afterward, finding those groups, not feet, the basis of meter in English. (It is not too much to say and not surprising that Saintsbury's foot-enthralled *History of English Prosody* takes Guest's *History of English Rhythms* as its antagonist.) In another work of the nineteenth century, hence well before the "age of free verse," Shadworth Hodgson took partial exception to Guest, but accepted his idea of sections, and, setting aside feet, declared that English meters "aim at a response of phrase to phrase, and sound to sound. . . ."[10]

Though it has had mostly a marginal status, we can trace a line of phrasalist thought from early on in this century. Mark Liddell, writing in 1902, dismissed the notion of feet, and spoke promisingly of "thought-movements" and "rhythm-waves," but these conceptions never became clear enough to threaten the system of meter he was trying to obliterate, let alone approach the "science" of verse be aspired to.[11] Cary Jacob, in a work published in 1918, made much of "the phrase" as the rhythmical unit in poetry. It could consist of a single word or a group of words "belonging together in thought," uttered "in a single exhalation," and marked on either side by a pause.[12] But this approach, commendable in itself, was unfortunately so handled by him as to dissolve the line as a significant unit, and to tie the phrase to an isochronous scheme. Three years after Jacob, Ezra Pound issued some advice to poets that included this directive: "Don't chop your stuff into separate *iambs*."[13] Five years later, in 1918, he listed as one of the principles he had agreed on with H. D. and Richard Aldington in 1912: "As regarding rhythm: to compose in the sequence of the musical phrase, not in sequence of a metronome."[14] This might be called

the most famous, perhaps the only famous, phrasalist statement
we have, but while Pound may have put it into practice, he did not
really expand in his critical prose on what he meant by it, and,
from my perspective, the linking of verbal phrases to music is
undesirable.

George R. Stewart, a timer, attempted in a book published in
1930 to take account of a poem's "phrases," though some of the
ones that emerged from his scansions seem questionable. Defining
a phrase as "composed of the smallest possible unit of pronunciation in actual speech, *i.e.*, metrically speaking, of the syllables
grouping themselves about a single stress,"[15] he gives us the following rendering of the opening line of Thomas Gray's "Elegy Written
in a Country Churchyard":

The curfew—tolls—the knell—of parting—day.[16]

Apart from offering us such truncated "phrases," Stewart could
not completely sever allegiance to the concept of the foot, though
he provides us with plenty of ammunition for questioning its
usefulness.

One phrasalist that Wright singles out, James G. Southworth,
writing in the 1950s and 1960s, was antagonistic to foot-based prosody as it was applied to Chaucer, and stressed the importance of
the virgule (/) in medieval manuscripts and those of Wyatt: "its
purpose was to indicate the 'sectional pause,' that is, a grouping of
syllables other than those defined by the foot.[17] Another phrasalist
(named as such by Wright), Ian Robinson, has told us of Southworth's liking for the term "the goddam iamb."[18] Robinson himself
has said "I do not think one can escape the conclusion that Chaucer's lines were thought in his own day and later to move in half-
lines as well as feet" (p. 41). This in itself would appear to be a
position tolerable to Wright, but Robinson, after noting that "The
half-line is the same as the syntactic phrase," adds "It seems true
that the best way of taking quite a number of effective lines in
Chaucer is to follow the half-line rhythms and forget any possible
feet altogether" (p. 155). Not the most consistent of prosodists,
Robinson backs off somewhat from this, but then goes on to take
an arresting stance that he does not qualify, one that marks him
as a phrasalist of phrasalists. He begins by saying that "The great
break in English poetic history comes not after Chaucer's death
but after Wyatt's" (p. 236). Taking note of John Thompson, who
spoke, to general acclaim, of the sixteenth century as the "found-

ing" period of English meter, Robinson sees it more as a time of dearth than birth:

> the rhythmic revolution after Wyatt virtually killed English poetry for fifty years. It was not until the new metres were forced to make some compliance with speech, not, that is, until the reintroduction—above all in Shakespeare's blank verse—of something akin to the phrasal element of Chaucer's metre, that there were again real poets in the land (p. 237).[19]

This is of course an overstatement, perhaps intended as a deliberate counterweight to the general celebration of Elizabethan lyric poetry, but it makes for a healthy reminder of the mechanical movement of much of that poetry, as in the case of George Gascoigne, the man whose *prose* Thompson relies on so heavily in advancing his thesis. Interestingly enough, Catherine Ing, who finds Gascoigne confused in his definitions, has insisted on thinking of Elizabethan lyrics as being composed in "phrases and lines rather than in . . . feet."[20] But her particular form of phrasalism is questionable, in my view, because of her apparent agreement with the notion she attributes to the Elizabethans, namely, that poetry is temporally ordered.

Other commentators who come under the phrasalist heading include John Nist, cited early in my study. An implacable enemy of foot-centered prosody, he rightly insists that "word groups . . . are the basic building blocks of English rhythm," and he provides a list of the forms such groups can take.[21] He defines these groups as lying between "major junctures," which are of two classes, the first optional and not requiring punctuation, the second obligatory and needing punctuation. (It has been pointed out that the word "juncture," a term from linguistics, would be better labeled "disjuncture," since it marks a point of separation, or better, a boundary.) "Both classes of major juncture . . . may occur at the termini of words or word groups that carry *maximum* stress, and they may occur at no other places within the syntax" (p. 76). Word groups can be divided into two basic types. The first is the "Endocentric," consisting of noun groups, verb groups, modifier groups, verbal [sic] groups, and conjunctional groups. The second sort of group is the "Exocentric," consisting of subject-predicate groups and prepositional groups. Terminal junctures are dictated by the "larger groups" (e.g., a prepositional group that contains a noun group would be marked by a terminal juncture) and these junctures "determine the cadences," with a cadence being defined as *"that rhyth-*

*mical pattern or accentual collocation which occurs between two
actualized major junctures"* (pp. 76–77; italics in original). In examining texts, Nist visually highlights their division into groups
through listing those groups vertically, one to a line.

There are several difficulties with Nist's approach. It is not clear
just what the distinction is between a "verb group" and a "verbal
group." Nor is it clear what the Exocentric groups have in common
that sets them apart from the Endocentric groups. Also, and this
is the most serious deficiency, having broken his chosen texts into
groups, Nist is somewhat sketchy and impressionistic in his analyses of how the resulting configurations function (for one thing he
does not point out the effects of their distribution of accents).[22] So
he proves to be stronger on the attack than in the exposition of
his alternative to using a metrical grid. Nevertheless, his intuition
that dividing a line into groups is more valid than its division into
feet, and his emphasizing the "variety" when he invokes the much-
used prosodic formula of variety-within-uniformity (p. 77), provides, as I eventually hope to show, a very useful direction for
prosody. Unfortunately, Nist's article, published in 1964, seems
not to have registered on the general prosodic consciousness (any
more than has his valuable essay applying what linguists call "distinctive features" of speech to poetry's sound patterns).[23]

But we do get D. W. Harding pointing out in 1976 that "The
sequence of strongly- and lightly-stressed syllables may be the
same in two lines and yet the rhythms be totally different because
the sense produces different groupings and therefore different
points of pause."[24] A year later Daniel Laferrière maintains that
"enough evidence is in to show us that the perception and/or production of normal spoken language involves rhythmic groups, and
it is therefore the business of metricists to somehow relate these
groups to metrical groups. . . ."[25] Attridge's *The Rhythms of English Poetry* (1982) acknowledges that "it is at the level of phrases
and sentences that we respond to the rhythms of poetry. . . ."[26]
Moreover, during the course of the last two decades we have seen
emerge, in addition to the passing remarks I have cited, approaches
bearing some similarity to Nist's focus on groupings, if not always
with his radical dismissal of the foot.

Charles L. Stevenson, cited earlier in the book, can be regarded
as a phrasalist, but one who assumes something of a fence-sitting
position with respect to the traditional concept of meter. He sees
himself as a follower of George Stewart in asking us to consider
"phrase-units," which "can be dissociated from feet and connected
with syllables that are variously grouped around metrical

stresses."[27] Stevenson defines a phrase-unit as "a minimally small group of consecutive syllables that 'want' to stay together, or else a single metrically stressed syllable that 'wants' to stay somewhat by itself" (p. 339). Stevenson is certainly on the right track here. His talking of syllables "wanting" to stay together can be seen as an intuitive registration of our tendency to group syllables when we speak, such groupings marked by the pauses spoken of in the preceding chapter. However, even though he rejects the foot, I see his invoking of a "metrically stressed" syllable keeping him tied to the traditionalist position he is supposedly avoiding, since in my view a syllable is stressed out of lexical, semantic, rhetorical, or phonological considerations, and not to maintain a "metrical" pattern, though its conformance to such a pattern may *follow* or attend. From this perspective, Stevenson is unduly solicitous of the traditional when he assures us that phrase units can greatly contribute to verse "without disturbing its recurrent metrical stresses," those stressees that are important in giving verse its "uniformity" (pp. 340, 343). Also, Stevenson's focus on the phrase as a "minimally small group," which appears to be an adaptation of Stewart's "smallest possible unit," can get him into a position that is not significantly different from that of the foot-bound prosodist. Here is his scansion and grouping of a line from *The Rape of the Lock* (each "group" is marked by an underline bracket):

The hungry, judges, soon, the sentence, sign . . . . .

He says:

> . . . in "The hungry" the article wants to stay with the noun, and the second syllable of the noun wants to stay with its first syllable [*sic*— in both cases where he says "noun" he must mean "adjective"]. And in "judges" the second syllable, once again, wants to stay with the first syllable. So these become the first and second phrase-units of the example. To a lesser extent, of course, all five of the syllables in "The hungry judges" want to stay together; but these syllables do not constitute a group that is minimally small, so for the purpose of obtaining phrase-units they must be subdivided after "hungry," where the want in question is least urgent (pp. 339–40).

What Stevenson offers us is certainly better than the results of foot scansion (The hung|ry jud|ges, etc.). But the separation of "judges" from the two words that precede it seems arbitrary, investing the "minimally small" with too much importance, the tail of the measuring unit wagging the dog of what is being measured.

Still, Stevenson's thinking in terms of entities that approach being phrases, even if they do not always make it to that status, serves as a valuable model, particularly since he is willing to extend his bracketing procedures to bring some of the phrase units together, as in "The hungry judges" (p. 340).

Publishing about the same time as Stevenson, and showing an awareness of the work of Jacob and Stewart, Roger Mitchell also falls into what I am calling the phrasalist tradition. In one essay, he considers the possibility of establishing a prosody for Whitman. While doing so, he attempts to effect a kind of bridge between what poets like Pope and Robinson do with their accentual-syllabic (and rhymed) verse and what Whitman does with his poetry. He initiates this by dividing up a set of consecutive lines of Pope into what he calls their "rhetorical" groups, counting and comparing the resulting numbers of groups per line, and commenting on their significance. The passage in question is from the "Second Pastoral":

> Where-e'er you walk,// cool Gales shall fan the Glade,
> Trees,// where you sit,// shall crowd into a Shade,
> Where-e'er you tread,// the blushing Flow'rs shall rise,
> And all things flourish where you turn your Eyes.

Mitchell says:

> The pattern of groups/line is: 2-3-2-1. This is a rhythmic parallel to the emotion of the speaker whose agitation over the nymph rises in the second line and then slowly disappears as his conviction takes stronger hold of him.[28]

Mitchell's groupings, as opposed to Stevenson's, are unexceptionable, their termini logically located, adhering tightly to the division points created by the punctuation. Still, his commentary here seems unpersuasive to me, crudely dependent on a "rising-falling" model of line movement.[29]

Working with Mitchell's divisions, I would say this about the Pope excerpt: The first and third lines are, in group or phrasal terms, something like fraternal twins, with the four-syllable—six-syllable composition of each reinforcing the elements that link them, namely, the anaphora of Where-e'er you walk—Where-e'er you tread, and the cause-effect structuring of the sense of each line. Lines 2 and 4 stand apart from the others, in opposed ways. Line 2, refusing, so to speak, to conform to the smooth cause-effect sequence found in lines 1 and 3, is initially choppy, a quality created by the two caesuras, their presence marking the obtrusive thrust of the "where you sit" phrase. Unlike Mitchell, I do not see line 2's phrasal organization as indicative of the speaker's rising agitation, but of something quite different, a posture that is at once genuinely complimentary and playful, producing a marvelous picture of trees responding to the presence of the "you" by bestirring themselves, pressing together to create a shady shelter—the "agitation" is all theirs. Also, the line's initial impedance by the two commas helps create, through contrast, a sense of quickening movement through the rest of the line, appropriate to the intense, if fanciful, action it describes: "shall crowd into a shade." Line 4 stands apart from all the others in its one-phrase construction, which undergirds its sweeping claim. That is, the all-encompassing effect of the nymph on her surroundings is appropriately expressed in an unchecked flow of words.[30]

In extending his grouping method to Whitman, Mitchell counts the number of speech stresses per group, and pays attention as well to group size. On the basis of his approach he speaks of "rhythmical variations" and their expressive function, and points to "tension" between the number of groups in a line and their respective sizes. He sees the "parabola" as "perhaps the commonest rhythmic feature of Whitman's poetry," by which he means an arithmetical patterning that expands and contracts, with the numbers referring to the stresses per line or number of groups per line (1609–10).

These notions come into play in his consideration of the first stanza in Section XII of "When Lilacs Last in the Dooryard Bloom'd," which he scans as follows:

Lo,// body and soul—// this land
My own Manhattan with spires,// and the sparkling and hurrying
    tides,// and the ships,
The varied and ample land,// the South and the North
    in the light,// Ohio's shores and flashing Missouri,
And ever the far-spreading prairies covered with grass
    and corn.

Mitchell comments that the last line is a deviant (having only one group while the others have three). This deviation helps give that line, focused on the prairie, importance. He also notes that

> As the groups/line tapers off at the end, the size of the groups expands irregularly though perceptibly throughout the stanza. . . . The group size pattern pulls against the groups/line pattern, allowing the poet both to expand his thought emotionally out toward the vision of the prairies, which are themselves "far-reaching," and to hone the thrust of his poem downward to the single point made in the isolated last group.

In terms of the speech stresses per line he finds a parabola pattern, which, he claims, "helps to control the emotion implicit in the expanding group size pattern" (p. 1609).

Here, too, I would take exception, at least partially, to Mitchell's reading. While I think he has nicely characterized the proportions of the passage, and is right in seeing the last line's use of a single large group as connected with a sense of expansion, I cannot go along with his formulation of the last line's effect. Mitchell apparently wants to find expansion and intensity at the same time, but does a focus on "far-spreading prairies" constitute a *honing* to a *point?* Nor do I see how the parabolic pattern helps control a rising emotion. The unbroken expanse of the last line does not suggest to me a reining-in of either scope or feeling.

But there are larger grounds for quarreling with Mitchell, valuable though his thinking in terms of groups may be. Apart from his relinquishing accentual-syllabic verse to the traditional concept of meter, he sets up criteria for "a genuine prosody" that appear to be very much conditioned by that concept. Thus, he tells us that a prosody must be "*continuous* and *whole,*" with this feature making for a poem's unity (p. 1606; italics in original).[31] It seems to me that standing behind this formulation is the bad old notion of the foot. As I have indicated earlier, metrical feet (by hook or by crook) can be made to appear *continuously* present. That is a good deal of their appeal; few other things can be. Therefore it is not surprising to find Mitchell concluding that, while Whitman "has taken significant steps toward devising [a prosody]," he falls short. A prosody should be flexible, but Whitman's is apparently too flexible (pp. 1610–11). While Mitchell shows a pleasing frankness in admitting that "there are a number of poems or parts of poems which are undoubtedly among Whitman's best that cannot be adequately measured by the theories I propose" (p. 1611), he unfortunately goes on to say of the wonderful opening lines of "Out of the Cradle Endlessly Rocking" that "Whitman's rhythmical effects in this stanza are fragmented and isolated within the stanza," that is, the first six lines are effective, the remaining sixteen something of a let-down into "the simple anaphora for which [Whitman] is known" (1612). Somehow the prosodist's confessed limitations have modulated into a defect of the poet. Not only does the opening stanza of "Out of the Cradle" fail to come up to snuff for Mitchell, but so does the last section of *Song of Myself*—there "Whitman was unable to achieve a unified prosodic effect," though Mitchell finds that section "magnificent" (p. 1612). What we have here is an illuminating case of a critic caught between his authentic response to a piece of verse not amenable to foot-analysis and his having been conditioned to think in terms of that analysis, even as he strives to get beyond it. Under these circumstances Whitman cannot do anything but receive a mixed review, and the prosodist cannot do anything but devise a scheme that, as he himself admits, comes up short in describing Whitman's rhythmic effects.

In a second essay, "Toward a System of Grammatical Scansion," a kind of logical extension of the essay on Whitman I have been discussing, Mitchell sets as his task the devising of a scansion that would "aid us enormously in making meaningful distinctions among the writers of nonmetrical verse."[32] He talks of "grammatical rhythm," and says that the key to it "is the group or, as it is sometimes called, the phrase" (p. 4). Providing a just, perceptive review of earlier prosodists who have thought in terms of groups, he comes to the conclusion, which I share, that "The most reliable way of identifying groups is through the pauses which sensible reading forces upon us" (p. 11). (It is because of their group-defining function that I paid the attention I did in the preceding chapter to the question of medial pauses.)

Up to this point, Mitchell has written a useful essay, but now his argument begins to blur. He first appears intent on drawing a distinction between end-stopped verse and run-on verse (confusingly identifying the first with grammatical English, the second with nongrammatical English—in general, Mitchell's use of "grammatical" in the essay is unfortunate). But having tried to establish a difference, he works around to finding common ground between the two: "Usually, the poet pays particular attention to the line ending in run-on verse, using it as a point of rhetorical as opposed to grammatical clarity and emphasis, thereby preserving most of the traditional sense of pause associated with the line-ending in end-stopped verse" (p. 14).

Coming rather belatedly to his chief task, he tells us that "A system of grammatical scansion" would require "A means of defining the varied nature of caesuras and line breaks." What this boils down to is setting up a scale of four degrees of pause, the first a "minimal juncture," the last a full stop, with the second and third being of an intermediate but otherwise undefined nature. "Grammatical scansion" would further require "A system for identifying the type of grammatical group created by the caesuras" (p. 18). We might see this as a more refined version of the scheme Mitchell offered in his piece on Whitman. Here, rather than simply addressing the number and size of groups that verse lines can be broken down to, Mitchell wishes to distinguish, in a manner reminiscent of Nist, between *kinds* of groups. His scheme here starts with a "group" consisting of a sentence, then moves down through groups designated respectively as clausal, subclausal (there are two classes of these), phrasal, and subphrasal.

While he began his essay by indicating that grammatical scansion would be very helpful "in making meaningful distinctions among the writers of nonmetrical verse," the first applications of his scheme are to passages by Dryden and Pope, respectively. Only then does he turn to a discussion of poems by Whitman, Williams, and Lawrence. In all cases, he uses his system of grammatical scansion in an attempt to register differences among the poets. While an approach that is applicable to formal as well as nonmetrical poetry is highly desirable (it is just such an approach that I am intent on working out), the results of Mitchell's scansions are somewhat flat. He points only once and briefly to a tonal effect created by a particular sort of pause, and, more importantly, does not deal at all with such expressive effects as might be generated by the use of different kinds of groups and their combinations. The group hierarchy would seem to furnish the basis for only a sort of bloodless taxonomy in sorting out the work of different poets, Mitchell being content to say, for example, that Pope shows more variety than Dryden in his choice of group sizes and arrangements.

In his concluding remarks, Mitchell himself says that his system suffers from "considerable" limitations, that, among other things, "the grammatical categories don't seem fine enough" (p. 27). The problem may not be lack of fineness, but Mitchell's failure to do enough with those categories—in his hands they lack sufficient point. Also, whereas he was too much under the influence of traditional prosody in his essay on Whitman, he seems here so wary of reverting "to artificial groups similar to the foot" (p. 19) that he foregoes dealing with stress entirely. But his work has been valuable because his analyses have kept alive the focus on groups, because the groups he points to are authentic assemblages, and because he takes pauses seriously.

Richard Cureton's insistent emphasis on "Raising Phrasing," that is, giving it greater weight in our prosodic theorizing and analyses, lends his work considerable interest for those who would go beyond foot-based prosody.[33] In an earlier chapter I tried to demonstrate how he was still under the influence of that prosody. This shows up, for example, at the level of "Metrical Realization" in his "multilevel" approach to rhythm. Here, once again, is how he depicts such realization in examining the last line of Stevens's "Sunday Morning"—the brackets indicate the way he breaks up the line:

[Dówn wărd] [tŏ dárk] [něss ŏn] [ĕx ténd] [ĕd wíngs][34]

As is so frequently the case, this sort of a representation seems to correspond more to a series of hiccups (e.g., [ness on]) than to a flow of words, and has nothing of interest to tell us. However, Cureton, while all too ready to retain the notion of foot-based meter, is very much a phrasalist, and the most considerable one of all those metrists who can be subsumed under that label.

In his approach to rhythm he uses various categories, or levels, that he dubs "Rhythm Phrases," "Tone Units," and "Larger Phrasing." In the next chapter I shall cite what he does with the line from Stevens at the level of "Tone Units," which seems to me to be the component of his elaborate scheme of rhythmic analysis that is most fruitful. Here I will confine myself to reporting his notion of "Rhythm Phrases" and commenting on his application of them to some passages of verse. Cureton characterizes such phrases as usually having "one stress per phrase" (this recalls Stewart and Stevenson) and "one to six or seven syllables—but deviations from this nor [sic] are possible" (Rhythm," p. 249). In my view, Cureton's rhythm phrases have, in practice, some of the arbitrariness of feet, as when, in analyzing the Whitman line, "One's self I sing, a simple separate person," he says that "a simple," "separate," and "person" each constitute a rhythm phrase ("Rhythm," p. 251).[35] That arbitrariness also manifests itself in his handling of lines 8 and 9 of Whitman's "A Noiseless Patient Spider." This is his breakdown of them:

Céasĕlĕssly/ mŭsíng,/ vénturĭng,/ thrówĭng,/ séekĭng/ thĕ sphéres/
        tŏ cŏnnéct thĕm,/
Tĭll thĕ brídge/ yŏu wĭll néed/ bĕ fórm'd,/ tĭll thĕ dúctĭle/
        ánchŏr hóld.

Cureton comments that

> In line 8, the stress-initial, one-word phrases ("venturing, throwing,")
> echo earlier rhythmic motifs in the poem in conveying the insistent,
> open-ended, "venturing" effort of the soul to connect with its surround-
> ings, while the solid, closed, stress-final rhythm phrases in line 9 dra-
> matically convey the completed connection (with the last three rhythm
> phrases contracting to a 'hold' on the last isolated monosyllable)
> ("Rhythm," p. 250).

In this reading Cureton allocates too many single words the status of "phrases," and there is certainly something arbitrary about
his groupings (or perhaps I should say his ungroupings) as in his
separating "seeking" from its object, "the spheres," and "ductile"
from the noun it modifies, "anchor." Still, he is onto something in
detecting a difference between the two lines in terms of where, in
their respective phrases, they place their stresses, a difference that
corresponds to the different kinds of action they describe. The
force of Cureton's remarks holds even if one is less ready than he
is to break up semantic units.

But, of more general importance, the valuable thing Cureton
has done is to have drawn our attention not simply to the phrasal
configuration *within* a line, but to the relationship between that
configuration and its counterpart in an *adjoining* line. It is true that
to the extent his "Definition of Rhythm" puts such relationships in
terms of "dilat[ing] and condens[ing] subjective time," he pulls us
back to isochrony-land.[36] But when he says simply that "One of
the major functions of rhythmic analysis is to allow us to compare
the appropriateness of rhythmic similarities and contrasts in various parts of a text," he is on firm ground.[37] His treatment of the
Whitman passage points up the usefulness of such comparison.

However, even when the principle is sound, a particular application of it may not be. A case in point is to be found in Cureton's
characterization of a stanza from Walter Savage Landor's "Rose
Aylmer," which reads:

> Rose Aylmer, whom these wakeful eyes
>   May weep, but never see,
> A night of memories and of sighs
>   I consecrate to thee.

Singling out "of memories" and "I consecrate," Cureton notes that
each may be described as

a four-syllable phrase with sharply falling, exclamatory energy contours . . . By their length and stress contours, these phrases are emphasized and linked (Both [*sic*], notice, have the same morphological structure as well: a monosyllabic function word followed by a trisyllabic content word).[38]

Apart from finding the initial characterization of the phrases ("sharply falling, exclamatory") somewhat overwrought, I think Cureton's case for an auditory parallel between them is dependent on our regarding them as phrases, aural-syntactic entities, to begin with, which I do not think they are, except technically. As with his treatment of the Whitman poem, he has been too ready to insert a phrasal terminus, though less radically here. What he sees, or rather hears, as phrases in the present case, I hear as fragments of larger groupings, "A night of memories" and "I consecrate to thee," respectively. I question whether the ear would catch the sound parallels between "of memories" and "I consecrate" as the lines flow past because I don't think either coheres into a gestalt. The parallels Cureton points to are undoubtedly there, but I see them as being detected not only after the fact (many sound patterns are so discovered, including some I point to) but, what is crucial, apart from the way the lines are really experienced. In general, Cureton's defining rhythm phrases so as to have them each built around a single stressed syllable makes for an artificial number of line constituents.

I have an additional quarrel with Cureton's reading of the "Rose Aylmer" passage, insofar as it illustrates his strong tendency to think of rhythm in terms of either that which rises or that which falls, whereas significant stress patterns may be detected in a poem, both individually and in the form of parallels, that are outside those categories, crucial as they are. (Risings and fallings of another order will, in fact, be attended to in the next chapter.) Still, whatever my differences with Cureton, I regard them, comparatively speaking, as a kind of family quarrel, a dispute between phrasalists, distinct in kind from the sorts of questionings I have brought to foot-based readings of lines, including Cureton's own.

What I think, then, is most usable in Cureton's elaborate approach to "rhythm," which, as indicated in an earlier chapter, explicitly takes on more than sonic effects, is the focus on groupings or phrases, both as they function in individual lines and between or among lines. In this he has, without mentioning him, reiterated and given somewhat more definition to the position taken by Nist. I count myself in the Nist-Cureton line, and in the readings I shall offer of individual texts, it is precisely a focus on groupings or phrases that will be at work. In the case of metrical poetry, these procedures will be used in combination with a *modified* form of traditional scansion.

My approach might best be demonstrated by first examining the foot-based reading of a Shakespeare sonnet that has been done by George Wright, he who has declared the limits of phrasalism, and then giving my version of how the poem moves. The work in question is Sonnet 116. After discussing Wright's findings, and his general stance on the status of phrases, I will formulate a revised notion of meter, or at least of iambic pentameter, and then offer a scansion of Sonnet 116 that will at once accommodate the revision and incorporate a phrasalist reading.

Before giving Wright's scansion it should be observed that he uses two kinds of marks to designate stress, the / for full stress, the \ for something less, *and that he habitually marks only feet that deviate from the iambic norm;* anything unmarked should be regarded as composed of one or more iambs. Wright's visual format may seem to put his scansion closer to my own than it actually is; we need to remember that every syllable in his scansion is part of a foot.

Here is his version of Sonnet 116, with "the normal iambic feet," as well as "some problematic phrases," temporarily "unmarked":

Let me | not to | the mar | riage of | true minds
Admit imped | iments, | love is not love
Which al | ters when | it alteration finds,
Or bends | with the | remo | ver to | remove.
O no, | it is | an ever fixed mark
That looks on tem | pests and | is never shaken;
It is | the star to every wand'ring bark,
Whose worth's unknown, | although | his height be taken.
Love's not Time's fool, though rosy lips and cheeks
Within his bending sickle's compass come,
Love al | ters not | with his | brief hours | and weeks,
But bears it out | even to | the edge of doom:
   If this be er | ror and | upon me proved,
      I never writ, nor no | man e | ver loved.

Wright finds an "unusually large number of pyrrhic feet," in the poem as a whole, which "indicates the quiet, confidential tones in which this sonnet, or most of it, is meant to be uttered."[39] He says that "The contrast between the muted pyrrhics and the positive iambs contribute to the impression of very clean and distinct assertions being made in the poem . . ."(p. 85).[40]

But as he goes on he indicates that there is something a bit disturbing or uncertain about the poem's assertions, and observes that "Let me not to" and "love is not love" are two of the poem's three phrases "whose meter is highly problematical . . . . The trochee-pyrrhic beginning [Lét mĕ | nŏt tŏ] is very unusual in Shakespeare's poems or in Elizabethan poetic practice generally" (p. 85).[41] For "love is not love" he offers three possible readings and then adds "If we were not constrained by the rhyme [sic— does he mean the rhythm?] to keep the last foot iambic, we might even imagine 'lóve ĭs nót lòve' . . . ." His comment is that "The difficulty of deciding among such alternatives may have the effect of casting some doubt on the speaker's certainty about love. Coming as it does just after he has refused to admit impediments, the phrase impedes the line" (pp. 85–86). (It will be shortly seen that I assent to the notion of the line showing impedance, but on entirely different grounds).

In addition to the problems of the first two lines, Wright gives special attention to line 9 and its assertion that "Love's not Time's fool," where "we may feel that the stresses could fall on any or all of the four syllables . . . . Whatever we decide, the tone here, as in line 2, can hardly escape sounding to some degree tormented . . . ." He contrasts the problematic areas with "the metrical ease of the rest of the poem," though he does note metrical alterations at the beginning of line 11 and in line 12 (the latter contains the poem's "only medial trochee")—the "Love alters not" statement is "faintly belied" by these alterations (p. 86).

I find that Wright's reading of the poem, though a very sensitive one, offers some difficulties in the way it handles both metrical characteristics and tone. First, I would make my standard objection that foot analysis generates some very peculiar entities, entities that we do not hear as such (in this case, for example, "pests and" in line 6 and "ror and" in line 13). I would also note that Wright's failure to assign a stress to "not" in the first line is decidedly odd, since this is a key term in the first quatrain of the sonnet, a quatrain whose strategy is to offer a definition of true love by negation. Moreover, the word "not" (along with other negatives) is a featured item of the poem, appearing no fewer than four times. Given Wright's reading of the poem's first two words as a trochee (Lét mĕ) did he reject a "not tŏ" reading because this would have made for a combination of two successive trochees, an opening he would have found even more uncomfortable than the trochee-pyrrhic pairing he does find? One can only speculate. At any rate "Lét mĕ nót" or "Lĕt m̆e nót" strikes me as making much more rhetorical sense than "Lét mĕ nŏt." Another place where I would differ with Wright's stress assignments is at the beginning of line 5, "O no," which he reads as just another iamb; I would read it as a spondee (and will shortly designate the effect of this reading). Yet another point at which Wright and I disagree is at the end of the sixth line, where he leaves "shaken" unmarked, and therefore, by his notational system, somehow to be taken as part of a normal iambic foot. (If he thinks of "is never shaken" as one of the poem's "problematical phases" he never discusses it as such.) A similar point could be made about his failure to mark "taken" at the end of the eighth line.

Differences of stress assignment aside, one might wish to ask, continuing the use of Wright's foot terminology, why a *contrast* of pyrrhics and iambs rather than a series of *consistent* iambs makes for the "clean and distinct assertions" about love that Wright finds. Moreover, after talking of such assertions, Wright has to backtrack and recognize problematical elements in the poem, some of them in lines—the first two—that offer precisely the combination of pyrrhics and iambs that he originally found generating those assertions. Also, while he rightly says that any or all of the syllables in "Love's not Time's fool" could be stressed, his layout of the poem's scansion blandly presents these syllables as composed of two iambs.

I should like now to offer a "phrasalist" reading of the poem. But before I do, it will be necessary to suggest a reformulation of "iambic pentameter," the mode of the sonnets, as of so much poetry in English. (I will retain the term for just a bit.) This reformulation derives from my characterization of that meter in Chapter 2, and is less an abstract paradigm or prescription than a description of poetic practice. "Iambic pentameter" is a form that commits itself fairly strictly to generating ten syllables per line, though lines of nine or eleven syllables should not astonish us.[42] (Where appropriate, allowance is to be made for the convention of syllable elision.) Also, "iambic pentameter" allocates stresses to *four or five* of the ten syllables. This adjustment of the usual definition, slight as it appears to be, immediately renders many lines, hitherto "variations," as simply part of the norm, not calling for special attention *per se*. The metrical "system" is thus being conceived of in a significantly loosened way.[43]

I would further define "iambic pentameter" as normally starting a line with an unstressed syllable, and, again normally, as using at least one such syllable to separate stressed syllables. In reading any given line, words of one syllable are assigned a stress or not in accordance with rhetorical and semantic considerations, those of two or more syllables are accorded the "natural emphasis" discussed in Chapter 5. Deviations from the norm as hitherto defined are to be examined for *possible* expressive significance. The foot as an a priori conception is simply dropped. (I should add that with my approach it is entirely possible for any line or set of lines to fall into a series of what have been called "feet," though I would eschew the term; the crucial point is that scansion would not begin by *assuming* the existence of such entities, or by conducting an eager, reifying hunt for them, and would not find it necessary to treat them, should they appear, as significant units in themselves. A wielding of Occam's razor simply slices such entities away.)[44] In light of eliminating the foot, I would re-christen "iambic pentameter" simply as "decasyllabic verse."

Implicit in all that I've been saying is the assumption made explicit in the preceding chapter, namely, that the line be regarded as the essential unit of the poem. My procedure calls for taking each such unit and dividing it into its phrasal constituents, whose terminuses might be thought of as often, if not inevitably, marked by pauses, however slight, with line-ending always followed by a pause. There would then take place the marking of the stressed syllables in each line as they are generated by ordinary pronunciation, as well as by rhetorical and semantic considerations. In the case of metrical verse, say "iambic pentameter," or decasyllabic verse, we would compare each line's pattern of stress distribution with the metrical paradigm's distribution norm, looking for possibly significant deviations. The next step would be to consider how the phrases of a given line compare with each other in terms of their respective lengths and stress distributions, and how they compare on those same grounds with phrases in adjoining lines. Here, we would be looking for structural parallels and contrasts that might be related to expressive effects.

Before moving on to specific applications of the proposed procedure, it is time to confront a question I have thus far skirted: What is a "phrase"? It is a term often taken for granted or defined in the most general sort of way, as in a recent work on grammar: "A combination of words that constitutes a unit of the sentence."[45] This does not take us very far, begging as it does the question "what is a unit?" (Is Cureton's "rhythm phrase" truly a "unit?" Not always, in my view, as I have already indicated.) Rather than starting from scratch to attempt a definition that is at once abstract enough to be sufficiently inclusive and concrete enough to be useful, perhaps we could flesh out the notion of "phrase" by having it designate any one of a series of word combinations that have been thought of by grammarians or linguists as constituting meaningful clusterings in treating the language at large (that language is my point of reference here as in the matter of assigning stresses). Transformational grammar offers us a handful of such combinations: noun phrase, verb phrase, prepositional phrase, adjectival (a structure that functions as the modifier of a noun), and adverbial (a structure that functions as the modifier of a verb). These will cover a lot of ground, but in a given instance may not be adequate or may offer some difficulty (I leave the illustration of this to the next chapter). Expanding the list, I would add entities that have traditionally been set off from phrases, namely, clauses, and here we might follow the traditional classification of these into independent and dependent, with a relative clause being a specific instance of the latter. The point of all this is not to come up with a taxonomy for its own sake, but simply to indicate that there are a number of standard ways of grouping words when we analyze language in general, and that a given poem can be fruitfully thought of as made up of such groupings. The names of the groupings are not essential, but the fact that there are such groupings is. Also, I am assuming that such groupings are experienced as such when we read.[46]

With this prologue out of the way, here is my scansion of Sonnet 116 with only stressed syllables marked (intralinear phrasal divisions have been indicated by the use of extra spaces).

> Let me not   to the marriage   of true minds
> Admit impediments.   Love is not love
> Which alters   when it   alteration finds,
> Or bends   with the remover   to remove.
> Oh no!   it is an ever fixed mark
> That looks on tempests   and is never shaken,
> It is the star to every wand'ring bark

Whose worth's unknown,   although his height be taken.
Love's not Time's fool,   though rosy lips and cheeks
Within his bending sickle's compass come.
Love alters not   with his brief hours and weeks,
But bears it out   even to the edge of doom.
   If this be error,   and upon me proved,
   I never writ,   nor no man ever loved.

Approaching the first lines in terms of the stress patterns that constitute variations from the iambic pentameter or, better, decasyllabic "norm," as I have earlier defined it, we observe that "true minds" stands out because it contains two adjacent stresses, half the line's total, with that half delivered at the last moment, so to speak. This highlighting is appropriate because it is the operation of such minds that the sonnet will focus on. We observe that there is another such variation, a pair of adjacent stresses on "not love," at precisely the corresponding point of line 2, that is, the closing of the line's terminal phrase. (I hasten to say that I recognize an alternative reading or "performance" of the line might render it as "love is not love.") The reading I have designated is closest to the one Wright could "even" imagine if we were not "constrained by the rhyme [rhythm?] to keep the last foot iambic." This second pairing, "not love," may be said to set up a counterforce to "true minds," the antagonistic relationship between the two sets of words brought out by the matching of their stress patterns and their corresponding line locations. The first two lines, then, in my reading, are in at least one respect metrical cousins, sonically and semantically tilted to the right.

If the first and second lines have a significant prosodic relationship to each other, so do the third and fourth, but in a fashion that is different and more delicate. Both the later lines may be regarded as consisting of three syntactic or phrasal units:

> Which alters   when it   alteration finds
> Or bends   with the remover   to remove.

That this is the case with line 4 does not, I think, need to be argued, but with line 3 some rationale for my analysis might be in order. The pause I have placed, in effect, after "it" is necessary because of the inverted syntax of the line ("it alteration finds," rather than "it finds alteration"); this pause enables us to take in and communicate the sense of the line. Another way of putting it is that the line produces a semantic hitch at the point where "it" meets up with "alteration," requiring a pause at an awkward place, after a pronoun functioning as a subject, which normally one would be inclined to join with its adjacent verb as soon as possible. (Here, it seems to me, is a real source of "tension," that is, between the way we would normally handle a pronoun-as-subject and the way we need to handle it here.) I go so far as to allocate a stress to "it," not to fill out a preconceived quota of stresses, but to aid the process of mastering the line's sense. (In doing this, incidentally, I find myself agreeing with and applying a principle set forth by Wright himself, namely, that "When syntactical inversion [so] requires [,] some unusual stress [may be placed] on a minor word to make the syntax clear" (p. 193).)[47]

The forced pause, so to speak, after "it" produces a movement in line 3 different from that in line 4, though the two lines are superficially similar, in that each, in my reading, is made up of three phrasal units. For unlike the "disturbed" effect of line 3, with its stressed and pause-marked "it," the units in line 4 and their accompanying pauses make for a flowing movement, for "natural" phrasing. In fact, that line, a variation from the iambic pentameter norm as I have defined it ("four or five stresses"), moves with decided ease and speed, partly due to its having only three stresses. The third and fourth lines, then, despite having the same number of phrases, are set off from each other in terms of their articulatory unfolding.

What is the significance of this in relation to their contents? That which I have called the hitch in line 3 might be said to register a sense of psychological disturbance on the part of the "love" that cannot transcend alteration when it meets up with change. The pause that I see at that point dramatizes a kind of repugnance, a distancing from the fact or alteration occurring outside oneself. On the other hand, the unopposed free-flowing movement of line 4 suggests the readiness with which false love itself changes when it encounters change. In short, the contrasting natures of the line movements are related to the semantic or tonal burdens of those lines.

In a sense, line 2—"Admit impediments. Love is not love"—is something of an oddball in relation to the others in the quatrain, not only (if one grants my breakup of line 3) in its possessing only two synactic units, but, more important, in its exhibiting a full stop in midline (a rare effect in the sonnets in general). This is another variation from a norm, but not the sort that foot-based prosody considers. One needs to ponder the significance of the poem allowing itself to be notably impeded, so to speak, just as it completes its declaration that it will admit no impediments. If there is a sense of "disturbance" in this line, a sense that the poem is questioning its own assertion, as Wright suggests, I believe it is in this full stop, or heavy pause, which renders the line problematical in a more acute way than does the metrical ambiguity he locates in the words following the stop. This is a case of a phrasal approach and a foot approach agreeing on an effect of a line but not on the means by which it is brought about.

As indicated earlier, the second quatrain, in my reading, begins not with an iamb, as Wright would have it, but with two successive stresses—Ó nó. This, of course, constitutes a variation from the iambic pentameter norm as I have defined that norm: stresses are usually separated by at least one unstressed syllable. But more than that, the *placement* of this variation *reverses* in two ways what is happening in the first quatrain. The beginning of the latter, if my reading is granted, is marked by two successive *unstressed* syllables—"Let me." Moreover, when the first quatrain allows itself the variation of two consecutive stresses, it places that variation at line's *end,* both with line 1 and line 2. The sound reversals I speak of correspond to the reversal of strategy the poem employs as it moves from the first to the second quatrain: it replaces attempting to define what love is not with an attempt to define what it is.

The whole "O no" line is of considerable sonic interest, though Wright would confine such interest to the portion of the line following "O no" (i.e., "it is an ever fixed mark"). For in his foot-based reading we have here a particular instance of a pattern whereby the poem's pyrrhic feet "help other phrases to stand out in bolder relief: 'it is' performs this service for the decisive iambs of 'an ever fixed mark'" (p. 85). I would say, rather, that after its opening two-stress phrase, marked off by a pause, the line delivers a second phrase, characterized by an initial run of three unstressed syllables—"it is an"—that is checked by coming up against the stressed first syllable of "ever." To put the matter slightly differently, the fifth line, in my reading, undergoes a kind of initial retardation and focusing, then a decided release as it passes through unstressed nondescript material, so to speak ("it is an"), before being checked and focused by "ever." That release gives particular force, by contrast, to the stressed syllable in "ever," and the configuration of that word is reinforced by the same configuration in the next word, "fixed" (which is, of course, pronounced as a disyllable). The stress parallelism of the "ever fixed" combination functions to give substance and solidity to the "mark" that concludes the line. Wright's reading would chop the two key words up—an ev | er fix | ed mark—and deny them their binding "trochaic" character, seeing them rather as part of a configuration of strongly marked iambs.

To sum up, Wright sees a march of feet in the line, all of them iambs except for one pyrrhic, with the words "ever fixed" fragmented by foot divisions. After finding an initial pairing of stresses in "O no!" my reading, respecting word integrity, sees "it is an ever fixed mark" as a single phrase composed of two distinctly different parts, the lightly uttered low-interest words of the first part—"it is an"—giving way to the forceful, crucial words of the second part—"ever fixed mark." There is some agreement between Wright and myself here: we both see a contrast in the line but disagree as to the contours of that contrast. Moreover, Wright is sharply different from me in flattening "O no" into just another iamb, not requiring comment, where I see it as a two-stress phrase calling attention to itself and distinctly set off from the rest of the line by a pause.

Wright does not say anything in particular about "That looks on tempests and is never shaken," and, as indicated earlier, does not even single out "shaken" as a "trochee." Read phrasally, the line splits neatly in two (I am assuming that "never" undergoes a standard contraction to a one-syllable word in order to preserve a ten-syllable line). This five-syllable, five-syllable structure, not usual in iambic pentameter, together with the presence of two stresses on either side of the mid line pause, as well as the symmetrical stress structures of the two respective terminal words—tempests, shaken—make for a sense of balance in the line, enhancing the effect of a love so stable that it cannot be moved by the most intense sort of disturbance. At the same time the relative positioning of stresses is not symmetrical, so one could see the line as slightly self-subverting.

Another line that Wright does not apparently regard as worthy of special comment is the tenth: "Within his bending sickle's compass come." This stands unmarked in his scansion, meaning that it is entirely regular, though he does say parenthetically that its "major words" are "trochaic" (p. 86). What Wright refers to in passing here, presumably because the trochaic words are absorbed into an iambic pattern for him, I regard as central to the line's effect. Joined here are three consecutive words—"bending sickle's compass"—that make up the heart of the single phrase the line consists of. Each term has a stressed-unstressed structure that, in my view, is *not* dissolved by some overriding "iambic" pattern. The single stressed syllable following on this "trochaic" trio of two-syllable words—come—can almost be said to create the effect of something truncated, or cut off. It is almost as if that fearsome sickle was doing its work at the end of the line, slicing away an unstressed syllable the ear has been prepared to hear by the repeating pattern of the three preceding words. Even if one does not wish to go that far, the three words joined by their stress pattern make for a decidedly intense effect.

Line 12—"But bears it out even to the edge of doom"—elicits from Wright the remark that its rhetorical climax "is signaled by the poem's only medial trochee" (p. 86); he is referring to what he reads as "éven tŏ" (p. 84). Such an analysis ignores what I regard as the strongly "trochaic" flavor of "bending sickle's compass" just two lines back, and indicates that we hear "even to" as a unit, which I say we do not. What I find of interest in this line is the speeded-up effect of "even to the edge" created in part by the contraction of "even" to "e'en" and in part by the two unstressed syllables that follow immediately. It is as though the quality of love the poem is attempting to define has not the slightest hesitation about moving to confront even the end of time. The speed of this line answers the speed of line 4—"Or bends with the remover to remove"—a line that depicts the action of inauthentic love.

There are some other differences between Wright's foot-based reading of Sonnet 116 and my own, but I hope I have said enough to indicate that a foot-free notion of meter, combined with a phrasal approach that keeps words and their groupings whole, has something to tell us about line movement that the traditional concept of meter does not, and operates, in my view, closer to our actual reading experience. Wright ostensibly makes a great deal of room for phrasing in his study of Shakespeare's verse, saying, as noted earlier, that his book rests on the belief that "there are always at least two structural orders simultaneously audible in iambic pentameter—the metrical and the phrasal . . . and their varied rhythmic interplay constitutes the great beauty of the form" (p. 12). But even though he entitles one of his chapters "The Play of Phrase and Line," and at its conclusion speaks of a "fourfold rhythm—of line, sentence, argumentative detail . . . and accumulating rhetorical impact," he tells us that at the heart of the "collective design" made up of these four elements is "the meter . . ." (p. 228). Others may come to regard feet "as intrusive markers," but not he. No matter how often the iambs might be intruded upon by midfoot pauses, no matter how often phrase boundaries might violate foot boundaries, Wright's claim is, as I pointed out in Chapter 3, that "The iambic body runs on, foot by foot . . . " (p. 213). It is meter, traditionally conceived, that engages his primary allegiance and that dominates his reading of Sonnet 116.[48]

I do not think my reading of the poem any poorer for ignoring its alleged feet. That reading is, to be sure, different from Wright's. It locates sonic evidence for the speaker's uncertainty in places that do not correspond to Wright's foot-based citations, which strike me as by and large forced. Also, my phrasalist reading points to effects that are not captured by Wright's approach and that he might well reject. The reader must decide for himself or herself which is the more persuasive account.[49]

I would like now to apply my phrasalist approach to specimens of free verse. While some prosodists, as indicated in Chapter 4, look at free verse through a metrical grid, here there will be no considerations of meter, even of the loosened sort I proposed earlier as a revision of the traditional notion of iambic pentameter. But, as with my handling of Sonnet 116, there *will* be a focus on the sonic structure of a poem's individual lines, broken up, where appropriate, into phrases, and a focus as well on the way a given line may compare with those adjacent or in close proximity to it.

The first free-verse text I wish to consider, a very short but very famous work, is one that in the form of its original printing encourages us to read it in a manner almost entirely like that I am advocating for all verse. Here it is, as Ezra Pound first presented it:

In a Station of the Metro

The apparition   of these faces   in the crowd:
Petals   on a wet, black   bough.[50]

One might reasonably assume that Pound's use of extra spacing is to be interpreted as a highlighting of the pausing attendant on the completion of a unit within a line. Granted this, if we except the separation between "black" and "bough," the layout here is identical to the one that would result from a phrasal reading of the poem, one that applied the rules of silent demibeat addition advanced by Elisabeth O. Selkirk—the words "apparition," "faces," and "Petals" each mark the end of a phrase, and in addition, fall under the category of "a word that is the head of a nonadjunct constituent," and so take on two extra demibeats (see chapter 5). Even without referring to Selkirk's rules, an ordinary breakdown of the lines into their grammatical units would come up with Pound's scheme, again with the exception of the separation of "black" and "bough."

Let me reproduce the poem again, this time with the stressed syllables marked, and with the original spacing kept except for the spacing between the final two words:

> The appari′tion of these fa′ces in the cro′wd:
> Pe′tals   on a we′t bla′ck bou′gh.

What can we say of the sonic configuration of the poem so displayed or conceived? The first line can be regarded as offering us an array of shrinking phrases, containing five, four, and three syllables, respectively. These diminishing packets of sound may be said to dramatize the term "apparition." Whatever it is we are looking at is melting away. Reinforcing the effect of insubstantiality is the fact that relatively few of the line's syllables are stressed. The second line may be described as, in one respect, continuing a pattern of the first, but also, and more prominently, sharply breaking with that line. The first phrase of the second line, a one-word, two-syllable affair—"Petals"—continues the pattern of phrasal shrinkage. At the same time it gives us its stress immediately, on the first syllable, as opposed to what might be called the deferred stresses of the first line's phrases. In addition, the next phrase of the second line expands decidedly, and has an abundance as opposed to a paucity of stresses in relation to its size. In overall terms, the first line gives us but three stressed syllables out of a total of twelve, the second four out of seven. The distinct differences in the packagings of sound respectively offered to us by the two lines corresponds to our moving from what seems insubstantial or questionable in the initial line, to the visual solidity in the second. The evidence of our ears is made to correspond to the evidence of our eyes, so to speak. As far as the pause that Pound inserted between "black" and "bough" is concerned, I can only conjecture that he did it for dramatic emphasis, for a last second suspension before the poem's terminal word clicked into place. But even with that additional pause, my observations on the different sound patternings of the two lines will hold.

As a longer specimen of free verse, I will take a poem mentioned in Chapter 3, Sylvia Plath's "Ariel." This, the reader may remember, had two of its stanzas reshuffled by Sandra Gilbert, so as to make them allegedly exhibit some sort of metrical pattern. The poem may be taken as the expression of an attempted escape from one's ordinary self, its fears and the claims on it of others, through an all-out commitment to furious motion, coming in the form of a horse ride.

Here is the poem:

> Stasis in darkness.
> Then the substanceless blue
> Pour of tor and distances.
>
> God's lioness,
> How one we grow,
> Pivot of heels and knees!—The furrow
>
> Splits and passes, sister to
> The brown arc
> Of the neck I cannot catch,
>
> Nigger-eye
> Berries cast dark
> Hooks—
>
> Black sweet blood mouthfuls,
> Shadows.
> Something else
>
> Hauls me through air—
> Thighs, hair;
> Flakes from my heels.
>
> White
> Godiva, I unpeel—
> Dead hands, dead stringencies.
>
> And now I
> Foam to wheat, a glitter of seas.
> The child's cry
>
> Melts in the wall.
> And I
> Am the arrow,
>
> The dew that flies
> Suicidal, at one with the drive
> Into the red
>
> Eye, the cauldron of morning.

I will attempt only a partial analysis, concentrating eventually on the stanzas rearranged by Gilbert.

Consider the first stanza:

> Stasis in darkness.
> Then the substanceless blue
> Pour of tor and distances.

What we have here are three lines, none of which need be broken down into phrases—each may be regarded as constituting a phrase to begin with. Taken together, these phrase-lines add up to two sentence fragments, the second considerably longer than the first, and in some sense working against it. The first fragment, line 1, has at its core the feeling of an oppressive fixedness; the line's sound patterning underscores this. Regard the fall of accents and the resulting structure.

$$\overset{/\ \ X\ \ \ X\ \ \ /\ \ \ \ X}{\text{Stasis in darkness}}$$

One way of describing what we have here is to say that we find an arrangement of syllables whose middle component is the un-stressed one-syllable "in" (it is the third in a series of five sylla-bles). "In" is the soft center of the line, surrounded, so to speak, in a symmetrical manner, that is, by a word on each side that has in common with the word on the opposite side not only that it is distinctly more imposing than "in," but that it is composed of two syllables, with the stress falling on the first syllable.[51] The effect of this symmetry, compounded by the period that appears virtually as soon as the poem has gotten started, is the sense of a distinctly stable state of affairs, one permeated by balance and fixity so to speak, and enforced by the absence of any verb. (This sense of the line will be somewhat qualified in the upcoming chapter, when we examine other aspects of its sonic nature.)

The function of the next two lines is to begin the welcome undo-ing of the stasis. They initially effect this by giving us a line that is not only not brought to the full arrest of the first, but that is strongly enjambed (an effect much favored in free verse). The ad-jective that ends the line, "blue," moves to join the noun the linea-tion has separated it from, "Pour." Moreover, the respective stress patterns of lines 2 and 3—

$$\overset{X\ \ \ X\ \ \ /\ \ \ \ X\ \ \ \ X\ \ \ \ \ /}{\text{Then the sub stanceless blue}}$$
$$\overset{/\ \ \ \ X\ \ /\ \ \ X\ \ \ /\ \ X\ \ \ X}{\text{Pour of tor and distances}}$$

have no manifest relation either to each other or to that of the
first line:

$$\overset{/}{\text{Sta}}\overset{\text{x}}{\text{sis}} \overset{\text{x}}{\text{in}} \overset{/}{\text{dark}}\overset{\text{x}}{\text{ness.}}$$

In the space of just three lines Plath has generated a strong sense
of stability and then its dissolution, moving from a condition of
being stuck to one of liquidity. (Even though, strictly speaking, we
no more have a verb in lines 2–3 than we did in line 1, we have
the feel of a verb in Plath's use of "pour.")[52]

Let us consider now the poem's closing lines, the very ones
tampered with by Sandra Gilbert. Here they are once again, in
their original format:

> And now I
> Foam to wheat, a glitter of seas.
> The child's cry
>
> Melts in the wall.
> And I
> Am the arrow,
>
> The dew that flies
> Suicidal, at one with the drive
> Into the red
>
> Eye, the cauldron of morning.

The first thing to be said, contra Gilbert, is: contemplate the
lines as they lie and do not attempt to rearrange them or squeeze
them into a metrical grid. The next thing is to note how Plath again
avails herself of what is so common in free verse, the willingness
to effect a severance through line ending of words otherwise tightly
bonded (a practice much abused in contemporary poetry but not
here). In two places where she does this—"And now I," "And
I,"—the first-person pronoun is hung out at the end of the line (an
effect decidedly vitiated by Gilbert's monkeying around). In my
reading, the "I" acquires prominence by this placement as well as
by attracting to itself a stress. Also, if we honor the principle of
line-terminal pausing, the "I" in both cases floats free for the moment of everything except its I-ness:

> And now I

> And I

At the same time each line calls for completion. So with each we get a sense of *precarious* self-containment. Plath's "I" is not, in the final analysis, gloriously separate in its glamorous rush toward freedom. It is bound and doomed, if only by its willed intensity. The pronoun "I" joins its verbs, has its sound echoed in "cry,"flies," and "Suicidal"—each of the relevant syllables receiving a stress. The sound of "I" is reembodied in a homonym, "Eye," and this time placed at the *beginning* of a line, made salient by that location, by receiving a stress, and by being momentarily isolated through the comma that follows immediately, which generates the equivalent of the line-ending pause attendant on each "I." This prominent repositioning of the *i* sound accords with the repositioning of the "I" or, we might say, with its *dual* position, that of powerful hurt-giver and powerless hurt-receiver, the two identities proving to be one and the same.[53]

The dramatization of oneness by the poem, its fusion of hurter and victim, observer and observee, male (arrow) and female (cauldron), is accomplished by the last-second generation of a one-line stanza. "Ariel," for all its irregular lines, for all its unpredictable expansions and contractions of those lines (an unpredictability that undergirds the I's sense of being in intense motion, in process, escaping a hated entanglement) has stuck to tercets. It now effects a radical variation (that dwarfs the sort of variations many prosodists are fond of locating in metrical verse, e.g., substitute "feet"), delivering just a single line. This is a piece of one-ness with a vengeance, a pattern Plath created for this particular occasion. In this line the ambitious, driving enterprise of the poem at once comes to a climax and collapses.

The line, considered phrasally, is decidedly lopsided in its proportions:

Eye, the cauldron of morning.

What might be called the one-word phrase, "Eye," is also just one syllable, and is followed by a phrase of six syllables. The effect of this on the line's movement is to provide a decided check early on, after only a single syllable has been uttered, and then, by contrast, a sense of release. But that release is only into a terminating phrase, the conclusion of the poem. The rush to freedom, the throwing off of restraints, enacts its own end, the line's progression embodying this theme.

I hope that these examples have demonstrated the usefulness of phrasalism, both with respect to "metrical" verse and free verse.

The analysis involved deals with what is palpably there, words in their usual pronunciations and combinations (at least within the lines), not forced into stress configurations to fit an a priori pattern, nor dismembered into foot divisions, nor disconnected from their semantic kin except insofar as line divisions may effect such severance. Foot-analysis, by comparison, appears perverse, at once breaking or overriding natural syntactic bindings within lines, and taking no account of syntactic fracturings that may be created by line endings. But the analysis offered here has focused largely, if not exclusively, on phenomena of stress. There is something else at work in the lines of poetry because there is something else at work in spoken language in general. It is to that something else that I now turn.

7

Tuning In: Towards Making a Place for
Intonation in Prosodic Analysis

INTONATION is an inherent and essential part of spoken language and, therefore, an inherent and essential part of poetry, insofar as we lift the words of verse off the page and breathe sound into them. To the extent that we do, intonation is inseparable from what has been a standard and central consideration in the analysis of a poem: its speaker's attitude toward his or her subject matter and/or toward the audience. As with speech in general, this attitude will be at least partly conveyed by the tone of voice the poem suggests it is employing, a tone that we therefore employ when we read the poem aloud (here again, of course, I am arguing for "performance"), a tone whose realization is largely a matter of intonation. The close connection between attitude and intonation is recognized in effect in the common use of "tone" to designate the former. Intonation, in poetry as in ordinary speech, can also mark focus or emphasis. If all this is agreed to, it must be conceded that the near-silence of prosodic studies on the matter of intonation amounts to a huge gap in our description and understanding of how poetry works, a gap not filled by the widespread, casual references to the "music" of verse.

Dwight Bolinger, an eminent linguist and the foremost American authority on intonation, once defined that subject as "the melodic line of speech, the rising and falling of the 'fundamental' or singing pitch of the voice. . . ."[1] Others have referred to intonation as "speech tunes" or "speech melody."[2] These formulations can be seen as extending into linguistics literary prosody's penchant for using musicalized terminology, a penchant that, while apparently inescapable, is more a tribute to music than an illumination of language.[3] Bolinger's acute sensitivity to the richly inflected ascents and descents of the human voice makes his use of such terminology understandable, but that vocabulary should probably

189

receive the same rebuke Seymour Chatman administered to its appearance in commentary on poetry. Chatman noted that "Intonation contours are not melodies, even though they are sometimes referred to as 'speech tunes.' They possess no exactness of pitch relation . . . or even simple tonality (in the sense of constancies of pitch)."[4] He also pointed out that "The pitch capacity of the speaking voice is very limited compared to that of the singing voice or musical instruments."[5]

An approach to intonation intent on avoiding the musical slant of Bolinger's definition, while appropriating one of its terms, might formulate that phenomenon as the series of changes in the fundamental frequency of an utterance, with "fundamental frequency" referring to the rate at which "'puffs'" of air (generated by vibration of the vocal chords) are emitted by operations of the larynx.[6] But this seems somewhat removed from ready application to the sonic analysis of poetry. It turns out that we can get help by turning to Bolinger himself. In *Intonation and its Parts,* Bolinger, more than thirty years after giving us his "musical" definition of intonation, once again equates intonation with "speech melody," pointing to the common element of pitch. But having said this he launches into a discussion that serves to drive speech and melody apart. He echoes Chatman's point about language's lack of true notes, which require pitch sustention; such notes in speech are the exception, not the rule. He observes that "For those who would like to see a close analogy between speech and music, the way to deal with this is through a rather sweeping idealization of certain critical points on a pitch curve as targets."[7] Such a view looks upon what happens between the targets as accidental and insignificant. This approach is tempting if only because it would make the notation of intonation an easy affair. But Bolinger rejects it. For *how* one gets from one note to another *is* important: "glides and jumps between levels are separately significant . . ." (p. 30). Bolinger does a good job of demonstrating this. While he does not relinquish the term "melody" (habits die hard, and the title of this very chapter has a punning musical component), he eventually produces a definition of intonation that retains only such linkage of speech to music as may inhere in the term they share, "pitch": intonation is "strictly the rise and fall of pitch as it occurs along the speech chain . . ." (p. 194).

Bolinger's attempt to cleave speech away from music is strikingly supported by evidence pertaining to the structure of our brains. Isamu Abe notes that "it turns out that the mechanism for perception of musical sounds is quite different from that for verbal sounds. A lesion of the left temporal lobe that destroys the ability to analyze phonemes leaves musical hearing undisturbed."[8] Unless one posits the notion that both lobes are simultaneously involved in the production and perception of speech, this seems like a definitive basis for separating spoken language and music. Such separation has consequences for poetics because an imputed connection between poetry and music has long served, at least intermittently, to blur the true nature, the language-specific characteristics of poetry's sounds.

In 1959, Edmund L. Epstein and Terence Hawkes wrote that "Pitch is still a mysterious element in prosody."[9] Not much has been done since that time to unveil the mystery, at least in discourse on poetry, thus extending a long tradition. Among the more than fifty headings and subheadings used by T. V. F. Brogan in his massive bibliography of writings on prosody, *English Versification, 1570–1980,* one looks in vain for the term "Intonation." (The same is true for the reader looking at the entries of the *Princeton Encyclopedia of Poetry and Poetics.*) The closest Brogan's table of contents comes to that word is "Pitch," and this rubric does not designate a category of literary prosody, but rather a branch of what Brogan has called "Linguistic Rhythm." Indeed, it turns out that the handful of items listed under "Pitch" were virtually all written by linguists. I am not pointing to a failure of taxonomic procedure or of data-gathering on Brogan's part—*English Versification* is as well-ordered and inclusive a work of scholarly labor as one could hope for from anyone with less than angelic powers. The paucity of items in it relating to intonation (and scattered under a variety of headings) simply tells us that of all the gallons of ink expended on literary prosodic analysis only a few drops have been employed to consider the matter of pitch patterns as one of some consequence. Brogan himself calls intonation "A subject widely important yet widely ignored."[10]

More will be said about this ignoring of intonation, but for now I wish to observe that to the extent that it *has* been engaged the results have not been very substantial. Consider for example Ronald Sutherland's attempt, in 1958, to apply the findings of structural linguistics to prosody by discussing Yeats's "After Long Silence." Sutherland's choice of poem was determined in part by its having been scanned in Brooks and Warren's *Understanding Poetry.* Their system, Sutherland says, "probably represents the peak of development in conventional metrics." Sutherland argues that the "prosodist's equipment" should be extended to include "linguistic information about pitch and juncture. . . ."[11] ("Juncture" may be thought of as a kind of pitch that marks a terminal or boundary-point in speech, and is associated with a pause.) But all Sutherland does, basically, is to reinforce what Brooks and Warren have said about Yeats's poems, plugging in phrases like "fading juncture" and "rising juncture" where they talk about a "heavy pause" or a "slight pause." He does register one slight disagreement with their reading, but taken as a whole, his piece is excessively deferential to them and to traditional prosody in general, his application of structural linguistics confined to terminological substitution. Yeats's poem does not receive more illumination by Sutherland than it did by Brooks and Warren. Equally disappointing is Seymour Chatman, in *A Theory of Meter*, who says that "No one as yet has used the Bolinger [pitch] accent analysis as a basis for metrical theory," and that his fifth chapter represents an attempt to do just that.[12] But on examination, we find that pitch figures only incidentally there, and eventually sinks out of sight, as Chatman works with his particular categorization of foot types, and not Bolinger's pitch-accent patterns.

J. Taglicht, drawing chiefly on the work of English linguists, considers intonation's capacity both to divide speech into segments and to highlight a part or parts of those segments. Curiously confining himself to specimens of decidedly minor verse, Taglicht delivers a series of observations of a minimal and purely formalist nature. He makes even less of a case than Sutherland for intonation having a significant role to play in poetry. Brogan rightly characterizes Taglicht's piece, "The Function of Intonation in English Verse," as "slender" (p. 139). On the other hand, Brogan calls Jan Mukarovsky's "Intonation as the Basic Factor of Poetry" an "important essay" (p. 679), but it is hard to see why. Showing a temperament opposite to the cautiousness of Sutherland or Taglicht, who favor a kind of plodding nuts-and-bolts approach, Mukarovsky indulges in a dubious theorizing that may well remind us of the Neoplatonic metrists referred to in Chapter 2, but he makes them look a little pale. He posits two intonational schemes that are simultaneously at work in verse and that may coincide from time to time: "One of them is bound to the semantic structure of the sentence, the other to the rhythmic nature of the line.[13] The intonation of verse "is always the resultant of the tension between [these] two forces" (p. 125). He goes on: "the duality of the intonational scheme in verse and the tension within this dual scheme exist independently of empirical sound and are the concern of the work alone" (p. 126). Neoplatonic metrists at least allow for one strand of empirical sound; Mukarovsky does not. One wonders what it is he hears when he listens to a line of verse. He does not help matters any in saying that even when the two intonational schemes he posits coincide the dual intonational scheme persists. Nor are we enlightened when he says that the intonational pattern resulting from a divide occurring after a word in prose will differ from the pattern resulting from a divide after the same word in verse: "In what this difference will consist is of little importance for us here; we are interested only in ascertaining its existence. This proves to us that the virtual duality of the intonational scheme in verse endures even if the verse intonation coincides with the syntactic intonation" (p. 124). If intonational analysis is to bear fruit for prosody, it will have to operate somewhere between the timidity of Sutherland or Taglicht, on the one hand, and the dogmatic audiomysticism and murky argumentation of Mukarovsky on the other.[14]

Whatever may be the limitations of the studies I have surveyed so far, our understanding of the role of intonation in poetry has suffered far more from the long-time inclination of prosodists simply to ignore or even snub the entire subject. David Crystal, the leading British authority on intonation, pointed out more than two decades ago that intonation had been "underestimated or ignored" in metrical theory.[15] Its importance or relevance, he noted, had sometimes been simply dismissed, "without any reason being given. . . ."[16] He cites a conference on style recorded in *Style in Language* (1960). There Rulon Wells spoke of abstracting the meter of a poem from a recording of it by "disregarding intonations," and John Lotz declared that "intonation patterns are not metrically relevant in English."[17] It turned out that of the two, Lotz proved to be the hard-liner. For in response to C. F. Voegelin's remark that in the statements he was hearing he missed "a discussion of intonation patterns" (203), Wells cited a line of Ben Jonson where considerations of intonation would enter, and said that "metrics . . . deals with more than meter," while Lotz said he had to disagree "with Mr. Wells about the metric role of intonation in English" (p. 204). The initial response to Voegelin's comment was made by John Hollander, who stated: "I presume that the reason [intonation] hasn't been mentioned is that the meter of English . . . doesn't schematize intonational levels" (p. 203). And that, apparently, for Hollander, was that.

In their classic piece, "The Concept of Meter: An Exercise in Abstraction" (which was itself published in "Abstract" form in *Style in Language*), W. K. Wimsatt and Monroe Beardsley, like Lotz, do not accord much importance to intonation, or at least they subordinate it to considerations of meter. Intonation is apparently significant only insofar as it may "change the meter," and they appear disinclined to offer examples of where this may happen, as opposed to examples of where it does not.[18] Wimsatt and Beardsley draw the latter from an article by Seymour Chatman, where he supposedly concerns himself with the role of intonation in Frost's "Mowing" (though actually, in the instances cited by Wimsatt and Beardsley, Chatman appears more preoccupied with pause and stress).[19] Interestingly enough, at the conference on style, Chatman—was he making a concession to Wimsatt and Beardsley?—said the following: ". . . I . . . do not believe that intonation is relevant to English metrics, at least not in terms of the present analysis of English which separates stress and intonation as different phonemic entities."[20] But as Crystal has noted, intonation has not been so much "argued against in the metrical literature," as it has been simply "ignored."[21]

It turns out that intonation has received less than its due not only in metrical studies but also—at least this was once the case—in linguistics itself. In his *Prosodic Systems and Intonation in English,* published in 1969, Crystal cited Alan Sharp, who, eleven years earlier, had characterized the study of intonation as "the Cinderella of the linguistic sciences."[22] In 1975, in *The English Tone of Voice,* Crystal said that "prosodic functions in general, and intonation in particular, have until very recently never held a prominent place in discussions of linguistic theory."[23] As recently as 1986, Dwight Bolinger said, without alluding to Sharp, that intonation was the "Cinderella of the communication complex."[24] Crystal and Bolinger between them have done much to make up for the one-time ignoring of intonation, which may derive from the difficulty of the subject. Bolinger himself has said that intonation is "physically . . . the most uniform element that the phonetician has to deal with; but this, instead of making for simplicity makes for complexity for, with its lack of contrast, intonation cannot be sliced up as other segments are."[25] Crystal has put Bolinger's position as follows: "Intonational features are not as formally discrete as phonemic segments . . . They are not as easy to delimit and organise into systems . . . as phonemes."[26] Crystal appears to be in agreement with this.

Intonation may be said, among other things, to register the emotions of a speaker, and Philip Lieberman has pointed up the difficulties of trying to measure this aspect of it. He focuses on the matter of fundamental frequency, which is designated in linguistics by the symbol F_0 or f_0. Lieberman says:

Some speakers apparently raise their average fundamental frequency when they are angry, but other speakers lower their average fundamental frequency. Extreme emotion may result in a wider f_0 frequency range, or it may result in a lowered and narrowed fundamental frequency range. Extreme emotion sometimes results in the speaker's breaking the sentence into many breath-groups. Emotion sometimes causes the speaker to extend breath-groups to extremely long durations. . . . all we can say at the present time, without knowing the idiosyncrasies of a particular speaker, is that emotion is marked by a departure from the normal speaking habits of the individual.[27]

Apart from the matter of individual idiosyncrasies, there is an inherent elusiveness about intonational patterns. After observing that "One of the more intractable problems in phonology has been the description of English intonation," the linguist Janet B. Pierrehumbert observes that "the same text [can] have many different melodies. . . ."[28] Intonation traced through an extended utterance can prove to be a Protean affair. Dwight Bolinger has said that "every [intonational] contour that is uttered is a 'new enactment,' with certain relatively constant configurations in the shape of accent profiles [this term will be explained later], but with slopes, intervals, intensities, lengths, and successions that answer to each moment's fluctuations of mood."[29]

In an essay that appeared in 1980, Philip Lieberman explicitly connected the difficulties inherent in the subject with its relative neglect.

Intonation is a difficult aspect of human communication to study. . . . The temptation naturally rises to ignore the role of intonation in human communication and to instead concentrate on the segmental elements [syllables]. Intonation thus is relegated to the dim and shadowy area of "paralingusitics" or the "expression of emotion." . . . Intonation according to this view is supposed to be a chancy, variable element that is subject to the whims of uncontrolled "stylistic" variation.[30]

Intertwined in this diagnosis (whose conclusions Lieberman does not share) are the elements of difficulty and "messiness," which, I think, account as much for the near nonpresence of intonation in literary prosody as for its shadowy status in linguistics, though more has been done to correct the latter than the former. A characterization of intonation, which involves one of the "suprasegmentals" of speech—pitch—is not easy to come by, from the point of view of either the metrist or the linguist. As Crystal points out, individual syllables ("segmentals") are the stuff of traditional metrics, whereas phrases and sentences are the focus of intonational study.[31] The ups and downs of those larger units, units that seemingly offer a variety of pitch options, appear much harder to track and put in neat packagings than the stress patterns of syllables making up individual words.

But also operating in the marginalization of intonation is the weight of tradition. Crystal asks:

> On what grounds, other than Tradition, has stress been singled out from the other phonological features of verse and been identified with metre? What experimental evidence is there to justify the priority of stress in this way? None has been provided; the assumption is axiomatic ("Intonation," p. 11).

Here, Crystal is concentrating on metrists in particular, but later he modulates from them to linguists, implicating the latter in the maintenance of a traditional approach that needs to be questioned. Linguists have used the syllable as the basis of their model of analysis, a model that has been "retained and applied further than its insights warrant." Returning to the question of analyzing poetry, Crystal says "the stress phoneme/syllable-unit model has far outlived its usefulness in metrics. . . ." He goes on:

> . . . I do not . . . want to throw away this model altogether. But in order to handle problems such as free verse, there seems little point (and a great deal of harm) in trying to force them into a syllable stress/foot framework (into which they will not go) when one could be trying to devise a fresh model which will handle these categories of poetry as well as the traditional ones equally readily. And the model I am suggesting uses the notion of line, expounded by reference to the intonation contour, and related prosodic features, as its basic element ("Intonation," p. 23).[32]

The reader may well recognize here a number of positions the present writer has advocated in earlier chapters. I found that these needed to be argued anew in part because the invaluable Crystal essay on which I have just been drawing, "Intonation and Metrical Theory," has, in the two decades since its appearance, hardly been attended to by prosodists. It has certainly not become the *locus classicus* it deserves to be.[33]

Remembering that intonation is a matter of pitch patterns, we can find several ironies attendant on its relative neglect in metrical theory. For one thing, the very term "prosody," under which metrical theory of whatever complexion is subsumed, derives from the

Greek word *prosōdia,* which "[i]n its technical sense . . . meant primarily accentuation as determined . . . by musical pitch. . . ."[34] Metrical theory has usually managed to ignore this aspect of its origins. Such avoidance applies even to the timer school of metrics, which, we should remind ourselves, was largely founded by a man who believed in the close kinship of poetry and music, Sir Joshua Steele, and who made a large place in his theory for pitch and pitch-change. Almost exactly a century later, in this country, Sidney Lanier propounded similar views, devoting the middle portion of *The Science of English Verse* (1880) to a consideration of "Tune." Temporal metrists after Lanier seem never to have heard of these matters or to have simply forgotten about them. Stressers too are involved in an irony in their resolute ignoring or dismissal of intonation. For while they have based all their theorizing on whether a syllable is stressed or unstressed, either in absolute terms or relative to adjacent syllables, and have identified stress with *intensity,* the element of stress has in fact increasingly been found by linguists to be a function of *pitch,* and hence implicated in intonation.

In examining this last point, we would do well to consider the comments on the terms *stress* and *accent* made by A. Cutler and D. R. Ladd, in a work published in 1983 (they are referring to linguists, but their first sentence can also be said to apply to metrists):

> *Stress* and *accent* have long been near-synonyms for prosodic features which render some syllables acoustically more prominent than others. . . . Until about thirty years ago *stress* was widely used to refer to prominence realised by greater intensity, and a distinction was sometimes drawn between stress accent (as in English) and pitch accent (as in Swedish). . . .
>
> Significant advances in phonetic research in the 1950s . . . showed clearly the interdependence of pitch and intensity . . . in the perception of prominent syllables, and made a redefinition of *stress* necessary. Since that time, work on *stress* has taken two main directions. One is based on Bolinger's . . . theory of pitch accent in English. . . . The second approach maintains the American structuralist insistence on distinguishing *stress* and *intonation*. . . .[35]

So even while they see pitch as an important component of language, American structuralists offer comparatively little threat to traditional metrists, who, eschewing pitch, make their home in considerations of stress. But what of Bolinger's theory of pitch accent? In 1958, in a landmark essay entitled "A Theory of Pitch

Accent in English," Bolinger, undaunted by the fact that "No other phenomenon in language . . . has more firmly resisted efforts to find out what it does" than pitch,[36] put forth a claim for its centrality that questioned the prevailing wisdom about its role in relation to stress. Pitch and stress, it had been thought, were phonemically independent, with changes in stress able to affect intonation somewhat. Bolinger's essay proceeds to deny this alleged independence, and to say that the respective roles of pitch (which is a "psychological term" whose physical correlate is fundamental frequency) and stress (whose physical correlate is intensity) are really the reverse of what had been assumed, and of a different order of magnitude, with pitch being "our main cue to stress" (p. 111). Bolinger makes it clear that by "stress" he was not referring to "word stress," which is the assignment of prominence to a given syllable of a word, as in the dictionary. *That* sort of designation, he says, simply indicates which syllable will be accorded prominence *if* a given utterance makes that particular word stand out phonetically. The syllable has merely *potential* prominence (p. 113), its realization dependent on being assigned the proper pitch.[37] Bolinger's favored term for indicating a point of realized prominence is "pitch accent" or simply "accent."[38]

Citing experiments done by others, as well as his own, Bolinger claims that listeners readily apprehended changes in pitch register as stress, and that changes in intensity had difficulty in competing with the pitch changes as a means of creating such apprehension. His conclusion is that "intensity is at best UNNECESSARY as a cue to stress and that pitch alone will serve so long as an utterance is kept reasonably close to the normal range of intensity and duration . . ." ("A Theory of Pitch Accent," p. 124). The ultimate thrust of Bolinger's article and of his subsequent work, particularly *Intonation and its Parts,* is that pitch is the queen of the three suprasegmentals—pitch, stress, and duration.[39] Acknowledging that "it is wrong to identify accent with any one of its various cues, there are reasons for believing that pitch is the one most heavily relied on."[40]

In his celebration of pitch as the key element in generating prominence, Bolinger is hardly to be regarded as a loner, a misguided enthusiast. Publishing their observation twenty-two years after the appearance of Bolinger's "A Theory of Pitch Accent in English," Georges Faure, D. J. Hirst, and M. Chafcouloff say that "Few linguists today would find fault with Dwight Bolinger's affirmation . . . that 'the primary clue of what is usually termed STRESS in the utterance is pitch prominence.'"[41] Also of interest here is the linguist Elisabeth O. Selkirk's statement that her approach to intonation and its relation to focus (i.e., the element of particular interest in an utterance, sometimes characterized as "new information"), "implies a theory of the intonation-stress relation that puts intonation first."[42] And while David Crystal was cited earlier as keeping a place for stress as an entity independent of pitch accent, he has shown considerable respect for Bolinger's views.[43]

If prosodists were to accord those views the same sort of respect they have been granted by linguists, traditional metrics would have to undergo a radical reevaluation. For one thing, continuing to ignore pitch so as to concentrate exclusively on stress could only be counted as perverse.[44] Moreover, an acceptance of Bolinger's distinction between word stress and accent would radically undermine orthodox scansion. There, words are considered in terms of their syllables, with those components regarded as stressed or unstressed. Even where shadings of stress are allowed, each stressed syllable takes its place as an equal partner with the other stressed syllables in a given line, in the sense that each of these entities contributes the same amount toward a realization of the alleged metrical pattern. But if we apply Bolinger's notions to poetry, we would have to consider the words of a line not as entities to be scanned one at a time in terms of their constituent syllables, but as parts of a larger configuration, with that configuration determining whether a given *word* should be regarded as prominent, and only *then* have its *potential* stress (on a particular syllable) be realized. This would certainly undermine the notion of the foot, or at least subordinate it, for the alleged regularity of stress occurrence that scansion-by-foot assumes would no longer be there, or would, at the very least, have to compete with pitch-determined locales of stress. According to Bolinger's theory, this would be no contest, for pitch, as opposed to intensity, is the main cue to stress; metrists ignoring pitch would be pushing aside the chief source of what they profess to be working with. Moreover, the appearance of pitch accent is likely to be a lot more irregular than that of the intensity-based points of stress the traditional metrist assumes are there, for such accent is a matter of semantic and attitudinal considerations that would have to be handled on a moment-by-moment, line-by-line basis.

Prudence Byers has remarked that "One of the reasons intonational phrases are ignored is that they are variable, and this variability hampers their description." The language is relatively firm on the matter of stress location, "far less" so on elements of intonation.[45] Bolinger has put the matter this way: "we can only conclude that any imaginable melodic shape can occur in actual speech" (*Intonation,* p. 257).[46] Given this wide range of possibilities, would regarding poetry as under the sway of intonation not only displace stress from its hitherto central position in our poetics, but threaten to replace the alleged orderliness and verifiability of metrical arrangements with a chaos of free, unpredictable configurations, a plethora of pitch-patterns coming out of the idiosyncrasies of each of the individual voices that might recite a poem? To paraphrase Stanley Fish, would there be a sonic text in the classroom, or merely a mélange of particular realizations of a given piece of verse? Would the pitch dimension of poetry simply furnish more toys for the playpens of indeterminancy that we have seen multiplying in recent years?

Let me begin to answer by saying that in subordinating the building block of meter—stress—to pitch, we are not in a real sense abandoning an agreed-on structure or series of structures. That putative entity, the metrical paradigm, either strictly defined, as in traditional prosody, or more loosely defined, as in the preceding chapter, is subjected to a variety of sonic interpretation as soon as the poem is voiced, even when that voicing is conceived of purely in terms of stress. The hostility to performance I spoke of in Chapter 2, to the danger it brings of different readings, was not focused on pitch-oriented readings but those based on stress. Performance is inimical to strict paradigms of any kind. To his credit, Seymour Chatman, in *A Theory of Meter,* not only illustrated the variety of stressing we get from different readers, but insisted on the inescapability of performance, saying that

> scansions can only derive from recitations—whether actually vocalized or 'silent,' that is, the scanner cannot but proceed by actually reading the words and coming to some decision about their metrical status. A metrist's proper task, then, is to try to discover by observation what people do when they perform metrical analysis.[47]

But, I would say, in making these observations the metrist cannot assume the possession of a privileged status, that of knowing the "real" meter of the poem, a knowledge that he holds in common with other professional readers. As noted in Chapter 1, Chatman says, and he is talking about traditional prosody, "1. Metrists do not agree upon the number of syllables in a given word or line; 2. Metrists do not agree upon whether a given syllable is prominent or not; 3. Metrists do not agree upon how the syllables are grouped."[48] In short, in moving from a focus on stress to one on pitch, we are not foolishly casting off a true covenant of understanding as to a given poem's sound structure.[49] Nor are we necessarily entering the realm of Chaos and Old Night.

The intonational contours of speech might be difficult to describe, but are not impossibly so. Nor does each person employ a repertory of such contours entirely peculiar to himself or herself. If this *were* the case we should hardly be able to communicate with each other. "Give me the hat," with the pitch accent on "me" would be appropriate to a desired message in one situation, while placing that accent on "hat" would be suitable to another, and speakers of English on the receiving end of either statement would certainly "get" what was intended.[50] Neither rendering is arbitrary if one wishes to convey a particular meaning. But the sharing of intonational cues goes well beyond being part of a particular language community. Before pursuing this argument in terms of language in general, I wish to take note in passing of T. Walker Herbert's contention that his experiments with performed poetry suggested "that there is a tone that belongs to a poem. [The experiments] . . . seem to say that the pitch pattern, as well as the pattern of time and intensity, will impose itself on the voice of anybody who reads the poem. . . ."[51]

Philip Lieberman was cited earlier as attributing linguists' neglect of intonation to their assumption that it was "a chancy, variable element that is subject to the whims of uncontrolled 'stylistic' variation." He continued by saying "Different dialects and different speakers supposedly have different styles of intonation that are a function of the speakers' varying backgrounds and the effects of chance." But his own comment on the matter is that "this view of the linguistic status of intonation is completely wrong."[52] Lieberman bases his dissent on human physiology, on "the role of respiratory and muscular mechanisms in the control and production of intonation" (p. 187). The fundamental frequency of the voice is produced, as indicated earlier, by those mechanisms, and as one example of the "innate" nature of intonation, Lieberman points to "The falling fundamental frequency contour, which is structured by the vegetative aspects of respiration, [and] is the universal language signal signifying the end of an 'ordinary' sentence" (p. 195). Far from being, then, the idiosyncratic property of an individual, intonation is rooted not simply in competence in a given language but in the articulatory mechanisms shared by the race.

Bolinger also conceives of intonation in terms of commonality rather than idiosyncrasy, though his ultimate focus is somewhat different. He says, "When we compare the descriptions of intona-

tion from language to language, we find resemblances that far sur-
pass anything that could be attributed to chance, and so widely
separated in space that they could hardly be the result of diffusion"
(*Intonation,* p. 197). He goes on to speak of a "commonality of the
gestural complex" in human beings, and offers some fascinating
examples of couplings of intonation and gesture, quoting Adam
Kendon: "it is as if the speech production process is manifested
in two forms of activity simultaneously: in the vocal organs and
also in bodily movement" (p. 199). Hands, shoulders, arms, facial
features—as the voice rises and falls, these may too, though not
necessarily in the direction taken by the voice. The upness and
downness of voice and gesture are, Bolinger points out, entangled
with commonly used up-down metaphors. One might say of an
excited speaker that "she's all keyed up." The intonation typical
of incomplete clauses "leaves the hearer up in the air . . ." (p. 202).
Bolinger's observations in these areas help locate intonation at the
center of our expressive energies.

But to pursue our subject per se, we must leave gesture and
metaphor behind, concentrating solely on the uses of the rises and
falls of the speaking voice. That is a challenging enough subject
but not totally unmanageable. For example, David Crystal undermines the notion that to engage intonation is to confront the messy
and arbitrary, the indefinable. He observes, with some understandable testiness, that

> it is not the case that prosodic . . . features [pitch, loudness and dura-
> tion] are on the whole ambiguous and undefinable. . . . intonation is
> usually mistreated in this way. It is often said, for example, that there
> is no one-to-one relationship between form and function in intonation—
> that it is impossible to define the meaning of the nuclear tone [the
> pitch movement of the most prominent syllable in a phrase, clause, or
> sentence] . . . because it can mean any number of things. This is a
> nonsensical criticism: the low rise [a particular intonational configura-
> tion] should not be discussed in this way. Any instance of a low rising
> tone has one meaning only *in one context*. One might just as well argue
> against the word 'table' on the grounds that it is ambiguous—of course
> it is, until one takes it in context. . . . the same considerations should
> also apply for intonation. . . .[53]

Nevertheless, the study of intonation is not without its difficulties. Prosodists need to go to linguists for help here, though they
will not always receive as much of it as they might want. Linguists,
understandably, tend to treat language at large rather than its literary manifestations; the expressive uses to which literature, poetry

in particular, puts language are well removed from what interests many linguists to begin with. We can get glimpses of this divergence as we consider the hunt for the intonational unit.

It would appear necessary, if one is to examine intonation either as it operates in language in general or poetry in particular, to have at hand a basis on which to break a given utterance into parts, rationalized clusters of pitch sequences, that is, intonation units.[54] The sentence, that elemental language entity, could be and has been regarded as one sort of intonational unit, with a resulting taxonomy of sentence types and their accompanying, allegedly characteristic "tunes." Crystal observes that "Most scholars make an initial classification of intonation patterns based on three or four major sentence-types: the most important structures seem to be statements, two types of question (those beginning with an interrogative word, and those requiring a yes/no answer), commands, and exclamations . . ." (*Prosodic Systems,* p. 253). Whatever the linguists' objections to this approach might be, and there are some (p. 254), from the point of view of poetics the sentence is just too large a unit to be useful, a macro-entity rather than the sort of smaller configuration that would be needed to illuminate the intonational characteristics of a line or even lines of poetry, since it often takes two or more lines to make up a sentence.

At least five conceptions of how an utterance might be broken into units shorter than sentences have been advanced, conceptions that are not necessarily mutually exclusive. Three of them are phonological in nature, that is, based on sound in one sense or another, two on grammar and/or meaning. One of the sound-based approaches takes the breath-group as the basic unit of intonation. A leading advocate of this is Philip Lieberman, who defines the breath-group as a universal of speech, generated by the act of expelling the breath from our lungs. It constitutes an intonational signal, which in its "archteypal" form moves from a medium pitch to a higher pitch and then subsides.[55] While Lieberman sees the breath group as the element that segments speech into sentences,[56] he also opens up the possibility that "a sentence can . . . be divided into two or more breath-groups."[57]

The notion of the intonation unit being made up of a breath group has the appeal of the elemental[58] and at least one poet, Charles Olson, has spoken of the breath-group as, if not the unit of intonation, the basis for a poet's lineation.[59] But unless we are prepared to monitor our reading by contriving and donning a kind of prosodic breatholator, a device that would measure the word-groups produced by our individual exhalations, the notion of the breath group does not appear to be a useful one for intonational scansion of a text (except for its drawing attention, if only implicitly, to the production of pauses in our reading, the question being where those pauses occur). Also, as Lieberman sees it, there is no correlation between the specific intonation pattern following from a sentence's division into breath groups and the attitude or emotion of the speaker. The breath-group is a purely phonological feature.[60] But for our purposes, studying the intonational contours of a poem takes its primary interest from their expressive potentials, particularly since, as Elisabeth O. Selkirk has contended, English in general

> is far richer than some languages [e.g., French] in its repertoire of pitch accents. . . . This means that the intonational contours of an utterance have the potential for making a much greater contribution to expressiveness in English than they do in these other languages.[61]

Nevertheless, a good deal of the investigation of intonation by linguists (including, ironically, that of Selkirk herself), shies away from focusing on intonation's expressive or "emotional" or "attitudinal" dimensions, preferring to treat its formal features. In *Prosodic Systems,* David Crystal displays such a tilt, saying he is "not primarily concerned with the referential nature of the meanings which [nonsegmental linguistic] contrasts may be said to carry." He observes that formalism is "such a regular part of modern linguistic methodology as to require no argued defence," but in effect he offers such a defense when he goes on to say that "considerations of meaning . . . do not enter in until a stable basis of formally defined features has been determined. Then a more satisfactory classification of meanings can be carried out" (p. 18). (Still, it turns out he *is* interested in the expressive dimensions of intonation.)

Janet B. Pierrehumbert presents a case of particularly severe formalism. She is intent on describing the intonational unit primarily in terms of a specific number of pitches, assigning them to stressed and unstressed syllables, and working out the "grammar" of phrasal tunes possible to English.[62] All the while she stays away from a concern with expressiveness or even meaning in a more general sense (p. 31). For this reason, her scheme seems to me not especially useful for the would-be analyst of a poem's intonational contours. But one thing we might employ is her saying that an intonation phrase boundary occurs "where there is a non-hesitation pause or where a pause could be felicitously inserted without perturbing the pitch contour" (p. 7).[63] Here again we have room being made for pause in a description of the speech stream.

Selkirk adopts Pierrehumbert's notion of the structure of the intonational phrase, and adopts as well, at least theoretically, her distancing herself from attempting to link intonational phrasing to a "'meaning' or discourse function . . . ."[64] But in fact, Selkirk's approach to intonation does show some concern for meaning, while setting clear limits to that concern. She notes that "Studies of intonational meaning in English have led to partitioning it into two components: one might be called the *expressiveness component,* and the other the *informational structure* or *focus structure component* . . ." (p. 198; italics in original). In light of her going on to say that "in English the burden of expressiveness is borne almost entirely by intonational structure" (p. 199), it seems almost perverse that she avoids dealing with that burden (though no more perverse than most *prosodists* in their avoidance of intonation entirely; Selkirk is a linguist). She does deal with intonation's role in establishing "focus," which has to do with a sentence's "presumed 'informational contribution' to a discourse" and which is equated roughly with the "new" information" that a statement is delivering (199–200). This is not a trivial function, and may well be of use to the prosodist, but expressiveness is left out in the cold. Moreover, this exclusion is not the only troubling thing for the prosodist about Selkirk's approach.

Lieberman had assumed a necessary congruence of intonational phrases and syntactic units.[65] This is an assumption that may be said to go as far back as the eighteenth century.[66] Prudence Byers has claimed that "Intonation depends so heavily on syntax . . . that no text really has an intonational shape, until a reader deciphers its syntax. Any analysis of intonation, therefore, demands syntactic analysis first."[67] Basing the statement on an experiment, Byers concluded that "Especially in scripted speech, the boundaries between [tone or intonation units] occur only at syntactic junctures . . . ."[68] Selkirk, however, insists on something that Pierrehumbert seemed to concede only reluctantly, namely, that there is no necessary congruence of intonational phrases and syntactic units.[69] Selkirk contends that an attempt to establish such congruence can fail to work in either direction. Syntactic considerations do not determine the intonational phrases of a sentence, and those phrases do not necessarily conform to syntactic units (pp. 285–87, 293).[70] The prosodist Richard Cureton apparently subscribes to a similar view, telling us that "syntactic units are not coextensive with prosodic units, and therefore one cannot convert a theory of syntax into a theory of prosody."[71] To sum up, then, we find that the honoring of a text's syntactic boundaries by its intonation units appears to be a fact for Lieberman and Byers, but certainly not for Selkirk and Cureton, nor, it would appear, for Crystal as well as some others.[72] (Of course, in traditional foot prosody, syntactic boundaries count for nought in the first place, so they present no difficulty to scansion.)

On the face of it, the Selkirk-Cureton-Crystal position is somewhat disconcerting. If intonational units do not map neatly onto syntactic entities, what forms *will* they take? And how, in tracing a poem's sound patterns, are we supposed to coordinate the role of nonsyntactic intonation units with the poem's syntactically organized phrases, for, as I have assumed hitherto, such phases undoubtedly shape our sense of sonic contours as well? Will we be thrust back into the position of "double audition" argued against in Chapter 2? That twofold hearing was originally required of us through the assumption of an ideal foot pattern running through metrical verse, a pattern we were supposed to pick up on along with the actual stress distributions. Now such stereo reception seemingly becomes necessary for *all* verse, in order for us to hear both an intonational "tune" and an organization of sound by syntax, assuming that one honors the latter notion, as I have been advocating, if not always explicitly, that we do. It should be added that in this particular case I would not argue against double audition per se, for it would consist of a registration of two sound patterns that are actually there, as opposed to one being strictly in the "mind's ear." Still, such audition would make for a complicated apprehension of a given poem's sonic unfolding.[73]

Have we simply circled back, then, to the *problematical* nature of intonation? Is the intonational phrase indeed the wild card in the phonology of language in general and poetry in particular, unconstrained as it is by syntactic boundaries, indeterminate in that important sense, and for all practical purposes unmanageable? Happily, no, not even for Selkirk, and not, I will argue, for the would-be analyst of poetry's sounds. For Selkirk has provided us with a decided grip on the intonational phrase by positing that it constitutes a "sense unit" (p. 286). In short, the ups and downs generated by the reading of a text will allow themselves to be mapped onto units that share their boundaries with units of sense. (The latter may even add up to syntactic wholes, but that, for Selkirk, would only be a by-product of their semantic integrity.) Here is at least a starting-point for the prosodist.[74]

Moreover, we may be able to reduce or dispose of the complication caused by syntactic units and intonation units supposedly failing to synchronize with each other. This splitting apart of syntax and intonation is, at least for Selkirk, apparently based on a transformational-grammar conception of the sentence, in which syntactic units are represented by a series of "trees," or brackets. Consider an example adduced by Selkirk (pp. 293–94), apparently one that has been used repeatedly in linguistics texts: "This is the cat that chased the rat that ate the cheese." One of the bracketings sets off as a syntactic unit, in this case a verb phrase, the words "chased the rat." A similar bracketing gives us "ate the cheese." But in vocalizing the sentence one is likely to say "This is the cat," then pause, then say "that chased the rat," then pause, then say "that ate the cheese." Such a *phonological* rendering sets up sound units that do not observe the respective initial boundaries of the syntactic phases, "chased the rat" and "ate the cheese." But there is nothing that *compels* us to describe this or any other sentence in transformational-grammar terms in order to characterize its structure. A perfectly acceptable alternative would be to see the sentence in question as composed of a main clause, followed by two relative clauses, each of which begins with "that." The three clauses, designated by Selkirk as intonation phrases, would give us a perfect fit between intonation and syntax.

To put together a number of the points that have been made thus far, if we think of syntactic units as constituting sense units, and if we go along with Selkirk in thinking of intonational units as being required to constitute sense units, we certainly have the *possibility* that syntactic entities and intonational ones will coincide within a given sentence. In addition, Dwight Bolinger has observed that "For the GRAMMAR of a sentence, the most important part of the intonational melody comes at TERMINALS—the end points of phrases, clauses, and sentences" ("Intonation," p. 25).[75] So one can think of syntactic units and intonational phrases as sharing terminals. Also, I would note that these terminals may well be marked by pauses (or the possibility of their occurrence), precisely the markers I attributed to the phrasal units featured in the last chapter, which were, in fact, syntactic units, except in cases of enjambment. Crystal, who speaks of "the presence of junctural features at the end of every tone-unit," says that "This usually takes the form of a very slight pause . . ." (*Prosodic Systems,* p. 206). What I am working toward is the position that what I have called phrases, which, as I have designated them, are both syntactic and sense units, coincide with the intonational units of a given poetic text (some adjustment of this proposition would have to be made in cases of enjambment). Moreover, the shared termini of all these units are marked by pauses.

In addition to the statement from him I have just cited, Crystal himself can be called on to support this view. As noted earlier, Crystal claimed, in *Prosodic Systems and Intonation in English,* that there were few instances of cooperation between grammatical structure and intonational phrasing. But in *The English Tone of Voice,* published six years later (1975), he seemed to take a very different stance, one that moves well beyond regarding the congruence of syntactic units and intonation units as unlikely. First, we might note, Crystal is in keeping with the "English" approach to intonation, which regards the accent assigned to the final "lexical" (major word) item in a tone-unit as the most important accent in that unit. It is designated as the "tonic accent," or "tonic," or "nuclear accent." In other words, the tonic will be found at or near the closing boundary of a tone-unit.[76] Starting with the model of a sentence consisting of one clause and assigned a single tone-unit, Crystal provides a series of rules for assigning a "prosodic operation" to each of a host of possible expansions of the model sentence, with those expansions conceived of as syntactic ones. The prosodic operation consists of adding one or two tone-unit boundaries for each expansion. For example, the insertion of a nonrestrictive medial clause calls for adding a tone-unit boundary (such a clause is designated by a virgule on either side of it, as in "/ my brother/ who's abroad/sent me a letter/."[77] The addition of an "adverbial" (this could be a single word or a phrase) at the end of a sentence would take a tone-unit boundary just before it, for example, "/I didn't ask him/anyway/."

Crystal presents a sentence that was transcribed from its oral delivery, with short and long pauses represented respectively by . and —, with words containing the tonic accent set in capitals, and with indication of the pitch movement over the stressed syllable marked by / for rising and \ for falling. This is how it reads:

the second deplorable thing ABOÚT it/—is the FAC̀T/. that. THÍS CH̀AP/ . a NEUR̀OTIC/—his mother calls him a NEURÓTIC/ from the age of TẂO/ . who can't stick in the army for twenty-four HOÚRS/ is the kind of PEŔSON/ who is made a public idol of the D̀AY/—(p. 20)

(I might note in passing that in five of eight cases here, tone-group endings are marked by a pause, and the others could easily have taken one.)

Crystal's point in exhibiting this sentence is to show how it conforms to the rules. That is, he starts out by considering a sentence not in the form of an actual and specific oral utterance but strictly as an abstract grammatical entity subject to various rules for the insertion of theoretical tone-unit boundary markings. It turns out that the intonational configuration of the cited transcribed sentence conforms exactly to the theoretical model. In fact, this was the case for the overwhelming majority of the specimens that Crystal tested. He therefore regards the rules he has formulated as *predictive,* claiming that "Out of the 12,000 tone-units examined [in the utterances he transcribed], about 100 were incapable of prediction from the . . . rules" (p. 21).[78] Careful linguist that he is, he worries the question of the exceptions, but what we might note is that the rules, which are formulated in terms of syntactic (if non-transformational-grammar) entities generating tone-unit boundaries, accounted for more than ninety-nine percent of the data. This means that for all practical purposes we can consider that syntactic units and tone-group units *are* congruent, with the important possible exception of what happens at the boundaries of enjambed lines (a matter to be considered later). Therefore, for those who might wish to go with Crystal's system, the phrasal approach recommended in the preceding chapter does not require modification when it comes to tracing intonation patterns.

If we agree that an intonational unit can be regarded as having syntactic as well as semantic integrity, what else can be say about its make-up in purely intonational terms? To turn to Crystal again, we find him characterizing a tone-unit's "maximal internal structure" as having the following components: Prehead, Head, Nucleus, Tail (*Prosodic Systems,* p. 208). "The head is that independently variable part of the tone-unit stretching from and including the first stressed and usually pitch-prominent syllable (here referred to as the *onset* . . .) . . . and extending as far as but not including the nuclear segment" (*Prosodic Systems,* p. 226). The prehead is made up of all the syllables before the onset syllable. The tail consists of all the syllables following the nucleus, that is, the most prominent syllable. Crystal embarks on what would appear to be an exhaustive taxonomy of the tone-unit components. He considers not only various pitch movements (rising, falling, and level) and combinations of such movements that can make up the nucleus, but also degrees of pitch height, and widened or narrowed pitch ranges. He distinguishes the various pitch paths that tails can take, classifies heads (at great length) and preheads (relatively briefly). When he adds to these matters consideration of the question of the relations of tone-units making up a sequence, the prosodist may well feel overwhelmed by the proliferation of analytic entities, and wonder about the possibility or even desirability of applying Crystal's scheme to the intonational analysis of verse.

Prudence Byers, one of the few people to consider seriously the intonation studies of linguists for the purposes of prosody, is aware of Crystal's work, and draws on it, but avoids anything like the minutely detailed scheme of his tone units. In an interesting essay, "based on a spectrographic study of six speakers' readings of both poetry and non-poetry," she comes to the conclusion that poetry is characterized by a slower speech rate, more pauses, a narrower pitch range, and shorter tone-units (which are "more nearly equivalent in duration" than those in nonpoetry).[79] Poetry is also characterized by a low average pitch, and a preponderance of "Simple falling melodies" and "Simple falling nuclei."[80]

In another essay, Byers manages to come up with a workable version of Crystal's model of the tone-unit. She focuses on the pitch of its "onset," that is, its first stressed syllable, and the pitch configuration of the syllables that make up the rest of the unit. Onsets are designated as either high or low (she lists seven main causes for a high onset).[81] She then considers how the tone-units making up a sequence compare with each other. Experimental data indicate that whether the materials are conversation, prose read aloud, or poetry read aloud, a "somewhat systematic" set of relations emerges between the respective onsets of successive units, making for a "typical 'phonic sentence,'" in which the onsets show a tendency to descend (p. 4).

Byers applies this to poetry but the results, unfortunately, are a bit confusing or somewhat flat. Using the criteria for high onsets, she says "predictions can be made about onset patterns in particular poems" (p. 8). But what the purpose of such predictions is, she does not say. At any rate, on the basis of the "prediction," the intonation patterns of the poem can be experimentally measured against the phonic sentence paradigm (that of descending onsets), to see if they conform to it. In the example she uses, the first stanza of Auden's "Alonso to Ferdinand," she finds a deviation, but apart from its helping us to distinguish this poem from others, she makes no case for its significance. The opening stanza of a second Auden poem, "Mountains," is said to show "more onset irregularity" than the first specimen, and this gives it a "conversational" quality because, Byers tells us rather belatedly, such irregularity, like other irregularities, "is more typical of conversation than of scripted speech" (p. 9). But irregularity does not inevitably make for conversational quality; its effect may sometimes be "simply to create tension." This notion, involving a gap between a paradigm and a particular verse instance, is, of course, very close to the concept of metrical tension, which Beyers explicitly links it with, saying that either can be used "to underscore thematic conflict" (p. 11). But her primary point, she says, is that intonation can be predicted. (p. 12) In my view, this formalist finding, along with Byers's other observations, constitutes rather poor pickings. Intonational analysis should have more to tell us about the pitch contours and their associated effects in a given poem.

It might be argued that had Byers included consideration of the attitudinal aspect of intonation and had she made use of the full dimensions of the tone unit as described by Crystal, she might have produced more fruitful results. While it must be conceded, as indicated earlier, that Crystal's scheme is a formidable one, this does not necessarily explain Byers's failure to employ it more fully than she does. Indeed, she finds his notational system "more iconic than most, and hence easier to use."[82] But the fact of the matter is that that evaluation is better merited by the work of another linguist, as we shall see in a moment.

Crystal requires us to keep our eye on two lines of text. The upper one contains the words themselves, along with a notation of the onset syllable, a notation of the other stressed syllables, and an indication, by means of various arrows, of any of the following: stressed syllables that are either pitched level with or unexpectedly lower than, or slightly higher than, or much higher than, the preceding syllable. (According to Crystal, it is the "norm" in English for a stressed syllable to be pitched slightly lower than the preceding one.)[83] This first level of notation also contains a marking for any unstressed syllable that is lower than the syllable preceding it, and additional notations for singling out the nuclear syllable and its pitch direction. The second level consists principally of a series of small dots and large dots arranged at varying heights: these represent, respectively, the sequence of unstressed and stressed syllables of the text and their relative pitch levels. The second line also, redundantly, indicates the nuclear syllable and its pitch direction.

While Dwight Bolinger, in *Intonation and Its Parts,* does not refer to Crystal explicitly, he does cite the breakdown of an intonation "contour" into prehead, head, body, nucleus, and tail, crediting the pioneering of the scheme to Harold E. Palmer. Though Bolinger himself will find a use for the term "tail," he claims that this overall arrangement doesn't distinguish one accent from another, or say anything of the contribution made by unaccented syllables, "or the

accenting or deaccenting of material between the major accents"
(p. 245). But if Bolinger prefers his approach because he finds it
more informative, we might well favor it because it makes things
much more manageable—for the prosodist, if not for the printer.
His method of transcription gives us but a single line of text, which
marks the locations of pitch accent, and, through the typography,
indicates the relative pitch levels of the syllables. This method,
along with Bolinger's unintimidating typology of pitch "profiles"
(to be discussed in a moment) and his insistence on the *emotive*
aspect of his subject ("Intonation is all emotion of some degree or
other," p. 260) makes him, I believe, with due respect to Byers,[84]
more useful than Crystal as a guide for the prosodist. Such is the
case, even though Crystal has cogently addressed the subject of
metrical theory, whereas Bolinger has pretty much ignored it. (As
I hope I have already suggested, a prosodist bent on a serious
consideration of intonation would do well to consult Crystal's writings on the subject.)[85] Noting that speech is not a medium simply
for conveying information, but one whose aim much of the time is
"to cajole, persuade, entreat, excuse, cow, deceive, or merely to
maintain contact," Bolinger describes it as imparting information
through "accents of interest" and attempting to impress though
"accents of power," though the two are not really separable (p. 74);
under accents of interest he handles what is commonly called the
"focus" or "new information" of an utterance.

Whatever the intention or effect of the pitch accents, which are
jumps up or down "from a relatively uniform line" (p. 130), they
generate shapes or "profiles." In Bolinger's system there are three
basic profiles, which can enter into a variety of combinations with
each other, forming contours. Those contours are to their constituent profiles "more or less what sentences are to words . . ."
(p. 254).

Profile A is characterized by an accent "at a relatively high pitch
followed by a jump down . . ." (139). Profile C Bolinger characterizes as "the mirror image of Profile A: the obtrusion is down instead of up. The accent is marked by 'downward to' rather than
'downward from': (p. 149). Profile B involves the upward aspect of
pitch: in it "the accent is jumped up *to*" (p. 152; italics in original).
The scope of a profile "is the limit of intonational movement that
can occur on a one-syllable [accented] word" (p. 141), but this does
not mean that the full enactment of a profile is necessarily limited
to such a word or to any single word.

Bolinger has many things to say about the contexts or uses associated with the respective profiles. In one instance, he opposes

Profiles A and B to each other along a separation-connection axis. "Where A singles things out, B ties them in . . ." (p. 166). At the same time, the two have a very important kinship. The pattern in perhaps "the majority of well-executed, longer" English utterances is sometimes described as a combination of "theme" and "rheme." The theme is the part "that lays the groundwork, that asks the question, that relates to what we already know or can guess . . . ." The rheme is the portion that "adds the figure to the ground, that answers the question, that supplies what was not already known" (p. 46). The accent typically attached to the theme is B, that attached to the rheme is A, so B + A may be said to give us the most frequently sounded contour of our language.[86]

The falling pattern of Profile A suggests "a coming-to-rest," "notions related to termination," (p. 341), the drop in A acting "as a sort of cutoff" (p. 166). Such termination can indicate one of a number of things, including certainty. Profile A "figures as the ASSERTIVE profile par excellence . . . ." This is "evident in its physical shape: the accented syllable is, more often than with any other profile, at the highest pitch, where it has greatest impact" (p. 164). Bolinger further says that "a string of As is the most assertive kind of utterance" (p. 341). He finds, as indicated earlier, that the "assertiveness" of this profile "links up with 'separateness'" (p. 165). In a related remark, he says that when we have one A joined to another, the drop in pitch that is part of the A profile signifies "separation of some kind," which may be "for sense or for power . . ." (p. 292). *The different levels that make up the profiles are typographically rendered.*[87]

To turn for a while from further exposition of Bolinger's profiles and their respective affects, consider how his remarks on Profile A might be applied to a poetic text. A prosodic *locus classicus* in Shakespeare is to be found in King Lear's lament over the dead Cordelia:

> Why should a dog, a horse, a rat, have life,
> And thou no breath at all? Thou'lt come no more,
> Never, never, never, never, never! (V, iii, 306–8)

The standard comment on the last of these lines is that it acquires its force in part by reversing the iambic norm, giving us a series of five "trochees." Perhaps. But it can also be argued that what we have here is a series of five A profiles, which would be rendered in Bolinger's format as:

Ne   ne   ne   ne   ne

ver   ver   ver   ver   ver!

These embody the qualities of the A profile I have just cited from Bolinger. The characteristic of *separateness*—each "never" would presumably be delivered as an entity unto itself—is strongly enhanced by the four distinct pauses that would be effectuated by the commas. (These too, incidentally, constitute a deviation from the "norm" of iambic pentameter—where we would expect one or at most two pauses in a line—though not the sort traditional prosody has been concerned with.) Such settings-off of the individual *never*s would lend emphasis to each. Moreover, the repeated word is *assertive* in the extreme, and, focusing on the most awful kind of absoluteness or termination, makes for a sequence of finality profiles. In addition, the high pitch of the accent of each "ne" syllable would presumably be given acute definition in any enactment of the line, so one might also say we have here a series of super-A profiles, with an accompanying intensification of the tonal qualities of that profile.

A further application of Bolinger's approach is possible in the *King Lear* passage, if we focus now on the B profile. We might well think of it as the reverse of A. The latter begins "up" with an accent and moves down from it, B begins down and moves up to accent. A and B can also be seen as opposed because B, we may remember, connects, whereas A separates. B, Bolinger tells us, "is common in listings where the speaker is mainly just reciting the list and not focusing on individual items" (p. 174). We have in "Why should a dog, a horse, a rat have life" a series of three sharply defined B profiles:

dog,   horse,   rat.

a   a   a

The items here constitute a list of *connected* terms, each having more in common with the others than any does with the dead Cordelia. At first glance, the prominent use of pause in this line appears to anticipate the make-up of the "Never" line, but what we are chiefly aware of is the sonic *opposition* of the two lines, the down-up of the B profiles, designating interchangeable animals that still live, contrasting with the up-down of the massed A profiles, designating the irrecoverability of the unique Cordelia. (I would even argue that the pauses suggested by the commas in the "Why" line are much less distinct than those in the "Never" line, and serve more as a basis for separating the two lines than for connecting them.)

Yet another way of looking at the relationship of the B and A profiles here is available to us. It involves, partly, one more instance of opposition. If A is, in general, the accent of assertion, finality, then B gives the effect "of 'something unfinished,'" when it occurs in "utterance-final position." This, according to Bolinger, is "the place where B is most conspicuous . . ." (p. 175). (It is commonly found at the ends of "yes-no" questions.) If we consider the whole of the question that Lear asks—"Why should a dog, a horse, a rat, have life,/ And thou no breath at all?"—we can say that the sequence of the B profiles in the first line here, pertaining to the animals, is extended to the next line, though the relative pitches of the latter's accented syllables might well be felt to descend, as follows:

thou

breath

all?

And no at

The question Lear asks can be seen as at once rhetorical and not—it *is* a question and leaves things up in the air. We then get, after the intervening "Thou'lt come no more" (more about this in a moment) the counterthrust of A profiles, a going down, an insistent finality that does not answer the question but that presents a terrible, incontrovertible fact. In its own way, this remarkable passage is based on the very common B + A configuration, but with each of its constituents multiplied.

We have yet to speak of Profile C in any detail. This one, involving an accent achieved by a *lowered* pitch, appears to be the most intriguing to Bolinger. As already indicated, he finds it the mirror image of A, seeing it so not only formally but also in its functions:

Where A tends to play up, to emphasize, to suggest contrast or newness, C plays down, deemphasizes, and often implies foreknowledge. If to accent something is to give it force, then the accent in C can be thought of as a reverse accent . . . the speaker needs to make the item stand out . . . but has opposite feelings about it. (p. 178)

When C enters into a contour with B, in the form of B + C, it can serve to convey "something repeated, hence routine, predictable" (p. 228). This effect can be enhanced by the use of a level tone, or monotone. The B + C contour is also associated with reassurance.[88]

We can see the application of these characteristics in the *Lear* passage, though I offer my remarks here tentatively. Consider the words that have not been commented on hitherto, "Thou'lt come no more." I would suggest that these generate a B + C profile as follows:

```
            come   no

      Thou'lt            more.
```

(Here, "come" receives accent by a raised pitch, "more" by a lowered one. I think this constitutes a truer representation of the words than what traditional scansion would give us, namely, a pair of iambs.) Am I saying that what we have here involves the routine, the predictable, or reassurance? Obviously not. But I think what Shakespeare has done is to generate a profile that may be said to be a quiet one, that is associated, to use Bolinger's terms, with a playing down, deemphasis, and indeed foreknowledge. However, Shakespeare has effected this mainly to provide a muted moment that will give, by contrast, even more force to the anguished series of *never*s appearing in the next line.

A more direct application of the B + C profile can be made to Frost's "Acquainted with the Night." Here is the poem in its entirety:

> I have been one acquainted with the night.
> I have walked out in rain—and back in rain.
> I have outwalked the furthest city light.
>
> I have looked down the saddest city lane.
> I have passed by the watchman on his beat
> And dropped my eyes, unwilling to explain.
>
> I have stood still and stopped the sound of feet
> When far away an interrupted cry
> Came over houses from another street,
>
> But not to call me back or say good-by;
> And further still at an unearthly height
> One luminary clock against the sky

Proclaimed the time was neither wrong nor right.
I have been one acquainted with the night.

Michael Cummings and Robert Simmons, have, commendably, tried to make a place for pitch in their "stylistics" approach to poetry, using "Acquainted with the Night" as an example.[89] The results, however, are distinctly peculiar. For one thing, Cummings and Simmons appear to divide the lines into units that are no less arbitrary than old-fashioned feet. The first line, for example, is divided this way:

I have been| one ac| quain ted| with the | night. (p. 48)

They appear to accept the notion of isochrony and of that paradoxical (and to me nonsensical) entity, "silent stresses," which they find "after the end of nearly every line" of this poem (p. 49). What isochrony and silent stresses have to do with the intonation or what they call the "tune" of the poem is not at all clear. They cite the notion of the "tonic" (that is, nuclear) syllable, the one showing the greatest pitch change, and employ curved arrows to designate the falling or rising pitch of the tonic (or so one infers—they are not as clear on the matter of their notation as they might be). They partially diagram line 2 as follows:

I have| walked| out in| rain-| and |back in |rain. (p. 48)

They say there is "a moderate rise on the first 'rain' . . . followed by a fall at the end of the line . . ." (p. 50). (I should note in passing that I disagree with this placement of the pitch changes.) They further say that "In line 2 there is a reversal of direction . . . in line 10 ['But not to call me back or say good-bye'] a presentation of two alternatives. In each case the tonic interrupting the flow of the line supports the sense" (p. 57).

All that this shows is that pitch analysis can be as guilty of imprecision and the same sort of glib impressionism as is not uncommonly found in stress-and-foot analysis. Just how does the tonic "interrupt the flow of the line" in the instances cited? Pitch change is *intrinsic* to English—it does not constitute an "interruption." Moreover, in line 2, that alleged interruption in the form of a pitch drop does not, according to Cummings and Simmons, occur at the point of reversal of direction, which is, presumably, "back." Let us reconsider line 2:

I have walked out in rain and back in rain.

Applying Bolinger's format, I would diagram the line as follows:

out in rain

and

I have walked

back in rain.

That is, there is a rise on "out" and a fall on "back," the line thereby assuming a pronounced B + C pattern, with "and" functioning as a kind of bridge, and with each of the profiles having a level tail (the tail being "the part of a profile that follows the accented syllable," (*intonation,* p. 253). A similar pattern, though realized over shorter stretches of syllables, shows up in line 13, which may be said to negate alternatives in the act of naming them:

wrong nor

Proclaimed the time was neither

right

The "routine" or "repetitive" quality assigned by Bolinger to the B + C contour, a contour enhanced by the monotone tails in the two lines under consideration, can be said to apply nicely in the first of these lines—"I have walked out in rain and back in rain." The suggestion of the words is that the activity in question has been performed more than once or that, at the very least, it has brought no looked-for change. The depressed quality of this line is matched by its pitch-pattern cousin, line 13, the latter making good use of the paradoxical nature of the C profile, which accents by playing down. "Right" in that line is highlighted by a lowering, thereby reinforcing the sense that the notion of appropriate timing is unavailable. To sum up, pitch movement is utilized here to suggest that whether one goes "up" or "down," there is no escape from the malaise depicted, just as there is no relief in walking out or walking back.

Other places in Frost's poem where pitch patterns may be said to lend expressive force are in lines 7 and 10. Here is the first of these:

I have stood still and stopped the sound of feet.

This ordinary reproduction of the line may at the same time be said to serve as a pitch-oriented diagram of it. That is, the principal words—stood, still, stopped, sound, and feet—all appear to be at about the same tonal level and at best only slightly raised above the level of the minor words (it is hard to see the element of "interruption" that Cummings and Simmons find here too, as they assign, for example, a rise to the word "still," p. 48). The absence of significant pitch change corresponds to the suspension of motion and of sound effected by the speaker.

Line 10 may be read as follows:

                    me   by
            back
    But not to call   or say good

Here we can be said to have a B + B contour,[90] which, Bolinger tells us, is associated with questions, "[u]nfinished assertions," a sense of being "'left-up-in-the-air'" (pp. 310, 309). Such a contour seems appropriate in this context, where the speaker is left unanchored by what he hears—it is a cry directed elsewhere. Of course the rise on "me" also serves to give stress to that word, the speaker saying "*I* have no connection with anyone in this setting I'm depicting."

Implicit in what I have been pointing to in the Frost poem is the notion that attending to its intonational patterns can yield a sense of shaped effects not captured by an analysis of its stress patterns. (Indeed, a stress analysis of the "But not to call" line might well see it as a perfectly regular series of alternating unstressed and stressed syllables, or, to put it in traditional terms, as a sequence of pure "iambs.") The focus on pitch configurations need not simply produce under other rubrics what stress analysis achieves, though there is of course an overlapping or reinforcement of results, no surprise when we remember that "stress" is entangled with "accent," the latter the result of pitch change.

To further demonstrate the fruits of investigating intonation, I would like to reconsider a work that was subjected solely to a phrase-and-stress treatment in the preceding chapter, Pound's "In a Station of the Metro." I shall reproduce it here in a typographical arrangement that both reflects pitch changes and honors the breakup into phrases I employed originally. My assumption (as with the Shakespeare and Frost passages) is that those phrases, which are syntactic units, correspond to intonation units, or, more precisely, profiles, to use Bolinger's terminology once again. In addition, the representation of the poem here corresponds to my sense of the heights of the intra-line and inter-line pitch accents relative to each other.

```
        ri
                            fa
                                                   crowd;
The appa    tion        of these      ces      in the

    Pe
                   wet black
                           bough.
    tals       on a
```

The B profile that marks the end of line 1, taken together with the fragmentary nature of that line, leaves things hanging, waiting to be completed by the second line, as they will be. More important, line 1's unfolding, and I have tried to indicate this by the typography, is in keeping with the notion stressed by Lieberman, that the pattern of the usual or "unmarked" utterance shows itself as a series of declining pitch levels (that is, decreasing fundamental frequencies). Also, if we think of the ends of the phrases as constituting articulatory breaks, then my arrangement is also in keeping with Bolinger's observation that "at points where speakers intend a break, their utterance—like an expended clock—'runs down.' There is a pitch correlate of this as well: more successive profiles within a contour show a falling tangent to their peaks than show a rising one . . ." (*Intonation,* p. 263).

The intonational effect here is different from that described in connection with the Frost poem, where one line contained a pitch pattern that was echoed by another. Here, there is a significant contrast. The descending pitch of the first line's accented syllables can be seen as a kind of ground against which the sharply elevated start of the second line functions as a figure. The declining energy level of the first line, so to speak, is strikingly arrested by the high pitch of the first syllable of "Petals" (which could be taken as an example of what David Crystal calls a "high booster," a pitch that is much higher than the next "previous pitch-prominent step-up syllable."[91] And even though "Petals" can be regarded as showing an A profile, its particular configuration is such as to separate it distinctly from both the A profiles and the B profile of the preceding line. All three of those profiles provide a kind of take-off space for their upward pitch changes; the A profile that initiates line 2 hits its peak instantly. Line 2 is further separated from line 1 in having two of its successive syllables—"wet black"—on a relatively high level (with only some descent to "bough"), whereas the first line juxtaposes same-pitch syllables only where they are low. The distinct sonic differentiation of the two lines through their respective pitch patterns helps dramatize the overall contrast between the two verses that was discussed in the preceding chapter.

"In a Station of the Metro" has all of its tiny domain mapped by the pitch patterns I have been describing, whereas, at least in my reading of it, "Acquainted with the Night" makes expressive use of intonation in only a few of its lines. I think it safe to say that the Frost piece is the more typical one in this respect. The use of intonation as a significant device is not to be assumed in every line of a poem any more than the presence of meaningful stress patterns should be. Assigning an a priori functional pervasiveness to either is a mistake; rather, both should be kept in mind as elements of poetry's sonic potential, part-time workers but important ones. Of course, some poets will give them much more frequent employment than others.

I should like now to draw on another poem already considered for its use of stress patterns enacted within phrases, Shakespeare's Sonnet 116, a poem that does in fact make heavy use of pitch patterns. Here it is again, in its entirety:

> Let me not to the marriage of true minds
> Admit impediments. Love is not love
> Which alters when it alteration finds,
> Or bends with the remover to remove.
> O no, it is an ever fixed mark
> That looks on tempests and is never shaken;
> It is the star to every wand'ring bark,
> Whose worth's unknown, although his height be taken.
> Love's not Time's fool, though rosy lips and cheeks
> Within his bending sickle's compass come;
> Love alters not with his brief hours and weeks,
> But bears it out even to the edge of doom.
>> If this be error and upon me proved,
>> I never writ, nor no man ever loved.

A stress analysis would, or at least could, as indicated in the earlier examination of this poem, assign stresses to each word making up the respective endings of lines 1 and 2, "true minds" and "not love." But in addition to that, a significant pitch change (in the form of a rise) would fall on the first word of each, in accordance with the implicit contrastive thrust of both lines (*true* minds as opposed to false ones, love that is *not* genuine as opposed to love that is.) This placement of pitch accent makes its own contribution to the effect, spoken of earlier, of the sonic symmetry linking the two lines, their setting of "true minds" and "not love" against each other as the antagonists, so to speak, of the poem:

<pre>
       true
           minds

       not
           love
</pre>

Another pitch effect that overlaps with the earlier stress analysis involves the word "it" in line 3. The reader may remember that that word was assigned a stress on the grounds that this would help untangle a statement made through a notably inverted syntax—"it alteration finds." Here it might be added that that stress is the result of the raised pitch that would be assigned to the normally lowly "it."[92]

In the instances so far cited, a focus on pitch simply reinforces what a stress analysis can discover. But concentration on pitch can yield some additional dimensions. Line 5—"O no, it is an ever fixed mark"—is particularly marked by intonational effects. The first two words constitute an obvious instance of the B profile, in Bolinger's terms, the "no" being just as obvious an instance of Crystal's "high booster":

<pre>
               no

       O
</pre>

The effect of raised pitch here is partly the result of the "background" generated by line 4, which I read as tending downward in its pitch accents:

<pre>
       bends
               mov
                           move
       Or   with the re   er to re
</pre>

The sharp B profile effect of the "O no" is a near-shrill protest against the sort of changeable love the poem has been describing.

Moving from that intense use of the B profile and the negative, which makes its own sort of assertion, line 5 of the sonnet shifts into a directly assertive mode, using the A profile (which, remember, Bolinger sees as the pitch signature of that mode). Two profiles that are both clearly A find themselves juxtaposed in the compound "ever fixed" in line 5,

```
      e       fix
        ver       ed,
```

and a similar combination occurs again in line 7 with "every wand'ring."

```
      ev      wand
        ery       'ring
```

In between, in line 6, a pair of such profiles have shown themselves, though not jammed together, but separated and placed so as to be respectively embodied in the hemistiches of the line:

```
               tem                    sha
   That looks on      pests   and is ne[v]er    ken
```

(I am assuming here that "never" is contracted to "ne'er.") This line, incidentally, offers a good example of how contemplating a verse with an ear to its intonation produces a different acoustic shape than that engendered by a focus on stress. In the latter case we would accord prominence to "looks" and "ne[v]er." Of course, one could allocate a somewhat raised pitch to those two terms as well, but I do not believe either merits the degree of raising I have assigned to "tem-" and "sha-."

As is the case with line 6, line 8 breaks up into hemistiches, but offers a different combination of pitch patterns:

```
            known                    tak
                                        en
   Whose worth's un      although his height be
```

Here the line may be said to be fully mapped as a B + B pairing (with the second B having a tail, -en, falling to a lower pitch). This, with its suggestion of suspension, or lack of resolution, seems appropriate to a description of an elusive entity. Once again, a stress-focused reading would accord prominence to other syllables, namely "worth's," "-though," and "height." But from the

viewpoint of a pitch-oriented reading, I regard these as being registered at a level *comparatively* near that of the non-stress-bearing
syllables.[93] As was the case in line 6, pitch here makes for two
cases of highlighting, not four or five.

We can find at least three more intonational effects operating in
the sonnet. The opening of line 9—"Love's not Time's fool"—
appears to be compressing into an epigram sentiments that the
poem had voiced in a comparatively expanded way in lines 5–6
and 7–8 respectively. It can be seen as exhibiting a B + A profile.

```
              not      Time's
     Love's                fool
```

Bolinger, surveying various examples of the B + A contour, one of
the most frequently encountered in English, remarks on the "tight
union" of the profiles therein (p. 292); such a union appears to be
at work here. Bolinger further remarks that some characteristic
instances of B + A represent "*comments* that the audience is expected to take at face value. Or not to take at all—B + A is the
normal contour when one is talking to oneself . . . " (p. 287; italics
in original). *Both* of these observations can be seen as applicable
to the present instance. The speaker is declaring something that
he apparently expects to go unchallenged, and at the same time,
as indicated in my original discussion of the sonnet, may be engaged in a form of self-address, designed to persuade himself more
than anyone else as to the durability of true love.

The final two instances of pitch management can be characterized quickly. Line 10, "Within its bending sickle's compass come,"
which I regard as a single syntactic unit, is dominated by the three
successive A profiles of "bending sickle's compass" ("come" can
be seen as the tail of the last such profile).

```
     bend-    sic-     com-
          ing      kle's      pass come
```

The juxtaposition of A profiles, as indicated above, is frequently
used for an effect of "power," according to Bolinger (p. 292), and is
so used here, to mark the destructive force of time. The respective
beginnings of lines 11 and 12 can both be seen as B profiles:

```
              not
     Love alters
```

```
              out
     But bears it
```

Here, pitch pattern is not so much an expressive device as an aid to bonding through symmetry. We have two consecutive line beginnings that are clauses, contain the same number of syllables, link up their terminal words in an off-rhyme, *not-out,* and display the same pitch pattern. This formal bonding underlines what may be regarded as their complementary relationship in terms of sense: Love alters not but bears it[self] out.

My readings thus far have worked sometimes with fragments of lines—beginnings, middles, and final sections—sometimes with whole lines. In doing so, those readings have favored the use of Bolinger's profiles and contours rather than Crystal's tone-units. But at this point I need to engage a question that Crystal raises. He disposes of it with relative ease, but in doing so only leaves us, from my perspective, with another problem. Crystal asserts that the verse line should be "taken as a primitive unit of metrical theory," and one that is phonologically defined and hence not dependent on its graphemic appearance. So far, so excellent, as Chapter 5 would suggest. Crystal continues by stating as one of his hypotheses that "the normal exponence of a line is a single tone-unit . . . this is usually sufficient to provide unambiguous indication of line-end boundary . . . " ("Intonation," pp. 24–25). In dealing with intonation patterns, my handling of final sections of lines or of whole lines has hitherto overlapped with Crystal's approach, in tacitly assuming that the terminus of a line marks an intonational boundary point. But this has been the case only because the specimens selected have not involved enjambments, or at least not what might be called acute enjambments—the lines in question have ended in such a way as to preserve some sort of phrasal integrity. But what of instances in which this is not true, as in a great deal of free verse, for example? Crystal says that "In these cases, the intonation contour is interrupted, and completed on the next line," though this is not inevitably the case (pp. 26–27). Crystal does not pursue the question for more than the space of a longish footnote. But we might linger over the matter for a while because it would appear to confront us with a whole series of instances, constituting at the very least a substantial subset of all enjambed lines, in which mappings through intonation contours would undermine the line as a sonic unit, just as enjambment has undermined it as a semantic and/or syntactic unit. What happens then to the notion of the line as the essential component of poetry.?[94]

We might begin consideration of this matter by looking at a text that has been the subject of intonational analysis by Richard Cureton, the ending of Wallace Stevens's "Sunday Morning."[95] Cu-

reton incorporates, in his "multilevel" approach to verse, the
consideration of "intonational units."[96] Here is his scansion of the
four concluding lines of Stevens' poem, with the symbol "|" mark-
ing the ends of the intonational units or phrases that he finds
(arrows indicate the continuation of such a phrase from one line
to the next:

```
  ,--------------------------------------->
And, in the isolation of the sky,
  >------------| ,--------------------------------------->
At evening, casual flocks of pigeons make
  >---------------------------| ------------>
Ambiguous undulations as they sink,
  -------------------------------------------------------------|
Downward to darkness, on extended wings.
```

As his arrows would indicate, Cureton has determined that "the
intonational phrasing in these final four lines is consistently enjambed," making, he says, for an "expansive, flowing" movement.[97]
This reading of the verse structure illustrates that a line that is
enjambed for one prosodist may not be for another, since I regard
only the second and third of the lines as run-over, with the former
obviously so and the latter showing itself as enjambed only as we
read on. Be that as it may, Cureton, who appears to be primarily
interested in the relative *lengths* of intonational phrases, finds the
last one, which he regards as "anapestic" (in terms of the "phonological phases" making it up), "more expansive and resolving than
the preceding . . . iambic phrases."[98] But apart from Cureton's
questionable use of "anapestic" and "iambic," to say this is to say
nothing of the nature and role of the pitch patterns involved, a
striking omission if one is supposed to be talking about
intonation.[99]

Before giving my own reading of the Stevens text, I should like
to make a general point about the status of the verse line in relation
to intonational analysis. Cureton's intonational phrases are allowed
to ride roughshod over line endings, moving into the next line to
complete themselves (in this sense his approach overlaps that of
Crystal). In keeping with my insistence on the centrality of the line
in poetry, and my thinking of it being, ideally, a meaningful entity,
the method of intonational analysis I propose is that we honor the
line-ending by seeing it as an intonational terminal. This principle
may come into conflict with another principle that I have advocated, namely, that prosodic analysis should respect a poem's
phrasings, its syntactic units. That is, a line-boundary/intonation-

terminal may cut into a syntactic or sense unit, as certainly happens in lines 2–3 of the Stevens passage: "casual flocks of pigeons make/ Ambiguous undulations . . . ." In such cases I would continue to regard the line-ending as constituting a genuine, pause-marked terminus (including the terminus of an intonation unit, be it profile or contour or both), and at the same time I would acknowledge how the enjambment's violation of syntactic or sense-unit boundaries affects the intonation. In this way both the fact of line-ending and the fact of enjambment are properly respected.

In my reading of the Stevens passage, for example, I find the enjambment of the second line assigning a distinct rise in pitch to "make," if only to indicate that the sense unit has not been completed (I venture to say that such raising of pitch will prove to be the most characteristic effect of enjambment). The B profile, coming at the end of a line that has been dominated by A profiles, keeps things in suspension:

```
                                    make
     ca          flocks      pi
         sual             of     geons
```

This rise matches the ending of the preceding line, which I read as unfolding at a level tone until the last syllable:

```
                                  sky
        And in the isolation of the
```

These two successive raised-tone endings are followed by one more such, "as they sink," and then by a lowered-tone ending in "on extended wings." The meaning of "sink" would seem to encourage a lowering of pitch on that word, but what proves to be enjambment operating at line-end results in a raising, so we get another B profile:

```
                    sink
        as they
```

The argument for seeing "on extended wings" as a lowered-tone ending, and, in fact, as a distinct example of a C profile, is somewhat more elaborate. By carefully enunciating the word that precedes it, "extended," thereby assigning full rather than reduced value to the third "e" of that word, the rise on the middle syllable, "ten," would be sustained through the last syllable, "-ded," or followed only by a qualified drop. Such a performance of "extended" would dramatize its meaning—we are extending the word, so to speak—and get the most out of its twice-used "d" sound, a phoneme the line has already featured in "Downward to darkness." In short, I am arguing for either

```
                    ten ded
          ex
```

or

```
              ten
                   ded
          ex
```

Either configuration provides an elevation from which "wings," though a word whose meaning more readily suggests ascent than descent, sinks in a characteristic end-of-utterance decline in fundamental frequency. As far as the first phrase of the line is concerned, the first syllable of "Downward," going counter to its meaning, would receive a pitch elevation, and the resulting configuration of the word would be echoed in the quickly-following "darkness." Represented in terms of pitch arrangements, the line, then, would come to this:

```
    Down          dark           ten ded
         ward to       ness on ex
                                       wings
```

(One might want to locate "wings" on a pitch level no lower than the other lowered ones, but in any event the word would I think, undergo a drop of some degree.) In Bolinger's terms the contour here is $A + A + B + C$.

To sum up, this reading would have it that three lines with raised endings (the second and third raisings effected by enjambment) are followed by one line with a lowered ending. The up-up-up-down sequence of these endings, along with the fact that "Down-" and "sink" and "wings" go counter, respectively, to their meanings or associations and to the intonational value we might be inclined to give them in other contexts, greatly enriches the lines. The pitch patterns weave themselves into a passage that can be thought of in two ways or as having two different emphases: it is, on the one hand, about a downward movement that suggests death but is simultaneously a sign of vitality, of life at its fullest, and, on the other hand, it is about life even at its fullest moving towards darkness and death. Down (as with "sink") entails up, and up down—the latter realized both by the general configuration of the line-endings and by the handling of "wings"—in this passage of ambiguous undulations. (It might be noted that in my reading here I have paid less attention to the attitudinal characteristics that generally accompany particular profiles, and have focused more on the particular dynamics of risings and fallings in a given passage of poetry, and on how these mesh with the thematic burden.)

To provide more instances of intonational analysis, and to show further how enjambment enters into intonation, I shall now move away from "Sunday Morning," an example of blank verse, and take up a sample of the mode that has produced even more instances of run-over lines, or more acute instances of such lines, free verse. The poem in question is Sylvia Plath's "Ariel." My observations will be confined to those portions of the poem that were looked at earlier in terms of their phrasal arrangements and stress patterns. Now I shall try to show how considerations of pitch might add to our understanding of the way those passages work. (I should note, and this goes for all my intonational schematizings, that the designated relative pitch levels represent something of an abstraction (but of a lesser degree of abstraction, I hasten to add, than the schemes produced by foot scansion), and might differ with different readers. What is set down in this case, as elsewhere, is what I regard as a performance likely to be rendered by many readers.)

Here again is the opening line of Plath's poem, this time in a pitch-pattern arrangement:

```
        Sta
                         dark
            sis
                 in
                      ness
```

Where my original reading produced a sense of line 1 as composed of two symmetrically stressed disyllabic words, balanced around "in," the present reading sees a line where the sense of balance is at once confirmed, by the presence of two A profiles back to back, but also qualified to an extent, by "in" being regarded as the initial component of the second of the profiles, giving the latter a somewhat different structure than the first. (In Bolinger's terminology, "in" is an instance of "takeoff," which consists of "the unaccented syllables, if any, that precede the accented syllable in a profile"; *Intonation*, p. 253). The sense of symmetry, or balance, is further qualified by the overall downward tilt of the line's pitch levels. The two successive A profiles, combined with the overall falling pitch, help give the line a sense of finality and low energy.

In distinct contrast, the second line can be seen as assuming a B profile followed, after a pause, by another such profile, though one of quite different proportions.

```
        Then                          blue
                        sub
            the        stanceless
```

Here I am reading "the substanceless" primarily as a relatively level takeoff for the accented "blue," though my format indicates that "substanceless" may be said to incorporate a subdued A profile. "Blue" is another instance of a word whose pitch level is raised by enjambment. The line thus gives us, primarily, two B profiles, which characteristically help create an "up in the air" feeling, one that is reinforced by the distinctly different dimensions of those profiles, and that suggests the possibility of movement, change. Line 2 thereby reverses the effect of the first line's falling pitch patterns, its downward slope.[100]

The third line might be rendered as follows:

```
        Pour        tor
                            dis
            of       and      tances.
```

This is a B + B + A array, with the first two profiles maintaining the energy level initiated in the preceding line, followed by what might be called the bringing-down-and-to-completion effect of the A profile, the fall of this profile being stretched over two syllables, which helps strengthen the sense of spatial expansion created by the meaning of "distances." (The reader might test this last assertion by comparing the effect of "distances" with that of the singular form, "distance.") Moreover, the proportions of the A profile here echo those of the A profile in line 2:

```
        sub
          stanceless

        dis
          tances
```

This similarity of pitch patterns helps link the words "substance-less" and "distances" in our ears (a linkage aided by the rhymes or near-rhymes of *-stance* and *-tance,* of *-less* and *-es.*) For all the presumable allure of those "distances," the word's sonic kinship to "substanceless" can be taken (at least with hindsight) as prophetic of the speaker's mad dash toward liberation-dissolution.

We might look now at the other section of "Ariel," considered earlier in terms of phrases and their stress patterns, namely, the poem's closing lines:

> And now I
> Foam to wheat, a glitter of seas.
> The child's cry
>
> Melts in the wall.
> And I
> Am the arrow,
>
> The dew that flies
> Suicidal, at one with the drive
> Into the red
>
> Eye, the cauldron of morning.

What strikes the ear about this passage is its domination by B profiles. Two in particular stand out because of each one's stretching of the raised pitch over two syllables, with the second syllable in both cases lending itself to an additional rise; the connection of these B profiles is cemented by rhyme.

$$\text{And} \quad \overset{\text{now}}{} \overset{\text{I}}{}$$

$$\text{The} \quad \overset{\text{child's}}{} \overset{\text{cry}}{}$$

These are perhaps the strongest instances of the B profiles' presence, both partly created by and reinforcing the prominent use of enjambment, serving to charge the passage with energy, with momentum. (Considering that the poem is about an imperious horse ride, I cannot resist noting here that Bolinger speaks of the use of "the sustained high pitch of the B" for an effect of imperiousness—in such instances "the speaker is 'on his high horse'" (*Intonation,* p. 286).)

More intonational effects are at work in the passage cited. Consider the lines

> Am the arrow,

> The dew that flies
> Suicidal, at one with the drive

In intonational terms they might be rendered as follows:

```
              ar
    Am the    row

         dew        flies
    The        that

        cid        one              drive
    Su i   al,     at       with the
```

The third line occurs close enough to the first to be in earshot of it, so to speak, and the word "Suicidal" recapitulates in itself the intonational shape of "Am the arrow."[101] In both cases we have an A profile with the accented syllable led up to by two unaccented syllables. The respective semantic contents or implications of "Am the arrow" and "Suicidal" would appear to pull away from each other, the first suggesting an embodiment of force directed against others, the second a force directed against oneself. But the intonational parallelism of the phrases makes sense when we realize that their respective meanings are in fact inseparable, aspects of the same drive; indeed, the grammar of the passage may be said to put the two meanings in apposition. Also, the two A profiles sandwich between them the B-dominated, exuberant "The dew that flies," keeping it in check.

But the B profile will not be immediately subdued. In fact, the next two lines generate four such profiles in a row:

```
          one              drive
    . . . at       with the

              red
    Into the

    Eye

                    caul           mor
               the       dron    of   ning
```

The last of these, "Eye," is perhaps the purest, a one-syllable embodiment of high pitch. But this is followed by a restraining, which has the final word or, perhaps one should say, the final sound. With "the cauldron of morning," the poem concludes with two consecutive examples of the profile that falls, the A, the resulting contour (knitted together by the sound overlap of *caul-* and *mor-*) reversing the feeling created by all the Bs, bringing the poem down and to rest.

The readings I have given have demonstrated, I hope, that a pitch-focused analysis of verse, while serving in places to reinforce what a stress-based scansion shows, can also reveal something about a poem's shape that eludes that analysis. In fact, if one believes with Bolinger, as I do, that it is pitch change, more than loudness, that creates salience (accent), then pitch analysis, the determining of intonational profiles and contours, should not only be included as one means of describing the formal shape of a line, it should be accorded pride of place.

How does pitch analysis's diagram of a line compare with the diagram generated by stress analysis? One might think of the two as layers of a palimpsest, separable by examination but working simultaneously in the poem's voicing. Each takes as its domain, its unit of attention, the line. In addition, each mode of analysis will, wherever possible, cluster a line's syllables into phrases, units of meaning, with the two sets of phrases by and large congruent. Exceptions to such clustering will occur in both modes, of course, with enjambment.

Pitch analysis reveals the essential structure of the whole of the line, the skeleton of its gestalt, a gestalt for which no a priori model need be invoked. *Stress* analysis, without, in my version of it, being predisposed to demonstrating the presence of a particular metrical paradigm, proceeds mainly on a word-by-word basis, using lexical stress as a frame of reference in making its determinations, in addition to weighing the semantic importance of each word. It will flesh out the linear skeleton, so to speak, pointing to a layer of lesser saliences than those that will dominate the intonational analysis. If the specimen under examination appears to fall into a traditional mode, the findings of stress analysis would be compared with the abstract model of that mode. To use Sonnet 116 once again, the first line, "Let me not to the marriage of true minds," will, under the gaze of intonational analysis, single out "not" and "true" as the most salient syllables. A stress analysis will add "mar-" and "minds," and then compare the overall stress configuration of the line with the abstract paradigm of the "iambic pentameter" line, renamed and redefined, I would hope, in the manner suggested in Chapter 6.

In one respect, that redefinition offers a model differing only slightly from the traditional one, substituting a "four- or five-stress" clause, so to speak, for the original stipulation of five stresses. But this small shift entails, as already indicated, major repercussions in the application of the metrical paradigm, automatically removing the label of "variation" from hundreds of lines, seeing them instead as instances of the norm. A large shift away from the traditional definition of iambic pentameter is at work of course, in my rejection of the foot in favor of the phrase. This featuring of the phrase, originally put in terms of stress, has now been enlarged to include considerations of pitch. Giving such weight to phrasing might make some metrists uncomfortable, for in place of the alleged unity, the totalism of meter, the finding of a slot in a sonic scheme for every syllable of a poem, phrasalism thinks in terms of ad hoc effects, of patterns that, when revealed, might not completely map or account for every syllable in terms of an ongoing pattern. But as I have already tried to show, the totalism of meter comes with the price of forced readings and the violating or ignoring of essential elements in the way we process the strings of sounds making up the lines of verse.

As indicated earlier, there is still room for a modified version of meter in phrasalism. However, it is not only a modified version but a shrunken one, no longer allowed to bully our conception of the sound-shapes of verse, to place the movements of the living language under the heel of a dubious formalism, to obscure or ignore the groupings, and the ups and downs, of the way we speak, when what we speak is poetry.

Epilogue: Epireading, Graphireading, and the Matter of Voicing

IN *Ferocious Alphabets,* Denis Donoghue, as part of his commentary on individual literary critics—English, American, Continental, most of them modern—speaks of two ways of regarding texts. The first he labels "epireading," from the Greek *epos,* meaning "speech or utterance."[1] For the epireader, "speech is the choice form of language" (p. 93). Writing is speech that has in effect been embalmed, since it is, compared to its source—vocalized utterance—"a dead thing" (p. 96). Donoghue calls the second way of looking at texts "graphireading," from the Greek *graphos,* writing. The graphireader "deals with writing as such and does not think of it as transcribing an event properly construed as vocal and audible" (p. 151).

Donoghue traces the notion of epireading back to "the Christian tradition in which the primal creative principle is identified as the Word of God," and back as well as to Plato's *Phaedrus,* in which writing is seen as a bastard son of living speech (pp. 93, 95). In the beginning, then, in both traditions, was the voiced word; writing is later, and lesser. The epireader wishes "to reverse chronology, go from the second stage to the first . . . making up for the tokens of absence and distance which he finds in written words." He wants to restore those words "to a source, a human situation involving speech, character, personality . . ." (pp. 98–99). Included among those named as epireaders by Donoghue are Georges Poulet, Kenneth Burke, and Harold Bloom.

The pedigree of graphireading is not nearly as long as that of epireading, but this comparative newcomer has figured potently in contemporary criticism. If there is a single originator of graphireading in Donoghue's scheme, it is Stephane Mallarmé, for whom "the pure work of poetry involves the disappearance of the poet's voice" (p. 153). The words on the page are primary, and the reader must be as self-effacing as the writer, not breaking the silence that surrounds those words. Mallarmé's ideology, says Donoghue, is utterly dependent on the written word, because if the word were conceived of as spoken, the author "would be dragged into the poem with every audible breath" (p. 155).

Immediately after his discussion of Mallarmé, Donoghue turns to the views of Jacques Derrida, whom he had already cited as a commentator on the *Phaedrus.* For Derrida, writing is not to be regarded as a fallen form of speech. He links speech to a metaphysics of presence (which he rejects), to the belief that uttered words successfully point beyond themselves to a nonverbal order of reality: "the formal essence of the signified is *presence,* and the privilege of its proximity to the *logos* as *phonē* is the privilege of presence" (cited in Donoghue, p. 159). Writing, in fact, is the primary form of language for Derrida, acknowledging by its nature a metaphysics of absence, including the absence both of a signifier and a transcendental signified. Writing is language that registers the play of absence and presence, a form in which the self forgets itself. Donoghue comments: "What is forgotten in writing is the self as it is understood in the midst of speech" (p. 161).

In *Reading Voices: Literature and the Phonotext* (1990), published almost a decade after *Ferocious Alphabets,* Garrett Stewart argues for and attempts to demonstrate at length a mode of reading that falls "[m]idway" between the "polarized concepts" of epireading and graphireading that Donoghue has given us.[2] This middle mode, which he calls "phonemic reading," would make room, as Donoghue does not, "for the reader's silent voice" (pp. 138–39). Perpetually present but perpetually inaudible, such a voice is indeed operative in the act of reading, as has been attested to by Ake W. Edfeldt's *Silent Speech and Silent Reading,* a work cited by Stewart. Edfeldt points to evidence indicating that our vocal apparatus is set in motion when we read, but at a low level of operation. So it seems that the sounding out of words that accompanied our first steps in learning to read is suppressed but not entirely obliterated in the act of silent reading.

What does our silent voicing produce, in Stewart's view? Not a text in its entirety (more of this later), but a series of decidedly scattered, decidedly local effects. These occur when the distinctions between some words, as conveyed by their graphic representations—bunchings of letters separated by white spaces—begin to dissolve, to slip and slide, to break and blur, under the pressure of a voicing that is recorded in "the . . . 'mind's ear' of the reader" (p. 117).[3] In these cases, the ending of one word is such that it can fuse with or appropriate or be appropriated by the beginning of the next word so as to produce a new meaning, one that coexists with the meaning established by the text considered purely in graphemic terms. The segment of one word drifts across the intervening space to link up with the word before or after. One example Stewart puts forth sees a dissolving interplay between the second and third words of a line from *Paradise Lost:* "With Serpent error wand'ring, found their way." This, he says, "can never be entirely free of 'serpent terror' . . . (p. 149). Another example is from a text that has figured prominently in this study, Shakespeare's Sonnet 116. According to Stewart, the phrase characterizing love as "an ever-fix'd mark" is simultaneously heard, through our phonemic reading, as "a never-fix'd mark" (p. 63).[4] One might think that such effects occur too rarely to serve as the basis for a goodly-sized, densely written book, but this is precisely what Stewart has produced.

What does all this have to do with the concerns of my own book? Let me start by saying that Stewart's characterization of his enterprise as falling "midway" between voice-centered epireading and voice-banished, or at least voice-subordinated, graphireading seems to me clearly a mismapping. Decidedly Francophile are his critical allegiances (French itself is his virtuoso and implicitly self-delighting way of responding to texts, of generating or manipulating critical abstractions with an almost sensuous satisfaction), and while he tries to establish a distance from that celebrated graphireader, Jacques Derrida, there is a decided qualification of the difference Stewart lays claim to. It is almost as though we are looking at the critical equivalent of the ambiguous, shifting nature of word boundaries he is so enamored of: Stewart is his own man, Stewart is an apostle of Derrida, both are true. For while, in supposed opposition to Derrida, he insists on making a place for the workings of voice in the experience of a text, those workings are only allowed to enter as a series of scattered guerilla operations; victory in the war as a whole has been conceded to the French philosopher. "The question is no longer the presence (or index) of voice in text but, instead, the presence *to* evocalization of any text when read" (p. 3). Stewart's italicized construction in the second half of his sentence seems to me obscure, but the allegiance of the first half of the sentence to Derrida is clear enough. Again:

Derrida's frontal assault on the primacy of voice in language might well seem to render any reading-with-the-ear a theoretically groundless pastime. If one recognizes, however, why the phoneme need not suffer the same fate of banishment from textuality as does the voice, such an acknowledgement secures a considerable phonotextual foothold within both the practices and the axioms of deconstruction (p. 103).

Stewart ultimately sees his work as an *extension* of Derrida:

> The linguistic refinement displayed in Derrida's apprehension of textuality, deconstruction's unprecedented grasp of the *play* of literary language (play in the sense of alternation, oscillation, give) . . . ought to be, though has so far not proved, widely enabling for an intensive reading of the literary text. In fact, one line of Derrida's thinking could lead, more or less directly, to what I have been characterizing as phonemic reading: a continuous response to those traces highlighted in literary language as a drift of functioning differentials (p. 107).[5]

All in all, Stewart appears to have no problem acceding to Derrida's assault on voice conceived of as establishing authorial presence, but Stewart insists that he himself is making a place for voice conceived of as that which the reader provides. What he means by his title, *Reading Voices,* he tells us, is that the act of reading gives voice to. But to what, we might ask: whole texts or even whole lines when the texts are poems? Not at all. In claiming to rescue the phoneme, Stewart does not have in mind the phoneme as something continually present in a text, but only the occasionally occurring, fickle phoneme, capable of breaking away from one word to join another. Reading voices what he calls "transegmental drift," intermittent slippage at the boundaries of words, and nothing more.

Even if one were to go along with Stewart's acceptance of the deconstructionist dissolution of the author, even if, swallowing hard, one were to look on the surnames of Donne, Milton, Dryden, and Pope as "merely the place-name[s] . . . for the site[s] of certain phonemic contingencies" (p. 80), and even if one were to agree with the insistence that the text is something that is produced by the reader (this last is at least partly true), Stewart's approach would be deeply troubling, finally perverse. Apart from his own characterization of transegmental drift creating an effect "dubious and ephemeral" (p. 107), the *voicing* that he claims to put at the center of his project is, in my view, an intolerably attenuated affair. (All the more ironic are Stewart's repeated references to something as large and substantial as the "body," when he talks about the reader's production of the phonotext—nothing as modest as "the organs of speech" for him—only the "body" will do).[6] For the reader-enacted "voicing" that engages Stewart is, he continually reminds us, silent, latent, soundless, not oral, "not sonic at all but phonemic," "under erasure" (p. 127), audible only to the "mind's ear," "silently heard—beyond the grounding of any Voice . . ."

(p. 118); deconstruction is contemputuous of the thought of such grounding.

The phonemic interplay between words that so fascinates Stewart would not, as I see it, automatically be ruled out if those words were to be truly sounded. But the chief thing to note here is that Stewart is not, from my perspective, much more of a friend of the sonic dimension of poetry (he discusses prose as well) than René Wellek and Austin Warren, whose views he explicitly pits himself against. He cites their saying "unless we are almost illiterate . . . we grasp printed words as wholes without breaking them up into sequences of phonemes and thus do not pronounce them even silently" (p. 23). Wellek and Warren, the reader might remember from Chapter 2, cautioned us against the danger of giving weight to the performing of the literary text, namely, attributing importance to the merely personal, thereby undermining the possibility of "a real science of rhythmics and metrics. . . ."[7]

Stewart of course contends, and rightly, that in ordinary reading we inevitably enunciate the words of a text silently, but my objection is to his *preoccupation* with that silence. While he insists on a place for a reader's voicing, it is only a minimal version of such voicing that he will allow. Everything I have said in this book is based on the assumption that the full consumption (or production, if one prefers Stewart's formulation) of a poetic text cannot be effected unless the words are given tongue, unless we bring to them the unbridled operation of our vocal apparatus. Even if Stewart were right in assuming that the particular effects he is interested in can only be generated by a silent reading, we would be paying too high a price for those effects, which are, after all, highly infrequent affairs and which do not even serve the deconstructive agenda of destabilizing, problematizing the text nearly as much as Stewart would apparently like us to think. For as far as I can tell, the overwhelming majority of the specimens of transegmental drift he offers us only reinforce what the text, considered without the meltdowns of adjacent words, already gives us. In the apparently extreme case of Sonnet 116, where "an ever-fix'd mark" yields its apparent *opposite,* "a never-fix'd mark," the sense of the poem as being in conflict with or subverting itself can be established on entirely different grounds; it need not be deconstructed by a phonemic, that is to say, silent reading.

Such a reading would certainly not render adequately what is *always* present in a poem, the movement of its lines. That is a question of stress and pitch configurations, of flows and pauses, which, while they may not be continuously significant, certainly blossom into significance with much greater frequency than do the occurrences of transegmental drift. The knottings and loosenings of verse lines, their ups and their downs, constitute a much larger dimension of their voicing than does the slippage of phonemes that so fascinates Stewart. To subject the poem to a silent reading so as to elicit that slippage (and thereby supposedly confirm or extend deconstructionist tenets) seems to me, at best, a Pyrrhic victory. I could not agree more with Clive Scott's contention that "Meaning . . . cannot free itself from the business of uttering,"[8] and everything I have said in this book is predicated on the assumption that, ideally at least, a poem is to be voiced, not subliminally, but out loud, and that we attend to what we are doing and hearing—with our actual ears, not the "mind's ear"—when we so deliver it, whether to others or to ourselves. I opt always for literally-heard melodies, and while our lives or the poems we are reading may not allow us to sing of summer or in ease, we should certainly not throttle our voices, not settle for anything less than the fullthroated.

Notes

PREFACE

1. Eniko Bollobas, *Tradition and Innovation in American Free Verse: Whitman to Duncan* (Budapest: Akademia Kiado, 1986), 11.

INTRODUCTION

1. John Nist, "The Word-Group Cadence: Basis of English Metrics," *Linguistics* 6 (1964): 73.
2. Karl Shapiro, "English Prosody and Modern Poetry," *ELH* 14 (June 1947): 82.
3. In 1964 Harvey Gross was saying that "metrics and versification are deemed contemptible studies." See his *Sound and Form in Modern Poetry: A Study of Prosody from Thomas Hardy to Robert Lowell* (1964; reprint, Ann Arbor: University of Michigan Press, 1968), 249. See also Roger Fowler, *The Languages of Literature: Some Linguistic Contributions to Criticism* (New York: Barnes and Noble, 1971), 141. Writing in 1976, Alan T. Gaylord, after characterizing prosodic criticism as a "hand-maiden," said: "It is not likely to have direct influence in any discourse on meaning, and is required in any case to harmonize its findings with meanings which others have already described." See his "Scanning the Prosodists: An Essay in Metacriticism," *The Chaucer Review* 11 (Summer 1976):72. Derek Attridge, one of the more considerable of contemporary prosodists, has said of works of metrical study that "by and large their undisturbed repose on the library shelves is not unmerited." See his *The Rhythms of English Poetry* (New York: Longman, 1982), 3. According to Edward L. Epstein and Terence Hawkes, prosody has been in bad odor for centuries. See their *Linguistics and English Prosody,* Studies in Linguistics Occasional Papers, no. 7 (Buffalo, N.Y.: University of Buffalo Department of Anthropology and Linguistics, 1959), 12. All these men have themselves written prosodic criticism.
4. See Alan Helms, "Intricate Song's Last Measure," *Sewanee Review* 87 (Spring 1979): 249–66; also Brad Leithauser, "Metrical Illiteracy," *New Criterion* 1 (January 1983): 41–46; also Brad Leithauser, "The Confinement of Free Verse," *New Criterion* 5 (May 1987): 4–14.
5. See Diane Wakoski, "Picketing the Zeitgeist: The New Conservatism in American Poetry," *American Book Review* 8 (May–June 1986): 3; see also "Picketing the Zeitgeist Picket: Replies to Diane Wakoski from Robert Mezey, Lewis Turco, David Radavich, Brian Richards, and Dana Gioia," *American Book Review* 8 (November–December 1986): 3; also Robert McPhillips, "Reading the New Formalists," *Sewanee Review* 97 (Winter 1989): 73–96; also Ira Sadoff: "Neo-Formalism: A Dangerous Nostalgia," *American Poetry Review* 19 (January–February 1990): 7–13. That Brad Leithauser's "Metrical Illiteracy" and "The

Confinement of Free Verse" appeared in the ideologically conservative *The New Criterion* undoubtedly contributed to the politicizing of the issue of New Formalism.

6. Timothy Steele, *Missing Measures: Modern Poetry and the Revolt Against Meter* (Fayetteville: University of Arkansas Press, 1990) 278.

7. See Philip Dacey and Robert Jauss, ed., *Strong Measures: Contemporary Poetry in Traditional Forms* (New York: Harper and Row, 1985); also Robert Richman, ed., *The Direction of Poetry: An Anthology of Rhymed and Metered Verse Written in the English Language since 1975* (Boston: Houghton Mifflin, 1985).

8. Karl Shapiro registered a strong sense of cleavage in the culture of American poetry as far aback as 1947, though in somewhat different terms than I have employed. See his thoughtful essay, "English Prosody and Modern Poetry," 90. An important exception to the denigration of free verse, and hence a document going counter to the cleavage is John Hollander's *Rhyme's Reason: A Guide to English Verse* (New Haven: Yale University Press, 1981), although Hollander has elsewhere scolded the abuse of free verse (see his "Poetic Schemes," *Partisan Review* 48 [1981]: 478–85) and he does not seem to have any quarrel with the concept of meter.

CHAPTER 1. IN THE MUDDLED KINGDOM OF METER

1. Cf. Derek Attridge's remark that "most comments on the rhythms of English poetry owe their existence to theories which bear the dust—or the patina—of centuries upon them." See his *Rhythms of English Poetry,* 4.

2. T. V. F. Brogan, *English Versification, 1570–1980: A Reference Guide with a Global Appendix* (Baltimore: Johns Hopkins University Press (1981), xiii.

3. Karl Shapiro, "English Poetry and Modern Poetry," 83.

4. Donald Wesling, *The New Poetries: Poetic Form Since Coleridge and Wordsworth* (Lewisburg, Pa.: Bucknell University Press, 1985), 89.

5. The original can be found in René Wellek and Austin Warren, *Theory of Literature,* (New York: Harcourt, Brace and World, 1949), 167.

6. T. S. Omond, *English Metrists: Being a Sketch of English Prosodical Criticism from Elizabethan Times to the Present Day* (1921; reprint, New York: Phaeton Press, 1968), 76.

7. Edgar Allan Poe, *Essays and Reviews* (New York: The Library of America, 1984), 26.

8. O. B. Hardison, Jr., *Prosody and Purpose in the English Renaissance* (Baltimore: Johns Hopkins University Press, 1989), 24, 31.

9. The author of the encyclopedia entry, "Poetry," is Theodore Watts; his citation of Hegel is noted in Raymond MacDonald Alden, *English Verse: Specimens Illustrating its Principles and History* (New York: Henry Holt and Company, 1903), 426–27.

10. Seymour Chatman, *A Theory of Meter* (The Hague: Mouton, 1965), 102.

11. Paul Fussell, *Poetic Meter and Poetic Form* (New York: Random House, 1965), 104.

12. Paul Fussell, *Poetic Meter and Poetic Form,* rev. ed. (New York: Random House, 1979), 100.

13. Cleanth Brooks and Robert Penn Warren, *Understanding Poetry,* 3rd ed. (New York: Holt, Rinehart and Winston, 1960), 124. An even more inclusive

conception of rhythm as a context for poetry, if such can be imagined, is to be found in Harvey Gross, who says "the rhythm of poetry is an image of 'vital process.' It conveys an awareness of the movements which actuate all physical life: the rhythm of the cell and the pulse of the modern physicist's perpetually self-renewing universe. . . ." See his *Sound and Form in Modern Poetry,* 312. Cf. the observation in the Princeton *Encyclopedia of Poetry and Poetics* that "Medieval theories of m[eter] . . . frequently assume that the pleasure man takes in m[eter] is an image of the pleasure he takes in the observation of the principle of order in a universe which is itself will and order incarnate" (497).

14. A typical and recent example of the critical strain I am talking about (together with a complementary hostility to the nonmetrical) can be found in Dana Gioia's untitled contribution to the January, 1989, issue of *Crosscurrents,* given over to the New Formalism and the New Narrative. (I shall have other occasion to draw on this issue.) Gioia's remarks embody the form-and-freedom variant of the meter-as-creator-of-synthesis argument. He says "Formal poetry always includes an element of performance where the writer, like an acrobat or dancer, by effortlessly overcoming predetermined obstacles creates an exhilarating sense of freedom. Though the formal restrictions may initially seem arbitrary, ultimately they prove valuable by challenging the artist to discover and develop new imaginative capabilities. In formal poetry, the imagination affirms its power by making each word—no matter how difficult the metrical pattern—seem not only natural but inevitable. A poet who constantly changes the rules in midperformance to suit his or her own convenience not only destroys the reader's pleasure, but more importantly never translates the formal pattern beyond a set of arbitrary obstacles to natural expression." In "Symposium," *Crosscurrents* 8 (January 1989): 88. See also Molly Peacock's untitled contribution to this symposium, 97–98.

15. Chatman, *Theory of Meter,* 103; cf. Henri Meschonnic, *Critique du rhythme: anthropologie historique du langage* (Paris: Editions Verdier, 1982), 224.

16. See Annie Finch, *The Ghost of Meter: Culture and Prosody in American Free Verse* (Ann Arbor: University of Michigan Press, 1993), 3–5.

17. Steele, *Missing Measures,* 283.

18. W. K. Wimsatt, Jr., and Monroe C. Beardsley, "The Concept of Meter: An Exercise in Abstraction," *PMLA* 74 (December 1959): 593

19. I find myself in perfect agreement with Brogan on this, if not on some other points. He says: "One must attend not to what a metrists *says* but to what he *does* . . .Go to the scansions last, if not first—that is where the real principles appear" (143; italics in original).

20. W. K. Wimsatt, Jr., "The Rule and the Norm: Halle and Keyser on Chaucer's Meter," in *Literary Style: A Symposium,* ed. Seymour Chatman (New York: Oxford University Press, 1971), 198.

21. George Saintsbury, *Historical Manual of English Prosody* (1910; reprint, New York: Schocken Books, 1966), 28.

22. Egerton Smith, *The Principles of English Metre* (London: Oxford University Press, 1923), 77.

23. John Crowe Ransom, "Wanted: An Ontological Critic," in *Essays on the Language of Literature,* ed. Seymour Chatman and Samuel R. Levin (Boston: Houghton Mifflin, 1967), 281.

24. Henry Lee Smith, Jr. "Toward Redefining English Prosody," *Studies in Linguistics* 14 (Winter 1959): 75.

25. John Thompson, *The Founding of English Metre* (London: Routledge and Kegan Paul, 1966), 144.

26. Gross, *Sound and Form*, 30.

27. Ibid., 31.

28. Wimsatt, "Rule," 198.

29. See Thomas Cable, *The English Alliterative Tradition* (Philadelphia: University of Pennsylvania Press, 1991) 123.

30. Finch, 39. In fairness to Finch I should note that she goes on to say that the line "could also—and perhaps even more properly—be scanned as iambs and anapests." She continues: "My choice to scan it as, and call it, dactylic . . . is not a judgment on the best way of scanning the line. I use the word *dactylic* as a sign for the rhythmic similarity and the semantic kinship between such lines and the many technically dactylic lines in Whitman" (39). Metrists, in my judgment, too often scan a given line in a particular way because of the nature of the lines that adjoin it. In characterizing a line in a particular way because it is akin to lines that may not lie near it, Finch is truly opening a can of worms.

31. John Nist, "The Word-Group Cadence: Basis of English Metrics," *Linguistics* 6 (1964): 75.

32. Even Paul Ramsey, who seems to me to be a traditional prosodist, has said "we can use feet in a comprehensible way in scanning accentual-syllabic poems. Apart from such scanning, the idea 'foot' has no visible meaning or use." See his "William Carlos Williams as Metrist: Theory and Practice," *Journal of Modern Literature,* 1 (May 1971): 580. Still, Ramsey is not prepared to discard the foot.

33. Wesling, 108–9. Wesling's position strikes me as particularly peculiar in light of the fact that he himself quotes Paul Fussell's observation that "there is no better way to appreciate the power of eighteenth-century prosodic conventions to perpetuate themselves almost indefinitely than to contemplate the prescriptive 'scansions' and regularistic exhortations which now and then offer themselves to the public view in various modern critical works and in the scholarly quarterlies" (Wesling, 99). Fussell does not mention the foot explicitly here but certainly the foot is typically invoked in prescriptive scansions.

34. George Saintsbury, *A History of English Prosody From the Twelfth Century to the Present Day,* 3 vols. (1906–10; 2nd ed., 1923; reprint, New York: Russell & Russell, 1961), 3:473.

35. Saintsbury, *Historical Manual,* 230.

36. Saintsbury, *History of English Prosody,* 1:4.

37. The temporal position, dating back to Sir Joshua Steele, and coming forward through Sidney Lanier, T. S. Omond and William Thomson, has been advocated in no uncertain terms. R. M. Alden stated that "The fundamental principle of the rhythm of English verse . . . is that *the accents appear at regular time-intervals*" (12, italics in original). Paul Verrier contended that "if rhythm does not rest on isochronism, it rests on nothing—it does not exist. . . ." See his "English Metric," *Modern Language Review* 7 (October 1912): 525. Despite such dogmatism, the temporal approach has some undeniable difficulties it has to face, apart from those it shares with the stresser approach. For one thing, measurements of the respective durations of feet as rendered by actual readers have shown them to be markedly different. See Warner Brown, *Time in English Verse Rhythm: An Empirical Study of Typical Verses by the Graphic Method.* Archives of Psychology, no. 10; Columbia Contributions to Psychology, 17, no. 2. (New York: The Science Press, 1908). But Brown allows for verse lines producing an

effect of equal time intervals. An appeal to such an effect is a standard tactic for those who wish to retain the notion of isochrony in the face of evidence that it is not objectively present. Still, Brown himself is far from being an uncritical espouser of isochrony. His sense of what enters into rhythm is too inclusive for that. A fairly strict dismissal of the notion of equal time intervals is to be found in Ada L. F. Snell, "An Objective Study of Syllabic Quantity in English Verse: Blank Verse," *PMLA* 33 (September 1918): 396–408, and her "An Objective Study of Syllabic Quantity in English Verse: Lyric Verse," *PMLA* 34 (September 1919): 416–35. See also Yuri Tynianov, *The Problem of Verse Language,* ed. and trans. Michael Sosa and Brent Harvey (1924; reprint, Ann Arbor: Ardis, 1981), 153n. The timer, or isochronous, position would seem to have been given a boost by the linguist David Abercrombie, who contends that English is a stress-timed language, that is to say, its stresses occur isochronously. If so, how is the stress pattern of verse to be distinguished from ordinary English? Abercrombie apparently doesn't think such a distinction exists. See his *Studies in Phonetics and Linguistics* (London: Oxford University Press, 1965), 20. I could not agree more with Brogan's characterization of Abercrombie's scansions as "especially forced and unnatural" (165). For a classification of timer theories, see Pallister Barkas, *A Critique of Modern English Prosody (1880–1930);* also see W. Sidney Allen, *Accent and Rhythm. Prosodic Features of Latin and Greek: A Study in Theory and Accentuation* (Cambridge: Cambridge University Press, 1973), 97–99. For materials that take a stance against isochrony see Yao Shen and G. G. Peterson, *Isochronism in English.* Studies in Linguistics Occasional Papers, no. 9. (Buffalo: University of Buffalo Department of Anthropology and Linguistics, 1962); see also David Crystal, *Prosodic Systems and Intonation in English,* 31; also Meschonnic, 130n. Brogan says that "very recent evidence" on the matter of isochrony is "mixed" (193).

38. Saintsbury, *Historical Manual,* 310.

39. Poe, 65.

40. Egerton Smith, 295.

41. Saintsbury, *Historical Manual,* 31.

42. Ibid., 270.

43. See Edmund L. Epstein and Terence Hawkes. *Linguistics and English Prosody.* Studies in Linguistics Occasional Papers, no. 7. (Buffalo: University of Bufalo Department of Anthropology and Linguistics, 1959), 6.

44. Sheridan Baker, "English Meter *Is* Quantitative," *College English* 21 (March 1960): 314, 315.

45. I might point out that Chaucer criticism has produced at least a pale imitation of Baker. Norman E. Eliason, in *The Language of Chaucer's Poetry: An Appraisal of the Verse, Style, and Structure, Anglistica,* vol. 17 (Copenhagen: Rosenkilde and Bagger, 1972), raises the question of how Chaucer himself recited his verse: "Did he emphasize the meter, beating it out strongly and insistently and producing a tum-ta, tum-ta effect that would appall us today? I suspect he did" (cited in Gaylord, 54). At least Eliason is appalled; Baker apparently is not.

46. John Frederick Nims, *Western Wind: An Introduction to Poetry* (New York: Random House, 1974) 254–55. The linguist Roger Fowler has conceded that "thoroughgoing linguistic exposition of the form of a text or texts is certain to be cumbersome and will perhaps be unpalatable. . . ." See his *Essays on Style and Language: Linguistic and Critical Approaches to Literary Style* (London: Routledge and Kegan Paul, 1966), 27.

47. In fairness to Nims, it should be stated that, apart from his allegiance to

the foot, his pages on the sound patterns of poetry are quite strong. In general, his *Western Wind* is a very fine book.

Chapter 2. A Further Look at the Foot: Prosody's Persistent Problematic

1. Attridge, *Rhythms*, 5.

2. Karl Shapiro and Robert Beum, *A Prosody Handbook* (New York: Harper and Row, 1965), 30; italics in original.

3. W. Sidney Allen has remarked that "The poet's analytical awareness of the abstract metrical patterns of his poetry is a widely variable factor, and this is likely to be particularly true of those metrical units which are not also units of composition" (124). What Allen may be saying in a rather circumlocutionary way is that some poets at least may compose in terms of the phrase or line and do not give primary consideration to the foot.

4. Attridge, *Rhythms*, 9.

5. I should acknowledge that, in personal communications to me, T. V. F. Brogan has indicated that "from the remarks by the Renaissance prosodists and by Donne, it would seem that scansion by feet, at least for Latin poetry, was commonly known to British schoolboys, some of whom grew up to become English poets. Whether or not these *poets* scanned one way or another we don't know, much. . . . As for whether *prosodists* scanned in feet, it is certainly true that the Classicizing impulse is most strongly felt in the second half of the 19th c. but the Ren. prosodists certainly knew how to." Largely because of the materials concerning the Renaissance shortly to be presented in the text, I tend to go along with Attridge's emphasis on the relatively *late* emergence of scansion by foot. This is not to say it was unheard of earlier, but it is to say it did not always have the dominant place it has assumed over the last century or so.

6. *Princeton Encyclopedia*, 135; see also W. Sidney Allen, 3.

7. Derek Attridge, *Well-Weighed Syllables: Elizabethan Verse in Classical Meters* (London: Cambridge University Press, 1974), 8.

8. Hardison, 34.

9. Attridge, *Well-Weighed Syllables*, 10.

10. Dennis Taylor, *Hardy's Metres and Victorian Prosody with a Metrical Appendix of Hardy's Stanza Forms* (Oxford: Clarendon Press, 1988), 10.

11. Thompson, *The Founding of English Metre*, 1.

12. The difference in priorities here is crucial. Conventional prosody has too often favored the "meter" at the expense of violating lexical pronunciation, a choice that Thompson himself appears to accept. I shall argue in a later chapter for ordinary pronunciation, for letting the stresses fall where they may, and then seeing what we have, not what we have imposed.

13. George T. Wright, *Shakespeare's Metrical Art* (Berkeley: University of California Press, 1988), 211.

14. Thomas Cable, *The English Alliterative Tradition* (Philadelphia: University of Pennsylvania Press, 1991), 118.

15. Ibid., 4.

16. Hardison, 8.

17. George Puttenham, *The Art of English Poesie*, ed. Gladys D. Willcock and Alice Walker (1936; reprint, Cambridge: Cambridge University Press, 1936), 67. Somewhat confusingly, immediately after talking of "not regarding . . . feete,"

Puttenham's statement continues this way: "otherwise then that we allow in scanning our verse. . . ." (See Hardison, 121, on possible interpretations of what Puttenham had in mind by adding this.) Yet, however much Puttenham might appear to give back the feet he has just taken away, the subsequent statement by him rejecting feet—I go on to quote it in the text—seems clear enough.

18. Ibid., 129.

19. Wright, *Shakespeare's Metrical Art*, 40.

20. For the Skeat material, see his "On the Scansion of English Poetry," *Transactions of the Philological Society* (1898): 484–503.

21. Otto Jespersen, "Notes on Metre," in *The Structure of Verse: Modern Essays on Prosody*, ed. Harvey Gross, rev. ed. (New York: Ecco Press, 1979), 82.

22. E. W. Scripture, *The Elements of Experimental Phonetics* (New York: Charles Scribner's Sons, 1902), passim.

23. Chatman, *Theory of Meter*, 88.

24. George R. Stewart, *The Technique of English Verse* (1930; reprint, Port Washington, N.Y.: Kennikat Press, 1966), 49.

25. Chatman, *A Theory of Meter*, 14.

26. James G. Southworth, *Verses of Cadence: An Introduction to the Prosody of Chaucer and his Followers* (Oxford: Basil Blackwell, 1954), 1.

27. Catherine Ing, *Elizabethan Lyrics: A Study in the Development of English Metres and their Relation to Poetic Effect* (1951; reprint, New York: Barnes & Noble, 1969), 121.

28. Charles L. Stevenson, "The Rhythms of English Verse," *Journal of Aesthetics and Art Criticism* 28 (Spring 1970): 327.

29. Ibid., 343.

30. As far as I am concerned, not much more can be said for this school, though I shall describe it in some detail in a later chapter. Generative metrists continue to speak, but, I think, only to each other. Readers wishing to see a full account of generative metrics as well as a critique of it would do well to consult Attridge, *Rhythms*, 34–55.

31. Attridge, *Rhythms*, 14–15.

32. I have not, in my survey of the antifoot camp, drawn on the works of Gerard Manley Hopkins, whom Wesling makes much of. While his poetry and theory go beyond foot-based verse, they do not challenge the foot *within* the mode of accentual-syllabic verse. The prosodists I have been citing wish to approach that verse without benefit of the foot.

33. Nist, "Word-Group Cadence," 82.

34. Fussell, rev. ed., 15–16.

35. Gross, *Sound and Form*, 179.

36. Cited in Gross, *Sound and Form*, 130–31.

37. Paul Ramsey, "Ways of Meditation," *Parnassus* 10 (Spring/Summer 1982): 175.

38. T. S. Eliot, *Selected Prose*, ed. John Hayward (Harmondsworth, Middlesex: Penguin Books, 1953), 88.

39. Cf. Attridge: "one of the weaknesses of the classical approach is that *any* succession of syllables can be divided into recognised feet" (*Rhythms*, 12; italics in original).

40. Miller Williams, "The Line in Poetry," *Antaeus* 30/31 (Spring 1978): 311.

41. See Taylor, 13ff.

42. Thompson, 12.

43. Gross, Introduction to Saintsbury, *Historical Manual*, xxiii, xvi–xvii.

44. Marina Tarlinskaja, *English Verse: Theory and History* (The Hague: Mouton, 1976), 6.

45. Donald C. Freeman, "Current Trends in Metrics," in *Current Trends in Stylistics,* ed. Braj B. Kachru and Herbert F. W. Stahlke (Edmonton, Alberta: Linguistic Research Inc., 1972), 78–79.

46. Cable, "Timers, Stressers and Linguists: Contention and Compromise," *Modern Language Quarterly* 33 (September 1972): 227, 235.

47. Cable, *English Alliterative Tradition,* 38.

48. Cable, "Timers, Stressers," 238.

49. Brooks and Warren, 562.

50. Wesling, 105.

51. Ibid., 143. Keeping in mind Wesling's association of system and "strong poetry," I might note that he characterizes the accentual-syllabic paradigm as "strong" (105).

52. Gross, introduction to Saintsbury, *Historical Manual,* xvi.

53. Fredrick Turner and Ernst Pöppel, "The Neural Lyre: Poetic Meter, The Brain, and Time," *Poetry* 142 (August 1983): 284.

54. See Leithauser, untitled contribution to "Symposium," *Crosscurrents:* 91.

55. Saintsbury, *Historical Manual,* 32.

56. Taylor, 7.

57. *Princeton Encyclopedia,* 740–41.

58. He may have had other deformations in view, but it is instructive to note that the nineteenth-century prosodist, Coventry Patmore, found that "The very deformities produced . . . in the phraseology of a great poet, by the confinement of metre, are beautiful, exactly for the same reasons that in architecture justify the bossy Gothic foliage" (cited by Taylor, 44).

59. Karl Shapiro pointed out the temporalist element in Saintsbury. See Shapiro, 81. I might observe that the same element is present in Brooks and Warren. They speak of encountering a line with a missing syllable and say that "we are likely to slow our reading in order to make up for that syllable" (130). The latest incarnation of *Understanding Poetry* is the middle section of *An Approach to Literature* by Brooks and Warren, and John Thibaut Purser (1975). Even before the authors get to the new sections on the role of "Time" in verse, that is, at a point where they have still focused only on stress, they speak of the "deficiency" of an "imperfect foot" being compensated for by the ear, which, "once accustomed to the metrical pattern, assumes a time interval in place of the missing . . . syllable." See *An Approach to Literature,* 5th ed. (Englewood Cliffs, N.J.: Prentice-Hall, 1975), 513. Thomas Cable thinks there needs to be "a kind of compromise between the extreme positions traditionally taken by stressers and timers," this to assume the form of keeping separate two levels of abstraction, as well as recognizing "temporal duration, pause, as a metrical element in certain lines with otherwise deficient feet" ("Timers, Stressers," 239).

60. Robert Bridges, *Milton's Prosody with a Chapter on Accentual Verse* (1921; rev. final edition, Oxford: Clarendon Press, 1965), 99. Having allowed himself to say this, Bridges once again puts on the metrical halter, albeit reluctantly, stating that he would have included Blake in the "Golden Treasury" anthology in 1861, but "when one is considering prosody and principles of rhythm, it is necessary to attend to that only; and I cannot admit that these verses are good as mere versification" (99).

61. Cited in J. Hoberman, "Harold Rosenberg's Radical Cheek," [*Village*] *Voice Literary Supplement* ([13] May 1986): 12.

62. Tarlinskaja, *English Verse,* 4.

63. Epstein and Hawkes, for example, assume that there is a "'stress clock' ticking away iambically in the minds of sensitive readers of English poetry. It ticks in possibilities of iambs exclusively, and the iambs it hears are unambiguous" (47).

64. Joseph B. Mayor, *Chapters on English Metre* (Cambridge: Cambridge University Press, 1901), 102.

65. John Crowe Ransom, "The Strange Music of English Verse," *Kenyon Review* 18 (Summer 1956): 475.

66. Baker, 310. Cf. Omond's saying of Cary Jacob "I could wish that Dr. Jacob recognized more fully the 'sing-song' effect as the chief feature in our mental rhythmizing . . ." (262).

67. Elias K. Schwartz, W. K. Wimsatt Jr., and Monroe C. Beardsley, "Rhythm and 'Exercises in Abstraction,'" *PMLA* 77 (December 1962), 671n.

68. Attridge, *Rhythms,* 289.

69. A severe sort of Platonism may be seen operating in Joseph Malof, though he doesn't use the term. His view is that the metrical design of a poem stands apart from meaning: "the poet's fluctuating emotions may be put into perspective by, or given substance by contrast to, the constancy of an unaffected meter." See his *A Manual of English Meters* (1970; reprint, Westport, Conn.: Greenwood Press, 1978), 146. This appears to have the messy emotions at once put in their place, and at the same time accorded respect. Malof's remarks might remind us of I. A. Richards, who said that through its artificiality "metre produces in the highest degree the 'frame' effect, isolating the poetic experience from the accidents and irrelevancies of everyday existence" (cited in Gross, *Structure of Verse,* 76). There is yet another brand of Platonism that is, self-admittedly, inconsequential. Ian Robinson says he doesn't deny the existence of an ideal metrical scheme "'deep in the mind'; I merely observe that . . . it remains in the mind without affecting any events; it is altogether disconnected from the reading of the verse." See his *Chaucer's Prosody: A Study of the Middle English Verse Tradition* (London: Cambridge University Press, 1971), 57.

70. Gross, *Sound and Form,* 40.

71. Cited in Gross, *Sound and Form,* 93.

72. Wellek and Warren, 159.

73. Ibid., 168.

74. C. S. Lewis, *Selected Literary Essays,* ed. Walter Hooper (Cambridge: Cambridge University Press, 1969), 280.

75. Wimsatt and Beardsley, 587; italics in original.

76. Chatman, "Mr. Stein on Donne," *Kenyon Review* 18 (Summer 1956): 450.

77. Chatman, *A Theory of Meter,* 96.

78. Ibid., 103.

79. *Princeton Encyclopedia,* 677. Cf. W. Sidney Allen's statement that "'metrical rules' are in the first instance descriptive, being abstracted from the compositional practice of poetry, and only subsequently may they take the form of positive or negative prescriptions" (108). But even with the concession of "only subsequently" it is no surprise to find him distinguishing between the poem itself and mere renderings of it; he says that tension "resides in the various levels of the *poem,* and their interrelationships, regardless of the particular performance" (112, his italics). Dennis Taylor's account of Victorian metrists has them "suggesting a sort of hermeneutic circle" regarding the question of the extrapolation of a poem's meter and the application of that extrapolation to the reading of the poem. He states their position as follows: "The metre must be induced from the given

language and imposed on that language. Once perceived, the metre enters into a dialectic relation with the language" (36–37). What Taylor calls a "hermeneutic circle" I find a bit of a muddle. The *imposing* of the perceived meter in the first statement is softened into the "dialectic relation" of the second. And just how does the dialectic work in practice? That is the essence of the matter.

80. Nist, "Word-Group Cadence," 74–75.

81. Gaylord, 76.

82. Fowler, *Essays on Style,* 9.

83. Abercrombie, 19.

84. See Ake W. Edfeldt, *Silent Speech and Silent Reading* (Chicago: University of Chicago Press, 1960).

85. See, e.g., John Buxton, "Correspondence," *Review of English Studies* 11 (August 1960): 20.

86. Robert Haas, "One Body: Some Notes on Form," *Antaeus* 30/31 (Spring 1978): 338. In citing Haas, I do not mean to suggest that he himself is an advocate of Neoplatonist metrics, though his formulation might be revealing a nostalgia for such prosody. The Haas essay I cite has been reprinted in his *Twentieth Century Pleasures,* where another essay, "Listening and Making" offers scansions close in spirit to the sort I shall go on to propose. I am grateful to Calvin Bedient for having called attention to this second essay.

87. Apparently one can be a monist and still retain a fundamental faith in meter. See Wright, *Shakespeare's Metrical Art,* 11, and my discussion of that book in the next chapter.

88. Wimsatt and Beardsley, 597.

89. G. S. Fraser, *Metre, Rhyme, and Free Verse* (London: Methuen, 1970) 82,2. Ian Robinson, rather confusingly, offers a similar opinion. He takes a very relaxed view of the iambic pentameter line, saying it can have anything from two to eight beats, or more (52). He also holds that "reading metrically is not necessarily pulling the stress-patterns towards some ideal. . . ." But immediately after producing this decidedly anti-Platonist stance, he goes on to say "the metre may rather help the reader to choose between alternative patterns all of which could occur in prose" (60). I find here a baffling inconsistency.

90. Samuel R. Levin, "The Conventions of Poetry," in *Literary Style: A Symposium,* ed. Seymour Chatman (New York: Oxford University Press, 1971), 181.

91. Shapiro and Beum, 30.

92. Wimsatt, 209.

93. Shapiro and Beum, 30.

94. See John Hollander, "The Music of Poetry," *Journal of Aesthetics and Art Criticism* 15 (December 1956): 232–44. I shall return to the linking of poetry and music in a later chapter, if only briefly, but for now I would observe that, curiously enough, prosodic studies given to massive linkings of poetry and music do not feature the notion of counterpoint. They tend, rather, to focus on the idea that verse, like music, is to be regarded as composed of units of equal duration. However, Hegel, who was among those linking poetry and music, is credited by Dennis Taylor as being "the first nineteenth-century source of the idea of metrical counterpoint" (27). But Hegel asribed this effect to classical verse, and did not find it in the German accentual line. "Here is where the English Victorians would step in and find a parallel art, between the pattern set up by the accentual-syllabic metre and the normal speech rhythm" (28; see also 32). In short, Taylor seems to be telling us, they would "find" counterpoint.

95. Chatman and Levin, 70.

96. Richard Cureton, "Traditional Scansion: Myths and Muddles," *Journal of Literary Semantics* 15 (December 1986)): 173.

97. See, e.g., Elias K. Schwartz in Schwartz, Wimsatt, and Beardsley, 673.

98. Thompson, 16.

99. Chatman, "Robert Frost's 'Mowing,'" 422; italics in original. Chatman's position is preferable to Thompson's, because Chatman at least finally settles for speech, whereas Thompson has us hovering in some misty kingdom of unvocalized counterpoint. Still, one's faith in Chatman's promotions or suppressions is not exactly strengthened by his comments on section 17 of Tenyson's *Maude*. The first eight lines read as follows:

> Go not, happy day,
> From the shining fields,
> Go not, happy day,
> Till the maiden yields.
> Rosy is the West,
> Rosy is the South,
> Roses are her cheeks,
> And a rose her mouth.

Chatman says that the occurrence of "Rosy" as the first word in lines 5–7 is so unequivocal a signal of ictus (stress) on the first syllable that the reader "finds himself promoting to ictus the metrical values of ordinarily humble monosyllabic words like *from, till,* and *and*" (*Theory of Meter,* 124). But the first two of these words initiate lines that occur *before* the first instance of "Rosy." So Chatman not only wants us to promote certain words, he wants us to do this retroactively.

100. Chatman, "Robert Frost's "Mowing, 424.

101. Chatman, "Mr. Stein on Donne," 449.

102. After writing this, I came upon Ian Robinson's statements that "In successful English verse there may be a tension between the expectations of metre and speech-rhythm as we are forming the verse to speak, but the tension is resolved in the spoken verse in a compromise or cooperation between the two rhythm systems" (61). I shall take up the question of "expectation" momentarily.

103. Schwartz in Schwartz, Wimsatt, and Beardsley, 673.

104. Wimsatt and Beardsley in Schwartz, Wimsatt, and Beardsley, 674.

105. Mark H. Liddell, *An Introduction to the Scientific Study of English Poetry* (New York: Doubleday, Page, 1902), 177–78.

106. See, e.g., Egerton Smith, pp. 204–6; Chatman, *Theory of Meter,* 207; Fussell, *Poetic Meter and Poetic Form,* 39; and Roy Fuller, "Boos of Different Durations," *Southern Review* 11 (October 1975): 835. Cf. Fuller's "The Fetish of Speech Rhythms in Modern Poetry," *Southern Review* 15 (January 1979): 11.

107. Enthusiasts of the idea of counterpoint have an additional problem. Gerard Manley Hopkins, who is strongly associated with the notion of counterpoint, observed that "in fact if you counterpoint throughout, since only one of the counterrhythms is actually heard, the other is really destroyed or cannot come to exist, and what is written is one rhythm only. . . ." (W. H. Gardner, ed., *Poems and Prose of Gerard Manley Hopkins* (Baltimore: Penguin Books, 1966), 7. We might extrapolate from this the conclusion that Hopkins had elucidated a device that the more one employs it, the more its effects diminish. Imagine a situation something short of that which Hopkins names, namely, a poem that employs a counterrhythm not exclusively but so frequently that it is a significant part of the ongoing texture; just what do we have then? I shall argue a little later that this

is precisely the situation we have in iambic pentameter. I might note here that Anthony Easthope appears to quarrel with the notion of counterpoint, but in a curious way; he retains the term even as he appears to give it a new meaning. He states that "It is not the case that the official pattern [of iambic pentameter] is a metrical 'abstraction' and its practice in counterpoint an 'actualization' of this abstraction; rather the counterpoint *is* the metre." See his *Poetry as Discourse* (New York: Methuen, 1983), 62 (his italics). Doesn't this reduce the two-ness of counterpoint to a oneness? What is the point of retaining the term?

108. Harvey Gross has said "All expressive rhythms are variations upon a pattern of expectation" (*Sound and Form,* 14). George Wright states "Variant lines depart not from a form we hear but from a form we *expect* to hear" (*Shakespeare's Metrical Art,* 11; italics in original). The notion of expectation might have originated with I. A. Richards, who stated that "all rhythmical and metrical effects spring from anticipation" (in Gross, *Structure of Verse,* 69). He also said "there can be no surprise and no disappointment without expectation" (71).

109. Egerton Smith, 295.

110. Chatman, "Robert Frost's Mowing," 436.

111. Fowler, *Languages of Literature,* 150.

112. Brogan, 356. Anthony Easthope makes the broader point that iambic pentameter is not to be considered natural to English, but as "a specific cultural phenomenon" (55).

113. For example, John Nist's trenchant attack on foot-based prosody is characterized by Brogan as "Simple myopia: the failure to distinguish between rhythm and meter" (267).

114. Saintsbury, *Historical Manual,* 167.

115. Jespersen, 71.

116. Paul Franklin Baum, *The Principles of English Versification* (Cambridge, Mass.: Harvard University Press, 1923), 134.

117. *Princeton Encyclopedia,* 78.

118. Paul Fussell, "English I. Historical," in W. K. Wimsatt, Jr. ed., *Versification: Major Language Types. Sixteen Essays* (New York: New York University Press for MLA, 1970), 196.

119. Taylor, 30.

120. Robinson, 151. I should note that Alan T. Gaylord has said that he suspects ". . . Chaucer liked iambics more than Robinson will allow" (46). But even with this disagreement between Chaucerians, the overall picture of iambic pentameter that emerges from the citations that follow in my paragraph seems persuasive enough.

121. Alden, 155.

122. Fowler, *Languages of Literature,* 165.

123. John D. Allen, *Elements of English Blank Verse: Shakespeare to Frost* (Johnson City, Tenn.: East Tennessee State University Press, 1968), 75.

124. Tarlinskaja, *English Verse,* 279–80.

125. Ibid., 11.

126. See Sebeok, 203.

127. Not confining himself to iambic pentameter, D. W. Harding has claimed that "It would be wrong to say that in more competent verse we expect the regular repetition of a stress pattern and then get a stimulating surprise . . . we are in fact expecting variety, though without foreseeing its precise form." See his

Words into Rhythm: English Speech Rhythm in Verse and Prose (Cambridge: Cambridge University Press, 1976), 48–49.

128. Raymond Southall, *The Courtly Makers: An Essay on the Poetry of Wyatt and his Contemporaries* (New York: Barnes and Noble, 1964), 118.

129. My arguing from the number of variations in iambic pentameter would presumably not impress Roger Fowler, who, pushing the notion of "metrical set," a reader's disposition "to impose a familiar reading on any metre which does not absolutely forbid it," argues that the norm of iambic pentameter "need never be realized in a poem" in order to make itself felt. On the other hand, Fowler does not seem to make very much of "tension," calling it a "misleading" term (along with "counterpoint") and saying that if it is applicable at all it is to the use "of disyllabic words with stress on the first syllable . . ." (*Languages of Literature*, 136, 166, 169.) His view of expectation seems, then, a much diminished version of the traditional one.

130. Even in territory outside iambic pentameter, instances of tension based on a strict norm are not guaranteed—consider the verse of Wyatt, Donne, and Hardy.

131. Cited in Taylor, 167.

132. Fussell, *Poetic Meter*, rev. ed.—see 70–71, 32, 18. While he does not mention him, Robert E. Abrams has given us an essay that amounts to an elaboration and extension of Fussell's view. Abrams says that "measure," that is, meter, "entails the deliberate arousal of abstract expectations of design nevertheless *meant* to be subverted and betrayed, but always such that orderliness is rediscovered by the ear on subtler, more intriguing terms." See his "The Skewed Harmonics of English Verse Feet," *Language and Style* 16 (Fall 1983): 479; italics in original). Abrams's piece is a sophisticated attempt to retain, in essence, the traditional concept of meter. While he seems to make concessions to those skeptical of that concept, he ends up in the conservative posture of reaffirming foot prosody. I am in agreement with the assignment of stress values in his scansions, but find him guilty in his own way of what is for me the traditional metrist's characteristic tampering with the empirical data of a line reading. Confronted with a verse where "the principle of identity between poetic feet begins to break down," Abrams invokes "mirror-like inversions," "analogic resemblances," "equivalence of syllables," and, in what is his distinctive contribution to the tradition of system-maintenance at any cost, the notion of "deaf spots." These are groupings of syllables that *we can simply pass over,* such groupings not conforming to the meter and existing *between* groupings that do exhibit the metrical pattern (491–93). That he models these deaf spots on what are actually silent intervals in a succession of abstract sounds doesn't appear to bother him.

133. See Sebeok, 403.

134. Harding, 47.

135. David Dooley, "Iambic in the 80s," *Crosscurrents* 8 (January 1989): 120.

136. Dooley appears to have a weakness for reversed fourth feet in lines that are highly irregular. Witness his calling attention to another such foot in a line by Allen Hoey, which reads: "at his hands chilled the short walk from the house." His comment is that the foot in question—walk from—"creates the sound of [a] spondee (short walk)" (126). Here Dooley manages to have a single word "walk" do double duty, first as the initial half of a trochee, and then as the second half of a spondee overlapping the trochee. Dooley appears to be saying that this slippery footwork has something to do with the poet "daringly" emphasizing monosyllables. What the daringness consists of eludes me.

137. In encountering prosodic commentary such as Dooley's, one is tempted to call the New Formalism the New Chutzpah.

Chapter 3. Recent Prosodic Commentary: Old Wine in New Bottles

1. Derek Attridge, *The Rhythms of English Poetry*, 17–18.
2. Turner and Pöppel, 284.
3. Susanne Woods, *Natural Emphasis: English Versification from Chaucer to Dryden* (San Marino, Calif.: Huntington Library, 1984), 8.
4. For a decidedly skeptical view of such notions as meter reflecting oceanic rhythm, see Henri Meschonnic, *Critique du Rhythme: anthropologique historique du langage* (Paris: Editions Verdier, 1982), 149–50.
5. Gilbert Youmans, "Introduction: Rhythm and Meter," in *Phonetics and Phonology, Vol. I. Rhythm and Meter,* ed. Paul Kiparsky and Gilbert Youmans (San Diego: Academic Press, 1989), 9.
6. Brogan, 299.
7. Youmans, "Introduction," 9.
8. Morris Halle and Samuel Jay Keyser, "Chaucer and the Study of Prosody," *College English* 28 (December 1966): 219.
9. The two men revised their findings somewhat in their *English Stress: Its Form, Its Growth, and Its Role in Verse* (New York: Harper and Row, 1971). Further citations of Halle and Keyser will be from their Chaucer essay.
10. It has been argued that Halle and Keyser have misrepresented the "standard theory of meter," because that theory considers variations from the abstract metrical pattern *part* of the norm. See C. C. Bowley, "Metrics and the Generative Approach," *Linguistics* no. 121 (February 1974): 5–19. From this point of view (whose formulation might be debated), Halle and Keyser are not offering us anything new. Here I might note that W. K. Wimsatt, in his extended response to the Halle and Keyser essay, says "it may be difficult to see the radical departure in method" that they claim to be making. "If we begin by throwing our empirical dragnet wide enough, we can always formulate an alternatively structured principle which will take care of everything which somebody else might wish to call an exception" ("The Rule and the Norm," 206). Here, for a change, I am not only in perfect agreement with Wimsatt, but cannot imagine a more cogent characterization of Halle and Keyser's enterprise.
11. See, once again, Wimsatt, "The Rule and the Norm," 206.
12. See the fuller exposition of their theory in their *English Stress,* 167.
13. Gross, *Structure of Verse,* 9.
14. Charles O. Hartman, *Free Verse: An Essay on Prosody* (Princeton: Princeton University Press, 1980), 119; italics in original. See also Attridge, though he is pushing his own program when he says that in generative metrics "the actual movement of the words *in a series of rhythmic alternations* is never brought to the centre of attention" (*Rhythms,* 54). I would drop the words I have italicized and say that generative metrics does not capture the movement of the words in a line, period.
15. Donald C. Freeman, "On the Primes of Metrical Style," in *Linguistics and Literary Style,* ed. Donald C. Freeman (New York: Holt, Rinehart and Winston, 1970), 452. But one has to wonder just how far Freeman himself is moving beyond the Halle-Keyser brand of generative metrics, since he says that "A useful

task for the future would be the construction of a framework for 'degrees of metricalness' . . ." (468). A consideration of such degrees is already present in Halle and Keyser with their notion of metrical "complexity." Freeman's exposition does not get into matters of a period style or the style of a given author, but only a miniscule portion of his essay is given over to showing the relationship of metrical style to expressive concerns (477–78). Even there the emphasis appears to be not on the individual passage of verse but on using it to arrive at a generalization about period style.

16. Brogan, 315. See also 316.

17. See Paul Kiparsky, "The Rhythmic Structure of English Verse," *Linguistic Inquiry* 8 (1977): 189–247.

18. Youmans, "Introduction," 9.

19. Maria Tarlinskaja, "General and Particular Aspects of Meter: Literatures, Epochs, Poets," in Kiparsky and Youmans, 126.

20. Ibid., 131.

21. Edward R. Weismiller, "Triple Threats to Double Rhythm," in Kiparsky and Youmans, 273, 287.

22. Elizabeth Closs Traugott, "Meter in Auden's 'Streams,'" in Kiparsky and Youmans, 291.

23. Youmans, "Milton's Meter," in Kiparsky and Youmans, 341.

24. Kiparsky, "Sprung Rhythms," in Kiparsky and Youmans, 337.

25. I do not wish to qualify this statement in any way, but I would like to add, in fairness to Kiparsky and others who have struggled with Hopkins, that that poet, like many metrists, wanted to have things both ways, making it difficult to get a handle on him. Kiparsky notes that Hopkins spoke of sprung rhythm as being able to effect a switch "from a rising to a falling movement," but wanted it always to be *scanned* as rising (325). Also, as Kiparsky further notes, Hopkins distinguished between stresses required by the sense (accents) and "metrical stresses" or "stresses of the verse" (307, 309). From my point of view, Hopkins, in this, was knuckling under to the "Platonic" strain of traditional prosody, which insists on having a regular metrical scheme, if only in the mind. At any rate, if we remember Hopkins's distinction between the two sorts of stresses, and the fact that, as Kiparsky reminds us, his own markings were of "'the metrical stress, marked in doubtful cases only'" (309), we can escape the discomfort induced in some Hopkins commentators by those markings. For such notations do not preclude a more "natural" reading of the lines, something Kiparsky may be forgetting when, as noted above, he airily dismisses the concern with such reading (though he might conceivably defend against this charge by saying that "natural scansion" to him is not the same as performance.)

26. Wright, "The Meter of 'Shall I Die,'" *Eidos* 3 (November 1986): 6, 11.

27. George T. Wright, *Shakespeare's Metrical Art* (Berkeley: University of California Press, 1988). Wright states flatly that most English meters are isochronous (3), but doesn't do anything to incorporate this view into his analyses, and so in terms of his practice he can be viewed as a stresser pure and simple, which is how I shall continue to treat him.

28. There may be some rare instances, as with the opening of Frost's "Directive," where our sounding of a line may have to be reconsidered in light of what comes afterward. But even in that poem, the reviewing of how the first line, "Back out of all this now too much for us," should be delivered, a reviewing prompted by the second line, "Back in a time made simple by the loss of detail," is not a matter of adjusting feet but of responding to a change in the use of "Back."

29. Curiously enough, when Brooks and Warren speak of "interplay" they see it operating mainly in free verse (179).

30. The absence of definition on this point is especially troubling because the term "rhythmic phrase" is of obvious importance to Wright. One is reminded of Saintsbury's simultaneous celebration of and fuzziness about the foot.

31. As I have tried to indicate, Wright's adaptation of "counterpoint" and "interplay" simply provides more ammunition for those who, like myself, question the usefulness of those terms in describing poetry. What I think "interplay" suggests is a dialectic rather than a simple, mutual enmity; it is the latter that appears to be operating in Wright's presentations. More accurate in describing the contents of those presentations, I think, would be an adaptation of Donald Wesling's terminology. He speaks of the "mutual interference" of "the cognitive and the aesthetic structures of a poetic text," each attempting "to reduce the other to a minimum." "Grammar is the cognitive, meter is the aesthetic. . . . While the line is scissoring the sentence, the sentence is scissoring the line" (123). What best describes the effects Wright points to might be put this way: the phrase scissors the line, the line scissors the phrase. But it is still the case that Wright gives much more weight to the former.

32. In another piece, Cureton claims that "The most widely used poetry texts today completely ignore recent achievements in prosodic analysis and persist in presenting what amounts to a *mythology* of rhythm—a hodgepodge of outdated misconceptions and misleading oversimplifications" ("Rhythm: A Multilevel Analysis," *Style* 19 [Summer, 1985]: 242; italics in original). But it should be pointed out that in her section on "Versification" in the fairly recent *Poetry in English: An Anthology*, ed. M. L. Rosenthal, (New York: Oxford University Press, 1987), Sally M. Gall incorporates a major innovation by making considerable use of Attridge's *The Rhythms of English Poetry;* still, whatever Cureton might think of this attempt to get beyond the outdated, I have, as indicated earlier, serious reservations about Attridge's book.

33. In fact, later in the essay Cureton will concede that "metrical variation can orchestrate emphasis in an important way," though he does say that traditional scansion "often tends to overgeneralize this function" (184).

34. Cureton, "Response to Alan Holder's Queries, Quibbles, and Caveats," *Eidos* 4 (December 1987): 14, 17.

35. This approach is developed in several places besides "Traditional Scansion," namely: "Rhythm: A Multilevel Analysis"; "A Definition of Rhythm," *Eidos* 3 (November 1986): 7–10; "Raising Phrasing: Phrasal Rhythm as a Central Concern of Prosodic Analysis," handout at 1986 MLA Convention panel on prosody; and "Response to Alan Holder's 'Queries, Quibbles and Caveats.'" Cureton claims both simplicity and a desirable complexity for his hierarchical scheme: he says "The great formal advantage of a grouping hierarchy is the schematic simplicity of the basic rhythmic group," and at the same time he claims that "It is largely through hierarchy that prosodic structures acquire the ability to complicate rhythmic articulation . . ." ("Raising Phrasing," 15, 23).

36. "Rhythm," 253. In discussing the opening two lines of *Leaves of Grass,* Cureton comes up with foot-designated rhythm phrases and what appear to be arbitrary and pointless "matchings" of them ("Rhythm," 251).

37. Ibid., 253.

38. See "A Definition of Rhythm," 8–10. For a statement of some difficulties I have with this particular essay, see Alan Holder, "Richard Cureton's 'Definition of Rhythm': Some Queries, Quibbles, and Caveats," *Eidos* 4 (December 1987): 10.

39. See "Raising Phrasing," 21, 36.

40. "Rhythm," 254.

41. It just so happens that in a piece he published in the year following the appearance of "Rhythm: A Multilevel Analysis," Cureton *did* see the rhythm so resolved, saying the line "resolves into regular alternation in the final four syllables" ("Traditional Scansion," 191). But in "Rhythm" itself, it turns out that the line is resolved for Cureton at another level, by the stress on "wings," a word that he designates as a "phrasal monosyllable" (254). Such a kind of phrase is certainly possible, but to invoke that term in this particular context, thereby justifying the separating of "wings" from "on extended," renders "phrase" or "rhythm phrase" (to use Cureton's terminology) very dubious terms, of a piece with Wright's "pyrrhic iamb" and "spondaic iamb." In another scansion, this one of two lines of Landor's "Rose Aylmer," Cureton, after dividing the lines up into a series of choppy rhythm phrases, finds a resolution on the metrical level (see "Traditional Scansion," 187).

42. "A Definition," 10.

43. "Raising Phrasing," 11.

44. "Response," 13.

45. In the essay in question he says as much, referring to the impending publication of a long manuscript setting forth his theory of rhythm (10, 13), but as of the time of my writing this, such publication has not yet occurred.

46. While Cureton has said that his "representation of meter makes no claims about isochrony" ("Response," 14), he also claims that grouping can create "rhythmic equivalents," and that "Units that are varied but recognized as equivalences structurally can dilate and condense subjective time" ("A Definition," 8). It is hard to see whether this passage per se adds up to an acceptance of isochrony or not, though it does seem to echo the passage cited in my text.

47. "Response," 17.

48. Ibid. See also his taking the scansion of the opening bars of "The Star-Spangled Banner" by the music theorists Grosvenor Cooper and Leonard Meyer as his model for the scansion of poetry. See "Traditional Scansion," 188–89, as well as "Raising Phrasing," 12–14.

49. See Meschonnic, Chapter 4.

50. "Raising Phrasing," 3.

51. "Traditional Scansion," 183–84.

Chapter 4. The Haunting of Free Verse

1. Philip Dacey and David Jauss, ed., *Strong Measures: Contemporary Poems in Traditional Forms* (New York: Harper & Row, 1986), 1.

2. T. S. Eliot, *Selected Prose*, 86, 88.

3. Ibid., 65.

4. This remark is cited in Stephen Cushman, *William Carlos Williams and the Meanings of Measure*, Yale Studies in English 193 (New Haven: Yale University Press, 1985), 7.

5. See Mike Weaver, *William Carlos Williams: The American Background* (Cambridge: Cambridge University Press, 1971), 82.

6. William Carlos Williams, *The Selected Letters of William Carlos Williams*, ed. John C. Thirlwal (New York: McDowell Obolensky), 135.

7. Steele, 67.

8. Ibid., 66; italics in original.

9. Richard Moore, "Of Form, Closed and Open: with Glances at Frost and Williams," *Iowa Review* (Summer 1988): 87.

10. Hugh McNaughton, cited in Brogan, 410. The title of McNaughton's essay was "Free Verse: A Parallel and a Warning," and appeared in *The National Review* 90 (1927), 88–96.

11. Yvor Winters, "The Audible Reading of Poetry," in Gross, *Structure,* 145.

12. Baum, 154.

13. Frederick Morgan, "William Carlos Williams: Imagery, Rhythm, Form," *Sewanee Review* 55 (Autumn 1947): 682.

14. Charles Allen, "Cadenced Free Verse," *College English* 9 (January 1948): 198–99.

15. Graham Hough, "Free Verse," *Proceedings of the British Academy* 43 (1957): 175.

16. Shapiro and Beum, 151. Earlier in their book they had ascribed mnemonic value to meter rather than rhyme; see 81, 82.

17. Fussell, *Poetic Meter* (1965), 39.

18. Ibid., 89.

19. Peter Viereck, "Strict Form in Poetry: Would Jacob Wrestle with a Flabby Angel?" *Critical Inquiry* 5 (Winter 1978): 208.

20. Attridge, *Rhythms,* 299–300.

21. Marvin Bell, "On the Freedom of Free Verse," *Ohio Review* No. 28 (1982): [51].

22. Reg Saner, "Noble Numbers: Two in One," *Ohio Review* no. 28 (1982): 14.

23. Donald Hall, "Notes on Free Verse and Fashion," *Ohio Review* no. 28 (1982): 26–27. Italics in original.

24. Turner and Pöppel, 307.

25. Ibid., 298.

26. Robert Richman, *The Direction of Poetry: An Anthology of Rhymed and Metered Verse Written in the English Language Since 1975* (Boston: Houghton Mifflin, 1988), xvi.

27. Ibid., xxi.

28. Dacey and Jauss, 5.

29. Ibid., 9.

30. Brooks and Warren, 172.

31. Eliot, *Selected Prose,* 90.

32. Wimsatt and Beardsley, 597.

33. Brooks, Purser and Warren, 540.

34. Ralph D. Mills, Jr., ed., *On the Poet and His Craft: Selected Prose of Theodore Roethke* (Seattle: University of Washington Press, 1965), 81.

35. This appears in Rory Holscher and Robert Schultz, ed. "A Symposium on the Theory and Practice of the Line in Contemporary Poetry," *Epoch* (Winter, 1980): 221.

36. See Scully Bradley, "The Fundamental Metrical Principle in Whitman's Poetry," *American Literature* 10 (January 1939): 437–59.

37. Wesling, 107.

38. Fussell, *Poetic Meter,* rev. ed., 85.

39. Shapiro and Beum, 67.

40. Fussell, *Poetic Meter,* rev. ed., 85.

41. "Reader's Forum [Exchange between Alan Holder and Marjorie Perloff], *Georgia Review* 36 (Winter 1982), 933.

42. Elizabeth R. Hewitt, "Structure and Meaning in T. S. Eliot's *Ash Wednesday*," *Anglia* 83 (1965): 431.

43. Brogan, 295.

44. Paul Ramsey, "Free Verse: Some Steps Toward a Definition," *Studies in Philology* (January, 1968): 105; italics in original.

45. Eliot, *Selected Prose*, 88.

46. Charles O. Hartman, *Free Verse: An Essay on Prosody* (Princeton: Princeton University Press, 1980), 117.

47. See, most notably, James A. Powell, "The Light of Vers Libre," *Paideuma* 5 (Spring 1979): 3–34. While Powell states that "In Pound's mature poetry, there is no metre. Rhythm is all" (13), he analyzes a number of passages in Pound by invoking all sorts of feet, including some that only a classicist would ever even have heard of. As long ago as 1910, Robert Bridges, who has himself been thought of as a classicist poet, complained that "metrists are now at pains to match the names of Greek quantitative feet" to the "irregularities of well-written free verse. . . ." (cited in Wesling, 139).

48. Fraser, 59.

49. Gross, *Sound and Form*, 131.

50. *Ibid.,* 208.

51. Hartman, 29.

52. Wimsatt and Beardsley, 598.

53. Ramsey, "Free Verse," 100–1.

54. See Ramsey, "William Carlos Williams as Metrist: Theory and Practice," *Journal of Modern Literature* (May, 1971): 585–88.

55. Ramsey, "Free Verse," 100.

56. Ramsey, "William Carlos Williams as Metrist," 581.

57. Ibid., 587.

58. Annie Finch, *The Ghost of Meter: Culture and Prosody in American Free Verse* (Ann Arbor: University of Michigan Press, 1993). Considering that the source of Finch's title is undoubtedly the T. S. Eliot passage quoted earlier in this chapter, her citation of that passage is curiously minimal; see Finch, 82.

59. In general, it would be hard to exaggerate how much weight Finch, in her preoccupation with the notion of "metrical code," assigns to the alleged presence of metrical lines (or pieces of lines) in the specimens of free verse she examines. Again and again in her analyses, meter may be said to assume the role of *subject* in a given passage, as it does in her treatment of the lines from Whitman discussed earlier. Better yet, meter with Finch tends to fuse with or become a poem's *protagonist* (or antagonist). Witness her handling of some lines from Stephen Crane. They read as follows: "Going ridiculous voyages,/ Making quaint progress,/ Turning as with serious purpose/ Before stupid winds." Breaking the passage up into eleven "feet," four of them dactyls, Finch says: "The dactyls now appear ridiculous, divorced from God and left to their own devices; they keep the appearance of sacred seriousness, but are actually at the mercy of the 'stupid' prevailing iambic and trochaic winds" (74). The opening section of "The Love Song of J. Alfred Prufrock" refers to "an overwhelming question." Finch says that "In terms of the metrical code, the 'question' involves the extent to which iambic pentameter is still the only truly viable metric for ambitious poetry, and the nature of the risks involved in either adopting or rejecting it" (101). Later in the poem, Prufrock wonders if it would "have been worth while . . . /To roll [the universe squeezed into a ball] towards some overwhelming question,/ To say: 'I am Lazarus, come from the dead, Come back to tell you all, I shall tell you

all'. . . ." Finch says "The 'overwhelming' metrical question mentioned at the beginning of the poem is evoked again. The figure of Lazarus, confirming that death can become life and a dead meter a living one, resolves the previous associations of the meter with dead voices. The two triple substitutions in the Lazarus line also point ahead to the redeeming value of the dactylic rhythm in Eliot's later poetry" (104).

60. Quoted in Wesling, 153.

61. Viereck, 214.

62. Jonathan Holden, "The Free Verse Line," in *The Line in Postmodern Poetry*, ed. Robert Frank and Henry Sayre (Urbana: University of Illinois Press, 1988), 2.

63. For a skeptical examination of that sort of linking see Henri Meschonnic, *Critique du Rhythme: anthropologique historique du langage* (Paris: Editions Verdier, 1982), particularly Chapter 13, "L'Imitation Cosmique."

64. Sandra M. Gilbert "Glass Joints: A Meditation on the Line," in Frank and Sayre, 47. Earlier, Gilbert says that at the time of writing *Ariel*, Plath "was still haunted by iambic pentameter" (46).

65. Turner and Pöppel, 288, 298, 306.

66. In a variation on this haunting approach to free verse, John Hollander transposes the matter from the aural to the visual, saying, in one of the self-illustrating examples he favors in his *Rhyme's Reason:*

> Some free verse is arranged in various
> graphic patterns like this that suggest
> the barely-seen but silent ghost of a
> classical verse form
> like a fragment of Sapphic . . . (27)

67. See Meschonnic, 657ff.

68. Pound, in Gross, *Structure of Verse,* 237.

69. Attridge, *Rhythms,* 314.

70. Donald Wesling, taking off from Benjamin Hrushovski's important essay "On Free Rhythms in Modern Poetry" (in Sebeok, 173–90), has said that in the study of free verse we need "to substitute a various and multiple prosody for a prosody comprised of one or two a priori units. Thereby we understand the poem, as Modern [*sic*] linguists understand language, as a system of relations rather than an addition of particles" (153). This splendidly expresses my own view, with one important exception, Wesling's use of the word "system." Here, if I may indulge in my own form of detecting ghosts, we are encountering a dangerous echo of traditional prosody, with its enamored notion of a meter-generated system controlling a given poem. A free-verse poem may have a system or it may not, but the existence of a system should not be assumed to begin with. It appears to me that Henri Meschonnic would be in sympathy with my notion of a poem offering us a series of individual entities, the lines, that may interact in ways we cannot predict. He distinguishes between meter, which measures, and rhythm, which participates in the risks of discourse (528). He also observes that the notion of meter isolates the line (531). I am after an approach in which lines may be seen as capable of playing off each other.

71. Brooks, Purser and Warren, 537n.

72. Clive Scott's *Vers Libre: The Emergence of Free Verse in France 1886–1914* (Oxford: Clarendon Press, 1990) came to my attention only after I had written this chapter. While, as his title indicates, Scott is concerned with French

poetry and prosodic thought, it is interesting to note that some of the same characteristics of prosodic criticism in English that I have pointed to in the chapter have their equivalents in French. Thus, for example, Scott says "It is . . . the dearth of critical attention paid to the prosody of free verse which is the principal justification of this book" (1). The papers delivered at a particular colloquium held in 1966 "are, on the whole, more concerned to demonstrate the survival of the regular in the free than to tackle the free on its own terms" (2). Like free verse, vers libre has elicited hostility. Back in the 1890s Edmond Haracourt said of vers libre that "Il supprime des difficultés pour les faibles, et des ressources pour les forts. . . . Il enlève toute cadence et n'offre rien en sa place." Scott says that this remark is "equivalent to Robert Frost's wry sally that free verse is like playing tennis without a net" (3). Scott notes that as recently as 1966 Rene Étiemble said "le verse libre concourt en effet à la veulerie générale, à l'abaissement auquel se rue notre civilisation" (6). Bringing us back in effect to one of the strains in English-language criticism I have pointed to, Scott conjoins further remarks of Étiemble with A. D. Hope's observations made in 1965: "Free verse has not died out. It is, I believe, happily on the decline, and few serious poets now bother with it. But it is still a very common, cheap, and popular substitute for poetry . . ." (4).

CHAPTER 5. PRELIMINARIES TO REVISION

1. The stress pattern of a given word in English may be affected by the context in which that word is found. For example, in stating someone's age, we might say, "she is thirteen," assigning the stress to "-teen." But that same number would be stressed differently if we were to say "There are thirteen women in the room." Here the "thir-" would receive the stress.

2. Roy Fuller, "The Fetish of Speech Rhythms in Modern Poetry," *Southern Review* 15 (January 1979): 1–15.

3. Eliot, *Selected Prose*, 58. In light of Eliot's focus on poetry as *speech*, it is somewhat ironic that Timothy Steele should take him (as well as other modernists) to task for holding up music as a model for poetry. It is that focus on music, according to Steele, that formed one of the dubious bases for the free-verse movement in our century (*Missing Measures*, particularly 203–23). There is further irony in Steele's position when we consider the fact that taking music as a model has long been the practice of many prosodists committed to meter.

4. Puttenham, 81.

5. Hardison, 100.

6. Brogan, 244.

7. Bridges, *Milton's Prosody*, 35, 100.

8. Pound, *Literary Essays of Ezra Pound*, ed. T. S. Eliot (New York: New Directions, 1954), 6.

9. Southworth, 5.

10. Ibid., 90.

11. Henry Lee Smith, Jr., "Introduction," 5.

12. D. W. Harding, *Words into Rhythm: English Speech Rhythm in Verse and Prose* (Cambridge: Cambridge University Press, 1976), 6.

13. Baum, 47.

14. The tracing of that separation can be found in the entry "Music and Poetry," by John Hollander, in the *Princeton Encyclopedia of Poetry and Poetics*, 533–36.

15. Eliot, *Selected Prose,* 58–59; italics in original.

16. Fraser, 5.

17. Harding, citing Thompson, finds such a suggestion "indefensible" (37). Anthony Easthope assumes a kind of fence-sitting position when he says that "Since pentameter consists neither of the abstract pattern itself nor the intonation of nonmetric language but is a function of the two in which both are active, actual performance will vary widely according to whether the voice tends towards the abstract pattern (though never losing hold on the intonation) or towards the intonation (though it could only become nonmetric speech by defying entirely the abstract pattern)" (64). The decided unhelpfulness of this statement is not mitigated by Easthope's setting a stress pattern against an intonational one instead of against another stress pattern.

18. Thompson, *Founding,* 69; italics in original.

19. Richard Cureton has impressively demonstrated the limitations of a number of such books, but not with respect to the matter of natural emphasis. See his "Traditional Scansion."

20. Brogan, 135.

21. The work in question is cited in Omond, 182.

22. See Wellek and Warren, 173.

23. Cited in Brogan, 149.

24. In Sebeok, 186.

25. Zdzislawa Kopczynska and Lucylla Pszczolowska, "Le Role de l'intonation dans la versification," in *Poetics, Poetyka,: First International Conference on Work-in-Progress Devoted to Problems of Poetics* (Warsaw: Polish Scientific Publishers, 1961), 215.

26. Shapiro and Beum, 45.

27. T. S. Eliot, "The Borderline of Prose," 158.

28. Hartman, 11.

29. Holscher and Schultz, 162, 163.

30. Impulse, instinct, the inscrutable, and the unconscious were all invoked as the poets, understandably enough, spoke about the line from the perspective of the creator. But the results did not give the reader or critic of poetry much to chew on. See "The Poetic Line: A Symposium," in *A Field Guide to Contemporary Poetry and Poetics,* edited by Stuart Friebert and David Young (New York: Longman, 1980).

31. Louis Simpson, "Irregular Impulses: Some Remarks on Free Verse," *Ohio Review* no. 28 (1982): 55.

32. Stewart, 161, 163. Stewart, cited earlier, is an interesting prosodist, a man who rebelled against the hegemony of the foot even as he seemed to retain that dubious unit. His book, *The Technique of English Verse,* can be viewed as incipiently adopting a phrasal approach to poetry, the sort of thing I will be focusing on in the next chapter.

33. Randy Weirather, "The Language of Prosody," *Language and Style* 13 (Spring 1980): 135–36.

34. Ibid., 136.

35. In Donald Hall, "The Line," in Friebert and Young, 74–75.

36. Cited in Brogan, 89.

37. Ants Oras, "Spenser and Milton: Some Parallels and Contrasts in the Handling of Sound," in *Sound and Poetry: English Institute Essays, 1956,* ed. Northrop Frye (New York: Columbia University Press, 1957), 114.

38. Donald Wesling has argued that "the crisis of the poetic line" occurred in

the period of 1855–1910, in both French and English poetry (88). But this dating of the matter is dubious at both of the designated ends. As indicated earlier, some have seen an undermining of the line as having begun with the rise of blank verse (this topic will be returned to later in the chapter). Also, the nature of the line has become *more* problematical since 1910, though Wesling would appear to think otherwise. He says the 1885–1910 period is "the historical moment when the new phrasal verse can violently force the old foot verse into perceptibility. But afterward the two types can be blended . . ." (101). Wesling's own observations later in his book would indicate that the line has fallen outside such a truce arrangement.

39. Holscher and Schultz, 179.

40. Ibid., 185.

41. Hayden Carruth, "Here Today: A Poetry Chronicle," *Hudson Review* 24 (Summer 1971): 326.

42. Frank and Sayre, xvii; see also Helms. Such sentiments echo the position taken by Richard Howard some years earlier. In a class given at Yale, Howard had put on the board a short poem by W. S. Merwin, writing it out as a single line, and then asking where it was cut in the free verse original. Howard reported: "invariably—no one gets it 'right.' . . . It means that Merwin's poem is not in verse. When you cannot arrive at a consensus as to where the lines end, then you are writing in prose.'" This is cited by Wesling (173), who retorts: "you are not writing in prose. You are writing badly" (217).

43. See my exchange with Perloff on the question of the line in "Readers' Forum," *Georgia Review* 36 (Winter 1982): 933–36.

44. Marjorie Perloff, "The Linear Fallacy," *Georgia Review* 35 (Winter 1981): 867.

45. Pound's remark can be found in *Literary Essays*, 5.

46. Perloff, "'The shape of the lines': Oppen and the metric of difference," in her *dance of the intellect: studies in the poetry of the Pound tradition* (Cambridge: Cambridge University Press, 1985), 121.

47. Perloff, "Williams and the visualization of poetry," *dance of the intellect*, 99.

48. Carruth, 326.

49. Perloff, "Williams," 91.

50. Prudence Byers, working with reading measurements of both prose and poetry, has found that the poet "creates more obligatory short units (those with one or two stressed syllables, punctuation fore and aft and no syntactic break in between) than the prose writer does: 35% of all units in poetry are obligatory short units, in prose only 3% are. . . . And the poetry reader, when the division of a long stretch of speech is up to him, breaks it into short units more consistently than the prose reader does. . . . Both writer and reader, therefore, seem to share the conviction that poetry should come in short spurts rather than long stretches." (I see the use of the line itself as showing a predilection by poets for short entities, though the line will not necessarily converge with the units Byers focuses on.) Byers also finds that poetry is spoken at "a slower, statelier rate of speech" than prose. See Byers, "A Formula for Poetic Intonation," *Poetics* 8 (August 1979): 370.

51. Brooks and Warren, 562.

52. Quasha, in Holscher and Schultz, 214. Charles O. Hartman says "My definition of 'prosody' centers on the control of attention. If lineation helps to enforce attention, it serves as a prosodic divide, whether the line is metrically

organized or not. . . . Poetry is usually written in verse because lineation promotes the attention which is necessary to prosody and essential to poetry" (52).

53. Jonathan Monroe, *A Poverty of Objects: The Prose Poem and the Politics of Genre* (Ithaca: Cornell University Press, 1987), 21.

54. Perloff, "Postmodernism and the impasse of lyric," in *dance of the intellect,* 189. In further fairness to Perloff, it should be noted that her position on the line in "The Linear Fallacy" is mild compared to that of Randy Weirather. For while Perloff attempts to undermine the theoretical centrality of the line by extending the notion of poetry to include examples of twentieth-century prose, Weirather seems to see the integrity of the line dissolving with the disappearance of Anglo-Saxon poetry. According to him, prosodists enshrining the line have been guilty of imposing the norms of Anglo-Saxon poetry—verse (i.e., line), hemistich, and caesura—on the accentual-syllabic poetry that followed it.

55. Ibid., 190.

56. In her "Linear Fallacy" piece Perloff mentions Beckett's prose, along with Ashbery's *Three Poems,* as employing patterns of recurrence and having a greater claim to being poetry than some contemporary verse. But Beckett himself, as witnessed by his own lineated *Poems,* seems not to have been as ready to question the importance of the line as is Perloff.

57. Donald Wesling says that the "basic unit of analysis" of the prose poem is the sentence (190), but he does not invoke the notion of the new sentence.

58. Ron Silliman, "The New Sentence," in *Claims for Poetry,* ed. Donald Hall (Ann Arbor: University of Michigan Press, 1982), 395, 397.

59. Christopher Ricks, "Wordsworth: 'A Pure Organic Pleasure from the Lines,'" *Essays in Criticism* 21 (January 1971): 22–23.

60. Peter Townsend, "Essential Groupings of Meaningful Force: Rhythm in Literary Discourse," *Language and Style* 16 (Summer 1983): 327.

61. Shapiro and Beum, 51.

62. Ricks, 19. This is cited by Townsend, 324.

63. Perloff, "Linear Fallacy," 857–58.

64. Ibid., 864; italics in original.

65. Stanley Plumly, "Chapter and Verse," *American Poetry Review* 7 (January/February 1978): 25. Perloff, too, thinks in terms of scannable prose, talking of the feet in an excerpt from Beckett's *How It Is* ("Linear Fallacy," 867–68; see also her *dance of the intellect,* 145). She thereby ignores the fact that the notion of feet presumes, as Charles O. Hartman observes, "a numerically regular system"; feet are not to be extrapolated here and there, existing apart from such a system. See Hartman, *Free Verse,* 117.

66. In a related if not identical, comment, Robert Haas said in 1978: "Free verse has lost its edge, become neutral, the given instrument. . . . Once [it] has become neutral, there must be an enormous impulse to use it . . . to establish tone rather than to make form." "One Body: Some Notes on Form," *Antaeus* 30/31 (Spring 1978): 341–42).

67. Denise Levertov, "On the Function of the Line," in *Claims for Poetry,* 265–67.

68. Wesling, 160–61.

69. See, for example, Alan Helms, "Intricate Song's Last Measure," *Sewanee Review* 87 (Spring 1979): 249–66.

70. Cited in Stephen Cushman, *William Carlos Williams and the Meanings of Measure,* Yale Studies in English 193 (New Haven: Yale University Press, 1985), 13.

71. I might note that, in an experimental study of pause that took *Paradise Lost* as its principal text, Ada L. F. Snell found that readers generally agree on the placement of pauses, but that a third more of those pauses appeared within the lines than at their ends. This would at least suggest that some line endings were not marked by pauses. See Ada L. F. Snell *Pause: A Study of its Nature and its Rhythmical Function in Verse, Especially in Blank Verse*. Contributions to Rhetorical Theory, no. 8 (1918; reprint, Norwood, Pa.: Norwood Editions, 1975).

72. Samuel R. Levin, "The Conventions of Poetry," in *Literary Style: A Symposium*, ed. Seymour Chatman (New York: Oxford University Press, 1971), 182.

73. See Puttenham, 376.

74. See Brogan, 220–21.

75. Cary F. Jacob, "Concerning Scansion," *Sewanee Review* 19 (July 1911): 358.

76. Egerton Smith, 34. It should be observed that with this last statement Smith places line-end pause close to the "ideal" stresses sometimes posited by traditional metrists. I will take up this point shortly.

77. Ibid.

78. Cited in Levin, 191; italics presumably in original.

79. Brogan, 110.

80. Gross, *Sound and Form in Modern Poetry,* 173.

81. Ibid., 174.

82. Mitchell, "Toward a System of Grammatical Scansion," *Language and Style* 3 (Winter 1970): 15. Cf. Jon Stallworthy's statement: "every line-break entails at least a fractional pause" (in Holscher and Schultz, 221).

83. Mitchell, "Toward a System," 15.

84. Levin, 183.

85. Ibid., 182.

86. Ricks, 2. In a postscript to the article where this remark appeared, F. W. Bateson questioned Ricks' attributing significance to the white spaces at the ends of lines in connection with Wordsworth's poetry, but what is of interest to the essential matter at hand is that Bateson also questioned Ricks' notion of nontemporal pauses, since actual pauses "are necessary in poetry because each line's metrical impact must be registered *as a line. . . .*" "Editorial Postscript" (29; italics in original).

87. Prudence Byers, "The Auditory Reality of the Verse Line," *Style* 17 (Winter 1983): 27.

88. I should acknowledge that Charles Olson argued, and in extreme terms, against automatically pausing at the ends of his lines, at least those that are enjambed: "The lines which hook-over should be read as though they lay out right and flat to the horizon or to Eternity" (cited in Wesling, 161). One can only ask what the line, then, is supposed to mean to the reader.

89. Byers, "Auditory Reality," 30.

90. Hollander, *Vision and Resonance,* 92.

91. Ibid., 91.

92. Byers, "A Formula," 370. The figure that she cites is one pause for every eight syllables of poetry.

93. Weirather, 133.

94. Cited in Hollander, *Vision and Resonance,* 91.

95. Omond, *English Metrists,* 206.

96. Stewart, 31–32.

97. C. S. Lewis, "The Fifteenth-Century Heroic Line," *Essays and Studies* 24 (1938): 29.

98. Fraser, 13; see also 43.

99. Chatman, *Theory of Meter*, 156.

100. Gross, *Sound and Form*, 40.

101. Levin, 184–85.

102. Omond, *English Metrists*, 7.

103. Fowler, *Languages of Literature*, 133.

104. See Brogan, 275.

105. David Abercrombie, *Studies in Phonetics and Linguistics* (London: Oxford University Press, 1965), 20; italics in original.

106. Cable, "Timers, Stressers," 234; italics in original.

107. While Cable attempts to be both a stresser and timer, he is, first and foremost, a metrical fundamentalist of such purity that even Wimsatt and Beardsley seem to fall short of his standards (see 235).

108. Attridge, *Rhythms*, 90.

109. Cable, "Timers, Stressers," 229.

110. J. Milton Cowan and Bernard Bloch, "An Experimental Study of Pause in English Grammar," *American Speech* 23 (April 1948): 94.

111. William E. Cooper and Jeanne Paccia-Cooper, *Syntax and Speech* (Cambridge, Mass.: Harvard University Press, 1980), 106.

112. Elisabeth O. Selkirk, *Phonology and Syntax: the Relation between Sound and Structure* (Cambridge: M.I.T. Press, 1984). In addition to Selkirk, see Mark Liberman and Alan Prince, "On Stress and Linguistic Rhythm," *Linguistic Inquiry* 8 (Spring 1977): 249–336; also Alan Prince, "Relating to the Grid," *Linguistic Inquiry* 14 (1983): 19–100; and Bruce Hayes, "A Grid-based Theory of English Meter," *Linguistic Inquiry* 14 (Summer 1983): 357–92.

113. Selkirk, 7. It may occur to the reader that this bears a striking similarity to the standard prosodic matching of the words of a line of poetry with the abstract metrical pattern allegedly governing that line. But there are important differences. For one thing, Selkirk's metrical grid allows for a range of hierarchical values rather than the two-value system (stressed, unstressed) of traditional metrics, at least in its purer form. Secondly, Selkirk says that "there is nothing in the grid representation itself that specifies the nature of the periodicities of the pulses (metrical patterns) on any metrical level" (11); that is, the configuration of a particular grid does not exist a priori and as something to be imposed on a series of sentences; it is the result of investigating a particular utterance. There are, to be sure, certain general laws governing the assignment of values to particular grid positions. But these laws as well as the grid itself are attempts to account for the empirically observed speech patterns of the language; they are not, as metrical patterns too often are in the hands of prosodists, devices for bending those patterns into a presupposed shape. We might also note Selkirk's characterization of "the foot," which has seen separate service as a linguistic tool. She says "In this function, as Prince . . . argues quite effectively, the foot has been supplanted by the metrical-grid theory of stress. It is important to note, moreover, that there is relatively little evidence that the foot itself serves as a domain for phonological rules" (31).

114. Dooley, 117.

CHAPTER 6. PHRASALISM

1. George T. Wright, *Shakespeare's Metrical Art*, 11–12; italics in original.

2. One gathers that Karl Shapiro has been no happier with the notion of

phrasalism than Wright, and only finds it tolerable when allied with foot-based meter. In speaking of poetic practice as opposed to critical theory, Shapiro had this to say about prosody that attempted to overthrow the traditional one: "At its worst, as in the *Cantos* of Pound, this prosody was founded on the rhythm of phrases. . . . At its best, as in the more ambitious poems of Eliot, the prose phrase was used in juxtaposition with the orthodox prosodic foot to create a variety of movement which satisfied some of the conditions of traditional prosody . . ." ("English Prosody," 91). But, rather confusingly, in speaking of Hopkins and Coleridge, Shapiro says they "stood for the prosody that sounds in the ear and therefore does not 'scan,' and this is the prosody of nearly all English lyric poetry, the poetry of cadences, versicles, sections, vers libre, 'visual' poetry, *poesie orchestrale*—and every other tendency in verse that is not fully explained by the laws of foot-arrangement . . ." (89). The wording of this would appear to place not only Hopkins and Coleridge in or at least near the camp of the phrasalists but Shapiro himself.

3. Wesling, 101–2.

4. Ibid., 108.

5. Josephine Miles, *Eras and Modes in English Poetry,* 2nd. ed. (Berkeley: University of California Press, 1964), 11.

6. Ibid., 250.

7. Wright, *Shakespeare's Metrical Art,* 301; italics in original.

8. Hardison, 4. Here we might think of the sixteenth-century poet, Thomas Wythorne, cited by Raymond Southall as maintaining that it was Aristoxenus who "speaketh of that miuzik which standeth in sownd and vois, and not of that which konsisteth in meeterz, rithms, and verses" (120). Southall himself, one of the prosodists named as a phrasalist by Wright, sees Wyatt's poetry as forming "patterns of sense rather than permutations of feet" (125). He further claims that "In order to read [early Tudor] verse successfully it is only necessary to remember that it should be read phrase by phrase and not line by line" (137). (As will be made clear later, I do not regard one of these methods as incompatible with the other.) Southall spoke of several devices in early Tudor poetry that seemed to him to point to construction by phrases: capitalization, spacing, punctuation, and alliterating internal rhyme (139, 142).

9. Hardison, 4.

10. Cited in Omond, 203.

11. Liddell didn't help his cause in positing the four kinds of "stress" that he did: sense, word, emotion, and rhythm (303).

12. Cary Jacob, *The Foundations and Nature of Verse* (New York: Columbia University Press, 1918) 145, 193.

13. Pound, *Literary Essays,* 6; italics in original.

14. Ibid., 3.

15. Stewart, 12.

16. Ibid., 33.

17. James G. Southworth, *Verses of Cadence: An Introduction to the Prosody of Chaucer and his Followers* (Oxford: Basil Blackwell, 1954), 6; see also 46–47. T. V. F. Brogan, generally unfriendly toward Southworth, seems to think that his notion of the virgule's function has been brought into question by the work of another scholar, but I do not regard Brogan's formulation of the matter (576) as substantially undermining Southworth's view that the virgule marks off a significant entity not defined by feet.

18. Ian Robinson, *Chaucer's Prosody: A Study of the Middle English Verse Tradition* (London: Cambridge University Press, 1971), 12.

19. Brogan said this of Thompson's *The Founding of English Metre:* "Should become the *locus classicus* on Renaissance metrics and, indeed, on the more general subject of the nature of English accentual-syllabic meter in its staple form, the iambic pentameter line" (160). Unsurprisingly, Brogan is less than respectful toward Robinson (see 569).

20. Catherine Ing, *Elizabethan Lyrics: A Study in the Development of English Metres and their Relation to Poetic Effect* (New York: Barnes and Noble, 1969), 198.

21. Nist, "Word-Group Cadence," 76. It may be no coincidence that Nist, like Guest, was an Anglo-Saxon scholar; his training in the reading of a poetry that operates in half-lines might well have made him feel the imposition of the classical foot on the English verse line as particularly cramping. He speaks of the Norman Conquest's having "wrenched the native tradition of the Anglo-Saxon alliterative line into the French syllable-counting technique of Chaucer and all those main-stream poets who were to swim after him in the muddy waters of the so-called iambic pentameter" ("Word-Group Cadence," 73). Nist is actually conceding too much here to foot-based prosody.

22. In place of such data, prosaic but necessary for persuasive commentary, Nist offers us, in speaking of a passage from Shakespeare's *Henry V,* such things as "the intimacy of the three closing appositions," "the sublime assertion of the second full-line cadence," and the "two final intimately democratic and tear-filled incremental expansions" (78).

23. Referring to Nist's essay on distinctive features, "Sound and Sense: Some Structures of Poetry," Brogan asks "Why has no one else extended such an analysis?" (67). On the other hand, Brogan is dismissive of Nist's piece on word-groups (267).

24. Harding, 76.

25. Daniel Laferrière, "Free and Non-Free Verse: A Response to Howard McCord's 'Breaking and Entering,'" *Language and Style* 10 (Spring 1977), 80. As suggested earlier, I am not happy with the term "rhythmic groups" and much prefer Nist's "word groups." Also, as should be evident by now, I see no inevitable need to take account of "metrical groups," that is, feet; stress counts and distributions are another matter. I might note that Richard Cureton uses the term "rhythm phrases," which I shall deal with later in the chapter.

26. Attridge, *Rhythms of Poetry,* 113.

27. Stevenson, 340.

28. Mitchell, "A Prosody for Whitman?" *PMLA* 84 (October 1969): 1608.

29. Reliance on such a model has been common enough among prosodists. See, for example, Stewart, 37, and Herbert L. Creek, "Rising and Falling Rhythms in English Verse," *PMLA* 35 (March 1920): 76–90. Richard Cureton invokes rising and falling rhythms in "Definition," 8.

30. An alternative reading of the line might see two groups: And all things flourish//where you turn your eyes. This would move the line closer to lines 1 and 3 in terms of overall feel, but here a perfect balance of syllables would be achieved, 5–5, as opposed to the 4–6 construction of the other two. This balance, along with the line's inverting of the cause-effect sequence of lines 1 and 3, stamps the line with its own character.

31. Mitchell opposes to a genuine prosody a reliance on "local effects," such as "random alliteration or internal rhyming" (1606). Taking a rather different view

of the matter, I would say that the traditional conception of prosody has suffered from not paying *enough* attention to local effects, as opposed to seeking a specious continuousness or unity. Mitchell is a conservative in this, as in his linking Whitman to "a principle of unity-in-variety, comparable to that practiced in accentual-syllabic verse . . ." (1610). Just how much does this tired old formula tell us about a given text?

32. Mitchell, "Towards a System of Grammatical Scansion," 3.

33. "Raising Phrasing" is the title of a handout Cureton distributed to a section on prosody that he participated in at the MLA convention held in New York City in 1986.

34. Cureton, "Rhythm: A Multilevel Analysis," 253.

35. Admittedly, Cureton's rhythm phrases are not *quite* as arbitrary as feet, which frequently dismember words.

36. See his treatment of *"Equivalence"* in "A Definition of Rhythm," 8, and see my "Richard Cureton's 'Definition of Rhythm': Some Queries, Quibbles, and Caveats," *Eidos* 4 (December 1987): 10.

37. Cureton, "Traditional Scansion," 186.

38. Ibid.

39. Wright, *Shakespeare's Metrical Art,* 84.

40. He also says the pyrrhics "set off some spondees ('-riage of true minds')" (85); without seeing a need for foot terminology I agree with his description of the effect. I should add that it is good to see Wright talk of spondees, in seeming recognition that two consecutive syllables in English can receive stress, but notice how he combines this terminology with the allegation that the second stress is stronger than the first; in short, it has an "iambic" structure. Thus he has his spondee and his iamb too, in effect joining a fair number of metrists who have difficulty accepting the existence of spondees.

41. I find "Let me not to" as arbitrary a phrase as some of Cureton's specimens.

42. John Nist simply declares that Shakespeare's blank verse has "a line of from nine to eleven syllables. . . ." "Word-Group Cadence," 77.

43. There are prosodists who believe that beneath iambic pentameter there beats the Old English four-accent line (see e.g., Frye, xvii–xviii). My "four or five" formulation might be seen as accommodating this view, though such is not its purpose.

44. I might note here that my procedure for dealing with iambic pentameter could be extended to other meters. That is, one would start with the meter defined in terms of a fixed number of syllables, allowing for a deviation of plus or minus one. In the case of "anapestic," a norm would be assumed in which the line would be defined as starting with two unstressed syllables, and in the cases of "trochaic" and "dactylic," the norm would have the line starting with a stressed syllable. In the case of trochaic, the norm would have stresses separated by at least one syllable, in the cases of anapestic and dactylic by two syllables. In all cases no consideration would be given to feet.

45. Martha Kolln, *Understanding English Grammar,* 2nd ed. (New York: Macmillan, 1986), 357.

46. Just how much of a role grouping into phrases plays in the act of reading is pointed up by the work of Thomas Bever, a professor of psychology and linguistics at the University of Rochester. He has found that inserting spaces at the end of phrases contributes materially to students' reading comprehension. See Blair

Claflin, "Reading Between the Lines," *New York Times Education Life Supplement* (August 4, 1991): 10.

47. How special a case the assigning of stress to "it" amounts to is indicated by Dwight Bolinger's statement that "The word *it* comes as close as one can get to an inherent lack of stress . . ." See Bolinger, *Intonation and its Parts: Melody in Spoken English* (Stanford, Calif.: Stanford University Press, 1986), 185. Cf. Selkirk's observation that "the unfamiliarity of a word or of its appearance in a certain phrasal collocation apparently may influence its timing and in particular may give rise to a pause before it" (183). Here the unfamiliarity consists of a noun following immediately upon the word "it."

48. Wright is not the only true believer in feet who has seemingly made room for phrases. Marina Tarlinskaja has also done so, in a manner of speaking. She asks if "metrical laws . . . influence . . . the choice of grammatical categories of words and their syntactic combinations in verse." See her "Rhythm-Morphology-Syntax-Rhythm," *Style* 18 (Winter 1984):1. She employs the concept of the "metrical word," which is "a graphic word or a group of adjacent graphic words united by one strong ictic stress." The principle of segmenting a line into metrical words, she says, is "semantic and syntactic." On the face of it, this would seem to agree with or at least overlap my approach, but in practice her commitment to the "one strong ictic stress" principle can make for some arbitrary segmentations, as when she divides a line from Pope up as follows: "But secret/Cares/the pensive /Nymph/ oppress'd" (5). Also, after going through a strenuous statistical approach reminiscent of her treatment of feet, she makes no attempt to show how her findings illuminate the communicative effect of the poetry she has examined. She simply says: "The expressive functions of word boundary rhythm await further study" (23).

49. There is further disagreement between us. Part of the reason Wright thinks in terms of "interplay" appears to be that he identifies "meter" with the notion of the line as essential verse unit, and he finds that a poem's phrases will sometimes overrun line boundaries (213–23). But in my view, the line is not a creature of meter, it is the essential verse unit for everything I regard as poetry, as indicated in the preceding chapter. If a phrase overruns a line ending, that is something we can consider without invoking "meter."

50. See *Poetry: A Magazine of Verse* 2 (April 1913): 12.

51. While rhyming effects are beyond the boundaries of this study, it should be noted that the sense of symmetry here is reinforced by the two surrounding words making for an internal rhyme: *sis-ness*.

52. *At the same time,* to take account of rhyme once again, lines 2 and 3 are not totally opposed in their sonal characteristics to the first. Apart from the internal rhyme of *Pour-tor* in line 2, cousin if not sibling to the *sis-ness* of line 1 (*Pour-tor* comes on accented syllables, the other not), there is the subtler but undeniable cross-rhyme of sub*stance*less and di*stances,* which, because of its occurrence in unstressed syllables and its own use of the short *i* and *s* sounds, has a kinship to the first line's internal rhyme. That is to say, the apparent radical break lines 2–3 make with line 1 in terms of their overall structure and feel is qualified by these sonal overlappings. What if anything is the significance of this? At the risk of pushing the matter perhaps too far for some readers, I would say that the stanza's structure, producing an echoing of line 1 in lines 2–3 through the use of nonend rhyme, even as it separates lines 2–3 from line 1 in terms of enjambment and stress arrangement, is suggesting that escape from stasis is not an absolute condition—it is qualifying that escape. Indeed, as the poem concludes,

it indicates that the escape after all is one into the sadomasochistic and suicidal: "I/Am the arrow . . . at one with the drive/ Into the red/ Eye, the cauldron of morning." What lies just beyond the boil of the last line is the stasis of death.

53. This effect has been anticipated on a lesser scale by having the verb attached to the second I—"am"—share its vowel sound with the "arrow" that I claims to be. Perhaps a closer analogue is the binding through assonance of words in the last line that, strictly in terms of their connotations, would appear to pull in opposite directions: "Cauldron," with its suggestion of danger, even death, and morning," with its suggestion of a fresh start, or rebirth.

CHAPTER 7. TUNING IN

1. Cited in Isamu Abe, "How Vocal Pitch Works," in Linda R. Waugh and C. H. van Schooneveld, ed. *The Melody of Language* (Baltimore: University Park Press, 1980), 5.

3. Rose Nash and Anthony Mulac, for example, say that "There is little doubt that the overall reactions to pitch movement are universal, and that they apply to music as well as speech. In both, melody always rises to its emotional climax, and falls to its denouement." In "The Intonation of Verifiability," Waugh and Schoonevelt, 240.

3. Katherine M. Wilson went so far as to say that "poetry resembles music rather than speech. . . . Poetry is almost one branch of music." *Sound and Meaning in English Poetry* (1930; reprint., Port Washington, N.Y.: Kennikat Press, 1970), 167.

4. Seymour Chatman, *A Theory of Meter,* 189.

5. Ibid., 188.

6. See Philip Lieberman, *Intonation, Perception, and Language* (Cambridge, Mass.: M.I.T. Press, 1967), 7.

7. Bolinger, *Intonation and its Parts,* 28.

8. Abe, 22.

9. Epstein and Hawkes, 20.

10. Brogan, 139. Elsewhere, Brogan says that "The patterning of stresses in English verse is now reasonably well understood, but the distribution of other intonational features—pitch, duration, pauses—has so far either been slighted or misconceived in scholarly investigations" (110). In this chapter I myself shall be concerned first and foremost with matters of pitch, and give brief consideration to pause insofar as it is related to intonation units; duration is outside my purview. A little later in the text I shall return to the subject of the slighting of intonation, but for now I would note that the entry under "pitch" in the *Princeton Encyclopedia* is very short. I would also note Raymond Southall's having made the following observations: "The fundamental character of the rhythm [in Wyatt] is due to the requirements of intonation, a feature that receives no recognition from classical prosody. This principle is not peculiar to Wyatt, and anyone fairly competent at reading Donne, Shakespeare, or Hopkins will have little difficulty in reading Wyatt. In each of these poets, as in speech, the pause, marking the completion of one intonation pattern, or 'tune,' is of extreme rhythmical importance and is often made to carry considerable emphasis . . ." (126–27).

11. Ronald Sutherland, "Structural Linguistics and English Prosody," *College English* 20 (October 1958): 13.

12. Chatman, *A Theory of Meter,* 100.

13. Jan Mukarovsky, *The Word and Verbal Art,* ed. and trans. by John Burbank and Peter Steiner, Yale Russian and East European Studies, no. 13 (New Haven: Yale University Press, 1977), 121.

14. As indicated in the preceding chapter, I have my differences with George T. Wright, but his difficulties with Mukarovsky are similar to my own. See Wright, *Shakespeare's Metrical Art,* 299–300. While it cannot be accused of mysticism, another work on intonation by a Slavic metrist does have something of Mukarovsky's dogmatism about it. Maciej Pakosz contends, with no empirical backup, that verse exhibits a greater uniformity of pitch patterns than is found in speech. At the same time, interestingly enough, Pakosz appears to call for a laboratory sort of empiricism: "any intonational analysis of a poem is bound to be carried out in very general terms unless substantiated with a corpus of instrumental data." "Some Aspects of the Role of Intonation in English Versification," *Studia Anglica Posenaniensia* 5 (1973): 163.

15. Crystal, "Intonation and Metrical Theory," *Transactions of the Philological Society* (1971), [1].

16. Ibid., 8.

17. See Thomas A. Sebeok, ed. *Style in Language* (Cambridge: M.I.T. Press, 1960), 199, 138, respectively.

18. Wimsatt and Beardsley, 586.

19. See Chatman, "Robert Frost's 'Mowing,' 431–32.

20. Sebeok, 205. I shall shortly comment on the matter of that separation. Chatman also rejected pause as relevant to English metrics, though he himself had shown, in his piece on Frost, how essential pause placement is to the understanding of "Mowing."

21. Crystal, "Intonation," 19.

22. Crystal, *Prosodic Systems and Intonation in English* (Cambridge: Cambridge University Press, 1969), vii.

23. Crystal, *The English Tone of Voice: Essays in Intonation, Prosody and Paralanguage* (London: Edward Arnold, 1975), [1].

24. Bolinger, *Intonation,* 3.

25. Cited in Abe, 5.

26. Crystal, *Prosodic Systems,* 197.

27. Lieberman, *Intonation,* 122.

28. Janet B. Pierrehumbert, *The Phonology and Phonetics of English Intonation* (Bloomington: Indiana University Linguistics Club, 1987), 1, 2.

29. Bolinger, *Intonation,* 335.

30. Lieberman, "The Innate Central Aspect of Intonation," in Waugh and Schooneveld, 187.

31. Crystal, "Intonation, 22.

32. Earlier, he had said that "Any account of metre in terms of syllabification and stress alone is bound to lead to the recognition of two formal categories of poetry—a distinction difficult to maintain on semantic or critical grounds . . ." (11). He is referring, of course, to the division into metrical poetry and free verse.

33. I should add that for all the desirability of Crystal's insistence on the relevance of intonation to the study of poetry, his own conception of how it would be applied is itself colored by the traditional metrics he appears to be challenging. He cites a participant in the conference on style alluded to earlier who had said that the discussion of meter and stress had omitted free verse, and that what is needed is "a formula based on some general principle of equivalence. . . ." (The original statement can be found in Sebeok, 207). Crystal's rejoinder is that "this

general principle is primarily intonational in character" ("Intonation," 13). Later he says that "In metre . . . equivalences . . . are the thing, whereas in prose these are very few . . ." (31). And of course he is right, in the sense that in traditional prosody, "equivalences" consist of feet, or number of feet. What he appears to be looking for in his work on intonation is, again, equivalence, but now enacted with different materials, pitch-centered entities—for example, tone units. In my view, this simply extends the essence of traditionalism, which thinks of lines primarily as abstract equivalents of each other, as I noted in Chapter 1. With intonation as with stress patterns, we should not be committing ourselves in advance to look for equivalence, but be open to a possible play among the entities we discover, which may involve differences as well as parallels.

34. *Princeton Encyclopedia*, 135.

35. A. Cutler and D. R. Ladd, ed. *Prosody: Models and Measurements* (New York: Springer, 1983), 141–42. The key work of American structuralism is *An Outline of English Structure* by George L. Trager and Henry Lee Smith, Jr. (1951); reprint, Washington, D.C.: American Council of Learned Societies, 1956). For a study in linguistics, this enjoyed a vogue among some metrists that was virtually unprecedented and that has been unduplicated since. The sort of metrical approach it encouraged was one of the targets of Wimsatt and Beardsley. Trager and Smith posited four levels of stress in English, as well as four levels of pitch. In his attempt to apply Trager and Smith to the analysis of poetry, Harold Whitehall spoke of pitch, which he found "not usually regarded as important in prosody. Nonetheless, the higher pitches usually occur at points of primary stress and reinforce the stress peaks in both the metrical and isochronic line. . . ." (419). Whitehall here appears to be acknowledging stress as primary. That view has not gone unchallenged, as the reader will see in a moment. In the meantime, it should be noted that distinguing stress from intonation is not confined to American structuralists. Crystal himself has said "it seems wise to treat accented syllables [i.e., syllables made prominent by pitch change] and stress as largely independent phenomena" (*Prosodic Systems*, 158). But of course both the American structuralists and Crystal are in favor of taking pitch into consideration as an important element of language, and Crystal, it goes without saying, extends this to metrics.

36. Bolinger, "A Theory of Pitch Accent in English," *Word* 14 (August–December 1958): [109].

37. In 1926 the British phoneticians L. E. Armstrong and I. C. Ward had pointed out the obverse, that the stress pattern of a word spoken in isolation might be dropped when that word appeared in connected speech. See Lieberman, *Intonation,*176. As for Bolinger's notion of potential prominence, it might be argued that, in effect, traditional scansion also regards a given word or part of a word as having potential stress, realized if and when the metrical pattern calls for it. But Bolinger is concerned with semantic content or, even more, attitude as the determiner of stress, rather than with an array of abstract feet or a quota of such feet being the basis for judgment.

38. See Bolinger, *Intonation*, 14–15.

39. In *Intonation and its Parts,* Bolinger indicates that there are two other devices for conferring prominence in an utterance, rhythm and vowel quality (17–19).

40. Ibid., 21–22.

41. Georges Faure, D. J. Hirst, and M. Chafcouloff, "Rhyme in English: Isochronism, Pitch, and Perceived Stress," in Waugh and Schooneveld, 71.

42. Selkirk, 203.

43. This can be seen by the references to Bolinger in his *Prosodic Systems*. Also, Crystal cites A. C. Gimson as concluding that "the only realisations of stress which are linguistic, in that they are capable of creating an effect of relative prominence, of accent, in a listener's mind, are those which are effected with the complex help of pitch, quantity and quality variations." Crystal comments that "This may be a little extreme: intensity may at times be a sufficient indication of a linguistic contrast . . . but it is undoubtedly the right emphasis, and is in accord with the results of [D. B.] Fry . . ." (*Prosodic Systems*, 119). Fry's researches were also cited by Bolinger in his 1958 piece and by Cutler and Ladd in their discussion of accent and stress. Writing in 1930, Katharine M. Wilson could contend that "accent tends to raise the pitch" (94), but the current climate of opinion that Bolinger has done so much to create sees the cause-and-effect relation of pitch and stress as just the reverse.

44. Apart from ignoring Bolinger, metrists who would continue to dismiss pitch in favor of stress would also be ignoring the physiological linkage of the two. "The interrelation between intensity and fundamental frequency [a measure of pitch] has a physiological basis. Intensity and fundamental frequency are regulated by the same mechanisms (increase in pulmonary effort and in subglottal pressure, tension of the vocal folds, etc.), and as may be expected, higher fundamental frequency is generally correlated with an increase in intensity. . . . Similarly, the F_0 decrease at the end of sentences is matched by an intensity decrease." Jacqueline Vaissiere, "Language-Independent Prosodic Features," in Cutler and Ladd, 62).

45. Prudence Byers, "Intonation Prediction and the Sound of Poetry," *Language and Style* 13 (Winter 1980): 3.

46. Bolinger acknowledges that a given shape might be inappropriate to particular use, and recognizes that Janet B. Pierrehumbert is in disagreement with the notion that in intonation everything is possible (*Intonation*, 391).

47. Chatman, *A Theory of Meter*, 103.

48. Ibid. Chatman himself thinks a poem is possessed of a meter, but defines it in a way that keeps it tied to variety of rendering: it is "a structure or matrix of possibilities which may emerge in different ways as different vocal renditions"; it is "the matrix of all meaningful scansions" (*Theory of Meter*, 103, 104).

49. There is a larger issue of covenant associated with the use of stress-based meter, what John Hollander calls the "metrical contract," in which the metrical choice for a poem "establishes a kind of frame around the work as a whole. Like a title it indicates how it is to be taken, what sort of thing the poem is supposed to be . . ." (*Vision and Resonance*, 189). Critics who have alluded to the "metrical contract" in ways that endorse the traditional concept of meter have failed to acknowledge how the essay that gave us the term is at the same time concerned with "metrical evolution" with the notion that "the metrical forms take on new modal significances with each new use, and with different sorts of awareness of past ones" (196). In short, the presence of meter (which we can assume is based on stress, for Hollander) does not necessarily guarantee a timeless stability or significance, from which we fall in engaging intonation. The metrical contract appears to have a great deal of elasticity.

50. Lieberman quotes Kenneth Pike as saying "all speakers of the language use basic pitch sequences in similar ways under similar circumstances. In English, many intonation contours are explicit in meaning" (*Intonation*, 184).

51. T. Walker Herbert, "Tones of Poetry: Experiments in Recognition," *Emory University Quarterly* 16 (Fall 1960): 165.

52. Lieberman, "Innate," 187.

53. Crystal, *Prosodic Systems,* 192–93.

54. P. L. Garvin has noted that "the basic objective of descriptive linguistics" is one of defining the units of which language is made up and of their relations. "In terms of concrete analytic practice, defining the units means being able to ascertain their boundaries. . . ." Cited in Crystal, *Prosodic,* 205.

55. Lieberman, *Intonation,* 27.

56. See, e.g., Lieberman, "Innate," 192.

57. Lieberman, *Intonation,* 108.

58. Janet B. Pierrehumbert also appears to take the breath-group as the domain of the intonation unit (34).

59. Appropriately enough, the leading apostle of the breath-group, Philip Lieberman, along with Marcia Lieberman, put to the test the notion that each of the lines of Charles Olson's poems "is delimited by a unitary breath. . . " Lieberman and Lieberman, "The Breath-Group as a Constructive Element in Charles Olson's 'Projective Verse,'" *Proceedings of the Seventh International Congress of Phonetic Sciences,* edited by Andre Rigault and Rene Charbonneau (The Hogue: Mouton, 1972), 949. A recording made by Olson himself furnished some of the data. In at least one instance, Olson read four consecutive lines with only a single breath (950). Allen Ginsberg has talked of Olson as an influence on him in terms of scoring the words of the poem on a page in such a way as to indicate what "phrases would be all in one breath, and what phrases would be in short breaths; what single words like 'Oh' might be all by themselves in single breaths taking all that weight and time. The breath of the poet ideally is reproduced by the breathing of the reader" (Ginsberg, 162).

60. Lieberman, *Intonation,* 121; see also 2.

61. Selkirk, 265.

62. For her, the intonational unit or "string" consists of an optional "boundary tone," one or more tones making up a "pitch" or "nuclear" accent," a "phrase accent" (placed shortly after the nuclear accent), and a final boundary tone, with pitches being defined as high or low. At least, this was her original scheme.

63. In actual speech, she notes, the boundary may be marked by lengthening of the phrase's last syllable rather than a pause (7). Marian Nespor and Irene Vogel also talk of boundaries, calling them intonation breaks, and like Pierrehumbert associate such points with lengthening preceding the break, or "insertion of a pause, or the potential for inserting a pause." "Prosodic Structure above the Word," in Cutler and Ladd, 130.

64. Selkirk, 295–96.

65. Lieberman, "Innate," 188.

66. See Crystal, *Prosodic,* 22.

67. Byers, "Intonation Prediction," 12.

68. Byers, "The Auditory Reality," 28. In fact, she went so far as to say that, according to her findings, the modern poet "cannot count on line-end to create for him a sound unit distinguishable from others and manipulable for purposes of rhythm" (30), but that the tone-unit *is* so available.

69. In admitting this, Pierrehumbert said: "a syntactic account of phrasing is put on the defensive by examples in which surface non-constituents [i.e., elements falling outside a syntactic unit] appear to be intonational phrases, but . . . it may yet be salvaged by finding alternative interpretations of these examples" (9).

70. Among other things, Selkirk uses the simple sentence "Jane gave the book to Mary" to illustrate her point. This statement lends itself to any number of

readings, in one of which the intonation might group the words "gave the book." But these, says Selkirk, do not add up to a syntactic unit (293), although it is not clear why.

71. Cureton, "Response," 14. Cureton appears to be almost disdainful of a syntax-centered approach to prosody, saying that his own theory "does not construct its groups on syntactic principles. The theory is much larger than a theory of syntax, and entirely distinct theoretically" ("Response," 14).

72. Crystal says, and I believe he is using "grammatical" as equivalent to or overlapping with "syntactic," that "in actual fact, there are very few cases where a grammatical structure and an intonation sequence operate in a one-to-one relation" (*Prosodic Systems*, 239). When Marian Nespor and Irene Vogel talk about intonation breaks, they add: "A comparison of the syntactic and prosodic treatments of this phenomenon will reveal that syntax does not explain a number of problems that prosodic structure does." In Cutler and Ladd, 130.

73. For Cureton, double audition is apparently no problem, and his "multi-level" approach to rhythm would apparently have us attending to a lot more than two lines of sound. Even Byers, who sees a congruence of intonation and syntax, has her own version of double audition, saying that the person reading a poem aloud "can hear, in his auditory imagination, both the performance that ignores and the one that observes [line-endings]; and he can delight in the difference" ("Auditory Reality," 34).

74. Actually, the identification of an intonation unit with a sense unit can be traced back to L. E. Armstrong and I. C. Ward, in their *Handbook of English Intonation* (1926), where they spoke of "sense-groups." Cited in Lieberman, *Intonation*, 176.

75. Bolinger's use of "grammar," as was the case with Crystal, appears to overlap with "syntax."

76. What I have described thus far is "English" in its terminology, but not exclusively so in its conceptualization. Bolinger, an American, notes that "the last accent in an utterance—the one that tends to gravitate toward final position—is usually regarded as the most important one. It is sometimes called the 'sentence accent,' 'sentence stress,' or 'nucleus.' Our term for it . . . is RHEMATIC ACCENT" (*Intonation*, 49). Bolinger apparently is not making a sharp distinction between a sentence and an intonational phrase because he later says that "The tonic (often also called the nucleus) is roughly what we have called the rhematic accent." (362; see Cutler and Ladd, 142). Also relevant is his saying that "There is . . . a tendency, within an intonational phrase, to give greater prominence to the first and last accents" (376).

77. Crystal, *English Tone of Voice*, 18.

78. I realize, as Crystal himself does, though not precisely in the terms I have in mind, that there may be something circular about his procedure, namely, having the transcription process place a boundary marker at the completion of a syntactic unit to begin with (see *English Tone of Voice*, 21n). But if we see those placements coming at the end of sense units—for example, after "it" in "the second deplorable thing ABOUT it"—the charge of such circularity can be avoided. Even if there were circularity, it would only point up how easily an intonational phrase and a syntactic unit can be fitted together. I should add that, apart from the question of sense units, Crystal's approach is hardly *doomed* to circularity in transcribing. Once we grant him his definition of a tone-unit as having "one peak of prominence in the form of a nuclear pitch movement" (*Prosodic Systems*, 205) the end-boundary of that unit can be determined by measurable or audible phonetic phe-

nomena. He talks of "very slight" pauses, "but there are frequently accompanying segmental phonetic modifications (variations in length, aspiration, etc.) which reinforce this. . . . it seems safe to infer from the presence of a pause after the nucleus that the end of the tone-unit has come. . . . These phonological criteria suffice to indicate unambiguously where a tone-unit boundary should go in connected speech in the vast majority of cases" (206).

79. Byers, "A Formula," 373–74. Crystal appears to come to a different conclusion on poetry's pitch range; see "Intonation," 228–29.

80. Byers, "A Formula," 373.

81. Byers, "Intonation Prediction and the Sound of Poetry, 7–8.

82. Byers, "A Formula," 368n.

83. See Crystal, *Prosodic Systems,* 144.

84. In fairness to Byers I should note that her calling Crystal's system, as expounded in his *Prosodic Systems,* "More iconic than most, and hence easier to use" ("A Formula," 368n), occurred well before the appearance of Bolinger's *Intonation and its Parts,* whose approach, in my view, is far more iconic and easier to use than Crystal's.

85. Moreover, Crystal does address the attitudinal aspect of intonation. See, in particular, *Prosodic Systems,* 304–6, and "The Analysis of Nuclear Tones." But if intonational studies have been polarized into an emphasis on grammatical function and a focus on attitudinal indication, Crystal's work may be said to occupy a middle ground, while Bolinger's is virtually at the attitudinal pole.

86. See Emily Rando, "Intonation in Discourse," in Waugh and Schooneveld, 255. As indicated earlier, Bolinger notes that what he calls the "rhematic accent" is roughly the equivalent of the terms used by British linguists, "tonic" or "nucleus" (362). In further discussion of the B + A pattern, he says it tends to show up in "Frozen expressions," such as "Never again." (280)

87. For example, the B profile might occur in the response "Yes?" to someone who has called you, and would be rendered as:

es?

Ye-

In addition to such "jumps" in pitch level, Bolinger also speaks of glides, which are "more or less smooth up or down movement[s] . . ." (253); here is an example:

In my own use of Bolinger, I shall generally not include glide notations, on the assumption that the intonational contours of verse can be adequately represented without them, important as they may be to ordinary speech, and to differentiating between speech and the sequence of clearly differentiated pitch levels we get in music. This assumption is partly based on my own sense of how we read poetry, and partly on T. Walker Herbert's discovery, based on experiment, that compared to prose, "the tunes of poetry are characteristically based on longer, more gradual rises and falls in pitch extending over a number of syllables" (Herbert, 172). "Gradual" here might argue for glides, but not when we recognize that Bolinger tends to locate these on individual words or syllables, which would indicate a sharper change over a given phonetic stretch than Herbert seems to have found. Herbert's gradualism might better be represented by what Bolinger calls "tilts," which he places midway between glides and monotones (*Intonation*, 253). The prosodist might well want to include tilts as an option in both representations of a line, and in fact I shall invoke the notion of tilt a bit later. See note 90.

88. Besides the basic triad of the A, B, and C profiles, Bolinger posits some others: CA (low-up-abruptly down—"a sort of intensification of A," 181); AC (an A profile ending in a rise, used for admonition and emphasis *et al*); and CAC (a C profile followed by a rise, a fall, and an upward glide—it can be used for emphasis, but also restraint, or for incompleteness). I believe that we can dispense with these relatively uncommon configurations in applying the profiles to prosodic analysis. With respect to the principal profiles, Bolinger points to cases of ambiguity, where it is not certain if a C has a B preceding it, or if an A has a B preceding it. There are also instances where there may be a question of whether to interpret a preceding profile as an A or a B (186). I do not think this constitutes a major problem for prosodic analysis, and that such decisions can be handled on a case by case basis. Context is everything.

89. See Michael Cummings and Robert Simmons, *The Language of Literature: A Stylistic Introduction to the Study of Literature* (New York: Pergamon Press, 1983), 49ff.

90. I read "me back" as making for a B profile instead of an A profile, on the grounds that the "back," while lower in pitch than the "me," does not make for the real drop of an A, but rather keeps the phrase "me back" at a relatively high pitch. In fact I would say that "back" might be most accurately rendered not as inhabiting a single pitch level but as exhibiting an upward movement, a tilt at least, if not a glide. So "me back" might be best represented as:

me

ᵦack

To appreciate what I am arguing for here, consider, by way of contrast how "me back" might be sounded in the following hypothetical directive: Don't call Jim back, call me back.

91. Crystal, *Prosodic*, 145.

92. Bolinger remarks that "we are uncomfortable with [it] when it is heavily accented . . ." (*Intonation*, 111).

93. A more precise rendering of the line might employ three levels of pitch, to differentiate between the three syllables in question and the unstressed syllables, but even in that arrangement, which would give us a B + B pairing in the first hemistich, and a B + B + B arrangement in the second, I would keep "known" and "tak-" on a higher level of their own.

94. As indicated earlier, Mukarovsky recognizes a distinction between the intonational scheme of a line and that of a larger unit, the verse sentence in which the line is situated. This would seem to be relevant to the question I have raised, but apart from saying that there is a "tension" between the two, he has nothing useful to offer.

95. See Cureton, "Traditional Scansion," 193–94.

96. In "Traditional Scansion," Cureton refers to Crystal's work on intonation, and that of Selkirk, but not to Bolinger's (203). He may be showing the influence of Crystal when he says that "In the normal case, poetic lines tend to form natural intonational phrases" (194). His notion of the extent of an intonation unit seems

to me somewhat inconsistent, tending to the longer in one essay (see "Traditional," 194), and the shorter in another ("Raising"; see Chart #2 (unpaginated) of that piece). In the latter, he appears to identify such units with phrases, and finds clauses often made up of "at least two intonational units (subject and predicate) . . ." (16).

97. Cureton, "Traditional," 194.

98. Ibid. In one more instance of how a traditional mindset can persist even when one is ostensibly working out a fresh approach (the burden of Chapter 3 of the present work), Cureton not only adapts the terms "iambic" and "anapestic" to a consideration of phonological phrases, he assigns breves and macrons to those phrases. The phonological phrases are made up of "clitic phrases . . ." one of which is perceived as more salient than the others" ("Traditional," 193); it is the prominent phrases that are assigned the macrons.

99. Strangely enough, in his "Rhythm" essay, Cureton, treating only the last line of the Stevens passage, *does* seem to take account of pitch. He speaks there of "Tone Units," as opposed to the so-called intonational phrases of the "Traditional" essay, such a unit being a grouping of syllables containing a single pitch slide. Taking the first half of the last line "Downward to darkness," Cureton sees it as "falling," and the second half, "on extended wings," as rising, and says this of the whole: "At the highest level, the line is a balanced diminuendo as two sentence-final phrasal tone units pivot around a central pause. Each of these tone units conveys a side of the emotional paradox—descent to uncertainty and mortality on the one hand (the first half-line) and emotional ascent, extension and independent support on the other (the second half-line)" ("Rhythm," 254). While I would argue that the two half-lines each exhibit more than one change in pitch, I find this a much sounder treatment than the one Cureton accords Stevens in his "Traditional" essay.

100. As with stress-oriented scansions, the pitch-oriented scansion of a given line may produce variant readings. In the present case there is at least one:

Then   blue

the substanceless

That is, by keeping all of "substanceless" pretty much at one level, a move encouraged by the meaning of the word, the line can be seen as assuming a B + B shape. This would, like the first reading, certainly make for a very sharp contrast with the pitch shape of the first line. Also, read in this way, the line might be said to create one of the possible effects Bolinger attributes to the B + B contour, namely, "Implications of 'alert,'" (*Intonation,* 310). However, I favor the first reading I have given of this line, because it honors the fact that "sub" is likely to be raised at least slightly above the two syllables, and also because when so read, *substanceless* enters into a profile relationship with the next line, as my text is about to claim.

101. As I noted in the previous chapter, Richard Cureton has argued for the presence, in Walter Savage Landor's "Rose Aylmer," of parallel phrasal groups in two consecutive lines, those groups being defined by their stress configurations. I thought that this particular claim was forced, but endorsed the general notion that parallel phrases, occurring in lines that are close to each other, might be

at work in a given poem. Here I am arguing for such phrases conceived of in intonational terms.

EPILOGUE

1. Denis Donoghue, *Ferocious Alphabets* (Boston: Little, Brown, 1981), 98.

2. Garrett Stewart, *Reading Voices: Literature and the Phonotext* (Berkeley: University of California Press, 1990), 138.

3. Stewart does not ascribe the phrase the "mind's ear" (which he uses without quotation marks on p. 73 of his book) to anyone in particular, nor to a prosodic tradition in general, but I would remind the reader how the notion of the mind's ear, treated in Chapter 2, has been repeatedly evoked by those who hear two lines of sound as they read a metrical poem. Stewart requires a silent speaking and a "hearing" of its inaudible productions.

4. As indicated earlier, in my reading of Sonnet 116, I read "an ever fixed" mark as employing "fixed" as a disyllable, but this is not relevant to Stewart's reading.

5. Stewart also says: "My whole project in aural reading begins, in one sense, by accepting the Derridean reversal . . . of origin [speech] and supplement [writing]—as a quintessential case of the deconstructive agenda in action . . ." (134).

6. One example is: "texts are ultimately produced by the latent mouthing of the reader's body . . ." (129).

7. Wellek and Warren, 159.

8. Clive Scott, *Vers Libre: The Emergence of Free Verse in France 1886–1914* (Oxford: Clarendon Press, 1990), 49.

Works Cited

Abe, Isamu. "How Vocal Pitch Works." In *The Melody of Language,* edited by Linda R. Waugh and C. H. van Schooneveld, 1–24. Baltimore: University Park Press, 1980.

Abercrombie, David. *Studies in Phonetics and Linguistics.* London: Oxford University Press, 1965.

Abrams, Robert. E. "The Skewed Harmonics of English Verse Feet." *Language and Style* 16 (Fall 1983): 478–503.

Alden, Raymond MacDonald. *English Verse: Specimens Illustrating its Principles and History.* New York: Henry Holt and Company, 1903.

Allen, Charles. "Cadenced Free Verse." *College English* 9 (January 1948): 195–99.

Allen, John D. *Elements of English Blank Verse: Shakespeare to Frost.* Johnson City: East Tennessee State University Press, 1968.

Allen, W. Sidney. *Accent and Rhythm. Prosodic Features of Latin and Greek: A Study in Theory and Accentuation.* Cambridge: Cambridge University Press, 1973.

Attridge, Derek. *The Rhythms of English Poetry.* New York: Longman, 1982.

———. "Linguistic Theory and Literary Criticism: *The Rhythms of English Poetry* Revisited." In *Phonetics and Phonology, Vol. 1, Rhythm and Meter,* edited by Paul Kiparsky and Gilbert Youmans, 183–99. San Diego: Academic Press, 1989.

———. *Well-Weighed Syllables: Elizabethan Verse in Classical Meters.* London: Cambridge University Press, 1974.

Baker, Sheridan. "English Meter *Is* Quantitative. *College English* 21 (March 1960): 309–15.

Barkas, Pallister. *A Critique of Modern English Prosody (1880–1930).* Studien zur englischen Philologie, vol. 82. Halle: Max Niemeyer, 1934.

B[ateson], F. W. "Editorial Postscript" to Christopher Ricks, "Wordsworth: 'A Pure Organic Pleasure from the Lines." *Essays in Criticism* 21 (January 1971): 1–32.

Baum, Paul Franklin. *The Principles of English Versification.* Cambridge: Harvard University Press, 1923.

Bawer, Bruce. "The Poetic Legacy of William Carlos Williams." *New Criterion* 7 (September 1988): 14–26.

Bell, Marvin. "On the Freedom of Free Verse." *Ohio Review* number 28 (1982): [51]–53.

Bolinger, Dwight. *Intonation and its Parts: Melody in Spoken English.* Stanford, Calif.: Stanford University Press, 1986.

———. "A Theory of Pitch Accent in English." *Word* 14 (August–December 1958): 109–49.

Bollobas, Eniko. *Tradition and Innovation in American Free Verse: Whitman to Duncan*. Budapest: Adademia Kiado, 1986.

Bowley, C. C. "Metrics and the Generative Approach." *Linguistics,* no. 121 (February 1974): 5–19.

Bradley, Scully. "The Fundamental Metrical Principle in Whitman's Poetry." *American Literature* 10 (January 1939): 437–59.

Bridges, Robert. *Milton's Prosody with a Chapter on Accentual Verse*. 1921. Revised final edition. Oxford: Clarendon Press, 1965.

Brogan, T. V. F. *English Versification, 1570–1980: A Reference Guide with a Global Appendix*. Baltimore: Johns Hopkins University Press, 1981.

Brooks, Cleanth and Robert Penn Warren. *Understanding Poetry*. 3d ed. New York: Holt, Rinehart and Winston, 1960.

———, John Thibaut Purser, and Robert Penn Warren. *An Approach to Literature*. 5th ed. Englewood Cliffs, N.J.: Prentice-Hall, 1975.

Brown, Warner. *Time in English Verse Rhythm: An Empirical Study of Typical Verses by the Graphic Method*. Archives of Psychology, no. 10; Columbia Contributions to Psychology, 17, no. 2. New York: The Science Press, 1908.

Buxton, John. "Correspondence." *Review of English Studies* 11 (August 1960), [305].

Byers, Prudence. "A Formula for Poetic Intonation." *Poetics* 8 (August 1979): 367–80.

———. "The Auditory Reality of the Verse Line." *Style* 17 (Winter 1983): 27–36.

———. "Intonation Prediction and the Sound of Poetry." *Language and Style* 13 (Winter 1980): 3–14.

Cable, Thomas. *The English Alliterative Tradition*. Philadelphia: University of Pennsylvania Press, 1991.

———. "Recent Developments in Metrics." *Style* 10 (Summer 1976): 313–28.

———. "Timers, Stressers, and Linguists: Contention and Compromise." *Modern Language Quarterly* 33 (September 1972): 227–39.

Carruth, Hayden. "Here Today: A Poetry Chronicle." *Hudson Review* 24 (Summer 1971): 320–36.

Chatman, Seymour. "Robert Frost's 'Mowing': An Inquiry into Prosodic Structure." *Kenyon Review* 18 (Summer 1956): 421–38.

———. "Mr. Stein on Donne." *Kenyon Review* 18 (Summer 1956): 443–51.

———. *A Theory of Meter*. The Hague: Mouton, 1965.

———, ed. *Literary Style: A Symposium*. New York: Oxford University Press, 1971.

——— and Samuel R. Levin, eds. *Essays on the Language of Literature*. Boston: Houghton Mifflin, 1967.

Claflin, Blair. "Reading Between the Lines." *New York Times Education Life Supplement* (August 4, 1991): 10.

Cooper, William E. and Jeanne Paccia-Cooper. *Syntax and Speech*. Cambridge: Harvard University Press, 1980.

Cowan, J. Milton and Bernard Bloch. "An Experimental Study of Pause in English Grammar." *American Speech* 23 (April 1948): [89]–99.

Creek, Herbert L. "Rising and Falling Rhythms in English Verse." *PMLA* 35 (March 1920): 76–90.

Crystal, David. "The Analysis of Nuclear Tones." In *The Melody of Language*, edited by Linda R. Waugh and C. H. van Schooneveld, 55–70. Baltimore: University Park Press, 1980.

———. *The English Tone of Voice: Essays in Intonation, Prosody, and Paralanguage*. London: Edward Arnold, 1975.

———. "Intonation and Metrical Theory." *Transactions of the Philological Society* (1971): 1–33.

———. *Prosodic Systems and Intonation in English*. Cambridge: Cambridge University Press, 1969.

Cummings, Michael and Robert Simmons. *The Language of Literature: A Stylistic Introduction to the Study of Literature*. New York: Pergamon Press, 1983.

Cureton, Richard D. "A Definition of Rhythm." *Eidos* 3 (November 1986): 7–10.

———. "Raising Phrasing: Phrasal Rhythm as a Central Concern of Prosodic Analysis." Handout at 1986 MLA Convention panel on prosody.

———. "Rhythm: A Multilevel Analysis." *Style* 19 (Summer 1985): 242–57.

———. "Response to Alan Holder's Queries, Quibbles, and Caveats." *Eidos* 4 (December 1987): 10, 13–17.

———. "Traditional Scansion: Myths and Muddles." *Journal of Literary Semantics* 15 (December 1986): 171–208.

Cushman, Stephen. *William Carlos Williams and the Meanings of Measure*. Yale Studies in English 193. New Haven: Yale University Press, 1985.

Cutler, A. and D. R Ladd, eds. *Prosody: Models and Measurements*. New York: Springer, 1983.

Dacey, Philip and David Jauss, eds. *Strong Measures: Contemporary Poems in Traditional Forms*. New York: Harper & Row, 1986.

Donoghue, Denis. *Ferocious Alphabets*. Boston: Little, Brown, 1987.

Dooley, David. "Iambic in the 80s." *Crosscurrents* 8 (January 1989): 116–28.

Easthope, Antony. *Poetry as Discourse*. New York: Methuen, 1983.

Edfeldt, Ake W. *Silent Speech and Silent Reading*. Chicago: University of Chicago Press, 1960.

Eliason, Norman E. *The Language of Chaucer's Poetry: An Appraisal of the Verse, Style, and Structure*. Anglistica, vol. 17. Copenhagen: Rosenkilde and Bagger, 1972.

Eliot, T. S. "The Borderline of Prose." *New Statesman* 9 (19 May 1917): 157–59).

———. *Selected Prose*, ed. John Hayward. Harmondsworth, Middlesex: Penguin Books, 1953

Epstein, Edmund L. and Terence Hawkes. *Linguistics and English Prosody*. Studies in Linguistics Occasional Papers, no. 7. Buffalo, N.Y.: University of Buffalo Department of Anthropology and Linguistics, 1959.

Faure, G., D. J. Hirst, and M. Chafcouloff. "Rhythm in English: Isochronism, Pitch, and Perceived Stress." In *The Melody of Language*, edited by Linda R. Waugh and C. H. van Schooneveld, 71–79. Baltimore: University Park Press, 1980.

Finch, Annie. *The Ghost of Meter: Culture and Prosody in American Free Verse*. Ann Arbor: University of Michigan Press, 1993.

Fowler, Roger, ed. *Essays on Style and Language: Linguistic and Critical Approaches to Literary Style*. London: Routledge and Kegan Paul, 1966.

———. *The Languages of Literature: Some Linguistic Contributions to Criticism.* New York: Barnes & Noble, 1971.

Frank, Robert and Henry Sayre, eds. *The Line in Postmodern Poetry.* Urbana: University of Illinois Press, 1988.

Fraser, G. S. *Metre, Rhyme, and Free Verse.* London: Methuen, 1970.

Fredman, Stephen. *Poet's Prose: The Crisis in American Verse.* New York: Cambridge University Press, 1983.

Freeman, Donald C. "Current Trends in Metrics." In *Current Trends in Stylistics,* edited by Braj B. Kachru and Herbert F. W. Stahlke, 67–80. Edmonton (Canada): Linguistic Research Inc., 1972.

———. "On the Primes of Metrical Style." In *Linguistics and Literary Style.* Edited by Donald C. Freeman, 448–91. New York: Holt, Rinehart and Winston, 1970.

Friebert, Stuart and David Young, eds. *A Field Guide to Contemporary Poetry and Poetics.* New York: Longman, 1980

Frye, Northrop. *Sound and Poetry: English Institute Essays, 1956.* New York: Columbia University Press, 1957.

Fuller, Roy. "Boos of Different Durations." *Southern Review* 11 (October 1975): 825–37.

———. "The Fetish of Speech Rhythms in Modern Poetry." *Southern Review* 15 (January 1979): 1–15.

Fussell, Paul. "English I. Historical." In *Versification: Major Language Types. Sixteen Essays,* edited by W. K. Wimsatt Jr, 191–203. (New York: New York University Press for MLA, 1970).

———. *Poetic Meter and Poetic Form.* New York: Random House, 1965.

———. *Poetic Meter and Poetic Form,* rev. ed. New York: Random House, 1979.

Gardner, W. H., ed. *Poems and Prose of Gerard Manley Hopkins.* Baltimore: Penguin Books, 1966.

Gaylord, Alan T. "Scanning the Prosodists: An Essay in Metacriticism." *The Chaucer Review* 11 (Summer 1976): [22]–82.

Gilbert, Sandra M. "Glass Joints: A Meditation on the Line." In *The Line in Postmodern Poetry,* edited by Robert Frank and Henry Sayre, 41–50. Urbana: University of Illinois Press, 1988.

Ginsberg, Allen. *Allen Verbatim: Lectures on Poetry, Politics, Consciousness,* ed. by Gordon Ball. New York: McGraw-Hill, 1974.

Gioia, Dana. Untitled contribution to "Symposium" in *Crosscurrents* 8 (January 1989): 88–90.

Gross, Harvey. *Sound and Form in Modern Poetry. A Study of Prosody from Thomas Hardy to Robert Lowell.* 1964. Reprint. Ann Arbor: University of Michigan Press, 1968.

———, ed. *The Structure of Verse: Modern Essays on Prosody,* rev. ed. New York: Ecco Press, 1979.

Haas, Robert. "One Body: Some Notes on Form." *Antaeus* 30/31 (Spring 1978): 329–42.

———. *Twentieth Century Pleasures: Prose on Poetry.* New York: The Ecco Press, 1984.

Hall, Donald. "The Line." In *A Field Guide to Contemporary Poetry and Poetics,* edited by Stuart Friebert and David Young, 73–75. New York: Longman, 1980.

———. "Notes on Free Verse and Fashion." *Ohio Review* no. 28 (1982): 25–30.

———, ed. *Claims for Poetry.* Ann Arbor: University of Michigan Press, 1982.

Halle, Morris and Samuel Jay Keyser. "Chaucer and the Study of Prosody." *College English* 28 (December 1966): 187–219.

———. *English Stress: Its Form, Its Growth, and Its Role in Verse.* New York: Harper and Row, 1971.

Harding, D. W. *Words into Rhythm: English Speech Rhythm in Verse and Prose.* Cambridge: Cambridge University Press, 1976.

Hardison, Jr., O. B. *Prosody and Purpose in the English Renaissance.* Baltimore: Johns Hopkins University Press, 1989.

Hartman, Charles O. *Free Verse: An Essay on Prosody.* Princeton: Princeton University Press, 1980.

Hayes, Bruce. "A Grid-based Theory on English Meter." *Linguistic Inquiry* 14 (Summer 1983): 357–92.

Helms, Alan. "Intricate Song's Last Measure." *Sewanee Review* 87 (Spring 1979): 249–66.

Herbert, T. Walker. "Tones of Poetry: Experiments in Recognition." *Emory University Quarterly* 16 (Fall 1960): 164–73.

Hewitt, Elizabeth R. "Structure and Meaning in T. S. Eliot's *Ash Wednesday.*" *Anglia* 83 (1965): [426]–50.

Hoberman, J. "Harold Rosenberg's Radical Cheek." [*Village*] *Voice Literary Supplement* ([13] May 1986): 10–13.

Holden, Jonathan. "The Free Verse Line." In *The Line in Postmodern Poetry,* edited by Robert Frank and Henry Sayre, 1–12. Urbana: University of Illinois Press, 1988.

———. "Postmodern Poetic Form: A Theory." *NER/BLO* 6 (Autumn 1983): 1–22.

Holder, Alan. "Richard Cureton's 'Definition of Rhythm': Some Queries, Quibbles, and Caveats." *Eidos* 4 (December 1987): 10.

H[ollander], J[ohn]. "Music and Poetry." In *Princeton Encyclopedia of Poetry and Poetics,* edited by Alex Preminger, Frank J. Warnke, and O. B. Hardison, Jr., 533–36. Princeton: Princeton University Press, 1965.

———. "The Music of Poetry." *Journal of Aesthetics and Art Criticism* 15 (December 1956): 232–44.

———. "Poetic Schemes." *Partisan Review* 48 (1981): 478–85.

———. *Rhyme's Reason: A Guide to English Verse.* New Haven: Yale University Press, 1981.

———. *Vision and Resonance: Two Senses of Poetic Form.* New York: Oxford University Press, 1975.

Holscher, Rory and Robert Schultz, eds. "A Symposium on the Theory and Practice of the Line in Contemporary Poetry." *Epoch* (Winter 1980): 161–224.

Hough, Graham. "Free Verse." *Proceedings of the British Academy* 43 (1957): 175–77.

Hrushovski, Benjamin. "On Free Rhythms in Modern Poetry." In *Style in Language,* edited by Thomas A. Sebeok, 173–90. Cambridge: M.I.T. Press, 1960.

Ing, Catherine. *Elizabethan Lyrics: A Study in the Development of English Metres and their Relation to Poetic Effect.* 1951. Reprint. New York: Barnes & Noble, 1969.

Jacob, Cary F. "Concerning Scansion." *Sewanee Review* 19 (July 1911): 352–62.

———. *The Foundations and Nature of Verse.* New York: Columbia University Press, 1918.

———. "Rhythm in Prose and Poetry." *Quarterly Journal of Speech Education* 13 (November 1927): 357–75.

Jespersen, Otto. "Notes on Metre." In *The Structure of Verse: Modern Essays on Prosody,* rev. ed., edited by Harvey Gross, 105–28. New York: Ecco Press, 1979.

Kiparsky, Paul. "Sprung Rhythms." In *Phonetics and Phonology, Vol. 1. Rhythm and Meter,* edited by Paul Kiparsky and Gilbert Youmans, 305–40. San Diego: Academic Press, 1989.

——— and Gilbert Youmans, eds. *Phonetics and Phonology, Vol. 1. Rhythm and Meter.* San Diego: Academic Press, 1989.

Kolln, Martha. *Understanding English Grammar.* 2nd ed. New York: Macmillan, 1986.

Kopczynska, Zdzislawa and Lucylla Pszczolowska. "Le Role de l'intonation dans la versification." *Poetics, Poetyka, First International Conference on Work-in-Progress Devoted to Problems of Poetics,* edited by Donald Davie et al, 215–24. Warsaw: Polish Scientific Publishers, 1961.

Kunitz, Stanley. "Action and Incantation." *Antaeus* 30/31 (Spring 1978): 283–95.

Laferrière, Daniel. "Free and Non-Free Verse: A Response to Howard McCord's 'Breaking and Entering." *Language and Style* 10 (Spring 1977), 79–85.

Lanier, Sidney. *The Science of English Verse.* 1880. Reprint. New York: Charles Scribner's Sons, 1901.

Leithauser, Brad. "The Confinement of Free Verse. *New Criterion* 5 (May 1987): 4–14.

———. "Metrical Illiteracy." *New Criterion* 1 (January 1983), 41–46.

———. Untitled. In "Symposium," *Crosscurrents* 8 (January 1989): 90–93.

Levertov, Denise. "On the Function of the Line." In *Claims for Poetry,* edited by Donald Hall, 265–72. Ann Arbor: University of Michigan Press, 1982.

Levin, Samuel R. "The Conventions of Poetry." In *Literary Style: A Symposium,* edited by Seymour Chatman, 177–96. New York: Oxford University Press, 1971.

Lewis, C. S. "The Fifteenth-Century Heroic Line." *Essays and Studies* 24 (1938): 28–41.

———. *Selected Literary Essays,* edited by Walter Hooper. Cambridge: Cambridge University Press, 1969.

Liberman, Mark and Alan Prince. "On Stress and Linguistic Rhythm." *Linguistic Inquiry* 8 (Spring 1977): 249–336.

Liddell, Mark H. *An Introduction to the Scientific Study of English Poetry.* New York: Doubleday, Page, 1902.

Lieberman, Philip. "The Innate, Central Aspect of Intonation." In *The Melody of Language,* edited by Linda R. Waugh and C. H. van Schooneveld, 187–99. Baltimore: University Park Press, 1980.

———. *Intonation, Perception, and Language.* Cambridge, Mass.: M.I.T. Press, 1967.

Lieberman, Marcia and Philip Lieberman. "The Breath-Group as a Constructive

Element in Charles Olson's 'Projective Verse.'" *Proceedings of the Seventh International Congress of Phonetic Sciences.* [949]–56, edited by Andre Rigault and Rene Charbonneau, [949]–56. The Hague: Mouton, 1972.

McNaughton, Hugh. "Free Verse: A Parallel and a Warning." *The National Review* 90 (1927): 88–96.

McPhillips, Robert. "Reading the New Formalists." *Sewanee Review* 97 (Winter 1989): 73–96.

Malof, Joseph. *A Manual of English Meters.* 1970. Reprint. Westport, Conn.: Greenwood Press, 1978.

Mayor, Joseph B. *Chapters on English Metre.* Cambridge: Cambridge University Press, 1901.

Meschonnic, Henri. *Critique du rhythme: anthropologie historique du langage.* Paris: Editions Verdier, 1982.

Miles, Josephine. *Eras and Modes in English Poetry.* 2nd ed. Berkeley: University of California Press, 1964.

Mills, Jr., Ralph D., ed. *On the Poet and His Craft: Selected Prose of Theodore Roethke.* Seattle: University of Washington Press, 1965.

Mitchell, Roger. "The Fifteenth Century Again." *American Poetry Review* 17 (November–December 1988): 23–25.

———. "A Prosody for Whitman?" *PMLA* 84 (October 1969): 1606–12.

———. "Towards a System of Grammatical Scansion." *Language and Style* 3 (Winter 1970): 3–28.

Monroe, Jonathan. *A Poverty of Objects: The Prose Poem and the Politics of Genre.* Ithaca: Cornell University Press, 1987.

Moore, Richard. "Of Form, Closed and Open: with Glances at Frost and Williams." *Iowa Review* (Summer 1988): 86–103.

Morgan, Frederick. "William Carlos Williams: Imagery, Rhythm, Form." *Sewanee Review* 55 (Autumn 1947): 675–90.

Mukarovsky, Jan. *The Word and Verbal Art,* edited and trans. by John Burbank and Peter Steiner. Yale Russian and East European Studies, no. 13. New Haven: Yale University Press, 1977.

Nash, Rose and Anthony Mulac. "The Intonation of Verifiability." In *The Melody of Language,* edited by Linda R. Waugh and C. H. van Schooneveld, 219–41. Baltimore: University Park Press, 1980.

Nemerov, Howard. "On the Measure of Poetry." *Critical Inquiry* 6 (Winter 1979): 331–41.

Nespor, Marian and Irene Vogel. "Prosodic Structure Above the Word." In *Prosody: Models and Measurements,* edited by A. Cutler and D. R. Ladd, 123–40. New York: Springer, 1983.

Nims, John Frederick. *Western Wind: An Introduction to Poetry.* New York: Random House, 1974.

Nist, John. "Sound and Sense: Some Structures of Poetry." *College English* 23 (January 1962): 291–95.

———. "The Word-Group Cadence: Basis of English Metrics." *Linguistics* 6 (1964): 73–82.

Omond, T. S. *English Metrists: Being a Sketch of English Prosodical Criticism from Elizabethan Times to the Present Day.* 1921. Reprint. New York: Phaeton Press, 1968.

Oras, Ants. "Spenser and Milton: Some Parallels and Contrasts in the Handling of Sound." In *Sound and Poetry: English Institute Essays, 1956,* edited by Northrop Frye, 109–33. New York: Columbia University Press, 1957.

Pakosz, Maciel. "Some Aspects of the Role of Intonation in English Versification." *Studia Anglica Posenaniensia* 5 (1973): 153–63.

Peacock, Molly. Untitled. In "Symposium," *Crosscurrents* 8 (January 1989): 95–98.

Perloff, Marjorie. *The dance of the intellect: studies in the poetry of the Pound tradition.* Cambridge: Cambridge University Press, 1985.

———. "The Linear Fallacy." *Georgia Review* 35 (Winter 1981): 855–69.

———. "Lucent and Inescapable Rhythms: Metrical 'Choice' and Historical Formation." In *The Line in Postmodern Poetry,* edited by Robert Frank and Henry Sayre, 13–40. Urbana: University of Illinois Press, 1988.

Perry, John O. "The Temporal Analysis of Poems." *British Journal of Aesthetics* 5 (July 1965): 227–45.

"Picketing the Zeitgeist Picket: Replies to Diane Wakoski from Robert Mezey, Lewis Turco, David Radavich, Brian Richards, and Dana Gioia." *American Book Review* 8 (November–December 1986): 3.

Pierrehumbert, Janet B. *The Phonology and Phonetics of English Intonation.* Bloomington: Indiana University Linguistics Club, 1987.

Plumly, Stanley. "Chapter and Verse." *American Poetry Review* 7 (January/February 1978): 21–32.

Poe, Edgar Allan. *Essays and Reviews.* New York: The Library of America, 1984.

Pound, Ezra. "A Few Dont's." *Poetry* 1 (March 1913): 200–6.

———. *Literary Essays of Ezra Pound.* Edited by T. S. Eliot. New York: New Directions, 1954.

———. "Treatise on Metre." In *The Structure of Verse: Modern Essays on Prosody,* rev. ed., edited by Harvey Gross, 234–40. New York: Ecco Press, 1979.

Powell, James A. "The Light of Vers Libre." *Paideuma* 5 (Spring 1979): 3–34.

Prince, Alan. "Relating to the Grid." *Linguistic Inquiry* 14 (Winter 1983): 19–100.

Princeton Encyclopedia of Poetry and Poetics, Edited by Alex Preminger, Frank J. Warnke, and O. B. Hardison, Jr. Princeton: Princeton University Press, 1965.

Puttenham, George. *The Arte of English Poesie,* edited by Gladys D. Willcock and Alice Walker. 1936. Reprint. Cambridge: Cambridge University Press, 1970.

Quasha, George. Untitled. In "A Symposium on the Theory and Practice of the Line in Contemporary Poetry," edited by Rory Holscher and Robert Schultz. *Epoch* (Winter 1980): 213–18.

Ramsey, Paul. "Free Verse: Some Steps Toward Definition." *Studies in Philology* 65 (January 1968): 98–108.

———. "Ways of Meditation." *Parnassus* 10 (Spring/Summer 1982): 172–84.

———. "William Carlos Williams as Metrist: Theory and Practice." *Journal of Modern Literature* 1 (May 1971): 578–92.

Rando, Emily. "Intonation in Discourse." In *The Melody of Language,* edited by Linda R. Waugh and C. H. van Schooneveld, 243–78. Baltimore: University Park Press, 1980.

Ransom, John Crowe. "The Strange Music of English Verse." *Kenyon Review* 18 (Summer 1956): 460–77.

———. "Wanted: An Ontological Critic." In *Essays on the Language of Literature,* edited by Seymour Chatman and Samuel R. Levin, 269–82. Boston: Houghton Mifflin, 1967.

"Reader's Forum." [Exchange between Alan Holder and Marjorie Perloff]. *Georgia Review* 36 (Winter 1982): 933–36.

Richards, I. A. "Rhythm and Metre." In *The Structure of Verse: Modern Essays on Prosody,* rev. ed., edited by Harvey Gross, 68–76. New York: Ecco Press, 1979.

Richman, Robert, ed. *The Direction of Poetry: An Anthology of Rhymed and Metered Verse Written in the English Language Since 1975.* Boston: Houghton Mifflin, 1988.

Ricks, Christopher. "Wordsworth: 'A Pure Organic Pleasure from the Lines.'" *Essays in Criticism* 21 (January 1971): 1–32.

Robinson, Ian. *Chaucer's Prosody: A Study of the Middle English Verse Tradition.* London: Cambridge University Press, 1971.

Rosenthal, M. L., ed. *Poetry in English: An Anthology.* New York: Oxford University Press, 1987.

Sadoff, Ira. "Neo-Formalism: A Dangerous Nostalgia." *American Poetry Review* 19 (January–February 1990): 7–13.

Saintsbury, George. *Historical Manual of English Prosody.* 1910. Reprint. Introduction by Harvey Gross. New York: Schocken Books, 1966.

———. *A History of English Prosody: From the Twelfth Century to the Present Day.* 3 vols. 1906–10. 2nd ed. 1923. Reprint. New York: Russell & Russell, 1961.

Sandeen, Ernest. Untitled. In "A Symposium on the Theory and Practice of the Line in Contemporary Poetry," edited by Rory Holscher and Robert Schultz. *Epoch* 29 (Winter 1980): 218–19.

Saner, Reg. "Noble Numbers: Two in One." *Ohio Review,* No. 28 (1982), [6]–15.

Schwartz, Elias K., W. K. Wimsatt, Jr., and Monroe C. Beardsley. "Rhythm and 'Exercises in Abstraction.'" *PMLA* 77 (December 1962): 668–670, 671–674.

Scott, Clive. *Vers Libre: The Emergence of Free Verse in France 1886–1914.* Oxford: Clarendon Press, 1990.

Scripture, E. W. *The Elements of Experimental Phonetics.* New York: Charles Scribner's Sons, 1902.

Sebeok, Thomas A., ed. *Style in Language.* Cambridge: M.I.T. Press, 1960.

Selkirk, Elisabeth O. *Phonology and Syntax: The Relation Between Sound and Structure.* Cambridge: M.I.T. Press, 1984.

Shapiro, Karl. "English Prosody and Modern Poetry." *ELH* 14 (June 1947): 77–92.

——— and Robert Beum. *A Prosody Handbook.* New York: Harper and Row, 1965.

Shen, Yao and Peterson, G. G. *Isochronism in English.* Studies in Linguistics Occasional papers, no. 9. Buffalo, N.Y.: University of Buffalo Department of Anthropology and Linguistics, 1962.

Silliman, Ron. "The New Sentence." In *Claims for Poetry,* edited by Donald Hall, 377–98. Ann Arbor: University of Michigan Press, 1982.

Simpson, Louis. "Irregular Impulses: Some Remarks on Free Verse." *Ohio Review* no. 28 (1982): [54]–57.

Skeat, W. W. "On the Scansion of English Poetry." *Transactions of the Philological Society* (1898): 484–503.

Smith, Egerton. *The Principles of English Metre*. London: Oxford University Press, 1923.

Smith, Jr., Henry Lee. "Introduction" to Edmund Epstein and Terence Hawkes. *Linguistics and English Prosody*. Studies in Linguistics Occasional Papers, no. 7. Buffalo, N.Y.: University of Buffalo Department of Anthropology and Linguistics, 1959. 5–8.

———. "Toward Redefining English Prosody." *Studies in Linguistics* 14 (Winter 1959): 68–76.

Snell, Ada L. F. "An Objective Study of Syllabic Quantity in English Verse: Blank Verse." *PMLA* 33 (September 1918): 396–408.

———. "An Objective Study of Syllabic Quantity in English Verse: Lyric Verse." *PMLA* 34 (September 1919): 416–35.

———. *Pause: A Study of Its Nature and its Rhythmical Function in Verse, Especially in Blank Verse*. Contributions to Rhetorical Theory, no. 8. 1918. Reprint. Norwood, Pa.: Norwood Editions, 1975.

Southall, Raymond. *The Courtly Makers: An Essay on the Poetry of Wyatt and his Contemporaries*. New York: Barnes and Noble, 1964.

Southworth, James G. *Verses of Cadence: An Introduction to the Prosody of Chaucer and his Followers*. Oxford: Basil Blackwell, 1954.

Stallworthy, Jon. Untitled. In "A Symposium on the Theory and Practice of the Line in Contemporary Poetry," edited by Rory Holscher and Robert Schultz. *Epoch* 29 (Winter 1980): 221–22.

Steele, Timothy. *Missing Measures: Modern Poetry and the Revolt Against Meter*. Fayetteville: University of Arkansas Press, 1990.

Stevenson, Charles L. "The Rhythm of English Verse." *Journal of Aesthetics and Art Criticism* 28 (Spring 1970): 327–44.

Stewart, Garrett. *Reading Voices: Literature and the Phonotext*. Berkeley: University of California Press, 1990.

Stewart, George R. *The Technique of English Verse*. 1930. Reprint. Port Washington, N.Y.: Kennikat Press, 1966.

Sutherland, Ronald. "Structural Linguistics and English Prosody." *College English* 20 (October 1958): 12–17.

"Symposium." *Crosscurrents* 8 (January 1989): 87–128.

Taglicht, J. "The Function of Intonation in English Verse." *Language and Style* 4 (Spring 1971): 116–22.

Tarlinskaja, Marina. *English Verse: Theory and History*. The Hague: Mouton, 1976.

———. "General and Particular Aspects of Meter: Literatures, Epochs, Poets." In *Phonetics and Phonology. Vol. I. Rhythm and Meter*, edited by Paul Kiparsky and Gilbert Youmans, 121–54. San Diego: Academic Press, 1989.

———. "Rhythm-Morphology-Syntax-Rhythm." *Style* 18 (Winter 1984): 1–25.

Taylor, Dennis. *Hardy's Metres and Victorian Prosody with a Metrical Appendix of Hardy's Stanza Forms*. Oxford: Clarendon Press, 1988.

Thompson, John. *The Founding of English Metre*. 1961. Reprint. London: Routledge and Kegan Paul, 1966.

Townsend, Peter. "Essential Groupings of Meaningful Force: Rhythm in Literary Discourse." *Language and Style* 16 (Summer, 1983): 313–33.

Trager, George L. and Henry Lee Smith, Jr. *An Outline of English Structure.* 1951. Reprint. Washington, D.C.: American Council of Learned Societies, 1956.

Traugott, Elizabeth Closs. "Meter in Auden's 'Streams.'" In *Phonetics and Phonology. Vol. I. Rhythm and Meter,* edited by Paul Kiparsky and Gilbert Youmans, 291–304. San Diego: Academic Press, 1989.

Turner, Frederick and Ernst Pöppel. "The Neural Lyre: Poetic Meter, The Brain, and Time." *Poetry* 142 (August 1983): 277–309.

Tynianov, Yuri. *The Problem of Verse Language,* edited and translated by Michael Sosa and Brent Harvey. 1924. Reprint. Ann Arbor, Mich.: Ardis, 1981.

Vaissiere, Jacqueline. "Language-Independent Prosodic Features." In *Prosody: Models and Measurements,* edited by A. Cutler and D. R. Ladd, 53–66. New York: Springer, 1983.

Verrier, Paul. "English Metric." *Modern Language Review* 7 (October 1912): 522–35.

Viereck, Peter. "Strict Forms in Poetry: Would Jacob Wrestle with a Flabby Angel?" *Critical Inquiry* 5 (Winter 1978): 203–22.

Wakoski, Diane. "Picketing the Zeitgeist: The New Conservatism in American Poetry." *American Book Review* 8 (May–June 1986): 3.

Warren, James Perrin. "'The Free Growth of Metrical Laws': Syntactic Parallelism in 'Song of Myself.'" *Style* 18 (Winter 1984): 27–42.

Waugh, Linda R. and C. H. van Schooneveld, eds. *The Melody of Language.* Baltimore: University Park Press, 1980.

Weaver, Mike. *William Carlos Williams: The American Background.* Cambridge: Cambridge University Press, 1971.

Weirather, Randy. "The Language of Prosody." *Language and Style* 13 (Spring 1980): 120–45.

Weismiller, Edward R. "Triple Threats to Duple Rhythm." In *Phonetics and Phonology, Vol. I. Rhythm and Meter,* edited by Paul Kiparsky and Gilbert Youmans, 261–90. San Diego: Academic Press, 1989.

Wellek, René and Austin Warren. *Theory of Literature.* New York: Harcourt, Brace & World, 1949.

Wesling, Donald. *The New Poetries: Poetic Form since Coleridge and Wordsworth.* Lewisburg, Pa.: Bucknell University Press, 1985.

Whitehall, Harold. "From Linguistics to Criticism." *Kenyon Review* 18 (Summer 1956): [411]–21.

Williams, Miller. "The Line in Poetry." *Anteaus* 30/31 (Spring 1978): 309–13.

Williams, William Carlos. *The Selected Letters of William Carlos Williams,* edited by John C. Thirlwal. New York: McDowell Obolenskyh, 1957.

Wilson, Katharine M. *Sound and Meaning in English Poetry.* 1930. Reprint. Port Washington, N.Y.: Kennikat Press, 1970.

Wimsatt, Jr., W. K. "The Rule and the Norm: Halle and Keyser on Chaucer's Meter." In *Literary Style: A Symposium,* edited by Seymour Chatman, 197–220. New York: Oxford University Press, 1971.

———, ed. *Versification: Major Language Types. Sixteen Essays.* New York: New York University Press for MLA, 1970.

——— and Monroe C. Beardsley. "The Concept of Meter: An Exercise in Abstraction." *PMLA* 74 (December 1959): 585–98.

Winters, Yvor. "The Audible Reading of Poetry." In *The Structure of Verse: Modern Essays on Prosody,* rev. ed., edited by Harvey Gross, 129–46. New York: Ecco Press, 1979.

Woods, Susanne. *Natural Emphasis: English Versification from Chaucer to Dryden.* San Marino, Calif.: Huntington Library, 1984.

Wright, George T. "The Meter of 'Shall I Die?'" *Eidos* 3 (November 1986): 6, 11–12.

———. *Shakespeare's Metrical Art.* Berkeley: University of California Press, 1988.

Youmans, Gilbert. "Introduction: Rhythm and Meter." In *Phonetics and Phonology. Vol. 1. Rhythm and Meter,* edited by Paul Kiparsky and Gilbert Youmans, 1–14. San Diego: Academic Press, 1989.

———. "Milton's Meter." In *Phonetics and Phonology, Vol. I. Rhythm and Meter,* edited by Paul Kiparsky and Gilbert Youmans, 341–379. San Diego: Academic Press, 1989.

Index

293